RED
SUMMER

RED
SUMMER

The SUMMER of 1919 and
the AWAKENING of
BLACK AMERICA

Cameron McWhirter

A John Macrae Book
Henry Holt and Company
New York

Henry Holt and Company, LLC
Publishers since 1866
175 Fifth Avenue
New York, New York 10010
www.henryholt.com

Henry Holt® and 🏛® are registered trademarks of Henry Holt and Company, LLC.

Library of Congress Cataloging-in-Publication Data

McWhirter, Cameron.
    Red summer : the summer of 1919 and the awakening of Black America /
Cameron McWhirter.—1st ed.
        p. cm.
    "A John Macrae Book."
    Includes bibliographical references and index.
    ISBN: 978-0-8050-8906-6
    1. African Americans—Violence against—History—20th century.
2. African Americans—Social conditions—20th century.
3. Racism—United States—History—20th century.
4. Lynching—United States—History—20th century.   5. Race riots—
United States—History—20th century.   6. United States—Race relations—
History—20th century.   I. Title.

E185.61.M4794 2011   2010042111
305.800973—dc22

Henry Holt books are available for special promotions and premiums.
For details contact: Director, Special Markets.

First Edition 2011

Designed by Meryl Sussman Levavi

Printed in the United States of America

1 3 5 7 9 10 8 6 4 2

To Blythe and Finn

Contents

1. Carswell Grove   1

2. Things Fall Apart   12

3. The World Is on Fire   18

4. The NAACP   25

5. National Conference on Lynching   33

6. Charleston   41

7. Bombs and the Decline of the West   55

8. Ellisville   68

9. Cleveland   76

10. Longview   82

11. Washington   96

12. Chicago Is a Great Foreign City   114

13. The Beach   127

14. Like a Great Volcano   149

15. Austin   162

16. Knoxville   170

17. A New Negro   183

18. Omaha   192

19. Phillips County   208

20. Let the Nation See Itself   236

21. Capitol Hill   246

Coda. Carswell Grove   265

Acknowledgments   273

Notes   275

Bibliography   325

Index   339

RED

SUMMER

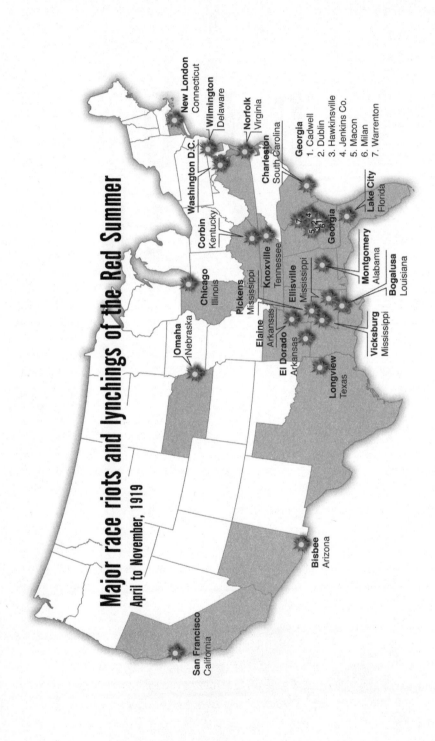

Major race riots and lynchings of the Red Summer

April to November, 1919

New London
Connecticut

Wilmington
Delaware

Norfolk
Virginia

Washington D.C.

Charleston
South Carolina

Georgia
1. Cadwell
2. Dublin
3. Hawkinsville
4. Jenkins Co.
5. Macon
6. Milan
7. Warrenton

Corbin
Kentucky

Lake City
Florida

Chicago
Illinois

Knoxville
Tennessee

Georgia

Pickens
Mississippi

Ellisville
Mississippi

Montgomery
Alabama

Omaha
Nebraska

Elaine
Arkansas

Bogalusa
Louisiana

El Dorado
Arkansas

Vicksburg
Mississippi

Longview
Texas

Bisbee
Arizona

San Francisco
California

1.

Carswell Grove

*[T]here has been nobody suffered in this matter like I
have. I did not do nothing at all to cause that riot.*

JOE RUFFIN

APRIL 13, 1919, WAS PERFECT FOR A CELEBRATION. AS JOE RUFFIN
set out to do his morning chores that Sunday, the sky was cloudless and
blue. The temperature was in the high 70s—normal for spring in east
Georgia.

The sixty-year-old man started the day at his barn, rushing to feed his
pigs, cows, and horses so he would not be late. He had sent his children
ahead to the Carswell Grove Baptist Church in one of the family's two
cars, a Buick Six. Ruffin would follow later. The church festival was to
mark its fifty-second anniversary. Preachers from several counties were
coming to deliver sermons. The choir would give a special performance.
More than three thousand people would be on hand for a gala cookout of
roast pig and fried chicken. Though Ruffin was not a Carswell Grove
member, he had been asked to speak as a prominent black Mason and
treasurer of another black church.

Ruffin had lived his entire life amid fields of cotton and sugar cane
east of Millen, the seat of Jenkins County. The land he tilled was once
part of the plantation where his parents worked as slaves. Ruffin remained
on good terms with the Daniel family, the former slave owners. Ruffin
owned almost 113 acres.[1] He ran five to seven plows a season—a substantial operation for anyone in that part of Georgia at the time and a major
accomplishment for a black farmer. Unlike many blacks in the area, he

could read and write, though census records did not report him having any formal education.[2]

Many of the years had been tough. Several times Ruffin had to mortgage tracts of land. He even took out loans on his mules and horses to cover debts.[3]

He had a large family. The 1910 census recorded three sons and four daughters living with him, plus another son and his family down the road. Ruffin was a widower.

Two sons—John Holiday, twenty-six, and Henry, thirteen—lived at home. Louis Ruffin, in his late twenties, farmed nearby.[4] A fourth son, Joe Andrew Ruffin, twenty-four, served with the U.S. Army in France. He was due home in time for the fall harvest.

Whatever Ruffin's past struggles, 1919 was shaping up to be profitable. Cotton was fetching extraordinary prices, averaging more than 35 cents per pound, the highest ever.[5] The Great War, which the United States entered in April 1917, was a boon for cotton. Textile mills needed tons of it for uniforms and other goods. The war's end the previous November had opened a broader market for cotton; mills across the world needed it for civilian clothes. Supply was limited as the ineluctable spread of the boll weevil reduced production in many parts of the South, including Georgia. Higher prices, fueled in part by cotton scarcity, helped farmers. The previous month, Congress boosted the price of cotton further by passing an amendment to the federal Cotton Futures Act, making it easier for speculators to make bids.[6] As global demand for cotton increased, futures skyrocketed. This spike was a windfall for Ruffin and millions of other southern farmers from Virginia to Texas.

Jenkins County, Georgia, lay in the lower third of a swath of cotton farmland that extended from eastern Virginia into southern Alabama. From colonial days, the region had evolved into a network of plantations, cotton storehouses, and small towns grouped along a major road that later supported a railroad running south from Augusta to the Atlantic port of Savannah. Jenkins was rural and poor, like most counties in the region. Blacks accounted for almost two-thirds of its population.[7] Many blacks in the county were illiterate, and election records indicate that only a handful were allowed to vote. All county government officials, from commissioners to police, were white.

Most blacks in Jenkins County were sharecroppers renting land from white landlords, but a growing number owned property, a phenomenon occurring all over the South. In the first decades of the twentieth century, despite the legal barriers imposed by Jim Crow, the number of acres owned by black farmers rose. In Georgia, black ownership jumped by 75 percent from 1899 to 1919.[8] These landowners formed the "respectable" classes of black society in southern towns. They sat on church boards and led social groups. They generally had good relations with white business owners and politicians, serving as go-betweens when racial friction erupted. In the late morning of this particular April Sunday, Joe Ruffin was the embodiment of this new class, having spent a lifetime navigating the racial restrictions of southern life. Through luck and hard work, he had prospered and never gave "offense to any white man in the county."[9]

By the late afternoon of that April 13, however, almost every white man in Jenkins County wanted Joe Ruffin dead.

Around 11:30 a.m., Ruffin's youngest son, Henry, came back to the farm to get his father.[10] Masons at the festival had asked for him.[11] Ruffin changed into his best Sunday clothes, then got in his second car—a late-model, high-powered Ford touring car—and headed down the road. Henry stayed at the farm. The 15-mile drive from Ruffin's farm near Billies Branch to the church was cut with swampy creeks and hollows.[12] The roads were unpaved. The car drove past acre upon acre of young cotton plants, very low to the ground with thin waxy leaves. Jenkins County is in the middle part of the state near the Savannah River Valley, where Georgia's Piedmont slopes gradually toward the coast. Georgia's famous red clay is sandier in this part of the state and a paler shade of orange. Ruffin could see cultivated land for miles, broken up by copses of loblolly pine and scrub oak as well as thickets of holly and cypress. Hawks and buzzards circled the sky.

Sometime after 2 p.m., Ruffin reached Big Buckhead Church Road, the final road leading to the festival. The dirt road had been around since the earliest settlers cut through the forest. As he crossed Buckhead Creek Bridge, Big Buckhead Church—one of the oldest inland white congregations in the South—was on his left. Across the road, mossy obelisk grave markers of Confederate veterans stood in a small cemetery.[13] In the closing days of the Civil War, when Ruffin was a young boy, Union and Confederate cavalry battled here.[14] The rebels lost; hundreds were killed.[15]

Carswell Grove was founded two and a half years after the battle in the midst of the social turmoil caused by the Confederacy's collapse.

After the war, whites at Big Buckhead Church kicked out blacks, who for generations had sat in segregated pews. Porter W. Carswell, a white judge who owned nearby Bellevue Plantation, gave black congregants two acres of scrubland to erect their own place of worship just down the road. The congregants named their new church in his honor. By 1919, Carswell Grove Baptist Church boasted more than a thousand members, most of them sharecroppers. The yearly celebration of the church's founding was one of the largest African American gatherings in east Georgia.

As Ruffin drove up the low ridge, he saw throngs of black men, women, and children milling about the grounds. They were talking and laughing—it was the cacophony of a large, joyous group. Ruffin parked his car and joined them. After a short time, Ruffin remembered that he had left the door to his house unlocked and decided to drive home. He got in his car, but the swelling crowds blocked the road. He drove as far as he could, almost to Big Buckhead Church, when he was forced to stop and wait for people to move along.

As he sat there, an older Ford drove up behind him and then pulled alongside. People scrambled off the road to get out of the car's way. It stopped abruptly and Ruffin looked over at its occupants: two white law-men and a distraught black man in handcuffs. Ruffin knew the black man: Edmund Scott, his longtime friend.[16] The driver was W. Clifford Brown, a Jenkins County police officer. In the back of the car with Scott sat Thomas Stephens, a Millen police night marshal. When he saw Ruf-fin, Scott frantically shouted to the white officers, "I can get him to stand my bond."[17]

Why the two white officers were at the black gathering is unclear. They had no warrant. Marshal Stephens was not even in his jurisdiction. In all likelihood, they were in search of illegal alcohol. Brown and Stephens were known for going after stills and liquor joints known in many parts of the South as "blind tigers."[18] That spring, the National Prohibition Act was making its way through Congress. It would enforce the Eighteenth Amendment, which banned the sale of liquor nationwide. But in Georgia, the ongoing murky contest between police and those who made, sold, and drank liquor was an old game. In 1907, the Georgia legislature, bowing to pressure from Baptists, passed a law banning alcohol.[19] The law was enacted partly in response to the Atlanta race riot of 1906, when white mobs attacked blacks for three days. Twenty-five blacks and one white were killed. White opponents of alcohol argued that heavy drinking in downtown saloons had been a catalyst for trouble, which they blamed primarily on blacks. The law, however, did little to suppress Georgia's thirst. By 1919, a thriving underground network of alcohol manufacturers and distributors operated across the state. The police, who were always white, played a running game of cat-and-mouse with still operators, many of whom were black. Sometimes police destroyed confiscated booze. Sometimes corrupt officers resold it. One newspaper reported that Brown, in only three months on the force, filed more than a hundred cases against gamblers and liquor manufacturers. The same report said Brown suspected Scott and the Ruffins of running a still.[20]

L. W. Beach, a white superintendent over black sharecroppers at a nearby plantation, told a different story. Beach was at the festival that day, driving impoverished blacks who did not own buggies or wagons to and from the church for one dollar a ride. He said Brown and Stephens were not investigating Scott or Ruffin. The white law officers claimed they arrested Scott, the festival's marshal of ceremonies, only after he brandished a weapon when they almost crashed into his car.[21]

Scott, who was driving a minister from another county to the fair, was infuriated by the officer's wild driving. Beach heard Scott say, "That is the way with some people, they haven't got a damn bit of manners." Brown and Stephens then arrested Scott, charging him with possession of an unregistered firearm. They were heading back to the Millen jail with Scott when they passed by Ruffin's car and Scott shouted for help. Officer Brown stopped his car and called for Ruffin. Ruffin got out of his car, walked over and stood on the running board of the police car.

"What is the trouble with Edmund?" Ruffin asked. Officer Brown said they had found a concealed pistol in Scott's car. Beach, positioned about thirty feet away, saw Ruffin take out a checkbook and offer to write a bond check for his friend. The officer told him he needed cash. Ruffin said he could not get that kind of money, $400, on a Sunday. Brown then said, "God damn it, I am going to carry him in."

A large crowd immediately gathered around the car, including two of Ruffin's sons, Louis and John Holiday. People who were there said Ruffin reached in and tried to pull Scott out. Brown became incensed and shouted, "God damn it, get back." He pulled out his pistol and struck Ruffin in the face. The gun went off, hitting Ruffin on the left side of his head, knocking him to the dirt. Ruffin said later he was unconscious for a few minutes. Others said he got up right away.

One person who was there said Louis, Joe's oldest son, rushed the car, wrested the gun from Brown and shot the police officer in the head, neck, and body, killing him. Two others said that the father, Joe Ruffin, killed Brown, pulling out his own pistol and firing into the police car. Others said Officer Stephens, a short, heavyset man, stepped out of the car, hunkered down with his pistol drawn. Another round of gunfire erupted. Scott, caught in the middle and handcuffed, was shot to death as he struggled to get out of the way. Stephens was wounded and slumped to the ground.

"It was just like a package of poppers [firecrackers]," said Ed Tancemore, a white man who saw the shooting, adding that it took no longer than a finger snap. In an instant, Brown and Scott were dead, slumped in the blood-smeared Ford. Stephens lay on the ground, bleeding but conscious. Black men in the crowd attacked him. Some said Ruffin's two sons led the assault. Tancemore watched as Stephens was beaten: "Every time he would get up, they would knock him back until they got him down the side of the car, and one of them placed his foot in his breast and the other handed him an oak limb, and right there they stopped him."

Police later found a blood-soaked oak branch beside Stephens's mutilated body. A newspaper account described Stephens as "a shapeless mass."[22] He took as long as two hours to die.

Ruffin said that after he was shot, he "fell to the ground and did not know anything at all until my boy J. Holiday and Willie Williams picked me up off the ground, and went walking with me off to my car." Ruffin said his friend Williams tried to hand him the checkbook that he dropped when he was shot. Williams also offered him a gun.

"No, keep them," Ruffin said. "I have got no use for them now at all. I better go to the doctor because I believe I am going to die."[23]

Someone, perhaps one of his sons, perhaps Williams, started Ruffin's Ford. Ruffin sat in the passenger seat, his head gushing with blood, his ears ringing from the gunshots. Smoke stung his nostrils as he looked upon the contorted corpses of a friend he had known his whole life and a white law officer. The other officer, Stephens, writhed on the ground, mortally wounded. Surveying the scene, Ruffin knew immediately he would be lynched when the white mob came for him. And there was no doubt it would come—if he lived that long. Word of the incident spread farmhouse by farmhouse across the county. The word traveled along two distinct vectors: black and white. Blacks hid in their homes while hundreds of white men grabbed their guns and headed toward Carswell Grove.

As Ruffin was rushed from the scene, he asked to be taken to the home of the only person who could help him—Jim Perkins, the most powerful white man in Jenkins County, whose farm was three miles from the shooting. Perkins, the chairman of the board of commissioners, had known Ruffin his whole life. Perkins was waiting at a nearby train depot when a black man told him a wounded Joe Ruffin had arrived at his farm. Perkins rushed home.

Ruffin recalled telling Perkins, "I was only trying to offer him [Brown] a bond for Edmund, and he got mad and shot me down for nothing."

Perkins remembered Ruffin telling him, "Mr. Brown shot me and it made me so mad I jumped up and emptied my pistol at him."

Perkins was baffled that Ruffin was in trouble. "I consider he came to me because he didn't know where to go or what to do," he said later.[24]

Perkins got the county jail physician, J. R. Littleton, to bandage Ruffin's head, and then drove to meet the county sheriff, M. G. Johnson, at the scene of the shooting. The two men saw the dead Brown and Scott and the dying Stephens. When the gathering white farmers learned Ruffin was alive and at Perkins's house, they became incensed. Perkins and Sheriff Johnson rushed back to protect him.

Ruffin sat bandaged on a cot in a cook's shed when Perkins and Johnson burst in. "Joe, come on, a mob is coming after you," they yelled. They had Ruffin lie in the back of Perkins's Cadillac, then drove north as fast as they could. Cars filled with angry white men pursued them all the way to Waynesboro, the seat of the next county. Perkins and Johnson then decided to drive on to the nearest big city, Augusta, about 45 miles away. They arrived about 6:30 p.m. and put Ruffin in the jail there. Ruffin recalled his jailer told him he had "better be proud Mr. Johnson and Mr. Perkins brought me for safekeeping and I told him I was."[25]

As Ruffin lay in his cell, mobs took vengeance in Jenkins County. In the first of many acts of violence that night, white men with guns charged the church at Carswell Grove, firing as they came. Congregants jumped through windows and took off into the woods. Mothers tossed children through the windows, and then scrambled behind them.[26] The mob torched the building.[27] Smoke and flames could be seen for miles as dusk descended.

White men went to Ruffin's farm and grabbed his youngest son, Henry. No account mentions the whereabouts of Ruffin's daughters. They apparently fled. Somewhere near the church, the mob also grabbed another Ruffin, John Holiday. Louis Ruffin escaped. The mob took Ruffin's car and drove the two boys back to the roaring fire at the remains of the

Carswell Grove church. The mob burned Ruffin's car, one of the clearest symbols of the black man's relative wealth. White men then hung a wagon "trace" chain around one son's neck and a rope around the other's. They threw both of Ruffin's sons into the flames. It is not clear whether they were dead when they were tossed into the fire. At some point, the bodies were shot. When the corpses were examined the next day, it was impossible to tell which son suffered the chain and which got the rope.

The mob next moved south to Millen. Three black Masonic lodges were torched. At least two more cars owned by blacks were destroyed. One black man was shot and wounded; mob members told a reporter that the man was at fault for acting suspiciously by running away when they approached. There were reports of other blacks murdered in remote sections of the county.

The crescendo of the mob's work in Millen was the abduction and lynching of Ruffin's friend Willie Williams, who had helped him get up after being shot. Sheriff's deputies took him into custody, presumably for his own safety. First they put him in the county jail near the courthouse. When they learned a mob was searching for Williams, they hid him in a nearby stable. But a mob easily found Williams. They dragged him three miles outside of town to a remote swamp hollow. They tortured him, and then shot him to death. Word came from the mob that before he died, Williams confessed to a plot to kill Brown because of his anti-liquor activities, though he would not tell the mob where Louis Ruffin, allegedly wounded, was hiding.[28] Blacks lured the white law officers into a trap, the story went. Another black man who was arrested, Jim Davis, also "confessed" to the plot and his life was spared. The story made its way, without any evidence or attribution, into news accounts of the lynchings, offering white readers moral justification for what happened. Whites cast the killings as all lynchings were presented, as *lex talionis*—the law of retribution.

The morning of April 14, the *Augusta Chronicle* ran a front-page, banner headline in capital letters: "RACE RIOT AT MILLEN; NEGRO IN JAIL HERE." The *Macon Telegraph* reported the day after the lynchings that hundreds of whites came to Carswell Grove and "found the church a charred ruin. The bodies of the two Ruffins—what was left of them—were still lying on the ground."[29] White reporters filed stories from the telegraph office at the Millen Depot, spreading the news across the country. The *Telegraph* reported Millen's blacks circulating a petition asking whites not to burn down any more of their churches. Black Masons in

Jenkins wrote to the *Atlanta Independent*, the main black newspaper in the state, to solicit donations to rebuild their destroyed lodges. The letter never mentioned the lynchings but only pleaded for money "to help us in our trouble as none of us know just where and when our troubles are coming."[30]

The published accounts were full of inaccuracies, ranging from minor misspellings to confusion over whether the mob had lynched Louis Ruffin. No newspaper—white or black—ever definitively reported how many people were killed; the number ranged from four to seven. In many of the stories, hearsay blended with fact, and prejudice assumed the guise of accepted wisdom. White mob members were not quoted or named. Blacks were not interviewed. White newspapers discounted the riot as a regrettable aberration as soon as it was over.

"All is quiet again," assured Jenkins County journalist John Gordon Ellison in the April 16 *Atlanta Constitution*. "The innocent will have nothing to fear."

Black newspapers, in the midst of a golden age of growth across the country, ran the Jenkins County story and put their own agenda onto the bare facts. At the time, the *Chicago Defender* was the nation's largest black newspaper, with a circulation of more than 100,000. Much of that circulation penetrated the Deep South, where most of America's more than 10 million blacks lived.[31]

The *Defender's* defense of black rights, sharp criticism of Jim Crow, and ardent call for southern blacks to migrate to northern cities aroused deep hatred from southern whites. Southern legislators moved to ban its distribution. Black readers loved it. On April 19, the *Defender* picked up the Jenkins County story with the headline: "White Officer Is Killed for Breaking Up Church." The *Defender* story laid blame on the white police officers for trying to break up a revival meeting and turned the piece into a pro-migration story.

"It appears to have been another case of too much of the 'Southern Idea' of interfering with our people, this part of the country representing the usual type of Georgia civilization," the article read.

Some suggested whites were threatened by the economic success that black men like Ruffin embodied. William Pickens, famed dean of the black Morgan State University in Baltimore, wrote about the clash on the front page of the *Washington Bee*, a newspaper serving what was then the nation's largest black urban population. Pickens wrote that Ruffin, "one of the wealthiest Negroes in Jenkins County," had been shot and his sons lynched in part because whites were jealous of his wealth.[32]

"This disposition of the South to govern the Negro without his consent or participation, to really 'keep the Negro down,' will make trouble to the end of it," he added.[33]

The *Savannah Tribune*, a black weekly, declared the violence was a reaction to the rising economic status of southern black farmers. The root cause, it argued, was "a deep-seated envy and animosity toward a few thrifty and industrious Negroes there who committed no worse wrong than to appropriate to themselves the right and privilege to own pleasure automobiles to enjoy and break the monotony of their Sundays."[34]

The editorial stated: "The tension and stress of racial hate and envy is so unnecessary and so unwarranted that it cannot obtain for many years more. Negro progress will continue: the attitude and opposition of the lawless, shiftless lynching elements must yield."

But the white mobs did not yield. They roamed Jenkins County for days. They grabbed a black man from neighboring Burke County, believing he was Louis Ruffin. Only when the terrified man was brought back to Millen and properly identified did they turn him loose. The mob made threats to get Joe Ruffin from jail in Augusta. When his jailers heard a mob was headed their way, they sent Ruffin to a jail in Aiken, South Carolina. Even out of state, Ruffin had no idea whether a white mob might show up some night to lynch him. Sending mobs far distances to kill people was not without precedent in Georgia. Georgia led the nation in lynchings in 1918 and had the most lynchings of any state since anyone had cared to keep records.[35] In a notorious case in 1915, a mob traveled over several counties to kidnap Leo Frank, a Jewish businessman, and lynch him for the alleged rape and murder of a young white girl, Mary Phagan. Hugh Dorsey, the prosecutor handling the Frank case, had been mortified by the lynching, which made national news and outraged Jews across the country. Dorsey became governor after Frank's death in part due to a promise to crack down on lynching.

In early 1919, Dorsey drafted legislation to authorize the state to seize control of sheriffs's departments and levy fines against county officials who did not suppress lynching. A day after the Carswell Grove lynchings, a reporter found Dorsey at a hotel in Macon and asked him about the violence.

"I have put in a call for the sheriff," he said. "And if the county authorities wish any state aid, the National Guard organizations at Savannah can be quickly rushed to the scene of the trouble."[36]

No such request was ever made; Jenkins County would handle the "trouble" itself. The county prosecutor charged Joe Ruffin with the murders of officers Brown and Scott and ordered that he be returned for trial. If Ruffin made it to trial without being lynched, his conviction was certain and his hanging would follow. No white person was ever arrested or charged with any crime relating to the riots and lynchings of April 13 or the destruction of the church and other buildings. Perkins, the county commission chairman who had rushed Ruffin to safety, ruled that no inquest regarding the white attackers was necessary.

At some point, someone—perhaps a jailer who read newspaper accounts of the lynching—told Ruffin that two of his sons were dead.

"This is an awful thing. It is awful!" Ruffin moaned later. "I am sorry for Mr. Brown. I am also sorry for Mr. Stephens; I am sorry for their families, but there has been nobody suffered in this matter like I have. I did not do nothing at all to cause that riot."[37]

The Jenkins County riot was not an isolated tragedy. In coming months, similar horrors would afflict cities and towns across America. The violence that April Sunday was only the beginning of what would become known as the Red Summer of 1919, when riots and lynchings spread throughout the country, causing havoc and harming thousands—yet also awakening millions of blacks to fight for rights guaranteed them, but so long denied.

2.

Things Fall Apart

America, will you let us fall,
After we so bravely answered your call?
Now why! Oh why! Is Freedom's Door
Closed against us as it was before?

—Burris Alexander, *black soldier*

THE YEAR 1919 WAS SUPPOSED TO BE ONE OF TRIUMPHANT PEACE and universal fellowship. Speaking in the United Kingdom as 1918 drew to a close, President Woodrow Wilson declared the world had united to defeat autocracy. With the war over, he said, "We shall now be drawn together in a combination of moral force that is irresistible."[1]

In the United States, many people—including black families with returning soldiers—fervently hoped 1919 would usher in a new epoch of peace, prosperity, and freedom. Black soldiers and workers believed their participation in the effort to make the world safe for democracy had earned them the equal rights they had been promised in the Constitution since the close of the Civil War.

Emmett J. Scott, assistant to Secretary of War Newton Baker and the highest-ranking black official in the Wilson administration, predicted the black soldier would return home with a broader vision of American citizenship and an appreciation of what liberty and freedom really meant.

"He will be anxious to renew and strengthen the friendly relations he left behind, confident that a spirit of justice abides in the land to which he is returning," Scott told dignitaries at the Tuskegee Institute in Alabama.[2]

But African Americans received no such welcome, despite their service in France. The lynchings and burning of Carswell Grove Baptist Church proved to be the tocsin of antiblack riots and lynchings that would sweep the nation from April to November 1919, as racial unrest rolled through the South, North, Midwest, and into the nation's capital.

It would be the worst spate of race riots and lynchings in American history. Even in the disordered 1960s, famed black historian John Hope Franklin considered 1919 as "the greatest period of interracial strife the nation has ever witnessed."[3]

James Weldon Johnson, the field secretary of the National Association for the Advancement of Colored People in 1919, called this season the Red Summer because it was so bloody. The violence enveloped towns, counties, and large cities from Texas to Nebraska, Connecticut to California. Though no complete and accurate records on the months of violence were compiled, analysis of newspaper accounts, government documents, court records, and NAACP files, show at least 25 major riots and mob actions erupted and at least 52 black people were lynched. Many victims were burned to death.[4] Riots were often over in hours, but some immobilized cities like Chicago, Washington, Knoxville, and Elaine, Arkansas, for days. Millions of Americans had their lives disrupted. Hundreds of people—most of them black—were killed and thousands more were injured. Tens of thousands were forced to flee their homes or places of work. Businesses lost millions of dollars to destruction and looting. In almost every case, white mobs—whether sailors on leave, immigrant slaughterhouse workers, or southern farmers—initiated the violence.

———

Some had predicted this trouble as black soldiers and stevedores returned home after fighting for democracy in Europe.

"The return of the Negro soldier to civil life is one of the most delicate and difficult questions confronting the Nation, north and south," wrote George Haynes, Fisk University professor and director of Negro Economics for the United States Department of Labor.[5]

In the first months after the war's abrupt end, blacks hoped they had won a new place in American society. It was a "plastic moment," as historian Richard Slotkin put it, when racial boundaries seemed to undulate and the social order expanded, possibly to allow a new place for blacks.[6]

On February 17, 1919, three thousand black soldiers of the 369th Infantry Regiment of the 15th New York National Guard paraded triumphantly through Manhattan up to Harlem. The Harlem Hellfighters, as they were called, had distinguished themselves in combat, and they returned home to cheers from New Yorkers—most of them white—lining the avenues. A *World* reporter declared the soldiers' dark skin "made no difference in the shouts and flagwaving and handshakes that were bestowed upon" the regiment.[7]

But soon race relations frayed and goodwill from the war dissipated. Many whites resorted to threats and violence to reassert their old dominance. Most politicians did not see the rising potential for riots or lynching. Some openly endorsed such antiblack violence when it came. Others said there was little they could do to stop it. Most delayed and bungled when faced with crises.

Blacks, who had seen themselves on the cusp of true equality, became confused and angry. Corporal Burris Alexander, who served with engineers in France, composed a plaintive poem that captured black sentiment.

America, will you let us fall,
After we so bravely answered your call?
Now why! Oh why! Is Freedom's Door
Closed against us as it was before?[8]

Yet something amazing happened as the mobs rose up. They encountered black men and women transformed by their experiences during the war, whether in European trenches, on the factory floors of northern cities, or in the cotton fields of the South. The economic, social, and political dynamics of black-white relations were changing. African Americans fought back in large numbers. They retaliated immediately, picking up guns and firing on approaching mobs. They also organized and transformed political organizations, primarily the NAACP, to challenge the violence in the political arena and the courts. The white attacks, and importantly the black reaction to them, emboldened blacks across the country and made 1919 a turning point in American race relations.

William Edward Burghardt (W. E. B.) Du Bois, head of the NAACP's publications and editor of its monthly magazine *The Crisis*, saw black troops returning from victory in Europe as a civil rights vanguard.

"By the God of Heaven, we are cowards and jackasses if now that the war is over, we do not marshal every ounce of our brain and brawn to fight a sterner, long, more unbending battle against the forces of hell in our own land," he announced.[9]

Black journalist William Allison Sweeney declared early in 1919 that the idea of keeping blacks oppressed after the war was "the graveyard yawp of a dying monster."[10]

"The day has dawned and the start has been made," Sweeney wrote in his popular *History of the American Negro in the Great World War.* "Before the noontime, America will be prouder of her Negro citizens and will be a happier, a more inspired and inspiring nation; a better home for all her people."[11]

Average black men also felt this energy. Stanley B. Norvell, a black veteran awarded French medals for bravery, wrote to a white newspaper editor that the war had aroused desires for true equality and freedom.

"The five hundred thousands [sic] Negroes who were sent overseas to serve their country were brought into contacts that widened both their perceptions and their perspectives, broadened them, gave them new angles on life, on government, and on what both mean," wrote Norvell, then living in Chicago. "They are now new men and world men, if you please; and their possibilities for direction, guidance, honest use and power are limitless, only they must be instructed and led. They have awakened, but they have not yet the complete conception of what they have awakened to."[12]

In the first months of 1919, black culture and society radiated a new vitality and hope. In New York, Harlem expanded with theaters, cabarets, restaurants, and a budding literary scene. Caribbean immigrants poured in, bringing new forms of music and poetry and espousing fresh political theories. Jazz sank roots in Chicago's South Side, the black capital of the Midwest. Black theaters became popular. A black film industry developed. Black communities, including many in southern towns, launched publications modeled after the established and profitable *Chicago Defender.* The NAACP's *The Crisis* gained tens of thousands of readers. Black clubs and Masonic lodges attracted members. Black-themed books drew healthy sales. The year saw the first mass manufacture of black dolls for children.

"Teach your children pride of race and appreciation of race," an advertisement for the dolls read.[13] Fittingly, one was a soldier in uniform.

Yet despite this uplift, blacks had virtually no political power in early 1919. The last black congressman had left office in 1901. Across the South, governments disenfranchised blacks. In the North, their votes only mattered when concentrated in a few urban areas.

But the young black writer Jean Toomer, in one of his first published writings, declared the riots to be the start of a new era in American race relations. "As long as the Negro here was passive the true solution of the race problem could wait," he wrote in a socialist New York newspaper. "The South burned and lynched, and the North aided by its silence. But now, with the Negro openly resolved and prepared to resist attacks upon his person and privileges, the condition assumes a graver aspect. Immediate steps toward cooperative relations are imperative. It now confronts the nation."[14]

The violence hit the United States amid a profusion of other national and international crises that swirled about after a war so bloody, damaging, and horrific that all anyone could think to call it was the Great War. A new map of Europe emerged, with nations born from collapsed empires. Radicals saw the Bolshevik Revolution in Russia as an opportunity to reorder the world. The rest of the world trembled. White Russian armies, aided by American and British troops, fought the Reds from the Baltic to Siberia. Marxists led uprisings in German cities, only to be crushed by right-wing Freikorps. Bela Kun tried to establish a Communist state in Hungary, but the revolt was put down. British colonial troops mowed down rioters in India, Jamaica, and elsewhere. The genocide of Armenians by the Turks, begun in 1915 and resulting in one million deaths, came to light in early 1919. Thousands of Jews were killed in pogroms in Ukraine. Influenza, which had killed tens of millions around the world, continued to take lives. William Butler Yeats captured the pervading dread and worldwide chaos in his poem "The Second Coming":

> Things fall apart; the centre cannot hold;
> Mere anarchy is loosed upon the world,
> The blood-dimmed tide is loosed, and everywhere
> The ceremony of innocence is drowned.[15]

In the United States, the Allied victory did not mean peace. Instead, uncertainty permeated political discourse and social interaction. For the first time, census takers found that the majority of Americans lived in cities. In 1919, women secured the right to vote. Prohibition was set to become national law. The year would see the founding of two American Communist parties, a national crackdown on subversives, and an explosion of strikes and labor unrest. Amid the chaos, blacks were attacked with impunity.

The 1919 racial violence came at a pivotal moment in American history, ushered in by a confluence of forces, including the rise of Jim Crow, the

Great Migration and urbanization, plus an economic downturn exacerbated by hundreds of thousands of job-seeking veterans home from the Great War. The nation appeared to be collapsing before the challenges.

A growing fear was radicalism. Talk of revolution and the rise of white supremacist movements unnerved many Americans. The Red Summer arrived in tandem with the Red Scare, which was rolling across Europe and into America. Clearly, the old social order was breaking down. Race played a major role in the unrest.

Small-minded politicians and irresponsible journalists seized on racial violence to promote agendas and careers. The rising black press worked to counter biased coverage, but most white newspapers, from the *New York Times* to the *Jackson Daily News* in Mississippi, favored whites in their reports, blaming blacks for initiating trouble.[17] Those who spoke out in favor of the rule of law were shouted down. Courageous political leaders were largely absent. It seemed the Great War had upset everything, settling nothing.[17]

3.

The World Is on Fire

We have found from bitter experience, and this case is no exception, that we cannot depend upon the police, the posse of the sheriff, or the militia.

—CHICAGO DEFENDER, April 5, 1919

THE JENKINS COUNTY RIOT WAS NOT AN ISOLATED EVENT. IN MANY places, whites battled blacks over where they lived, where they worked, and how they voted. On April 13, the same day blood was shed at Carswell Grove, a group of white men in Metcalfe, Mississippi, kidnapped a black minister. A week later, the Reverend John H. F. West was still missing.[1]

Around 3 a.m. on April 14, a mob looking for a black man accused of shooting a white police officer attacked a plantation near Fitzgerald, Georgia. The mob could not find him, so it burned down a black church on the property.[2] On April 22, a scuffle between three white military guards and black civilians near the naval yards at Newport News, Virginia, led to a "near riot" after a guard shot a black girl in the foot. Military police later arrested sixteen black men, but they escaped when hundreds of others rushed the jail. In what was to become a standard line in news reports during 1919, the story ended: "The authorities declare that they are anticipating no more serious trouble."[3] Yet an armed mob stopped a train on April 29 near Monroe, Louisiana. George Holden, a black man, was dragged from the train, then shot to death. He was accused of writing an insulting note to a white woman. A coroner's jury convened later that day declared that Holden "came to his death by unknown causes."[4]

Racial violence was not limited to the South. In Chicago, black and Irish gangs fought along Wentworth Avenue, one of the city's racial dividing lines.

"Brickbats, clubs and bullets were used promiscuously and many on each side were hurt," the Associated Press reported. "Racial feeling has been gaining in intensity, the police say, since the encroachment of Negroes from what is known as the South Side 'Black Belt' into a district further southward."[5]

The article did not mention another cause of tension: on April 1, Mayor "Big Bill" Thompson, a Republican, won a second term after a campaign labeled "perhaps the most acrid ever waged in Chicago." Black support for Thompson inflamed his white opponents, who saw him as using blacks to check their advance. "All the prejudice tom-toms were sounding furiously," an observer noted.[6]

In the North, returning veterans had trouble finding jobs, since few factories were hiring and southern black migrants had filled many jobs.[7] On April 19, a federal official in Chicago, working to place veterans in jobs, reported to superiors that he was urging blacks to return to the South. Black migrants were not receptive, he said, because the black worker knew "what conditions and wages are and there is nothing that I know of that could induce him to return if he prefers to stay north."[8]

In the South, employers grew desperate for black labor. On April 22, John D. Baker, head of the Chamber of Commerce in Jacksonville, Florida, wrote to a federal veterans employment office in Chicago begging for cheap black workers.

"We people of the South understand the Negro laborer," he wrote, "and the large employers of labor in this section of the country prefer the working of Negro's [sic] to the white man, especially in the turpentine camps, saw mills, and upon the plantations, for these men understand this work, and give better satisfaction than the white man."[9]

That spring, Emmett Scott, the black assistant secretary at the War Department, sent a special report to the director of the National Defense Council. The war had completely upset the American economy and race relations, he wrote, "thus presenting social and economic problems—UPON THE PROPER SOLUTION OF WHICH WILL LARGELY DEPEND THE FUTURE SECURITY, WELFARE, and PROSPERITY OF BOTH WHITE AND COLORED AMERICANS."[10]

In early April, the nation was reminded of a recent spasm of racial violence with the murder conviction of Leo Bundy, a black dentist and local political leader from East St. Louis, Illinois. An all-white jury found that Bundy conspired to murder white detectives and incited a riot on July 2, 1917. National news coverage of Bundy's trial and conviction awakened ugly memories of the young century's worst race riot. Thousands of whites had attacked black neighborhoods of the factory town known with derision as "the Hoboken of St. Louis."[11] An estimated 6,000 blacks fled across the Mississippi River to St. Louis as white mobs burned and ransacked black homes and businesses. Future international entertainer Josephine Baker, then an eleven-year-old living in St. Louis, likened it to the Apocalypse. "The entire black community appeared to be fleeing," she recalled.[12] At least forty blacks and eight whites were killed.

White union members, fuming at black union busters, led the riot. Illinois militia were sent to quell them, but did little to protect black victims. In some instances, soldiers participated in the violence. When asked by a congressional committee what he saw soldiers doing during the riot, a white witness replied tersely, "Shooting Negroes."[13] The 1917 riot shocked a nation that had entered the European conflict claiming to end German atrocities against Belgian civilians. Black activists and journalists across the country were outraged. White leaders were embarrassed. President Woodrow Wilson's press secretary found accounts of the riot too sickening to read. Yet despite national calls for a presidential investigation, Wilson remained silent.[14] A political cartoon in the *New York Evening Mail* pictured an East St. Louis black mother cowering with two children and pleading to Wilson: "Mr. President, why not make *America* safe for democracy?" A hatchet-faced Wilson glared without comment.[15]

Bundy, who had argued that blacks should use force to defend themselves against white mobs, was charged with the murder of two police officers. Scant evidence linked Bundy to the shooting, but he was extradited from Cleveland. At first, black activists and white liberals set up committees for his legal defense. Newly appointed NAACP field secretary James Weldon Johnson organized a 10,000-person silent march down Fifth Avenue in New York to protest the East St. Louis riot and lynchings in general. The NAACP sent a delegation, including Johnson, to the White House with a petition declaring, "No nation that seeks to fight the battles of civilization can afford to march in blood-smeared garments." Wilson declined to see the visitors.[16]

All this ugliness was revived in the spring of 1919 with Bundy's trial, held in the small community of Waterloo, Illinois, 20 miles from East St. Louis. Bundy's lawyers savaged prosecution witnesses and provided ample evidence that Bundy was not involved in the murders or in the riot that followed. The jury still found him guilty.[17] Blacks across the country were livid. The *Chicago Defender* called it "a shameful miscarriage of justice," saying Illinois governor Frank Lowden caused the riot by waiting too long to send in the militia and did little to enforce troop discipline once he finally did.

"A little exercise of executive backbone at the proper moment might have resulted in the saving of many lives and in preventing the destruction of thousands of dollars' worth of valuable property," a *Defender* editorial stated on April 5, 1919. "It might have kept the great state of Lincoln and Grant from stepping into the same column with Texas and Mississippi."[18]

The editorial closed with a declaration that would prove prescient: "There is but one way to deal with a mob—that is to prepare for it, and when you see it in action move to meet it with every weapon at your command. We have found from bitter experience, and this case is no exception, that we cannot depend upon the police, the posse of the sheriff, or the militia."[19]

Claude McKay, a twenty-nine-year-old Jamaican immigrant, railroad porter, and aspiring poet, published a poem that April in the New York–based leftist publication *The Liberator*. The poem was called "The Dominant White," and it served as a muscular rebuke of the prevailing attitude that whites were a superior race destined to rule the world:

> God gave you power to build and help and lift;
> But you proved prone to persecute and slay
> And from the high and noble course to drift
> Into the darkness from the light of day.

The poem closed with an explicit threat:

> Oh White Man! You have trifled with your trust
> And God shall humble you down to the dust.[20]

McKay was little known at the time. Within months, however, he published "If We Must Die," a poem that would make him famous as the de facto poet laureate of the cause of black self-defense.

A few whites picked up on the shift in black attitude. In January, the seventy-three-year-old Moorfield Storey, a Boston Brahmin lawyer and the NAACP's first president, noted that discharged black soldiers—just beginning to return to the country—were not "disposed to accept the treatment to which they have been subjected. . . . I foresee a serious crisis."[21]

But most whites did not see this seething racial tension in the spring of 1919. In fact, many assumed race relations were improving. On the same day as the Carswell Grove violence, the *New York Times* published a letter to the editor titled "After-the-War South: An Improvement in Social Temper and Racial Feeling With Return of Troops." Progressive educator James Hardy Dillard argued that the war had smoothed relations:

> People in the South know that the race problem is there; know from time to time, in this place and that, some fool or fools of one race or the other will act according to their folly and make trouble. But there is a mysterious wisdom in the great body of the people, in the South and elsewhere, which keeps them going on with their ordinary lives and in a sort of subconscious way guides them as if they had reasoned out the fact that time alone can cure some ills and that meantime occasional aches and pains will occur. . . . You could easily make a month's tour in the South and forget all about lynching and other damnable things.[22]

Dillard was no Jim Crow apologist. His credentials as an advocate for black education and racial harmony were unequaled among southern whites. Born to Tidewater Virginia aristocracy in 1856, Dillard seemed destined for a comfortable life within the confines of the elite institutions of southern education. Instead, he spent his life monitoring race relations and working to improve educational opportunities for blacks. A key goal, he wrote, was to help "transform the average white man's attitude towards the Negro."[23] Dillard was president of two national funds for black education.[24] He cofounded the Southern University Race Commission, which attempted to lead a Christian men's movement against lynching.[25] In 1918, he engineered formation of the Atlanta-based Commission on Interracial

Cooperation. The group of religious leaders and academics worked to set up biracial committees to ease tension in every county of every state in the South. Many Americans considered Dillard one of the keenest experts on what was called "the Negro Problem." So when the sixty-two-year-old wrote the *Times* from his home in Charlottesville, editors gave the letter prominent display. Dillard had finished a three-week tour of the South, talking with "people of both races, men and women, educated and uneducated." He recounted meeting a white Alabama Baptist minister roughly his own age on a train. When the minister saw black soldiers standing on a railway platform, he remarked that the men should get the right to vote if they met qualifications. Dillard took this anecdote as a sign of progress. Dillard wrote to the *Times* with one clear purpose: to allay concerns regarding racial tension. Mob violence, he argued, was on the wane.[26]

Most blacks considered Dillard's views deluded. Walter White, the NAACP's young assistant field secretary, wrote an internal memo to James Weldon Johnson about Dillard's piece.

"The colored man of the South is not satisfied nor is he so busy that he doesn't think of the race problem," he wrote. "Not a day can pass but he is reminded vividly of it and such constant reminders are not conducive towards forgetting."[27]

Dillard was not the only Pollyanna. A group of southern university professors, from institutions like the University of Alabama, the University of Mississippi, and the University of North Carolina, banded together several years earlier and issued pamphlets calling for white college men to be more sympathetic toward blacks. They fell far short, however, of calling for equality. On April 26, 1919, the professors issued "A New Reconstruction," asking white college men "to seek by all practicable means to cultivate a more tolerant spirit, a more generous sympathy, and a wider degree of cooperation between the best elements of both races, to emphasize the best rather than the worst features of interracial relations, to secure greater publicity for those whose views are based on reason rather than prejudice—these, we believe, are essential parts of the Reconstruction programme by which it is hoped to bring into the world a new era of peace and democracy."[28] On the eve of unprecedented racial violence, many white political leaders and journalists embraced this romantic sentiment. For two years, Americans had been told incessantly that the war's end would bring global peace and prosperity and that the nation was the most unified and patriotic on earth.

But this propaganda began evaporating in the spring of 1919. War and economic hardship roamed the world, and the United States came close to being torn asunder along fault lines of race and labor. Isaac Frederick Marcosson, the popular economic and political writer, predicted in his *The War After the War* in 1917: "Peace will be as great a shock as War."[29]

While Germany and the Allies worked to finalize a treaty of surrender at Versailles, the world beyond the grand château's terraced gardens was falling apart. On April 13, the same day as the Carswell Grove incident, British troops in Amritsar, India, fired on unarmed protesters, killing at least 379 men, women, and children, and wounding at least 1,100 more. Novelist John Dos Passos presented the global mood in his novel *1919*:

> The world's no fun anymore,
> only machinegunfire and arson
> starvation lice bedbugs cholera typhus.[30]

Victory left America feeling anxious and exhausted, not robust and triumphant. H. L. Mencken summed up the mindset of the average American: "There is always something just ahead of him, beckoning him and tantalizing him, and there is always something just behind him, menacing him and causing him to sweat."[31] In the spring, while working to negotiate a European peace in France, the prosaic President Wilson confided to his personal physician: "The world is on fire."[32]

Many Americans felt the same way. In late April, the black editors of the *Cleveland Gazette* wrote sardonically: "Nero thought he was some pumpkins when he fiddled for a few days while the city of Rome burned. Now we fiddle around five months while the whole world burns."[33]

4.

The NAACP

Make way for Democracy! We saved it [in] France, and by
the Great Jehovah, we will save it in the United States of
America, or know the reason why.

—W. E. B. Du Bois, "Returning Soldiers,"
The Crisis, May 1919

As Carswell Grove church smoldered in Georgia, twelve men and one woman gathered Monday, April 14, in the Manhattan offices of the NAACP. It is unlikely anyone there knew of Carswell Grove. A small item on the killings appeared in New York newspapers the next day.

But this band of social workers and intellectuals was about to have its organization irrevocably transformed by the violence now spreading out from places like Jenkins County. Other black rights groups operated at the time, some older and better financed than the NAACP. William Monroe Trotter, editor of the black publication *Boston Guardian*, headed the National Equal Rights League, which traced its origins to the abolitionist movement of the 1840s. The National League on Urban Conditions Among Negroes, known as the Urban League, worked in industrial cities to improve the lives of black migrants. Black political organizations arose in different communities across the United States. The Lincoln League, founded in Memphis in 1916, was a Republican Party group for blacks that had set up chapters across the South and was about to establish the national Lincoln League of America. In 1917, Marcus Garvey established a division of his Universal Negro Improvement Association in his new home in Harlem. It was the first division of his organization out-side of his native Jamaica. The UNIA flourished with chapters in major cities, including many in the South. Garvey promoted the UNIA with the group's weekly newspaper, *The Negro World*. All of these organiza-tions played a role reacting to bloody 1919, but the NAACP would domi-nate. As the violence unfolded, blacks needed to channel a political response. In overwhelming numbers, they chose the NAACP.

Just as the *Chicago Defender* became a main news source for blacks, the NAACP became the primary civil rights organization. After its founding in 1909, it was a small, somewhat sleepy group led by white do-gooders. But that began to change as it approached its tenth anniversary. Howard University professor Kelly Miller, one of the country's most well known writers on black rights, wrote after the East St. Louis riot: "The United States thus becomes the world's most interesting laboratory for working out the intricate issues of race adjustment."[1] The interplay between the NAACP and the Red Summer was to be one of that laboratory's most interesting experiments.

Despite the organization's name, only three of those gathered for its April board meeting were black. What is obvious from the minutes, how-ever, is that these three men—an intellectual lion, a literary and political dynamo, and a fearless young organizer—dominated the meeting with their reports. Soon they would dominate the organization, growing it to a size, strength, and reach never imagined by its white leaders. Their hard work and influence brought thousands of African Americans into the NAACP, helping it arise as the first sustained national black civil rights organization.

The three had considerable talents and egos that sent them on differ-ent trajectories after the bloody eight months, but for that crucial period they complemented each other greatly and propelled the NAACP's trans-formation and growth.

By far the most influential was W. E. B. Du Bois. The fifty-one-year-old Du Bois, balding with a Vandyke goatee and searching eyes, led a life marked by brilliant successes and tempestuous public arguments. Though Du Bois was greatly admired by many black and white activists, others found him imperious. Black writer George S. Schuyler, an army veteran who was living in Harlem in 1919, satirized Du Bois as a pompous ass in his novel *Black No More*: "Dr. Shakespeare Agamemnon Beard...whose haughty bearing never failed to impress both Caucasian and Negroes."[2] Du

Bois often fought with the NAACP board and as the Red Summer began, he was battling with them over expenses for his recent trip to France. He knew he could be trying, and once wrote fellow NAACP board member Joel Spingarn, "I do not doubt in the least but that my temperament is a difficult one to endure. In my peculiar education and experience it would be miraculous if I came through normal and unwarped."[3] He was the first African American to earn a doctorate at Harvard. His most influential book, *The Souls of Black Folk*, was published in 1903, and sparked controversy by criticizing Booker T. Washington, the era's famous conservative black leader and academic. Du Bois argued Washington had limited intellectual ambitions for African Americans and acquiesced to segregation.[4]

Du Bois was the only African American among the five people who founded the NAACP. In July 1910, he moved to New York to launch *The Crisis*. Under Du Bois's editorship, it grew in prestige, circulation, and advertising revenue.[5] In its pages, Du Bois advocated his program of fostering black leadership, which he called the "Talented Tenth," his term for the favored few. Du Bois believed in elite education rather than work-study programs of the sort favored by Booker T. Washington.

"No organization like ours ever succeeded in America; either it became a group of white philanthropists 'helping' the Negro like the Anti-Slavery societies; or it became a group of colored folk freezing out their white co-workers by insolence and distrust," he wrote Spingarn, his closest white friend, in 1914. "Everything tends to break along the color line. . . . How can this be changed? By changing it. By trusting black men with power."[6] The organization started doing just that, bringing on black staffers whom Du Bois recommended.

Another black man at the April meeting was James Weldon Johnson, the group's energetic field secretary. Du Bois recruited Johnson away from his life as an accomplished writer. "I am inclined to think that contact with human beings would be an incentive rather than a drawback to your literary work," Du Bois told him.[7]

Since joining the group, round-faced, gregarious Johnson traveled the Northeast and South, giving eloquent speeches and recruiting thousands of members. Using skills honed from years as a diplomat in Central America, Johnson also lobbied politicians in New York and Washington. Johnson, who considered himself a literary man, had found little time to write since taking the hectic job, which required constant travel and public speaking. "I simply cannot find the time, or better the leisure to write poetry," he wrote to a friend in May 1919.[8] Despite his peripatetic lifestyle, Johnson had produced some poems while on the road, until 1919 when he became too busy. At that April meeting, the forty-seven-year-old Johnson was just back from a two-week speaking tour to drum up support for an upcoming anti-lynching conference—the first such national meeting—in New York City.

The third black man, fair-skinned and with eyes so blue he could easily pass for Caucasian, was Walter White. At twenty-five, he was the youngest in the room. He had just returned from a speaking tour of black churches and civic groups in New England, Virginia, and the Carolinas. Johnson had lured White, a natural salesman, from a career in insurance. Raised in Atlanta and a witness to that city's 1906 race riot, White attended Atlanta University, where Du Bois had taught and where Johnson had earned a degree.[9] In 1917, White helped set up an Atlanta branch of the NAACP. His enthusiastic letters to the New York office impressed Johnson, who offered him a job as his assistant field secretary where "you can put enthusiasm and draw out inspiration."[10] Soon White went undercover to investigate lynchings throughout the South. The pawky White claimed it was so easy for him to pass for Caucasian he once was deputized to kill blacks while investigating a riot.[11] This dangerous "sleuthing," as he liked to call it, was perfect work for the chameleon-like White. Wrote biographer Kenneth Robert Janken: "His easy manner, Atlanta roots and white appearance gave him sources in mobs and Ku Klux Klan circles that were the journalist's envy."[12]

By April 1919, the three men had done much to help the NAACP grow. *The Crisis* was approaching a circulation of 100,000. Johnson and White set up dozens of chapters and recruited thousands of members. In January 1918, the NAACP had 9,200 members.[13] By April 1919, it had 51,023. Almost all of these new members were black and most came to the organization by reading *The Crisis* or by hearing speeches from one of the three men.

Still, the NAACP had yet to be tested politically, and critics discounted the organization as a gaggle of East Coast parlor socialists. The roster of board members present at the April meeting showed the criticism had some basis. The board's chair, Mary White Ovington, was a socialist and suffragette who helped found the NAACP. Spingarn, who that year founded the publishing house of Harcourt, Brace and Company, was a wealthy advocate of progressive causes and a former literature professor at Columbia University. Both he and his younger brother, prominent lawyer Arthur Barnette Spingarn, supported the NAACP from its inception and served in various roles in the organization. The two Jewish brothers had both recently returned from serving in the army in Europe. The NAACP's leading white staffer, John R. Shillady, was an Irish American social worker who had worked for several causes before joining the organization as secretary.[14]

Mary Ovington personified the white "do-gooder" leadership that dominated the NAACP's early years. Born in Brooklyn to left-leaning parents, she spent her life as a social worker helping New York's poor. As a young woman, she became interested in improving conditions for blacks after hearing Frederick Douglass speak. In 1904, she began a correspondence with Du Bois after reading *The Souls of Black Folk*. Following the Springfield, Illinois, race riot of 1908, she brought together the group that formed the NAACP a year later. Throughout her involvement, Ovington embraced a genteel reserve that set a tone for other whites on the board. They worked for the "advancement of colored people," but it was unpleasant to discuss ugly matters like lynchings and race riots.

"I can think of no more nauseating work for a kindly set of people," she wrote.[15]

In 1919, blacks found they needed more than paternalistic or maternalistic aid. They needed black leaders who listened to them and who commanded the respect of whites.

At the April meeting, NAACP board members heard sobering reports of how southern politicians continued to dismiss them as gadflies and meddlers. Shillady read off accounts of lynchings in March. After the lynching by 1,000 people of a black man accused of rape in Florida, Shillady sent a protest letter to Governor Sidney Johnston Catts, calling for those responsible to be brought to justice. The governor wrote back, arguing that the NAACP was promoting "lawlessness among Negroes" and should spend its efforts educating blacks, not defending black criminals. He failed to acknowledge that the man who was lynched was never convicted of the crime.

Shillady also talked about another lynching in early March in Belzoni, Mississippi. Eugene Green, a black pauper charged with wounding a marshal, was dragged from jail, hanged, shot, and dumped in a river. Shillady sent Governor Theodore Bilbo a telegram asking what steps had been taken by the Mississippi authorities to deal with the situation.[16] Bilbo ignored the telegram, as he had previous NAACP inquiries.[17] But the *Jackson Daily News,* a Bilbo ally, did respond to a duplicate telegram. In an article, the newspaper called the NAACP "a body of Northern extremists on the Negro question," adding the organization "need not remain in the dark concerning the fate of Green. He was 'advanced' all right from the end of a rope, and in order to save burial expenses his body was thrown in the Yazoo River."[18] Such contempt for the organization was common.[19]

In contrast to Shillady's dour report at the April meeting, the three black staffers brought optimistic news. Since the last board meeting, Johnson and White helped the NAACP found twenty-one new branches, from Spokane, Washington, to Baton Rouge, Louisiana, adding 1,366 new members.

Du Bois told the board about his trip to France. While some board members griped privately about the trip's cost of more than $2,000, Du Bois accomplished much. He was a key organizer of the Pan-African Congress in Paris, in which blacks from across the globe gathered to pass a resolution calling for racial equality to be presented to negotiators at Versailles. The French press wrote extensively about the congress and Du Bois. French officials treated him as a dignitary, further enhancing the NAACP's prestige and inflating Du Bois's ego.

While in Europe, amid white freethinkers, Du Bois began to view his homeland as hopelessly prejudiced. It did not matter that he was brilliant and accomplished, he thought. All that mattered in America was his skin color. In the April issue of *The Crisis,* Du Bois wrote about going to dinner in Paris and how liberating it was not to be trapped in American racial roles. His enjoyment of this simple pleasure, he wrote, made him angry. "It was simply human decency and I had to be thankful for it because I am an American Negro and white America, with saving exceptions, is cruel to everything that has black blood—and this was Paris, in the year of salvation, 1919."[20]

In France, Du Bois also collected evidence of the mistreatment of black soldiers. During the Great War, the United States enlisted 367,710 black men—most from the South—into the armed forces. About 200,000 were sent to France and about 50,000 of those saw combat. The vast majority served in supply units.[21] As one journalist observed, "They were doing the drudgery, the dull routine, the monotonous labor; still they were the foundation and groundwork upon which the whole army was built."[22] Black soldiers, segregated into their own units, were subjected to racial insults and accusations of cowardice and licentiousness. The news infuriated African American families who had sent their men off to war. Reverend Francis J. Grimké, brother of NAACP board member Archibald Grimké, told black war veterans in Washington that April: "I know of nothing that sets forth this cursed American race prejudice in a more odious, execrable light than the treatment of our colored soldier in this great world struggle that has been going on, by the very government that ought to have shielded them from the brutes that were over them."[23]

Though most African American troops were used in support units, those who did see combat acquitted themselves well. The 369th New York Infantry, made up of volunteers from Harlem, served more days under continuous fire than any other regiment in the American Expeditionary Force and suffered 40 percent killed and wounded.[24] It did not matter. White soldiers regularly disparaged black soldiering and portrayed blacks as lazy and unpatriotic.

The *Cleveland Gazette* wrote on its editorial page on April 12, 1919, "The Afro-American soldier overseas certainly had a hard time of it, with the Germans in front of him and prejudiced Southerners on all three of his other sides."

This treatment was somewhat expected at home, but it embittered black Americans risking their lives in war. At a field near Metz on November 23, 1918, a black regiment that had been in hard fighting at Champagne was ordered to sing "My Country, 'Tis of Thee." The roughly 3,000 men stood in silence as six white officers sang.[25]

Du Bois spent months reporting firsthand in Paris and at American military bases in the French countryside, documenting mistreatment of black officers, privates, and stevedores. At his prodding, the NAACP board passed a resolution at the April meeting demanding "a congressional investigation of the treatment of colored soldiers in the United States and France." Du Bois had already penned one of his most famous essays, "Returning Soldiers," which he planned to publish as the lead article in the May issue of *The Crisis*. He knew this story would increase circulation and enhance the reputation of the NAACP as a defender of black rights. Black Americans had a new energy after the war, and Du Bois wanted to harness that strength:

> For America and her highest ideals, we fought in far-off hope; for the dominant southern oligarchy entrenched in Washington, we fought in

bitter resignation, For the America that represents and gloats in lynching, disfranchisement, caste, brutality and devilish insult—for this, in the hateful upturning and mixing of things, we were forced by vindictive fate to fight, also.

But today we return! We return from the slavery of uniform which the world's madness demanded us to don to the freedom of civil garb. We stand again to look America squarely in the face and call a spade a spade. We sing: This country of ours, despite all its better souls have done and dreamed, is yet a shameful land.

The essay ended in heroic cadence:

We *return.*
We *return from fighting.*
We *return fighting.*
Make way for Democracy! We saved it [in] France, and by the Great Jehovah, we will save it in the United States of America, or know the reason why.[26]

With his galloping lyricism, Du Bois addressed black America not as a member of a white-dominated social welfare group, but as a black soldier at war for something inherently his—dignity and equal rights. Every black person was a veteran of racial prejudice, Du Bois proclaimed, and every black person was ready to force true democracy on the nation. As the violence opened up in earnest, Du Bois's metaphoric license would approach an ugly reality. The United States was about to become a battlefield.

5.

National Conference on Lynching

The nation is today striving to lead the moral forces of the world in the support of the weak against the strong. Well, I'll tell you it can't do it until it conquers and crushes out this monster in its own midst.

—James Weldon Johnson, May 5, 1919

Carnegie Hall in Midtown Manhattan was bustling on the evening of May 5, 1919. The elegant concert hall had been built twenty-eight years earlier by industrialist Andrew Carnegie to be New York's premier space for classical performance. On this humid Monday night, however, an estimated 2,500 black and white people gathered to learn about the ugly subject of lynching.

The keynote speaker of the National Conference on Lynching was Charles Evans Hughes, ex–New York governor, former United States Supreme Court Justice, and failed 1916 Republican candidate for president. Hughes told the crowd that black soldiers who demonstrated bravery, honor, and loyalty in Europe deserved equal protection under the law back home.

"We are hearing much these days of the drawing together of the nations in cooperation to establish international justice. . . . I say that duty begins at home," he declared. "The salvation of democracy must lie in the days of peace after victory."[1]

Hughes's remarks were directed, in part, at his political nemesis, President Wilson, who was in France developing the framework for the

League of Nations. Republicans like Hughes voiced skepticism of Wilson's grand plans. They argued America needed to solve its own problems, including racial violence. Focusing on lynching emphasized the GOP's ties to the Civil War and Lincoln, and highlighted the fact that Jim Crow and lynching were concentrated in the Democratic South. Wilson was a southerner, the first one elected president since the Civil War. Republicans, having just taken control of both houses of Congress in January, were eyeing the White House in the upcoming 1920 election. But the Republicans were not pitching racial equality. Hughes and other politicians stressed law and order instead. Mob violence in the United States, if unchecked by the rule of law, would spread from the South, Hughes told the crowd. He condemned lynching by using jargon from the war just finished. It was "the very essence of the Hun spirit," he said. "If lawlessness succeeds in one place it will break out in another."

The conference was the brainchild of Moorfield Storey, the seventy-four-year-old past NAACP president. Storey was a dean of the black rights movement and could trace the roots of his activism back to Ralph Waldo Emerson, whom he met while an undergraduate at Harvard.[2] Storey helped found the NAACP and served as its first president until 1915. He headed the legal team that won the Supreme Court ruling in *Buchanan v. Warley* (1917), which found municipal racial segregation laws unconstitutional. The case was a triumph of Storey's approach to advancing black rights: persuasive argument presented in the corridors of power.

The year 1919 saw Storey attempt this approach again. After the East St. Louis riot of 1917, Republican congressman Leonidas Dyer of St. Louis had proposed a bill calling for federal intervention and punishment of local officials in acts of lynching. At first Storey opposed the bill, arguing it was unconstitutional. His overriding concern was that the Constitution did not allow for federal intervention in state murder cases.[3] In 1918, Storey, Arthur Spingarn, and others decided to back a modified version of Dyer's bill to see if any constitutional issues could be resolved. The bill died that year but in the fall Dyer planned to resubmit a new version for 1919. Storey held a special meeting at his Boston home to persuade NAACP leaders that a national conference on lynching could pressure Congress to pass the bill.[4] He insisted such a gathering be held in Manhattan, close to prestigious law firms that he was convinced would join the cause.

The timing seemed right. Pressure for federal anti-lynching legislation was building from both white progressive politicians and grassroots black groups across the country. In December, the Texas NAACP petitioned Governor William P. Hobby to pass similar legislation. He told the group he "was in hearty sympathy" with their cause.[5] On January 1, 1919, the Lincoln Memorial Association and other black groups asked the South Carolina legislature to improve education for African Americans. "We ask for such fearless enforcement of the law as will abolish lynchings and all forms of mob violence," the association mentioned at the close of its petition.[6]

In February, an anti-lynching meeting in Washington filled one of the largest church auditoriums in the city. Crowds were turned away.[7] In March, Congressman Henry Ivory Emerson, a Republican from Cleveland, called for a constitutional amendment "authorizing Congress to enact legislation to prevent lynching." Two other Republican congressmen, Frederick Dallinger of Massachusetts and Merrill Moores of Indianapolis, submitted similar bills. Other bills were proposed in several state legislatures.[8]

By March, conference planning was well under way and those "fairly representative of the best citizenship of the country," including governors, senators, congressmen, university presidents, and judges, agreed to attend.[9] Organizers were optimistic as the two-day conference was announced and received widespread publicity in the white and black press. Madame C. J. Walker, the black cosmetics entrepreneur, gave $3,000 to sponsor the meetings.[10] At the NAACP board's May 5 meeting, held just hours before the anti-lynching conference, board members and staff were thrilled at the organization's momentum. NAACP branches had grown to 205. Overall membership had jumped to 52,540.[11]

As a final publicity push, the NAACP released a booklet that April titled *Thirty Years of Lynching in the United States, 1889–1918*. It was sent to politicians, churches, charities, and publications across the country. NAACP researchers compiled data from clippings files and reports. Researchers found at least 3,224 people were lynched from 1889 to 1918. At least 2,522 of them were black.[12] Most lynchings occurred in the South. Only 219 people were lynched in the northern states and 101 of those—45.6 percent—were black.[13] Georgia had the most documented lynchings, with 386. Just 26 victims were white.[14] Lynching decreased in the first part of the twentieth century, the report claimed, but had picked up again during the Great War.[15]

The booklet was clinical, presenting charts and graphs, and was devoid of hyperbole. It contained no photographs or narrative accounts. It focused on the sheer volume of incidents for impact. The report found that white claims that lynchings were usually a response to black men raping white women were not true. Reasons given for mob attacks ranged from serious accusations like murder to trivial ones, such as a black man speaking inappropriately to a white woman.

The New Republic found the numbers astounding. "We are a nation disgraced; and the disgrace deepens year by year," the editors wrote.[16] *Atlanta Constitution* editors warned that "sooner or later if the states do not put an end to lynching and mob outlawry the federal government will!"[17]

The white mainstream press covered the conference, with the *New York Times* publishing several stories. But the *Times* did not even mention James Weldon Johnson, the only black man to address the audience that night. If Moorfield Storey represented the rich past of the black rights movement—white, stodgy, legalistic, and northeastern—then Johnson represented the movement's future—black, engaging, activist, and southern. Here, at the precipice of the unprecedented antiblack violence, stood a black man ready to argue to the white American public from a position of moral indignation. The NAACP's field secretary did not come to meekly request aid for an oppressed minority. He came to present, in stark terms, the universal moral imperative: that lynching and rioting were social evils. In 1919, condemning lynching and race riots was not an obvious assertion. Many whites argued they were necessary social purgatives, that those lynched brought on the violence. Even fierce lynching opponents, like Georgia's Governor Dorsey, argued it would end only when the black community restrained its rapists and other criminals.[18]

With a booming voice and confident delivery, Johnson worked to make attending whites—from A. Mitchell Palmer, the newly appointed U.S. attorney general, to Booth Tarkington, winner of the 1919 Pulitzer Prize for fiction—so uncomfortable that they would press political leaders for a federal anti-lynching law. Usually Johnson was too friendly a person to adopt the stern persona presented by Du Bois. But Johnson suppressed his amiability that night, making his blunt words all the more persuasive.

"I ask not only black Americans but white Americans, are you not ashamed of lynching?" he said to the crowd. "Do you not hang your head in humiliation to think that this is the only civilized country in the world—no, more than that, the only spot on earth—where a human being may be tortured with hot irons and then buried alive? The nation is today striving to lead the moral forces of the world in the support of the weak against the strong. Well, I'll tell you it can't do it until it conquers and crushes out this monster in its own midst."[19]

Born in 1871 in Jacksonville, Florida, Johnson's multiple talents and varied interests made him a towering literary and political figure in black America, even before he joined the NAACP national staff. He was raised in comfortable black middle-class surroundings. His father was a headwaiter and his mother a public school teacher. He attended Atlanta University, where he had his first political awakenings.[20] After graduating in 1894, he earned a law degree, started a black newspaper, and lived in New York for several years composing popular music with his brother Raymond. They wrote, "Lift Every Voice and Sing," which later became known as "The Negro National Hymn." In 1900, the two men saw firsthand a race riot in New York.[21]

In 1904, Johnson returned to his alma mater for an honorary degree and met Du Bois, then a professor there. Johnson was appointed American consul to Puerto Caballo, Venezuela (1906), and Corinto, Nicaragua (1909), by Theodore Roosevelt. In his spare time, he anonymously authored *The Autobiography of an Ex-Colored Man*, published in 1912. The novel made him a leading literary figure in black America. In 1914, he quit the diplomatic service to become a contributing editor at the *New York Age*. He was involved in Republican politics and strongly supported former New York governor Charles Hughes against Wilson in the 1916 presidential election.

In 1916, at Du Bois's urging, Johnson joined the NAACP as field secretary. He threw himself into his work, and only took his first substantial break in early 1919, when his mother died. Soon he was back, traveling and recruiting.

He was liked by all factions within the NAACP, and despite strong views on equal rights and Jim Crow, he got along with many blacks who supported the late Booker T. Washington's accommodationist approach.[22] Johnson was also a lawyer and a writer who moved easily in both professional circles. His correspondence was wide ranging. He exchanged letters with black writers like novelist Charles W. Chestnutt and white writers like *Smart Set* editor H. L. Mencken.

That night Johnson declared "the race problem in the United States has resolved itself into a question of saving black men's bodies and white men's souls." Such a moral framing of the issue of racial violence thrilled blacks in the audience. Johnson's protégé, Walter White, sitting in a front row, wrote in admiration that he could discern shocked expressions on the faces of whites on the dais as Johnson spoke.[23] On the stage at Carnegie Hall stood a representative of what would come to be called the New Negro. His message was blunt: "There are millions of intelligent Americans who do not know, who are not concerned with the fact that every year atrocities are committed in this enlightened land that would cause envy in the heart of the most benighted Turk."[24]

When the conference wrapped up two days later, attendees voted on resolutions urging passage of federal anti-lynching laws, calling on the NAACP to set up committees to push similar state laws.[25] Attendees were hopeful. J. C. Wilson, the leader of the Mississippi Welfare League, one of the few white southerners to attend, said, "The colored people have not always been able to secure justice in the courts nor to have the best advantages of education, but the time has come when all these things must change."[26]

The NAACP launched a campaign to double its membership to 100,000 by its June 21 national convention in Cleveland.[27]

The efforts had some immediate success. Republicans in Congress responded well to the meeting. Liberal publications touted the effort.[28] Within days, the NAACP raised $9,300 for anti-lynching efforts.[29] At the NAACP's May board meeting after the conference, the New York branch reported a record 5,000 members. At the same meeting, the board learned that the monthly circulation of *The Crisis* had hit 100,000 for the first time ever.

"Our 'friends' are beginning to feel the punch of *The Crisis*; now while they are groggy, lets 'hit em again,'" a gleeful reader wrote to Du Bois.[30]

Johnson went on a West Coast tour, hitting ten cities in two weeks. New chapters were chartered from California to Virginia to Ontario. Several NAACP speakers hit the stump.

Other groups joined in. Within weeks, the New York Bar Association, the Churches of Christ, and a national Presbyterian organization, Woodrow Wilson's own faith, passed resolutions calling for new laws against lynching. A week after the New York conference, the Southern Sociological Congress, a group of leading academics and social workers, urged "the immediate exercise of all possible state and federal power to put a speedy end to these outrages throughout the country."[31] The group launched its own education campaign among white universities and churches against lynching.[32] In June, the conservative Southern Race Congress met in New Orleans and lobbied for southern governments to combat lynching, not only for moral reasons but for economic ones: a way to keep black workers from migrating North.

"We want the people of the South to understand that our people want to remain in the South," said E. P. Columbus, business manager of the accommodationist group. "This is their homeland: they are happier here and more contented than they ever can or will be in the North, and they know it."[33]

The black community, however, was not uniformly behind the NAACP's anti-lynching campaign. Harry Smith, editor of the *Cleveland Gazette*, mocked the NAACP's conference as "simply another of its many 'hot-air' affairs that are now so well known all over the country by our people particularly."[34]

The conference had only a limited impact—it was full of speeches delivered with force to the already converted. Storey was unhappy about what ended up being poor participation from the major law firms he had invited. The former president of the American Bar Association assumed the firms would show up when he asked.[35] They were not interested. And though the press covered the conference, the stories were pushed off front pages by news of chaos and revolution. Anarchists sent package bombs to politicians and business leaders. Labor riots broke out in many cities on May Day. The International Workers of the World, known as the "Wobblies," held a three-week-long convention in Chicago. Thousands heard leader "Big Bill" Haywood and others predict capitalism's imminent collapse.[36] Revolts, food shortages, epidemics, and economic strife gripped Europe and the Middle East.[37]

To keep lynching in the forefront, the NAACP issued press releases on the latest attacks. Shillady called for a national program "to make America safe for Americans." He demanded an end to lynching, and called for voting equality for black men and women. He also demanded that blacks have the right to a fair trial and equal education. He condemned the lynching of a white man, unfortunately named Jay Lynch, in Lamar, Missouri. Lynch had pleaded guilty to murdering a sheriff and a mob pulled him from his cell and killed him.[38] The NAACP stressed that whites too could be victims of lynch law.[39]

Political allies bolstered the NAACP effort. Congressman Frederick William Dallinger (R-Massachusetts), a Harvard graduate who was friends with Storey and sympathetic to the NAACP, submitted his bill on

May 30, calling for fines and/or imprisonment for state, county, and city officials who allowed lynchings in their jurisdictions. It was similar to legislation he had proposed the year before. The bill, like its predecessor, went nowhere.[40] Dallinger, however, and other sympathetic legislators, like Dyer of Missouri, continued to press their case.

The NAACP had more success with black Americans that May. Walter White was sent out on tour for most of the month to drum up support after the anti-lynching conference. The persuasive White recruited new members across the Midwest.[41]

With its growing name recognition and expanding list of chapters, the NAACP became the main vehicle by which blacks concerned with mob violence could communicate and organize. From uneducated to educated, northern migrants to southerners, factory workers to business owners, blacks turned to the NAACP. As the month came to a close, Shillady received a letter from Harry Pace, secretary-treasurer of the black-owned Standard Life Insurance Company in Atlanta, an activist in that city's chapter, and a longtime friend of Du Bois.[42]

Pace mocked a white editor of the *Tampa Morning Tribune*, who wrote that the NAACP was holding its annual conference in Cleveland because blacks living in the North were stirring up political trouble, but blacks living in the South were not.[43]

"If the Editor of this paper could see some of the branch meetings which are being held weekly in Bethel church [in Atlanta], he would have his eyes opened to a number of things," Pace wrote. "The old bromide that the southern white man knows the southern Negro better than anybody else is the greatest joke that ever has been perpetrated."[44]

About the same time, Shillady received a handwritten letter from a Horace Jones of Pittsburgh. Jones had migrated from South Carolina and his brother, Howard, sent him information about racial violence back home. Jones collected his own information as well as his brother's and sent it along to the NAACP for investigation.

"Is thare not a Law to Safeguard the Negro Sitizens of the United States against the mobs and lynchers of this country," he wrote to Shillady. "We cannot Stay in the South if this is not stopped and proper treatment Restored to humanite. We are proud to have you help us in this Shameful Distress and we do hope throue your organization to Gaine Liberty and Freedom again and Life Liberty and Happiness."[45]

6.

Charleston

The first requisite for success in riot tactics is prompt action.

—Henry A. Bellows, *A Treatise on Riot Duty for The National Guard*, 1920

At nine o'clock on the sweaty Saturday night of May 10, 1919, a group of white sailors gathered at the corner of King and George streets in the black "tenderloin" section of downtown Charleston, South Carolina. The men were standing outside a pool hall owned by a black man with the unlikely name Harry Police. The five white sailors on weekend liberty from the nearby naval yard felt cheated. They had handed money to a bootlegger for a quart of whisky, but they claimed the man never came back.[1]

"We are looking for a damn nigger whom we gave $8 to get us some bug juice," one of the sailors shouted.[2] The group started scuffling with some black men. Someone fired a pistol. The sailors, armed with brickbats, stormed into Police's pool hall and attacked patrons.

Published accounts and testimony from police stated the trouble flared into a riot after the white sailors shot and killed a black man named Isaac Doctor.[3] Within an hour, word of the street brawls and shooting got back to the Charleston Navy Yard and carloads of white sailors poured into the black district. Sailors broke into two nearby shooting galleries, stealing rifles and hundreds of rounds of ammunition.[4] The mob swelled to one thousand sailors plus many civilians.[5] Rioters broke into black homes, smashing furniture, doors, and windows.[6]

"Get a nigger!" sailors shouted as they prowled the streets. They attacked a cobbler's shop, smashing the window and shooting a black apprentice.

Augustus Bonaparte, a black man, was getting his hair cut when he saw sailors raid a shooting gallery. Rioters jumped him, beating him with clubs and sticks. One sailor said, "Let's see if he has got any money." After hitting him some more, one sailor said, "That's enough." They left him on the ground.

At Marion Square, they pulled a black man off a trolley, then beat and shot him. Another was taken from a car on King Street near Market Street and shot.

"Persons in a fashionable restaurant were unwilling spectators to this," the *Atlanta Constitution* reported. "All witnesses agree that the bluejackets were after Negroes only, as no white civilians were molested."[7]

About 11 p.m., sailors attacked a black hack driver, William Randall, beating him so badly that he died two weeks later. Leaving Randall unconscious in the street, the sailors drove his taxi around downtown.[8]

At 11:30 p.m., Cyril Burton, a black bricklayer from the British West Indies, was out walking when a group of sailors set upon him and beat him with hammers, mallets, clubs, and an iron pipe. "I was covered with blood," he later complained to the Navy. "And so severely injured I was immediately taken to the hospital."[9]

The 1919 mayhem marked the worst mass violence in Charleston since the Civil War. As a main port for the Deep South, Charleston occupied a peninsula at the convergence of the Ashley and Cooper rivers. It became one of the main Atlantic ports of the American colonies after its founding in 1670. African slaves were first sold in the Charleston market in the 1600s, and by the 1700s slaves outnumbered whites on the rice plantations in the surrounding low country.

Racial violence flared periodically. The most notorious incident came in 1822, when city officials arrested and hanged freed slave Denmark Vesey and thirty-four other blacks for plotting a slave revolt. Afterward, mistrustful whites imposed laws across the South restricting slave movements and gatherings. Charleston's most infamous role in the history of American race relations came on April 12, 1861, when secessionist South Carolina artillery opened fire on the federal garrison at Fort Sumter, signaling the start of the Civil War.

After the war, however, the city withdrew into a sleepy backwater for the next four decades. The city sloughed off its malarial ennui in 1900, when the Navy purchased marshy land near the city and opened the Charleston Navy Yard. During the Great War, the yard underwent a $5 million expansion, and by the close of 1918, it employed 5,000 people. Thousands of white sailors came to the adjacent Naval Training Station, as did thousands of black stevedores. All interaction between the races was segregated in accordance with military policy. By 1919, Charleston had 67,957 residents—an increase of more than 15 percent since 1910. Blacks were the minority, but just barely, making up about 46 percent of the population.

A black middle class developed in Charleston, and with it an active NAACP chapter headed by Edwin A. Harleston, a well-known portrait artist. In early 1919, the group successfully petitioned the city school system to allow blacks to teach in black schools for the first time.[10] But even though Charleston blacks won some victories, they still suffered the daily humiliations of segregation. Weeks before the riot, the local newspaper, the *News and Courier*, posted a notice inviting all patriotic citizens to visit the naval yard to welcome an arriving transport ship, the USS *Mercury*, from France. But Harleston and other blacks were turned away when they came to join the tribute. A furious Harleston wrote the editor: "It certainly caused a number of people an unnecessary and unwarranted humiliation. In future announcements state when possible whether it is the 'public' that is invited or 'whites only.' Perhaps, I do not need to tell you, Mr. Editor, that we know how to stay away."[11]

The black section of the city was home to what law enforcement labeled vice and what young men, particularly sailors, called a good time. With the dramatic expansion of the yard, Charleston's black neighborhood saw a commensurate increase in blind tiger liquor stores, houses of prostitution, jazz clubs, and gambling joints. The neighborhood earned a reputation as a place to cut loose, as the Charleston—the racy dance that embodied the Jazz Age—signified. White sailors and workmen visited in droves. Whites would not tolerate such businesses in their neighborhoods, but they flocked to them in the black areas. Blacks had no choice but to put up with these establishments in their midst. Though some profited from the vice, most did not.

From the war's outset, Charleston mayor Tristram T. Hyde, who won a contentious election in 1915, and Admiral Frank Edmund Beatty, who ran the Navy's southern headquarters from the Charleston Navy

Yard, coordinated police and naval response to tamp down vice and racial tension. These two officious older white men became unacknowledged heroes of the Charleston riot, simply by doing their jobs swiftly. Despite their competence, both would be out of their posts within months.

As early as March 1918, Hyde wrote Beatty asking for a provost guard to patrol the city on weekends in coordination with police to "eliminate some of the trouble we have had." Beatty endorsed the idea.[12] Hyde later complained that sailors were throwing pennies to black children in the streets. Beatty ordered the practice stopped.[13] In January 1919, Beatty issued a memo stating that "the largest hotels in Charleston are being used by men in uniform for immoral purposes." He ordered that navy guards be posted at the city's major hotels to watch for prostitutes, both "walkers" and "roomers." The same month Hyde added three plainclothes vice officers.[14] Despite those efforts, fights regularly broke out between sailors and civilians, with binge drinking fueling the friction. On April 24, 1919, Beatty finally issued an order that all liberty parties from ships had to include military police patrols, which would be based at Charleston Police Headquarters.[15]

Beatty was a career Navy officer. Born in Wisconsin in 1853, he spent his life following orders and delivering them. He commanded several ships, including the USS *Wisconsin*, which he took on a world tour before rising to rear admiral in 1912. In quasi-retirement when the war started, he was made commandant of the Sixth Naval District, headquartered at Charleston, overseeing operations for a large section of the Southeast's coast. Judging from his blunt orders, he was a taskmaster who believed in hard and fast rules.

His civilian counterpart, Mayor Hyde, was a conservative banker who also firmly believed in the rule of law. His political career, however, was chaotic. In 1915, Hyde, the candidate of Charleston's aristocracy, unseated John P. Grace, the city's first Irish American and Catholic mayor, in a bitter and bloody contest.[16] Hyde accused Grace of being pro-German. Grace countered by criticizing Hyde as being pro-war and pro-Wilson. After the election, Grace, who owned a newspaper, attacked Hyde, claiming his police were corrupt and vice was out of control. In 1919, Hyde was up for reelection and Grace was back to challenge him. Days before the riot, Mayor Hyde filed suit to keep his challenger's delegates from being seated in a city convention.[17] The last thing Hyde needed was a race riot.[18]

When the trouble started that Saturday, both military and civilian officials moved quickly. An hour after the first brawl, Beatty ordered marines to the city. Chief Joseph A. Black and military officers set up a command center at police headquarters. Black risked his life to arrest two white sailors, Jacob Cohen and Frank Holliday, who were charged with killing Isaac Doctor outside the pool hall.[19]

Black seized two .22-caliber rifles from Cohen and Holliday, then walked the men to the police station since he had no wagon. On the walk, the men admitted killing Doctor, saying he threw rocks at them. A score of sailors followed, threatening the chief and demanding he free their fellows. Black did not back down. By the time he arrived at the station, he had confiscated three rifles and several pistols—plus the two prisoners.[20] Later, a third sailor, Roscoe Coleman, ran to the station and begged Black to take him into custody. He said he had been involved in the shooting and "the walls [of the police station] looked better to him than the mob outside."[21]

Provost guards stationed at police headquarters reported a carload of blacks fired at them. Police and marines took control of city intersections and dispersed crowds. At one intersection, a white mob caught a black man with a pistol and was about to kill him when marines intervened.

Around midnight, a mob chased a black man into Fridie's Central Shaving Parlor at 305 King Street. Though it catered to whites, the barbershop was owned and operated by blacks.[22] The fleeing black man turned out the lights as he ran into the shop. The mob demolished the shop. Provost guards arrived to discover the intended victim had escaped out a back door.

Though the marines did begin to restore calm, they were not always disciplined. In one instance, marines shot a young black man named William Brown. He asked why they shot him, and they accused him of refusing to halt when commanded. He later died. Another black man, Isaac Moses, claimed marines knocked him to the ground, bayoneted his leg, and stole five dollars.[23]

After touring the riot area around midnight, Beatty sent one hundred additional marines into the city. The marines, armed with riot rifles with fixed bayonets, stopped all people and searched them for weapons. Blacks were ordered off the streets, under threat of arrest.[24] Bluejackets were ordered to get in waiting trucks to be driven back to base. Other sailors were kept in a holding area at the police station. Around 2:30 a.m., the last mob broke up on King Street. Marines ordered all uniformed men to stand in the middle of the street. They then marched them to the police station.[25] By the early morning hours of May 11, the Charleston riot was over.

Though marines and police stopped the riot, it was the most destructive in the city's history. Mobs had killed four black men. Another died later. Casualties crowded the local hospital. At least seventeen black men, seven white sailors, and one white police officer suffered serious injuries. Rioters had ransacked several stores.

Sunday night, naval and civilian leaders followed up their crackdown of the night before with tough talk. Base officials issued a public statement: "We will do everything in our power to come to the bottom of the regrettable affair and to make impossible the recurrence of another such night."

Mayor Hyde released a statement that, in the heart of the Jim Crow South, was extraordinary.

"Monday morning I will ask W. G. Fridie, whose barbershop was demolished by the sailors, to draw up a bill of damages to be presented to the city government," he stated. "This might set a precedent, but the Negroes of Charleston must be protected."

He also included a warning to troublemakers: "If the action is taken by the Negroes against whites, or vice versa, I will ask that martial law be established."[26]

Beatty kept restrictions on Navy men for months. The Saturday after the riot, May 17, Beatty issued commandant's order no. 73: "Until further orders, no enlisted men will be permitted on the streets of Charleston, S.C., between 8:00 p.m. and sunrise, except on official duty, or in the case of married men going to and from their homes."[27]

Beatty eased the restrictions three days later, allowing some night liberty to "all reliable men." But he stipulated, in bold letters: "NO LIBERTY WHATEVER WILL BE GRANTED ON SATURDAY OR SUNDAY NIGHTS." He also ordered fifty armed sailors, headed by a marine officer, to patrol Charleston daily.[28]

The underlying causes of any riot are multifaceted and fiercely debated. How to stop a riot, however, is not complicated: Get well-armed, disciplined troops in the streets to disperse mobs quickly. If two sides are battling, divide them and keep them apart with the threat of overwhelming force. These tactics were spelled out in May 1920 by a former colonel of the Minnesota National Guard, Henry A. Bellows, in a federal government pamphlet titled *A Treatise on Riot Duty for the National Guard.* Bellows based his study on the race and labor riots of 1919.

"The first requisite for success in riot tactics is prompt action," he wrote. "More lives have been lost in riots because of delay and hesitation than from all other causes put together. Delay in bringing troops on the scene gives the crowd a chance to become a mob; hesitation in employing them vigorously as soon as they appear destroys their best weapon: their moral influence on the crowd."[29]

Bellows described "getting there first" as "a cardinal principle of riot tactics."[30] The Charleston leaders understood this. Military and civilian authorities contained then ended the riot, just hours after it began.

As a result of changes in military rules during the war, they also had legal authority to act quickly and decisively. However, it was an authority few other jurisdictions would utilize during the violent months ahead. The Constitution made only passing reference to the federal government's authority to suppress domestic violence, such as insurrections, riots, and other forms of mayhem. Case law had never evolved a clear course of action for local, state, or federal officials. Over decades, a loose policy developed by which local authorities had to formally request aid from the state if they felt a situation was beyond their control. If a state militia could not handle the situation, a state legislature or the governor could ask the president directly for federal military aid. The president could then declare martial law and temporarily take direct military control.

It was a cumbersome process, layered with numerous opportunities for politicians to obfuscate and avoid responsibility. As a result, race riots and lynchings flourished throughout much of American history in legal and political gaps not foreseen by the Founding Fathers. Lives were lost and property was destroyed in part because of constitutional ambiguities that allowed bigoted or dithering politicians to hesitate in addressing what was happening on their streets. It also allowed federal authorities to delay their response.

As part of putting the nation on a war footing, however, Secretary of War Newton Baker circumvented many of these political hurdles in November 1917 by issuing War Department General Order No. 147. The order allowed local and state authorities to contact a local military garrison directly for help. This change allowed a rapid response that could prove critical in putting down a riot.[31]

If the government reaction in Charleston showed how to stop a riot, the aftermath underscored how ill prepared the legal system was to deal with one. Although it was possible to detain people, it was difficult to prosecute them later. The chaos of a riot overwhelmed officials and police, making building cases later against individuals often impossible. A race riot compounded the problem, when the prejudices of police and court staff were inflamed. In Charleston, forty-nine men—most of them white—were arraigned on charges from murder to rioting to assaulting police officers. Others were arrested but never charged with any crime. The Monday after the riot, police court fined eight men $50 each for carrying concealed weapons, then released them. Another man lost his $100 bond because he did not show up in court. Two black men and one white man were charged with inciting a riot but were later acquitted. One black man was held pending further investigation. The rest were released after a judge delivered a stern talk.[32] The coroner's inquest on May 15 found Isaac Doctor died of a gunshot to the chest by "unknown enlisted men during a riot." The killing of another black man, James Talbert, was caused by "party or parties unknown."[33] The city compensated damaged businesses. As for military justice, the three sailors charged with killing Doctor were court-martialed. Coleman, who had begged to be put in jail, was acquitted. Cohen and Holliday, both arrested by the police chief, were sentenced to one year at a naval prison, then dishonorably discharged.[34] Several other sailors received lesser punishments.[35]

Despite the lack of judicial follow-up, black leaders in Charleston seemed satisfied with the initial government response, though they wanted assurances of protection for the future. At a city council meeting in late May, black ministers and community leaders, including the NAACP's Harleston, commended the mayor for promising such a riot would not happen again. They gave the council "a number of suggestions for the protection of the colored people and improvement of their living conditions." In a letter published in the News and Courier, the group outlined their requests, including having blacks serve on the police force. They asked a committee be set up to improve race relations and "that social justice and a square deal be given to all people." There is no record that such a committee was created.[36]

The group also sent resolutions to Josephus Daniels, head of the Navy. He did not set up a special committee to investigate the riot, but did prosecute sailors charged with misconduct.[37]

Several victims petitioned the city and the Navy for compensation, but were rejected. One victim, Moses Gladden, hired a lawyer to file a claim for injuries. The city passed on his and several other claims, including one for the crippling of a thirteen-year-old boy, to the Navy.[38]

The Navy rejected them, arguing no specific sailors were convicted of crimes against these individual victims, so it was not responsible for their injuries.

Cyril Burton, the Caribbean bricklayer beaten by sailors, claimed damages of $225 for lost wages and injuries. He also wanted $25 in cash stolen by the sailors. The city forwarded this bill to the Navy. After two years of letters back and forth, the Navy agreed to repay Burton's $25, but nothing more.[39]

The Navy Department took Beatty off active duty two months after the riot. He retired that September.[40] In August, Hyde was narrowly defeated by his nemesis, Grace, in the Democratic primary. Grace went on to win the general election and retake the mayoralty.

———◁▷———

The *News and Courier* made no editorial comment on the riot. The *State,* the main newspaper of South Carolina's capital, Columbia, expressed a commonly held view that out-of-town naval men and blacks—not good southern, white Charlestonians—caused the riot.

"What happened Saturday night, with sailors and Negroes as parties, might have happened anywhere," the newspaper stated.[41]

Many southerners saw Charleston's quick action as a good sign. In the segregated South, they argued, white-established law and order could be maintained. Soon after Charleston, however, white mobs would form elsewhere, and local, state, and federal officials would act belatedly, if at all. The Charleston riot would be the exception during 1919.

Reports of the Charleston riot ran in newspapers across America. While newspapers at the time tended to use the word *riot* liberally, readers were surprised to see trouble in a sleepy backwater port. Accounts exaggerated the violence, reporting incorrectly that six people were killed.[42] Most accounts blamed blacks for starting the trouble.

White military personnel attacking black civilians outraged black Americans, offending their ideas of patriotism and fair treatment. By May, tens of thousands of black soldiers, sailors, and stevedores returned to the United States and were discharged. Black towns and neighborhoods greeted these men with parades and honors. Books praising black veterans ran through multiple editions.[43]

But whites repeatedly dismissed black service and patriotism. The newly formed American Legion considered forbidding blacks from membership.[44] Jokes portraying blacks as malformed and lazy were published in *Stars and Stripes,* the main newspaper for the American armed forces. In the newspaper's May 2 humor column, one joke consisted of a black drill sergeant yelling at a black private to stand at attention by pulling in his large lips and raising his drooping eyelids.[45]

The discrimination went far deeper than lame humor. High-level military officials pressured French counterparts not to treat black soldiers as equals.[46] In early 1919, the War Department reported that military tribunals executed 32 soldiers during the war for charges from murder to rape. Of those, 28 were black.[47]

In late May, blacks were further stung by reports that Eugene Bullard, a Columbus, Georgia–born black man who had served with distinction in the French and American air corps during the war, had been beaten to death by an American officer at a café in Paris. Though reports that Bullard was killed were false, they were widely circulated in the black press. Bullard, awarded France's Croix de Guerre, was in fact beaten unconscious, apparently for bumping into a white officer as he stood up.[48]

On top of these events, Du Bois published "Returning Soldiers" in the May *Crisis* magazine. The essay and accompanying report on maltreatment of black soldiers stunned readers.

"I do not know that I have ever read anything so clean-cut and convincing based upon first hand evidence," black Detroit attorney Robert Barnes wrote to Du Bois.[49]

The *Chicago Defender* compared how white military personnel were treated for rioting in Charleston to how black soldiers were treated for rioting in Houston two years earlier.[50] In 1917, about 150 black troops mutinied after white police arrested a black soldier. Fifteen white civilians and four black soldiers were killed. Later a court-martial condemned 14 black soldiers to death by hanging. Another 41 were given life sentences. Black leaders and editorialists pleaded with President Wilson for leniency. He ignored them. To many blacks, Charleston underscored a double standard. A black war veteran, Paul Filton, wrote an angry letter to a Brooklyn newspaper announcing blacks were not going to stand for such mistreatment anymore.

"We are not the 'wards' of this nation, as are the Indians," he wrote. "We are component parts of this body politic. We have helped to gain the Victory for Democracy and we must share the fruits."[51]

Many whites had no plans of sharing, and violence flared up in several northern cities. On May 9, three white men were shot and wounded in a mini-riot involving 75 whites and 10 blacks at 25th and Pine streets in Philadelphia. The white mob attacked the house into which a black man and his family had just moved. Police arrested the black man but later released him.[52]

On May 29, at about 10:30 p.m., black and white sailors based at the port in New London, Connecticut, brawled outside a downtown hotel for blacks. At least two white sailors had their teeth knocked out. Marines with rifles were trucked to the scene. Firemen stood ready to spray a crowd of five thousand with hoses if they did not disperse. About twenty black and white sailors were arrested, and marines had to patrol the city all night.[53]

While racial unrest grew in the North, lynching became epidemic in the South. On May 2, Benny Richards, a black farmer, was shot to death in Warrenton, Georgia, in front of a crowd of three hundred white farmers. Richards, accused of killing his ex-wife and wounding her sister, wounded four men while being pursued. The posse, led by the county sheriff, finally cornered Richards in a swamp and ignited gallons of gasoline to burn him out.[54]

On May 8, a white mob lynched two blacks outside Pickens, Mississippi. One was reportedly a recently discharged soldier and the other a woman.[55]

Four days after the Charleston riot, as many as a thousand white men bashed down three sets of steel doors to get into the county jail in downtown Vicksburg, Mississippi. The mob overpowered the sheriff and twelve deputies and dragged a black prisoner, Lloyd Clay, from his cell. The mob marched him to the heart of the city and hanged him from an elm tree.

"At the same time placing a bonfire under him, after saturating his head with oil," according to a news account, "the Negro died while a fusillade of shots were being fired into his body."

One white onlooker was fatally shot in the head by a rioter firing at Clay. Another white was shot in the arm. Clay was accused of attempted rape of a white woman. The woman, who was not injured in the alleged attack, later told authorities she was not sure her assailant was Clay.[56] No one was ever charged in the lynching. The NAACP dispatched its newly appointed publicity director, twenty-seven-year-old New York writer

Herbert Seligmann, to Mississippi to investigate for ten days.[57] One doctor in Vicksburg told Seligmann that "the government was responsible" for race tensions because it drafted blacks into the army, making them equal to whites. The doctor, who did not know he was talking to an NAACP investigator, predicted "the best people" of the South would begin joining the KKK in large numbers.[58]

On May 15, two black men in Georgia were lynched in separate incidents: James Waters, a farmhand in Dublin, and Henry Prince in Hawkinsville.[59] On May 21, Frank Livingston, accused of killing his white boss and the man's wife, was burned alive in broad daylight in El Dorado, Arkansas.[60] On May 25, a seventy-two-year-old black man, Berry Washington, was lynched in Milan, Georgia, after he came to the defense of two young black girls being harassed by two drunken white men, John Dowdy and Lewis Evans.[61] The men attacked the girls' house late at night, brandishing weapons and demanding they open the door. The girls ran to Washington's house for protection. Washington, the steward of a local black church, came out with his shotgun and killed Dowdy in a gun battle. Washington turned himself in to the sheriff. The night after the shooting, a mob of 75 to 100 whites pulled him from jail, hanged him from a post, and then shot his corpse to pieces. No one was ever arrested. The story was barely covered in the white press, but gained wide circulation in the black press. It was reported to Governor Dorsey that the black people of Milan left town en masse the night of the lynching to hide in neighboring towns.[62] Dorsey offered a $1,000 reward for information leading to an arrest of a lyncher. He used the crime to push legislation giving him authority to fire any law officers who did not stop lynching or prosecute lynchers. The *Atlanta Constitution*, which backed Dorsey, called the Washington killing "one of the most horrible that has ever stained the pages of Georgia's criminal history."[63] His reward brought no convictions and the legislation failed.

A May 15 daylight lynching in Johnson County, Georgia, was typical. A deputy was driving a black prisoner out of the county when 150 men armed with rifles stopped him at a bridge over the Ohoopee River. The prisoner, Jim Waters, had been accused of rape. The men took the prisoner, then sent the deputy back the way he came. An hour later, Waters's bullet-riddled body was found tied to a tree by the river. By afternoon, the coroner ruled Waters died "at the hands of unknown parties." The deputy said he could not recognize any of the kidnappers. The sheriff closed the case that day.[64]

Even in communities where blacks were not killed or injured by white mobs, racial tension rose to levels not seen since Reconstruction. Starting around 11 p.m. Tuesday, May 27, until 3 a.m. Wednesday, May 28, night riders burned down at least five black churches and two black lodges in and around Eatonton, the county seat of Putnam County in central Georgia. A black minister speculated that white rumrunners were behind it. White leaders raised a reward fund to find the culprits, but no one was ever charged with the arson.[65]

The same day the fires started in Putnam, J. A. Martin, a prominent black preacher in Macon, traveled to Milledgeville, about 35 miles east, to deliver a speech to black high school graduates. When he arrived, he found the town up in arms because the white and black high schools chose the same school colors. The trivial matter had escalated to where both sides were arming themselves for a race war. Martin wrote to Du Bois that more than a hundred black men were patrolling their neighborhood, armed with "rifles, pistols, and shot guns."[66] Martin noted a new attitude among the black community: "The males carried their guns with as much calmness as if they were going to shoot a rabbit in a hunt, or getting ready to shoot the Kaiser's soldiers."[67]

In New Hebron, Mississippi, Mose Demper, a black man charged with shooting at a white man, was taken by a mob from jail. The crowd carried him to the woods and were set to hang him, when the sheriff persuaded them to whip him with a buggy trace instead. Some southern newspapers praised the whipping as a sign of progress, since the prisoner was not killed.[68]

All this tension spread to Atlanta, the economic capital of the South with the largest black urban population in the former Confederacy. On Saturday, May 18, the new Ku Klux Klan, revived in 1915 and headquartered in Atlanta, held a large parade through downtown.[69] William Simmons, the KKK's self-styled "Imperial Wizard," issued a proclamation that heralded the superiority of the white Anglo-Saxon race, but at the same time attacked "grossly false impressions" about the new Klan.

"This great order will not compromise its dignity by stooping to foster or encourage any propaganda or religious intolerance or racial prejudice—we are pure Americans," he declared.

The march set off a panic among Atlanta's blacks, Simmons's vague statements notwithstanding. On May 20, black leaders went to police headquarters to discuss rumors of an imminent race riot. "Any law-abiding Negro in Atlanta is just as safe as any white man," the leaders were told. But blacks remembered 1906, when white mobs controlled downtown Atlanta for days. The *Atlanta Constitution* reported it was being deluged with telephone calls from worried blacks and whites.[70]

At the western end of the Deep South, in Memphis, a riot almost broke out on May 22. A white streetcar conductor had been shot and a black man arrested for the crime. Lynchers tried to apprehend the man, but the sheriff, Oliver Hazard Perry, risked his life to stop them at the jailhouse doors.[71]

For days afterward, Memphis waited for a riot to erupt. "That there was no explosion was due to sheer luck," the *Commercial Appeal* opined. "Several days ago someone started a story that there was to be an outbreak of Negroes on Saturday. Others started the story that certain white people were going after the Negroes on the same day. . . . If a drunken white man or a drunken Negro had fired a shot Saturday in a crowded quarter there is no telling what would have resulted. . . . Somehow we have drifted into a tense racial relation."[72]

7.

Bombs and the Decline of the West

Where would you like to find the Negroes of the United
States, supporting law and order, or casting their lot with
rioters and anarchists?

—MOORFIELD STOREY, June 1919

SHORTLY AFTER 11 P.M. ON JUNE 2, 1919, CARLO VALDINOCI WALKED
up to the darkened front door of a house on R Street in an upscale neighborhood near Dupont Circle in Washington. Valdinoci, an anarchist in
his twenties, carried a bomb made of nitroglycerine, along with a pamphlet declaring war on capitalism and the government. The house was
the home of A. Mitchell Palmer, Woodrow Wilson's attorney general.
Palmer, dressed in his pajamas, had just finished reading in a front study
on the second floor. His wife and daughter were in bed.

At 11:15, Palmer switched off the light to go to sleep when the bomb
exploded, destroying the front of the house, showering Palmer with glass
and hurling a stuffed elk's head across the study.[1]

The blast shattered windows and doors throughout the neighborhood.
Franklin Delano Roosevelt, then assistant secretary of the Navy and living across the street, ran over and found a flummoxed Palmer wandering
the front yard.[2] The explosion so overwhelmed Palmer, Roosevelt recalled,
that he reverted to using the arcane "thee" and "thou" of his Pennsylvania
Quaker childhood.[3]

Valdinoci was "blown to butcher's meat," as one witness of the carnage put it.[4] Guts and bones showered the neighborhood. Valdinoci's
spinal column crashed through the bedroom window of the son of the

Norwegian minister living houses away.[5] Investigators speculated the anarchist tripped on the front walkway while leaning over to place the bomb. The detonation was the most dramatic of ten bombs exploded in eight cities across the country that night. Judges, legislators, and a Catholic church were targets.[6] The bombings, and earlier attacks in May, did not hurt many people and did minor damage overall.[7] Only Valdinoci died.

The bombings were orchestrated by a group of Italian anarchists dedicated to using terror to overthrow the government. No evidence exists that the group had any black members or cared about segregation, race riots, or lynching—beyond a standard anarchist position that race attacks were part of a broad capitalist conspiracy to divide the working masses.

Yet Valdinoci's theatrical obliteration would have a profound impact on federal reaction to racial violence in 1919 and beyond. Palmer and his General Intelligence Division, led by the ambitious young bureaucrat J. Edgar Hoover, saw the June 2 attacks as apocalyptic signs. Supported wholeheartedly by elected officials, a fearful Palmer made stamping out radicalism an overarching priority, launching a crackdown that would become known as the Red Scare. Palmer and his agents came to believe blacks were susceptible to Communists and anarchists because of their subservient status, so they set out to prove that revolutionaries were recruiting blacks.[8] Palmer defined radicalism broadly, and would include the legitimate political efforts of black activists.

President Wilson was predisposed to such a connection. That March, he remarked to his doctor that "the American Negro returning from abroad would be our greatest medium in conveying bolshevism to America." Black American soldiers were being treated as equals by the French, he worried, and "it has gone to their heads."[9] Now thanks to Palmer, and perhaps to the unfortunate Valdinoci, the phenomena known as the Red Scare and the Red Summer became enmeshed. Soon Palmer and his staff were loudly exaggerating the influence of a small number of blacks who supported Communism, the International Workers of the World, and similar causes as evidence of a broad conspiracy. Also many in the press believed black political activism and radical terrorism were connected. Even leaders of mainstream black groups like the NAACP warned of possible subversive infiltration of black communities if lynching and rioting did not cease. The net effect of all this public chatter was to warp white views toward black political activity, fusing it in many minds with both race riots and radicalism. Palmer and his department played a key role in shaping and legitimizing this notion.

Alexander Mitchell Palmer, born in 1872, was a progressive Democratic congressman from eastern Pennsylvania and a strong Wilson supporter. The president first offered Palmer the prominent post of secretary of war. Palmer declined because of his pacifist Quaker beliefs.[10] In 1917, Wilson appointed him "Alien Property Custodian," making him responsible for finding enemy financial assets. Palmer excelled, seizing millions of dollars in German bank accounts and real estate for the U.S. government. In spring 1919, Attorney General Thomas W. Gregory resigned, and Wilson put Palmer in the post. At first, Palmer took a more tempered approach than his predecessor to anti-sedition laws. Gregory had discussed arresting thousands of radicals, but Palmer stopped such talk when he took over the post on March 5.[11] He also broke ties with the reactionary anti-immigrant American Protective League, a move that infuriated conservative Democrats. Palmer openly supported the NAACP's anti-lynching effort as an attendee of its New York conference in May.

Yet the bombing of his home changed him, and undermining leftist movements became his crusade.[12] Within two weeks of the bombings, Palmer urged Congress to pass a peacetime law banning all "seditious utterances and publications."[13] Dozens of legislators introduced similar bills.[14] To many, Palmer became a frightening caricature, a paranoid subverting democracy while claiming to try to save it. The next year, the conservative *Chicago Tribune* ran a political cartoon titled "A. Mitchell Palmer Out for a Stroll," in which a perspiring Palmer rushed through a park where everyone, including little old ladies and babies in prams, had the bearded countenances of revolutionaries.[15] The man who once turned down a cabinet position because of his pacifism became known as "the fighting Quaker." Black activists initially saw Palmer as a highly placed ally. As attorney general, Palmer could have promoted anti-lynching legislation or pushed to protect black civil rights. Instead, less than a month after attending the anti-lynching conference, Palmer irrevocably shifted course.

Black civil rights fell off Palmer's agenda just as the summer's wave of racial violence got under way. But the government's interest in the writings and meetings of black political activists sharply increased. When Palmer issued a report on subversives to Congress months later, it cited *The Crisis* and other black publications as evidence that radicals had infiltrated organizations like the NAACP. As proof of black radicalism, the report quoted statements like a June 28 editorial from *The Veteran*, a small black publication that appeared for a few months in 1919. "The race man who determines that if he must die at all by the hands of the mob he will die game makes an incalculable contribution to the majesty of the law," the editorial read. In essence, federal officials considered it seditious to argue blacks should defend themselves from deadly attack.

During the war and after, some blacks—including soldiers—did join radical groups. Several Harlem-based black activists already identified with socialism, including A. Philip Randolph, editor of *The Messenger*, and Cyril Briggs, editor of *The Crusader*. Some went further, embracing political agendas like Communism, anarchism, and anarcho-syndicalism. Many more would join such groups in the early 1920s, when the Communist Party and others made a concerted effort to recruit blacks.[16] But during 1919, blacks did not join such movements in significant numbers. Black workers felt inhibited from participating in radical politics or the broader labor movement because of strains between nonunion black workers and unionized white workers. Though historians have focused much attention on black radicals, their numbers were small and their influence minimal during this period.

But reality played a small role in the Justice Department's investigations of black political organizations and publications during the Red Summer. Federal agents pored over *The Messenger* and *The Crusader*, searching for hints of Bolshevism's sinister hand guiding America's more than 10 million blacks. In truth, both publications were understaffed, sloppily edited, and poorly distributed. Circulation for both was minuscule compared to *The Crisis* and the *Chicago Defender*. Hubert Harrison, a leading socialist black agitator, formed the Liberty League in 1917 as a radical black political party and launched a newspaper, *The Voice*, as its party organ. The newspaper quickly folded and by mid-1919 the League itself collapsed.[17] Briggs, editor of *The Crusader*, relished the attention of federal agents and congressional committees in 1919, but he had few supporters outside of Harlem.

One white socialist bemoaned the lack of black participation in leftist causes in a private letter in May 1919: "There is a great need for missionary work among all people and especially among colored people. . . . Unless we make headway with the Negroes, the capitalists may use them in time of a social revolution."[18] Recruiting blacks was beyond the capacity of leftist groups. From May through August 1919, leftist parties in the United States were in turmoil. John Reed and others bolted from the Socialist Party to form the Communist Party and Communist Labor Party. The head of the Socialist Party, Eugene Debs, was serving a lengthy prison term for sedition. Federal agents were rounding up leftist organizers for incarceration and deportation. And trade union members still harbored deep prejudices against blacks, whom they considered scabs and management tools.

The International Workers of the World took a consistent stand against racism and launched an effort to recruit blacks in 1919, but the group was declining as a force in the labor movement.[19] Black leaders spoke kindly about the I.W.W., but most blacks did not consider joining. *Crisis* editors wrote in June that they respected the Wobblies but stressed, "We do not believe that the *methods* of the I.W.W. are today feasible and advisable."[20] Historian David Levering Lewis has noted that, "Du Bois and the NAACP were civil rights militants, not social revolutionaries—defenders of the Constitution, not exponents of class war."[21]

But in some instances the NAACP and other black advocates tried to use this fear of Bolshevism to gather support. During May and June, NAACP speakers warned that if whites did not end violence and segregation, blacks would turn to radicalism. On June 9, Moorfield Storey traveled to Columbia, South Carolina, and delivered the keynote address for the opening of Petigru College, which housed the all-white University of South Carolina's law school.

"Where would you like to find the Negroes of the United States, supporting law and order, or casting their lot with rioters and anarchists?" he asked the audience. "If things go on as they are going, what do you think is likely to be the outcome? The worm will turn."[22]

White America already saw black aspirations to equality as radical, because in their minds the concept of racial equality was radical. By the summer, two forms of racialism were entwined in American society, one ancient and one pseudoscientific. The one form, going back centuries, presented blacks as inherently inferior to whites in manifold ways. Since slave ships first carried shackled Africans to the colonies in 1619, the idea of black inferiority permeated American society. With slavery gone, this notion continued, flourishing from the end of Reconstruction in the 1870s through the Great War. In 1919, representations of blacks as lazy, stupid, lecherous, and dishonest were everywhere in popular culture.

Vaudeville performances included comics in blackface telling deroga-
tory jokes. Grocery stores advertised Brazil nuts as "nigger toes." Upper-
level seats set aside for blacks in segregated theaters were called "nigger
heaven."

Pseudoscientific books asserting proof of black inferiority and evil
were popular. *The Negro, A Menace to American Civilization*, first published in 1907 by retired Army medical doctor R. W. Shufeldt, asserted
blacks had smaller brains and larger penises and were prone to rape.
"Lynchings, in spite of everything, will continue to occur in the United
States of America just so long as there is a Negro left here alive, and there
is a white woman living for him to assault," Shufeldt wrote. "He can no
more help his instincts than he is responsible for the color of his skin."[23]

Shufeldt's solution? Castrate all black men.[24]

Another book was Charles H. McCord's *The American Negro as a
Dependent, Defective and Delinquent*, published in 1914.[25] McCord
argued that the brain weight of a black person was on average halfway
between the brain weight of a white person and a gorilla.[26] That same
year, author John Ambrose Price wrote that blacks were inherently "a race
of sycophants," and the United States "should remain strictly a white man's
government."[27]

During the first years of the twentieth century, white historians cast
race relations under slavery as wholesome, with white masters as paternal guides to childlike blacks. An example was British journalist Cecil
Chesterton's *A History of the United States*, published in 1919.[28]

"There can be little doubt that under Slavery the relations of the two
races were for the most part kindly and free from rancour, that the master
was generally humane and the slave faithful," wrote Chesterton, brother
of famed prolific author G. K. Chesterton. Almost fifty years after passage
of the Fifteenth Amendment, guaranteeing citizens the right to vote
regardless of race, creed, or color, Chesterton saw black suffrage as "a monstrous anomaly."[29] So did many American whites.

In 1919, David Wark Griffith's three-hour film *Birth of a Nation* was
still packing theaters four years after its initial release. NAACP efforts
to block showings had limited success, with bans in Chicago and some
other cities. Controversy fueled the film's notoriety. Starring Lillian Gish,
it was based on the best-selling 1905 novel *The Clansman* by Thomas
Dixon Jr., replete with black rapists, carpetbagger Svengalis, and heroic
white southerners. In the penultimate scene of the film, blacks come
out of their cabins on Election Day only to be met by armed Klansmen,

who force them back into their hovels. It is presented as the triumph of virtue. President Wilson saw the movie in a private showing with Griffith in the White House. He should have liked it. His two-volume *History of the American People* (1902), which extolled the Klan, was quoted in the film.

Despite racial stigmas, some blacks advanced in business, education, and other areas. But such attempts often were met with scorn and violence. W. E. B. Du Bois described this old brand of racism in *Darkwater*, a book of essays he completed during the Red Summer. In the book he described the repetitive aspect of white violence against blacks as "the logic of the broken plate, which, seared of old across its pattern, cracks never again, save along the old destruction."[30]

Two parallel efforts to establish national monuments in 1919 cast in stark relief the contrast between black aspirations to equality and white expectations of black subservience. Black "uplift" groups such as the New Jersey Federation of Colored Women's Clubs worked to raise money for a statue in Washington to commemorate black Great War veterans.[31] At the same time, white southerners pressed their plan to build a monument in Washington to black female slaves. In June, the United Daughters of the Confederacy convention in Knoxville supported the idea "to honor ourselves and our black mammies."[32] Neither statue was ever built.

<hr />

The other, newer form of racism that circulated in 1919 was grounded in pseudoscientific notions that evolved in response to decades of heavy European and Asian immigration, recent black migration to the North, and the ethnic chaos caused across the globe by the war. This racism was based on the belief that world history was an evolutionary struggle for domination by distinct racial groups. Though it had evolved over years, its influence reached a zenith in 1919. For generations, white culture dominated and ordered the world, but now "lesser" races threatened that rule, outnumbering whites and mixing with whites to weaken their bloodlines. Given a scientific underpinning by intellectuals, the theory melded with the older antiblack bigotry, infusing it with an urgency that made both whites and blacks anxious and unsettled. Whites, the logic went, had to act to save themselves and civilization.

But "white" was not easily defined. Many today who would be considered white were cast into stratified ethnic categories. Far from Theodore Roosevelt's "melting pot," the United States in 1919 was a cauldron of competing ethnic and racial groups. Most groups wanted to be white, or as close to it as possible. Fairer-skinned whites—people from northern Europe—looked down on whites with darker skin from southern Europe and elsewhere.

Black was not easily defined either. Millions of "blacks" were of mixed race. States passed legislation to try to set firm legal standards for who was black and who was not, yet untold numbers passed for white. Lighter-skinned blacks often looked down on darker-skinned blacks. In 1918, white sociologist Edward Byron Reuter published his influential *The Mulatto in the United States, Including a Study of the Role of Mixed-Blood Races Throughout the World*. The book derived its arguments from this idea of pigmentation hierarchy, even though Reuter considered himself an advocate of black advancement.[33]

"So long as the overwhelming majority of the notables of the race are yellow or near-white rather than brown or black, the ideal of the race will continue to be light rather than dark," he wrote.[34]

The upheaval caused by the war threatened the generally accepted hierarchical ladder of pigmentation. The collapse of centuries-old European aristocracies, colonial uprisings against European rule, and the rise of nonwhite empires like Japan unnerved self-defined whites.[35]

Respected intellectuals pushed a social Darwinistic worldview and framed it in scientific jargon. German philosopher Oswald Spengler's work *The Decline of the West* (*Der Untergang des Abendlandes*), a treatise on how white European society was collapsing before the rising power of blacks, Asians, and Arabs, was translated into English in 1919. That year, the philosopher became famous in Europe, winning a major award.[36] All history, Spengler argued, was a violent contest of races. As he would sum up in a later book: "Human history is war history."[37] American proponents of his theories included Madison Grant, chairman of both the New York Sociological Society and the New York Zoological Society. Grant co-founded the American eugenics movement, which advocated selective breeding for human populations. Educated at Yale and Columbia universities, Grant lectured widely on his view that the white race—which he divided into Nordic, Anglo-Saxon, and Teutonic groups—rightfully ruled the world but "bastard" races undermined its authority. In 1916, Grant's *The Passing of the Great Race* sold well, going through multiple editions. Grant wrote of race relations in declarative sentences dusted with the patina of scientific certitude.

"Negroes have demonstrated throughout recorded time that they are a stationary species, and that they do not possess the potentiality of progress or initiative from within," Grant wrote. "Progress from self-impulse must not be confounded with mimicry or with progress imposed from without by social pressure, or by the slavers' lash."[38]

Grant believed that if blacks lived close to whites they would eventually cause the downfall of white civilization through race mixing. He argued that blacks had to be kept in a subservient role and denied political rights, otherwise, "race bastards" would take over.[39]

Grant was not the only intellectual espousing scientific racism. Harvard-educated anthropologist Lothrop Stoddard spent much of 1919 writing what became the best-selling *The Rising Tide of Color Against White World-Supremacy*, published in 1920. The book was a clarion call for whites to save themselves from "servile races."[40]

"Democratic ideals among a homogeneous population of Nordic blood, as in England or America, is one thing, but it is quite another for the white man to share his blood with, or entrust his ideals to, brown, yellow, black or red men," Stoddard wrote. "This is suicide pure and simple, and the first victim of this amazing folly will be the white man himself."[41]

Academics like Columbia University anthropologist Franz Boas and others argued against Grant and Stoddard, but they had little sway on public opinion. George Haynes, the black sociologist, labor expert, and the Urban League's first executive director, acknowledged that Stoddard "voiced the attitude of a great many white people toward other races."[42]

White fear of losing preeminence pervaded American culture. Popular horror writer H. P. Lovecraft presented race mixing as an abomination. In 1916, Thomas Dixon, author of *The Clansman*, published another novel, *The Fall of a Nation*, about mixed-race plotters conspiring to undermine American war preparedness.[43] One of the chief villains was Professor Plato Barker, a malignant caricature of intellectuals like Du Bois.[44]

Common people also adopted this racial worldview. As he hitchhiked the South in the early 1900s, poet Vachel Lindsay stopped at a railroad depot to chat with a man who summarized this paranoid opinion.

"Why, the mixing that is going on is something scandalous," the man told the poet. "I had a nigger working for me once that was half-Spaniard and half-Indian. There are just a few white people, and more mulattoes every day. The white people ought to keep their blood pure. Russians are white people. Germans, English, and Americans are white people. French people are niggers. Dagos are niggers. Jews are niggers. All people are niggers but just these four. There is going to be a war in two or three years between all the white people and all the niggers. The niggers are going to combine and force a fight, Japan in the lead."[45]

Such views, coupled with anxiety over revolution, allowed a xenophobic organization like the revived Ku Klux Klan to thrive. The Klan grew dramatically in 1919 by presenting itself as progressive and patriotic. An advertisement, ornamented with skull and crossbones, in a June edition of the *Charlotte Observer* told whites, "Join the Loyal Order of Klansmen and you solve the problem of law and order in our Southland. With one million men enrolled in the Loyal Order of Klansmen, our land will have peace and security and prosperity."[46] An ex-Methodist preacher, William Joseph Simmons, incorporated the group in 1915 and established its national headquarters in a loft above a downtown Atlanta bank.[47]

Simmons was a racist George F. Babbitt, a club joiner haunted by delusions of greatness and obsessed with the belief that blacks and immigrants imperiled the United States, a nation divinely ordained to be ruled by white Anglo-Saxons. Atlantans knew Simmons as "a pious, prissy-walking big man. Lodge badges and charms were heavy upon him, and he carried this burden joyously."[48] Simmons devoted his life to the KKK, which he described as "my child."[49]

He was born in 1880 outside the small Alabama town of Harpersville, just east of Birmingham. Known by friends as "Doc" because he claimed some medical training, Simmons tried several ventures, including serving as a minister and selling insurance, before reviving the KKK. He said he formed the group in response to a spiritual vision of robed horsemen galloping in the sky, followed by a vision of a map of the United States.[50] Simmons established his KKK shortly after seeing *Birth of a Nation* and hearing news of the notorious lynching of Leo Frank outside of Atlanta. On Thanksgiving night in 1915, Simmons and fifteen friends hiked up the huge granite outcrop of Stone Mountain east of the city and held a ceremony Simmons had contrived.[51]

The Klan leader's bromidic speeches were strange and flowery. He once described himself as "He Who Traversed the Realm of the Unknown, Wrested the Solemn Secret from the Grasp of Night and Became the Sovereign Imperial Master of the Great Lost Mystery."[52] Simmons wrote numerous KKK tracts filled with breathless, confusing puffery. A pamphlet labeled *ABC of the Invisible Empire* declared the Klan's goals were "to shield the sanctity of the home and the chastity of womanhood; to maintain white supremacy; to teach and faithfully inculcate a high spiritual philosophy through an exalted ritualism; and by a practical devotedness to conserve, protect and maintain the distinctive institutions, rights, privileges, principles and ideals of a pure Americanism."[53]

The KKK's mission was to save "the white race" and "Anglo-Saxon civilization" from miscegenation and immigration.

"Our much boasted 'melting pot' has turned out to be a 'garbage can,' in which the nations of the earth dump their refuse," Simmons wrote in disgust. He once described jazz music as "the barbaric, meaningless medley of sounds . . . suggestive of the low and the lewd."[54]

The secretive rituals and clownish titles invited mockery.[55] The Klan's rulebook was called the "Kloran." A few years after 1919, a white Alabaman whose grandfather was a local leader in the original Klan told a visitor, "This club you've got here hasn't got as much relation to it as the Boy Scouts."[56] H. L. Mencken held up the new KKK as a prime example of why he called the United States "this Eden of clowns."[57]

Black America took note and worried about the new KKK. *Crisis* editors condemned "this revival of old-time terrorism" and urged blacks not to be cowed.[58]

Many whites, however, thought the Klan was just the answer to restoring the country. By June 1919, the KKK grew to several thousand members, mostly in Georgia and Alabama. Many more were just starting to hear about the group, which under Simmons's direction developed a middle-class respectability. It presented itself as a white answer to the swirling chaos of racial discord and labor unrest. Though founded in the Deep South and steeped in the symbolism of ex-Confederate vigilantism, the new Klan modeled itself as a civic club for Anglo-Saxon super-patriots, "the defender of Americanism and the conservator of Christian ideals." The white riots and reports of black resistance were boons to recruitment. The organization that claimed a few thousand members in early 1919 had tens of thousands by the year's end and more than a million by the early 1920s.[59]

In an exploded world where racial hierarchies were in flux, many whites were as frightened of "the darker races" as they were of Communism. Many saw them as the same thing. In the summer of 1919, Newell Dwight Hillis, a Congregationalist minister from Brooklyn and popular syndicated columnist, attacked Bolshevism on racial and ethnic grounds.

"Out of 384 rulers of Russia two are Negroes, thirteen Russians, fifteen Chinese, twenty-two Armenians and Georgians, more than 300 are

Russian Jews, of which 264 are, like [Leon] Trotzky [*sic*], apostate Hebrews from New York," Hillis wrote.[60]

Carl William Ackerman, a correspondent for the *Philadelphia Public Ledger* and well-known author, published in 1919 the first English translation of *The Protocols of the Elders of Zion*, the infamous fabricated tract that claimed a worldwide Jewish conspiracy. In a bizarre merging of fears—ethnic dilution and Communism—Ackerman substituted every use of the word *Jew* in that tract with the term *Bolshevik*.

Whites were not the only ones to adopt a Spenglerian view of race relations. The most influential black proponent of the pseudoscientific worldview of race competition was a loquacious, energetic, and rotund Jamaican named Marcus Garvey. June 1919 saw the start of his meteoric rise in popularity.

Garvey's politics were a unique amalgam of racialism, race-based entrepreneurism, and imagined imperialism—with himself as emperor. If whites did not want blacks as equals in their businesses, he argued, blacks should set up their own. If whites did not want them as equals in their governments, blacks should establish their own. Whereas the NAACP and other mainstream groups argued for an integrationist approach to black advancement, Garvey argued for separation.

"Cultures are organisms," Spengler wrote in *The Decline of the West*, "and world-history is their collective biography."[61] By 1919, Garvey saw the unified organism of the black race—400 million strong and stretching from the Americas to Africa—rising to lead human history. Born in 1887 in St. Ann's Bay, Jamaica, the dark-skinned Garvey was politically active in the British colony and in Great Britain. In 1914, he founded the Universal Negro Improvement Association (UNIA) in Kingston to unite the black "diaspora," set up black-run businesses, and create a black-run government of Africa. He admired Booker T. Washington and came to the United States in 1916 to meet him and to lecture. He settled in Harlem, finding work as a printer and lecturing on street corners at night. He befriended black socialist Hubert Harrison and other leftists. Garvey had no interest in socialism or Communism, however. Instead, his idea of black advancement involved cooperative businesses and his own autocratic leadership. The East St. Louis riot intensified his recruiting efforts. By 1918, he had opened a UNIA branch in the United States and established *The Negro World*, its weekly newspaper. Garvey was a gifted speaker and grandiose man, with clear views on race and even sharper visions of his own destiny to lead blacks worldwide. By April 1919, Garvey spoke about creating a black-owned ocean liner company called the Black Star Line, a foil to the widely known White Star Line.[62] By June, he began soliciting money from black people to buy shares. On June 27, the UNIA incorporated the Black Star Line in Delaware. Federal agents started looking at the UNIA, which had members with socialist tendencies. They also looked into Garvey's convoluted finances, a probe that would lead in the early 1920s to his indictment, conviction, imprisonment, and deportation. But in 1919, Garvey was still a fresh voice to most black Americans. His ideas thrilled tens of thousands. His separatism appealed to many blacks, and the UNIA grew rapidly. Soon it became a powerful, if lesser, rival to the NAACP. Both organizations grew stronger, with each lynching and riot, with each senseless killing reported in the newspapers.

"Lynchings and race riots all work to our advantage by teaching the Negro that he must build a civilization of his own or forever remain the white man's victim," Garvey once told supporters.[63]

The NAACP, with its integrationist view, held the loyalty of most politically active blacks, but the violence sparked blacks everywhere, regardless of their affiliations, to read, discuss, write, and act regarding their place in American society. The Red Summer accomplished something its ugly mobs never intended: it ignited a great political awakening that would transform twentieth-century America.

William Pickens, the leading NAACP activist and black academic, gave speeches in various cities during the Red Summer. In his standard speech, titled "The Kind of Democracy the Negro Expects," Pickens rejected the idea that blacks were becoming radicalized just because they were becoming political.

"There is less Bolshevism among the colored people than among the white, because the colored are more humble, more subservient, more used to inequalities," Pickens told cheering audiences.[64]

This new activism was not spurred by Moscow agents, anarchist pamphleteers, or separatists, he argued, but antiblack violence and Jim Crow restrictions.

"Brothers, I'll tell you who is the greatest agitator in this country," he said. ". . . The greatest agitator is injustice."[65]

8.

Ellisville

The door of hope is forever closed to the Negro, in so far as participation in politics is concerned, and there is no appeal from that decree.

—*JACKSON DAILY NEWS*, June 20, 1919

ON JUNE 26, 1919, AS MANY AS 10,000 WHITES GATHERED IN A FIELD just outside of Ellisville, Mississippi, to watch a bound and wounded black man named John Hartfield hoisted up the branch of a giant sweet gum tree. Vendors sold flags, trinkets, and souvenir photographs. Local politicians delivered speeches. Young boys crowded in the tree to look down at the wild-eyed, screaming Hartfield.

In the South that June, lynchings occurred every several days, as they had in May. In places like Jacksonville, Florida, and Clarksdale, Mississippi, mobs grabbed blacks accused of crimes and slaughtered them before large, cheering crowds.[1]

None would be as calculated and well publicized as what took place in Ellisville. It was like a county fair, political rally, and public murder rolled into one.

Lynchers cut off Hartfield's fingers. They let him dangle from a branch, then they shot him. They burned the corpse. The extrajudicial killing took place promptly at 5 p.m., as was publicized in advance in publications from New Orleans to New York. Everyone, from Ellisville citizens to Mississippi's governor to NAACP officials in the North, knew when and where it would happen. Those who could have stopped it did not. Those who wanted to stop it could not.

The lynching followed frenzied weeks in and around Ellisville. Posses with hunting dogs had searched for Hartfield for ten days before they caught him. The hunt began after a white woman named Ruth Meeks reported that he had attacked her on the night of June 9 as she walked home from her job as a hotel clerk. Hartfield threatened her with a pistol, she told police, then took her to a railroad trestle and raped her. He then took her under a sweet gum tree near a pasture and ran away with her clothes, she said. Police reported finding Meeks's clothing at Hartfield's house, and that he had fled into the forest.[2] Posses, which included some blacks, spotted Hartfield several times. White men shot and captured him on June 24 as he tried to board a train.[3] The sheriff held him in jail briefly, but a large party of whites soon took him away, with no resistance from the sheriff. From then on, this shadowy group of white men—none of whom were ever identified, though thousands saw them do their work—organized Hartfield's lynching. The lynching committee ordered a white doctor, A. J. Carter, to treat Hartfield's wounds and keep him alive until they could kill him. The doctor told them that they had better move fast: Hartfield would not last 24 hours. As the doctor treated Hartfield, the lynching committee set about gathering railroad cross ties and firewood. "Arrangements apparently had been made days ago," according to an Associated Press account.[4]

Ellisville, the seat of Jones County, was one of the oldest settlements in the "Piney Woods" section of southeastern Mississippi. It was a remote area where plantation farming was unprofitable and thus had an atypical history for the Deep South. In 1861, white farmers gathered at the Ellisville courthouse to protest what they saw as a "planters' war." When Mississippi voted to secede, the farmers declared a "Free State of Jones," with Ellisville as the capital. During the Civil War, a band of guerrillas led by a man named Newt Knight attacked Confederate units from a base in the Leaf River swamps.[5] Six decades later, Jones County's whites gathered near that same courthouse, this time to watch a black man die.

On June 26, thousands of people came to Ellisville from all over southeastern Mississippi. Alarmed NAACP officials sent a telegram to Governor Theodore Bilbo, asking him to intervene. On the day of the killing he issued a public statement that he was "utterly powerless."

"The Negro has confessed, says he is ready to die, and nobody can keep the inevitable from happening," he said.[6]

A reporter portrayed Hartfield as resigned to his coming death. "You have the right man," Hartfield supposedly said, then warned calmly for "all men, white and colored, to think before doing wrong."[7]

Such quotes hardly seem credible coming from a mortally wounded, uneducated field hand who had spent ten days in the woods running for his life.

White journalist Hilton Butler, who saw the lynching, claimed as many as 10,000 people came to the field that day.[8] Butler covered numerous lynchings in his career but would remain haunted by Hartfield's death. Years later, he recounted the grotesque carnival nature of the event in detail. T. Webber Wilson, the local district attorney, addressed the mob from a car's running board, he recalled. And the *Jackson Daily News*'s noon edition carried an eight-column, front-page story announcing Hartfield would be killed promptly at 5 p.m.

Hartfield's body was strung up and the crowd fired a volley at him.

"I had to drop from a tree behind him to escape bullets fired at his swinging body," Butler recalled. "Every time a bullet hit an arm, out it flopped like a semaphore. The legs didn't flop so easily. My newspaper account of it said that not less than 2,000 bullets were fired into his body. One of them finally clipped the rope. John's body fell to the ground, a fire was built around it, and John was cremated." An hour later, nothing remained of Hartfield but a pile of ashes. Ruth Meeks witnessed the killing, which took place about 200 yards from her house.[9]

Butler described how later that night he came across a ghoulish souvenir vendor in a nearby town:

A grinning man in Laurel exhibited to a sidewalk crowd a quart jar filled with alcohol, in which a finger cut jaggedly from a Negro's hand bobbed up and down.

"I got a finger, by God," the grinning man said. "And I got some photographs, too."

He passed them around. One showed John hanging from the tree, his bullet-riddled body naked except for a pair of olive-drab army breeches. Another showed a smoldering pile of ashes beneath a dangling rope.

"These photos," the grinning man said, "are twenty cents each." He sold out quickly. I bought some myself, as many as I could, and tore them up when I got out of sight.

"Ain't nobody can buy this finger," he announced proudly. "I cut it off'n him myself. Gosh, but that nigger was tough—tougher than the withers of a bull, by God. I like never to have to have sawed through it with a knife, but I did. He screamed like a woman when I done it, the yeller—."

He said it in expressive language.

"We orter kill more of 'em around here," he amplified. "Teach 'em a lesson. Only way I see to stop raping is to keep on lynching. I'm goner put this finger on exhibition in my store window tomorrow, boys, and I want you to drop around."

He grinned again.

"And don't forget to bring the ladies!"[10]

The next day, June 27, major newspapers from Los Angeles to Boston detailed the lynching. NAACP delegates meeting in Cleveland sent a telegram to Vice President Thomas R. Marshall asking for federal troops to be sent to Mississippi, a call that would be echoed decades later during the civil rights era.[11] The federal government did nothing. Days later, whites killed a black man in neighboring Perry County after hearing him mention Hartfield's death.[12]

Governor Bilbo said that stopping "the lynching of Negro rapists" was "practically impossible." He blamed the French for the increasing violence in the United States, claiming they had put ideas of equality in African American heads.

"This is a white man's country, with a white man's civilization and any dream on the part of the Negro race to share social and political equality will be shattered in the end," he said.[13]

That all lynchings were caused by society's indignation over black men raping white women was a pervasive notion. Even whites sympathetic to black advancement, like members of the Southern Sociological Congress or Georgia governor Hugh Dorsey, often mentioned that blacks needed to help end rapes against white women to stop lynching. Yet NAACP research found that most lynching victims were not killed for rape or attempted rape, but for other lesser crimes. Only 14 of the 77 black men lynched in 1919 were accused of assaulting a white woman.[14]

The NAACP and supporters stressed that the guilt or innocence of black lynching victims had not been determined and ultimately were not the point. The central issue was more basic: In a society of laws, each citizen deserved the constitutionally guaranteed right to a fair trial and due process.

The black *Baltimore Daily Herald* summed up: "No Negro man, woman or child is safe from the lynching, burning mob so long as the lowest and humblest Negro in the race can be strung up, shot or burned by an individual or mob with absolute security from punishment or even the inconvenience of trial."[15]

The fundamental problem with the mob was that once it formed, it needed a victim, no matter what.

"Is it likely that one of these mobs would 'call off' an interesting lynching party if at the last minute it were demonstrated that the accused was innocent?" wrote white academic Everett Dean Martin in his 1920 work *The Behavior of Crowds.* "The practice of lynching has been extended, from those cases where the offense with which the accused is charged is so revolting as justly to arouse extreme indignation to offenses which are so trivial that they merely serve as a pretext for torture and killing."[16]

To see governors treat these extrajudicial killings with nonchalance left blacks incredulous. Washington minister Francis Grimké, brother of NAACP board member Archibald Grimké, wrote to NAACP secretary John Shillady with a distinctly un-Christian message: "Gov. Bilbo says, 'Excitement is at such a high pitch throughout Mississippi that any armed attempt to interfere would doubtless result in the death of hundreds of persons.' What if it does? The best thing that could happen to Mississippi would be to have not only hundreds but thousands of those worthless lawless savages shot to death and gotten out of the way."[17]

Not all southern politicians and journalists were as unresponsive as Bilbo. At the end of June, Governor Thomas Walter Bickett of North Carolina blasted the KKK when he learned it had received approval to set up chapters in his state.[18]

"Such an appeal is desperately wicked," he said. "There is no good need for any secret order to enforce the law of this land and the appeal to race prejudice is as silly as it is sinful."[19]

In Georgia, Governor Dorsey delivered his inaugural address to the general assembly on June 28 and called for new authority to send in state militia to suppress mob violence and lynching. He also wanted power to fine counties that allowed lynching. If the legislature did not act, he warned, the federal government eventually would.[20] Tennessee governor Albert Roberts also spoke out against lynching, though he failed in his push to get anti-lynching legislation passed.

Despite isolated political efforts to curb racial violence or individual attempts to secure a fair trial, no national governmental effort developed to stop the antiblack rioting and lynching. So it spread like influenza, feeding off news accounts, deep-seated prejudice, and general anxiety.

In the South, white mobs attacked blacks with harrowing regularity. On June 7 in Macon, Mississippi, a white mob that included a leading banker, a deputy sheriff, and a city marshal attacked and beat a school principal, a merchant, and several other prominent blacks. The mob then looted several stores and ordered the victims, accused of trying to organize area blacks, to leave town and never return.[21] Other blacks were killed in Arkansas and Alabama.[22]

In the North, rioting and rumors spread. Fighting broke out on June 6 in New Brunswick, New Jersey, when about fifty white soldiers, most of them southerners, became raucous at a street fair, causing officers to send them back to their base. While marching through the black section of town, they attacked residents and smashed homes. Police fired above the rioters' heads to disperse them.[23] In late June, the 15th Infantry Regiment of the New York militia marched into Harlem to train for a "theoretical riot."[24] In downtown San Francisco, a riot started on June 30 between black and white soldiers on leave.[25] Sailors and blacks also brawled in Annapolis, Maryland.[26]

Great Britain saw similar racial battles that month. In Liverpool and Cardiff, white sailors and workers attacked immigrants from British colonies in Africa, the West Indies, and Asia who were brought to the United Kingdom to alleviate a labor shortage caused by the war. From January through August, such riots erupted in nine of the country's large ports, including London.[27] The worst trouble hit Liverpool on June 6 in the South End after a stabbing during a brawl between blacks and Danish workers. Whites threw a black man off Queen's Dock and the man drowned. Police rushed through black neighborhoods, waking up about a thousand blacks and taking them to the city jail for safety. News reports laid bare an economic motive for the attacks. "These men are taking the bread out of the mouths of the discharged soldiers," a white man told the *Manchester Guardian.* Ex-soldiers petitioned Liverpool's lord mayor to contact the colonial office and have the blacks sent back to the colonies.[28] Before that could happen, another riot erupted a week later. Mobs torched a black boardinghouse and killed two people. Several others were severely injured.[29] That same day, a white riot against black stevedores in Cardiff halted work on the docks for hours. As many as 2,000 ex-soldiers and ex-sailors armed with guns, razors, sticks, and stones paraded in the streets, smashing windows and attacking blacks and Arabs. Two blacks died.[30] By month's end, Cardiff officials "repatriated" more than 150 blacks to colonies.[31]

As race riots and lynchings were reported in major newspapers, cities everywhere became tense. The everyday places where blacks and whites intersected—trains, work, restaurants, bars, and the street—were transformed into potential battlegrounds. Small and fleeting confrontations threatened to explode into major crises. Even in Cleveland, where the NAACP national delegates met on June 24, about fifty white men and boys stoned black schoolchildren riding on a streetcar to the swimming ponds at Garfield Park.[32]

White concerns about black attempts to elevate their station, whether in the voting booth or a railroad car, reached a fever pitch. One minor incident showed how common these contests became. On June 6, 1919, four discharged black soldiers, returning to their homes on the New York-to-New Orleans train, ran into trouble after their Pullman sleeping car crossed the Mason-Dixon Line. The men remained in their sleeping berths in a white car, where offended white men complained to the staff and gathered a petition to send to the United States Railroad Administration. Several whites refused to sign, arguing "they did not intend to protest against Negro soldiers who had served their country," according to a Pullman car porter. The whites shouted at one another in heated argument. "The Negro soldiers as far as I observed were well-behaved and created no disturbance or trouble in any respect," the porter said.[33]

Everywhere, whites felt their long-assumed racial superiority was under assault—and they lashed out. The *Jackson Daily News* stated bluntly: "The door of hope is forever closed to the Negro, in so far as participation in politics is concerned, and there is no appeal from that decree."[34] Blacks learned quickly that the road to true equality would be perilous and long. In a rare down moment, James Weldon Johnson wrote in the *New York Age*: "One by one the idealistic war dreams are vanishing, and as they vanish the solid outlines of the old, pre-war conditions loom up clearer and clearer."[35]

As more clashes broke out, one of the Red Summer's first victims, Joe Ruffin, survivor of the April lynchings at Carswell Grove Baptist Church, languished in jail in eastern Georgia. Jenkins County citizens wanted him back, either to lynch him outright or convict him with an all-white jury and then hang him. They also sought his son, Louis, who was there when the shooting erupted at Carswell Grove. He was their other chief suspect in the deaths of the two white officers. On June 11, the county petitioned Governor Dorsey to offer a reward of $500 for Louis's whereabouts. Dorsey did not offer the reward. But he did not interfere with Jenkins County's efforts to extradite Ruffin back to Millen. If Ruffin had been a poor man, he could not have resisted extradition, but he had property in Jenkins County. Now that he could never go back there, he might as well sell it. He used land as collateral, and hired the best white lawyer he could find: Archibald Blackshear, a thirty-three-year-old Augusta blueblood with Confederate forefathers. Blackshear, trained in law at the University of Georgia and a former state representative, had a stellar reputation as a defense attorney with ties to east Georgia's key lawyers and politicians.[36] How the farmer Ruffin heard of Blackshear is not known, though both men were Masons. As soon as Blackshear took the case, he filed motions to move a trial as far from Jenkins County as possible. Unlike so many others that summer, Ruffin had a chance to fight for his life in court.

9.

Cleveland

What are you going to do with this organization?

—B. Harrison Fisher, a white delegate
to the NAACP's 1919 convention

By midyear, African Americans started to organize them-selves with an energy and in numbers not witnessed since Reconstruction. Black groups had struggled for civil rights through decades of Jim Crow, but black political activism did not become a substantial force in American politics until the Red Summer.

Black reaction to the violence, the return of legions of soldiers, an increase in earnings for many black workers, the migration of tens of thousands of blacks to the North, and an emboldened black press all combined in 1919 to create an unprecedented political awakening.

Young blacks voiced this new energy. On June 9, a student named Paul Robeson was the first African American to deliver a commencement address at Rutgers University. The six-foot-two, 200-pound Robeson endured harsh racism in his time at the New Jersey institution. White students even beat him in an attempt to get him off the football team.[1] Robeson, however, went on to succeed in both academics and athletics.

In his speech, titled "The New Idealism," Robeson declared to a white audience: "We of this less favored race realize that our future lies chiefly in our own hands. On ourselves alone will depend the preservation of our liberties and the transmission of them in their integrity to those who will come after us."[2]

Black ministers urged blacks to organize politically against rioting and lynching. Congregations responded enthusiastically.

"If there ever was a time in the history of a race that we get together it is now," Baptist minister C. H. Duvall, a popular speaker in black churches, told audiences.[3]

In New York, George Baker, a black man who called himself Major Morgan J. Devine (soon to become "Father Divine"), began preaching and recruiting large numbers of black followers on a message of racial harmony. Baker, born in Savannah, migrated north preaching a mystical Christianity, which presented him as the Messiah. Now in his early forties, Baker's message of racial harmony and equality brought blacks to his sermons. In October 1919, Father Divine and a handful of followers moved from Brooklyn to Sayville, Long Island. Father Divine was the first black homeowner in Sayville, and he purchased the house as the direct result of strife between two white neighbors of German descent. When one of the men changed his name to sound more English during the war, the other man mocked him. The argument between the two escalated until one of the men decided to move. He listed his home for sale explicitly to a colored buyer to spite his neighbor.[4]

———

It was the NAACP that drew more members than any other black organization. Name recognition, *The Crisis*, and lecture campaigns fostered spectacular growth. Speakers like Johnson, White, Seligmann, Storey, Shillady, and Du Bois fanned out across the country in May and June to promote the group's annual convention, set for late June in Cleveland. The perpetual traveling exhausted the NAACP speakers, but brought thousands of new recruits to the organization. Johnson wrote to family and friends about his grueling tour to the West Coast, which drew large crowds, including whites.[5] But the NAACP's more militant message alienated some traditional white backers who wished for a more docile effort, even in the face of lynchings and riots. Former Republican president William Howard Taft, in a nationally syndicated column published on June 4, cautioned black leaders that striking back at white violence would "only lead to worse things for the colored race." He promised, instead, "slow change for the better."[6]

Things were changing, and none of that change was slow. Whatever white support was lost by the NAACP in May and June, it was more than offset by dramatic growth in black membership. As the NAACP gathered for its convention in late June, the organization was undergoing a great expansion and fundamental change. As the Red Summer antiblack violence got under way, the NAACP transformed to meet the challenge. On June 22, members descended on Cleveland, described by Du Bois as "one of America's most beautiful cities—with broad, spacious streets, handsome buildings, and a Great Lake to temper the summer heat."[7] It would be the most important convention in the history of the NAACP.

John Hurst, a well-known black speaker and the African Methodist Church's bishop for Florida, told an excited crowd at the Cleveland Armory that blacks should reject those who counseled patience "until thru some Providence relief comes. No, my friends, we shall trust God of course, but we are going to do some fighting too. . . . We will fight. We will die, if need be, for what belongs to us. No matter how long the delay for it to come."[8]

Whatever Du Bois's misgivings about the NAACP leadership (he was bickering with board members over costs and editorial control of *The Crisis*), he was proud of the throngs convening in Cleveland. He called the gathering "the greatest assembly ever held by Negroes in the United States."[9] James Weldon Johnson and Walter White both arrived in Cleveland from speaking tours and were thrilled at the large turnout of black delegates. Though most NAACP board members were white, this convention was run by blacks, dominated by black speakers, and attended by a record number of delegates, almost all of them black. The convention adopted as its theme "The Battlefield of America," and the meetings took on a martial air. Two hundred and sixty-five delegates from 34 states met from Sunday, June 22, through Saturday night, June 29.[10] Du Bois estimated that 10,000 people attended the various meetings. The halls at the armory and the Technical High School were so crowded that hundreds were turned away.[11] Thousands more heard NAACP speeches at local churches and synagogues.

Southerner and northerner, factory worker and farmer, wealthy and poor, all came to hear one another's plight and share responses to white mistreatment and violence. The convention opened with a keynote speech by Emmett Scott, the assistant secretary at the War Department. Scott was fighting with Du Bois at the time over the May *Crisis* article that detailed poor treatment of black soldiers. But concerns about growing racial violence brought the two men together. Scott told the crowd that in "these dark and foreboding days of readjustment," black Americans "are expecting, yes, we are demanding that every such program [for equal rights and fair treatment] shall include all the men and women of America, black men and black women of America as well as of Europe and Asia." Though he made no overt reference to the increasing violence, the overtone of the speech was clear—blacks planned to defend themselves and get the respect they had earned on European battlefields.[12]

The specter of subversives was a constant theme. Speakers warned whites to halt lynchings or else blacks would turn from mainstream organizations like the NAACP and into the arms of Bolsheviks and Wobblies. A convention resolution read: "We warn the American people that the patience of even colored people can find its limit; that with poor schools, Jim Crow methods of travel; little or no justice in court or in things economic staring him in the face, while the colored man is called on to bear his part of the burden in taxation, in government loans, in civic affairs and in fighting the common foes of our government, we are inviting him to grasp the hands which the Bolsheviks, the I.W.W., and other kindred organizations held out to him."[13]

Southerners, for the first time, were strongly represented at an NAACP convention. Since its inception, the NAACP had held conventions in the North, with sparse attendance from Dixie. "The determined spirit of the southern delegates to fight for the ballot," Shillady noted, was "the most significant thing at the Conference."[14] Edwin Harleston, president of the 1,300-member Charleston branch, urged NAACP members to focus on getting blacks registered to vote. His branch, he said, launched a voter drive with the specific goal of voting as a bloc in upcoming local elections.

"I want the National Association branches all over the country to be thinking more of the extension of the franchise than perhaps any other one item on the program," he said, "because in all the discussions that have been engaged in, in all the speeches and reports, the idea has been brought out that after all methods have been tried, and after all the plans that we have devised have been used, it all reverts back to the ballot for our salvation."[15] Harleston made no mention of the Charleston riot in the previous month.

Rural southerners aired their problems. The Reverend G. W. Williams, from Dublin, Georgia, described how black sharecroppers were systematically mistreated.

"The white farmer has taken advantage of conditions that have grown out of the war," he said, "and as he gives the laborer better wages he runs up the rent in proportion to the increase of wages, so that the black man is practically on the farm just where he was before the war."

Violence was ever present: "Lincoln has declared that we are free citizens a long time ago, but the overseer is there yet. That overseer is backed by the Ku Klux Klan. If the Negro farmer rises to refute the overseer's word he is knocked down or he must reckon with the hang-rope and the torchlight."[16]

A white attorney, B. Harrison Fisher, a delegate from Toledo, posed the obvious question: What should the organization do with its newfound strength?

"I do not know whether I have any right to inject politics, but you have a splendid organization," he told delegates. "What are you going to do with this organization? We as delegates want to know, what is the Negro going to do with the National Association for the Advancement of Colored People as to getting all our rights by the ballot? . . . I look upon this Association as a group of the most intelligent people and if rightly conducted it can do inestimable good. Has the National Association any right to enter into politics?"[17] His answer: "The time for mincing words is past." The NAACP needed to join the political fray and harness black voting power.[18]

Not every attendee was happy with the mostly black crowd. Professor G. A. Gregg, a black delegate from Kansas City, told the audience: "I regret exceedingly that in these great meetings that we have had this week, assembled as we have from all over the United States, we are virtually speaking to ourselves, and that I might have stayed in Kansas and spoken to my family of the conditions which we endure. The only difference is that three hundred or five hundred of us have gathered together to talk over our troubles and our difficulties without other people present."[19]

Mary Ovington, white NAACP co-founder, was dismayed by the low participation of whites. But the energy of black delegates boosted her morale. The 1919 violence was changing black Americans, she realized, politicizing them and transforming the NAACP in a positive way.

"We were trying to direct and yet continually learning how little direction was needed," she said of herself, then board chair, and Shillady, the NAACP secretary. "Time has shown that white direction was short-lived."[20]

Shillady boasted to delegates about the organization's extraordinary growth. "I do not believe in miracles," he said. "The only kind that ever happened was the miracle that came through hard work and through purposeful effort."[21]

In January 1918, Shillady noted, the NAACP had 40 branches and 9,200 members. In May 1919 it had 229 branches and more than 62,000 members. Now it was closing in on its goal of 100,000 members.

"A year ago in Texas we had only four branches and less than 1,000 members," Shillady said. "Now they have the largest membership of any state in the Union. We have in Texas 24 branches and over 5,260 members."[22] Within weeks, that growth would bring the NAACP, and Shillady, into direct conflict with Texas authorities. The NAACP—thanks to the energy and attitude of its new members—was ready to take on violence and segregation in a new, bold way. Writing in *The Crisis*, Du Bois reported the dominant themes of the meeting were "FIGHT and VOTE."[23]

"Some feared that it meant a doctrine of bloodshed and murder in mad retaliation," Du Bois wrote. "It did not. It meant simply determination to secure the right to vote, education and law and order for twelve million people, and to secure these at any cost."

The convention passed resolutions calling for equal voting rights, fair trials, the right to sit on juries, equal rights to use public services and railroads, equal schools, equal rights to public and private employment, and defense against lynching and mob attacks.[24]

As the Cleveland convention wrapped up, the energized delegates headed home anticipating coming confrontations. In a gesture marking the NAACP's increasing confidence, as well as the burgeoning importance of the southern branches, delegates voted to hold the 1920 convention in Atlanta. Du Bois recalled the transformation in Cleveland in poetic terms for *Crisis* readers: "And so we came away—along the grey waters of the wide-thrown lake, above the thunder of Niagara, and I remembered the day when in fear and hesitation the Niagara Movement was born. I remembered the vague, uncertain birth of the N.A.A.C.P. Then in contrast I saw Cleveland—its crowds, its earnestness, its triumphant sense of power."[25]

They would need every ounce of that power for the coming month of July. Was the new black attitude Du Bois saw in Cleveland real? The nation was about to find out.

10.

Longview

We have been through the War and given everything, even our lives, and now we are going to stop bein' beat up.

—BLACK RAILROAD PORTER, ca. 1919

ON THURSDAY AFTERNOON, JULY 10, SAMUEL L. JONES, A BLACK schoolteacher known as the "professor," drove his automobile into downtown Longview, the seat of Gregg County, set amid the rich farmlands of East Texas. Jones parked on Methvin Street, across from the county courthouse, and went off to do some errands.[1]

When Jones returned to his car, three white men approached and demanded he come with them. He refused, so they grabbed him and beat him. One hit him with a wrench, cutting open his forehead. Jones, an overweight man in his early thirties, scrambled to run away but tripped. The men surrounded his prostrate body, demanding to know if Jones authored an offensive article in the latest edition of the *Chicago Defender*, which arrived by train that morning.[2]

The article was about the lynching of a black man, Lemuel Walters, who was arrested on June 16 in Kilgore, ten miles southwest of Longview. The story reported deputies took Walters to the jail in Longview, where that night ten white men used a key to enter Walters's cell, stuff handkerchiefs in his mouth, and drag him away.[3] His nude, bullet-ridden body was found the next day near railroad tracks south of Longview.[4]

"Despite the fact that every effort has been made by officials here to keep the outside world from learning of the lynching . . . the news has leaked out," the article stated.

The white men who attacked Jones did not care about that part of the story. They cared what the anonymous author wrote about an unnamed white woman.[5] Walters was arrested after he was discovered in the woman's bedroom in Kilgore. The story circulating among local whites was that the woman startled Walters, who fled. In this version of events, Walters claimed he only robbed the house.[6]

A July 5 article in the *Defender* presented a different scenario. The article stated that a mob lynched Walters "when a prominent white woman declared she loved him and that if she were in the North, she would obtain a divorce and marry him."[7] Two of the men beating Jones in the street that afternoon were her brothers.

Jones denied he wrote the article, but he was a likely suspect. Jones made extra money as an agent distributing black publications, including the *Defender*. On June 22, Jones visited the jail to drop off newspapers. Black and white prisoners told him of Walters's fate. He told local black leaders. Jones, his friend Dr. Calvin P. Davis, and nine other prominent black community leaders then met with Erskine H. Bramlette, Gregg County's judge. The men went as members of Longview's Negro Business League, the leading black organization in town. The judge asked them for the names of the whites who took Walters. They told him. He promised to look into the matter but warned them not to say anything in public. Nothing happened. Days later, the men returned and Bramlette told them the district attorney would not touch the case.

The *Defender* article then appeared and Jones was beaten. Though outnumbered, he escaped and fled to his friend Davis's office. Davis treated Jones's wounds, and the men rushed over to see the white secretary of Longview's Chamber of Commerce. They asked him to intercede, but he too grilled them about the article. Jones denied again that he wrote it and asked the secretary to telegraph the *Defender* to confirm he was not the author. Back at Davis's office, the two men received more bad news. A white deputy sheriff had whispered to a black jail worker to stay off the streets that night.[8]

Gregg County was almost half black, one of the highest percentages of blacks of any Texas county. It had never seen widespread racial violence.[9] Founded in 1871 as a stop of the Southern Pacific Railroad about 125 miles east of Dallas, Longview was set in piney woods country and a world away from cliché images of Texas cowboys and longhorns. By 1919, much of the flat wooded land was cultivated for cotton. Most of the county's more than 8,000 blacks were sharecroppers, many of whom migrated from the Mississippi Valley. Most of the whites were sharecroppers, too. To serve those farmers, Longview developed robust white and black business districts. Black businesses were clustered south of the railroad tracks. They all sold the *Chicago Defender*. Street vendors, including Dr. Davis's son, sold it as well. By the afternoon of the attack on Jones, it is likely every adult in town knew what the article said. The newspaper claimed: "Our people have been leaving this part of Texas in droves."[10] In the early morning hours of July 11, at least two black men would be forced to leave Longview forever.

With an injured Jones hiding in his office, Dr. Davis went downtown to see Longview's longtime mayor, the insurance broker and cotton buyer G. A. Bodenheim. "Bodie" was an obvious go-between. For years, he bought cotton from local black farmers while also dealing closely with white businesses.[11] He promised Davis he would check with white leaders about what was happening. Bodie and others talked to whites and thought they had the situation under control.[12] But later, Bodie learned a mob was forming. About 6:30 p.m., he sent a message to Davis and Jones: "Get out of town at once." Both men said they would not leave. Instead, they sent notes to about twenty-five other black men asking for help. All agreed to defend Jones.

The mayor held an emergency meeting that evening. Only white leaders were invited, but Davis heard about it. Risking his life, the tall and slender doctor armed himself with a pistol and drove to City Hall. He barged into the meeting. Take off your hat, he was ordered, a customary act of deference to whites. For maybe the first time in his life, the thirty-four-year-old Davis told the gathered white men, many of whom he knew on a first-name basis, that he would not.

"Yes! That's all 'you all' say to a colored man who comes to talk serious business to you: 'Take off your hat,'" Davis said. "I am not going to do it. I want to know what protection we colored citizens are going to have tonight."

Bodie replied, "You will have to take your chances."

The chief of police, Sam Matthews, warned Davis to calm down. "Now I've always been your friend," Matthews said. But he added ominously, "You'd better be careful or you mightn't get back to where you came from."

Davis stormed out. A white man named Tom Flanagan followed him into the street, demanding to know who wrote the article. Davis said he did not know and pulled his gun, making sure not to turn his back on Flanagan as he made his way to his car.[13] When Davis got to Jones's house, he met the twenty-five black men he had asked to defend Jones.[14] All were armed.

———◇———

The men gathered outside the house that hot afternoon represented a new spirit in black America. While economic and political forces sparked a great spasm of white mob violence in 1919, those same forces also awakened black resistance. No one had yet given it a name, but average black people—train porters, returning soldiers, farmers, factory workers, housemaids—realized something ubiquitous was gaining strength. It electrified the air and permeated the most mundane social exchanges wherever blacks and whites met.

The July issue of *The Messenger* expressed a growing black anger: "America, the chief ally in the fight for democracy, stands before the world with her garments dripping with blood and covered with shame."[15] Julius F. Taylor, editor and publisher of the Chicago black weekly *Broad Ax*, opined on July 12, "What a fearful and monstrous halo is overspreading this august race, this white race that feels itself called upon to rule the rest of mankind!"[16] A black railroad porter, talking to George Haynes, was more direct: "We have been through the War and given everything, even our lives, and now we are going to stop bein' beat up."[17]

Nothing more succinctly captured this spirit than Claude McKay's poem "If We Must Die," which first appeared in print that July. Like other black porters of the dining car crew on his Pennsylvania Railroad train, twenty-eight-year-old McKay read black weeklies in each city he visited. Bloody stories with lurid headlines about riots and lynchings appeared with increasing frequency in the "race press." McKay, terrified of being attacked, started carrying a revolver.

"Our Negro newspapers were morbid, full of details of clashes between colored and white, murderous shootings and hangings. . . . We Negro railroad men were nervous. . . . We did not separate from one another gaily to spend ourselves in speakeasies and gambling joints," he wrote later in his autobiography.[18] "We stuck together, some of us armed, going from the railroad station to our quarters. We stayed in our quarters all through the dreary ominous nights, for we never knew what was going to happen."

Feeling helpless and furious, McKay faked stomach trouble one day and hid in a railroad car toilet to scrawl poetry. In that locked bathroom, he wrote what would become his most famous poem:

If we must die, let it not be like hogs
Hunted and penned in an inglorious spot,
While round us bark the mad and hungry dogs,
Making their mock at our accursed lot.
If we must die, let it not be like hogs
So that our precious blood may not be shed
In vain; then even the monsters we defy
Shall be constrained to honor us, though dead!
Oh, kinsman! We must meet the common foe;
Though far outnumbered, let us still be brave,
And for their thousand blows deal one deathblow!
What though before us lies the open grave?
Like men we'll face the murderous, cowardly pack
Pressed to the wall, dying, but—fighting back![19]

McKay later wrote the sonnet "exploded out of me. . . . It was the only poem I ever read to the members of my crew. They were all agitated." One hardened man burst into tears.[20] Max Eastman, the white journalist who accepted a batch of McKay's poems for the July issue of his magazine *The Liberator*, was impressed with McKay's defiant sentiment. Race was never mentioned in "If We Must Die," but all readers knew what it was about and to whom it was addressed. Though blacks were outnumbered, the time had come to defy the monsters. Black publications across the country soon reprinted the poem, and it became a rallying cry.[21]

As dusk gathered, the men in Jones's yard set up defensive positions in and around the small clapboard house. Jones was sent to a relative's house to hide. The men waited. Around 11 p.m., Davis sneaked into town and saw armed white men gathering at the fire department. He rushed back to Jones's house, telling the men to flee if they wanted. All stayed.[22] Around midnight, the group of about twelve to fifteen armed whites made their way to Bodie Park, next to the railroad that divided the city.[23]

Within the hour, the mob made its way to Jones's front yard. Davis saw Tom Flanagan was a mob leader. The white men shouted for Jones to come out. No one answered. When the mob tried to force its way into the house, the black men waiting in ambush opened fire. Davis claimed he fired the first shot.[24]

The black men fired a volley and the startled whites fled, shooting as they retreated. More than a hundred rounds were exchanged.[25] Three white men, Elbert Kelley, Ed Nelson, and Louis Baer, were peppered with birdshot. Ernest White died from a fractured skull and other wounds after a hand-to-hand struggle with a black defender.[26] White's friends left him at the scene. Davis later claimed he killed White, striking him three times in the head with a bed slat. An hour later, whites returned in cars, gathered their wounded, and sped off.[27]

When news of the shootout reached Mayor Bodenheim, he sent off two telegrams to the *Chicago Defender* asking who wrote the article. He stressed he needed an immediate response as black lives were at stake. Bodie seemed ready to resolve the trouble by offering up to the mob the sole author of the article, thus containing the violence. The *Defender* never responded.

Newspaper accounts reported that the mayor and Judge Bramlette ordered the town's fire alarm bell to be rung, calling able-bodied white men to City Hall.[28] Other reports stated those who fled the shooting at Jones's house sounded the alarm.[29] Whoever rang the bell, as many as a thousand men responded.[30]

The local newspaper reported that the mayor and the judge warned the men not to do anything rash.[31] If the men did ask for caution, their pleas were lost on the mob. Men broke into Welch Hardware near the square, taking guns and ammunition. About 4 a.m., an armed mob headed to Jones's house.[32]

The rioters did not find Jones; he had fled. They torched the house. Next they marched down to a black dance hall and set it on fire. They destroyed several more black-owned buildings, including a grocery store, the Negro Business League's meeting hall, a lodge hall, and a drugstore.[33] The mob burned down Davis's office then prepared to burn his home with his family trapped inside. At the last minute, a black neighbor persuaded rioters to let Davis's wife and children escape before they set the house aflame.[34] In the conflagration, a car parked in front of the house caught fire and exploded.[35] The mob also burned the homes of two other black business owners. When one of the men and the wife of the other complained, the mob beat them.[36]

Davis hid in the home of his father-in-law, Marion Bush, as white lynchers searched the home twice. The first time, he hid behind a stack of large cans. The second time, he hid in the attic.[37] The doctor, who lived in Longview for ten years as a prominent member of the community, knew he had to leave immediately and forever. His escape would be harrowing.

At daylight, Davis changed into a borrowed army uniform.[38] He thought he would be safer disguised as a soldier and it would be easier to explain why a black man was traveling on a long train ride. He hoped to ride all the way to Dallas, where he had relatives. Instead, a conductor questioned him and he got off at Camp Switch, a black area outside of Longview, where friends hid him. Hours later, he went to the train station and pretended to be "a simple 'darky,'" as he put it. He said he drank soda and ate popcorn "ostentatiously." He then played craps with a white boy to look even more country. He lost fifteen cents.

When a train with black soldiers came, Davis rushed up to a window and greeted several as though they had been comrades in France. He jumped aboard and sat down among them, quietly pleading for help.

"Are you one of the Longview fellows?" a soldier asked. Davis nodded.

The soldiers encircled Davis, and gave him an overseas cap and a gas mask to make him look more authentic. Davis rode the train for hours and made it to Dallas, where he disembarked.[39] Jones, meanwhile, hid in Longview until the night after the shooting, then fled.

During the night of rioting, police did nothing to stop the rampage. Some reports said Bodie immediately telegraphed Governor William Pettus Hobby for help.[40] Other reports said Bodie telephoned Hobby at dawn, as the mob ended its work.[41] In either case, Hobby did not put state militia on alert until Friday morning. He ordered eight Texas Rangers from Austin and San Antonio to head to Longview.[42]

Judge Bramlette, worried about more rioting on Friday night, called Hobby again later in the morning and urged him to send in militia. Hobby agreed, ordering in a hundred guardsmen, who set up camp next to the courthouse Friday evening.[43]

In 1917, Hobby, a journalist with progressive, anti-lynching sympathies, had become the youngest governor in Texas history at age forty-one. In the spring of 1919, he pushed prohibition and suffrage bills in the Texas legislature.[44] But he also had strong ties to law-and-order politicians, many of whom were strict segregationists.

Hobby was wary of the NAACP, which he associated with radicalism because of its staunch opposition to segregation. In January 1919, the Austin chapter of the NAACP approached him with anti-lynching legislation, but the proposal went nowhere.[45] Despite the rebuff, the NAACP grew into a potent political force in the state as the year went on. In July alone, the national board accepted three new branches from Texas.[46] Longview, site of the worst Red Summer violence in Texas, did not have an NAACP chapter.

On the Friday after the riot, Texas Rangers and state militia patrolled Longview's streets. Both blacks and whites were arrested. Blacks were sent to Austin for fear they would be lynched if kept in Longview. Guardsmen were also sent to patrol nearby Kilgore. Federal agents were sent to Longview as well to look for Bolshevik activity among the black community. They found none.

The next day, Saturday, July 12, the Gregg County sheriff and another man went to the home of Marion Bush, Davis's sixty-year-old father-in-law. They told him they were taking him into protective custody. A frightened Bush refused and shots were fired. The sheriff emptied his pistol as Bush fled with a rifle and pistol. Bush escaped, but was later shot to death in a cornfield by a white farmer.[47]

Bodie and Bramlette heard of the killing and called Hobby for more soldiers. On noon that Sunday, Hobby dispatched 150 more troops to Longview and imposed martial law for all of Gregg County.[48] Guard officers imposed a curfew from 10:30 p.m. to 6 a.m., prohibited operators from placing long-distance calls, and ordered all citizens of Longview and Kilgore to turn in their guns. Guard officers warned that homes would be searched if residents did not cooperate. As many as 7,000 guns were turned in and stored in the courthouse.[49]

Eventually, Rangers arrested twenty-six white men for the attacks on black homes. Twenty-one black men were arrested on charges of attempted murder for the defense of Jones's home on early Friday morning. While the whites were freed on bond, the blacks were taken under guard to an Austin jail. Officials argued it was for their own safety. Eventually, all were released without trial.[50] On Friday, July 18, eight days after Jones was beaten, the governor lifted martial law. Before they left, the troops gave residents their guns back.[51]

White newspapers across the country reported the riot and after-math. Reports placed the blame on blacks and the *Defender*. Accounts said the white men were "waylaid and fired upon" by as many as 50 to 75 blacks.[52] The *Los Angeles Times* labeled the riot "Negro Trouble."[53]

A *Crisis* article, likely written by Du Bois, captured Longview's importance as a harbinger of coming trouble, as "a fair sample of the lawlessness which at present is stalking restlessly through the nation. Secondly, it is indicative of the attitude which Negroes are determined to adopt for the future."[54]

Who wrote the *Defender* article that sparked the trouble? No one ever claimed authorship and publisher Robert Abbott would not discuss it. Davis and Jones found themselves permanent exiles from Longview. Both made their way to a city where they were sure they would be safe: Chicago.

———

Though Longview got the most press of any racial incident in early July, black and white newspapers carried a flood of accounts of other racial violence, interspersed with chaos overseas, labor unrest, and alleged black-on-white crimes. The slightest incident triggered violence. Just days after Longview, blacks and whites brawled on a streetcar in Port Arthur, Texas, after a white man accosted a black man for daring to smoke in front of a white woman.[55] Riots and lynching were so prevalent by July that they became a joke. *Life* magazine suggested a mock constitutional amend-ment that "lynchings shall not be permitted on Sundays, legal holidays or after dark."[56]

July Fourth—traditionally a holiday of mixed emotions for many blacks—showed how frayed race relations had become.[57] On Indepen-dence Day, many blacks felt simultaneous pride and insult. Many whites saw the Fourth as *their* holiday, yet expected a patriotic acquiescence from blacks.

On July 3, whites and blacks rioted in the remote location of Bisbee, Arizona. Trouble in this dusty frontier town underscored how white authorities distrusted blacks, conflated racism with patriotism, and resorted to impulsive violence. It also showed blacks were set, in some cases eager, to fight.

Ten miles from the Mexican border, Bisbee, population 20,000, served

as the commercial center of a copper mining region in the Mule Mountains. It was a desert town of whites, blacks, Mexicans, and Native Americans, but it was clearly run by white businessmen who brooked little
dissent. In 1917, the town became infamous when 1,185 miners were
deported into the desert of neighboring New Mexico. In the early morning hours of July 12, 1917, Sheriff Harry Wheeler had deputized 2,000
vigilantes and sent them to round up strikers. Some of those rounded up
were members of the I.W.W., then engaged in a strike against the copper
mines. But others were not involved in the strike at all. They were all
herded into dirty boxcars and shipped into the desert. Wheeler considered himself a patriot for breaking a "Bolshevik" strike.[58] Not much had
changed by July 3, 1919, when black troops arrived to march in the
town's Fourth of July parade.[59] The soldiers, who came from Fort
Huachaca, 30 miles to the west, were members of the 10th Cavalry Regiment, the famed "Buffalo Soldiers" of the segregated Army. At the time,
the regiment was playing a pivotal role patrolling the border.[60] Mexico
was engulfed in civil war and Pancho Villa was a constant threat to
border towns like Bisbee.[61]

That night, the regiment's white officers went off to a prearranged
dance, while black cavalrymen visited "Brewery Gulch," Bisbee's red-light
district packed with saloons, brothels, and gambling joints. Around 9:30
p.m., five black soldiers got into a fight with a white policeman. Police
alleged drunken black soldiers yelled at the officer when he walked by,
starting a fracas.

The white commander of the 10th Cavalry, Lieutenant Colonel F. S.
Snyder, told the New York Times a different story. In a letter to the editor,
he "concluded that local officials had planned deliberately to aggravate
the Negro troops so that they would furnish an excuse for police and
deputy sheriffs to shoot them down."[62] Snyder also claimed the I.W.W.
was somehow involved against the black soldiers. Although it seems
implausible that Sheriff Wheeler and his men had been in cahoots with
Wobblies, Wheeler had a history of vigilantism and coordinated extra-
legal attacks on groups considered threats. In his minds, black soldiers
posed such a threat.

Whatever sparked the initial brawl, a "rough and tumble fight" spread
throughout the district as white police, sheriff's deputies, and "deputized"
white men moved to disarm black soldiers. Whites and blacks fought for
hours.[63] The two sides fired more than a hundred shots during running
battles throughout Brewery Gulch. Four black soldiers were shot, two

were beaten, and dozens were taken into custody. A deputy sheriff was severely injured. A Mexican woman was grazed in the head by a stray bullet.[64] Around midnight, police and deputies restored order. The next day, hundreds of white cavalrymen from nearby bases patrolled the streets while the parade continued with the Buffalo Soldiers, who were allowed to join the festivities under the careful watch of white troops and police.[65]

The Bisbee fighting, covered nationally, brought to the fore America's conflicted feelings about black participation in the war. Whites demanded black loyalty, but never trusted it. Early in July, General John "Black Jack" Pershing, commander of all American troops in Europe, proudly presented a medal to black private Sol Butler after Butler won the broad jump competition in inter-Allied games in France. More than 30,000 spectators, many of them white American soldiers, had cheered Butler on.[66] Yet less than a week after the award, Pershing's commanders barred American black troops from marching in an Allied parade on Bastille Day in Paris—even though black troops from British and French colonies joined in the parade.[67] An indignant black newspaper editor claimed it was "evidence of downright American prejudice and cussedness, practiced and evinced throughout the length and breadth of the globe."[68]

In Bisbee, officials had invited black soldiers to march in a parade marking the nation's most important holiday. Yet when they arrived, mistrust and tensions escalated and soon white authorities were battling "dangerous" black soldiers. It remains unclear how the violence spread beyond the initial altercation. But in subsequent days, newspapers picked up an Associated Press account that gave the police version of events. Such coverage reinforced white mistrust of blacks. A *Lexington Herald* headline was typical: "Negroes Cause Riot in Arizona."[69]

Days after Bisbee, race conflicts flared in the North and the South. In Pennsylvania, European immigrants clashed with southern black migrants in the town of Coatesville, west of Philadelphia. For decades, Coatesville had brought in immigrants and southern blacks to work in its two large steel mills. Race relations were fractious, with blacks segregated in the northeast section of the city fighting with white immigrants on either side. The town was notorious for a lynching in 1911, when a drunken black man, Zachariah Walker, a migrant from Virginia working in a mill, killed a white police officer in a brawl. A white mob dragged Walker from a hospital bed and burned him alive.[70] "Niggers, *now* you'll learn," men in the crowd had shouted. Fifteen white men and boys were indicted for their involvement in the killing, but all were acquitted.[71] The NAACP latched on to the Coatesville case for one of its first national anti-lynching efforts.

In 1919, race tensions arose again. During the war, thousands of blacks had showed up to work in the mills, but with the war over, demand for steel dropped, putting many out of work. And white unions pushed hard for nonunion blacks to be sacked. In the spring, Mayor A. H. Swing ordered police to round up unemployed blacks and ship them back to the South. The NAACP asked the United States Department of Labor to investigate.[72]

Now, in early July, a black veteran in uniform was arrested in Coatesville on charges of attempting to rape a white girl. Rumors circulated that a white mob was coming to lynch the unidentified man. But this time hundreds of blacks, remembering 1911, ran to the courthouse with baseball bats and pool cues, demanding the man be released for his own safety. The accused man was later released and the charges dropped.[73]

In the South, whites trumpeted such incidents to downplay troubles in their own region. The *Tuscaloosa News* crowed about racial fighting in northern cities:

"In all the tide of time there has never been a Negro ku-kluxed in the South for wanting to work; nor has there ever been an instance of where a quiet, law-abiding Negro had his house burned or been ordered to leave for the reason that it was near white neighbors," the editors wrote. "There are more than ten thousand Negroes right now in Chicago, jobless, drifting about, disliked by everyone and the objects of suspicion."

—————◇—————

Southern whites were not bashing the North solely out of regional pride. They were trying to stanch the loss of cheap labor. A *Wall Street Journal* correspondent from Birmingham noted on July 12, "Northern agents are inducing Negroes to leave southern industrial fields in numbers that have caused serious thought in the South. There is no surplus of labor now and a serious shortage this autumn and winter is threatened."[74]

For decades, southern sheriffs and local businesses had colluded to conscript thousands of black men, arrested on bogus or inflated criminal charges, to work farms, mines, mills, and factories for no wages.[75] But these forced laborers were not enough to meet the needs of southern agriculture and industry. The sharecropping system broke down, and many blacks fled to better-paying jobs in the North. Fearful white businessmen were desperate for blacks to stay. Most spent their energies not trying to improve the lot of southern blacks, but trying to discount criticisms of Jim Crow and antiblack violence as exaggerated. Many lashed out at comfortable targets such as northern black newspapers, Republicans, and the NAACP. A *Montgomery Advertiser* editorial in early July was typical. It condemned "inflammatory and erratic Negro newspapers" for "magnifying the difficulties of the Negro in the South."[76]

Some white officials were beginning to stand up for blacks, but such attitudes were rare. Governor Hugh Dorsey of Georgia, pressing his legislature for new anti-lynching powers, addressed 10,000 blacks at a Knights of Pythias convention in Atlanta on July 7. Dorsey told the crowd that black soldiers had "proven themselves loyal and they, too, gave their every effort to bringing the war to a successful close."[77]

Yet the next day, a shooting 130 miles south of Atlanta showed Dorsey could not, or would not, seek justice for blacks in every lynching. Just hours after Dorsey's speech, six white men came to the Dublin, Georgia, home of a black man, Bob Ashley, and riddled it with bullets.

The men, known to the authorities and the press, told police they went to the house in search of a black murder suspect. The men were relatives of the murder victim. When they knocked on the door and demanded to see the suspect, Ashley fired his shotgun through the door, fatally wounding one of the men, George Green, and wounding his brother, Clyde. The remaining men then opened fire, seriously wounding Ashley. So their story went.[78]

But Ashley's wife said the men were drunk and opened fire on the house as they approached. She insisted Ashley fired twice from his pistol before he was wounded, and never fired his shotgun, so he could not have injured Green. A reporter who examined the house shortly after the shooting substantiated the wife's story. He found shotgun bullets fired at the house but only two bullet holes coming from inside. "Ashley's shotgun was found in a corner showing plainly it had not been fired in some time. One officer stated that there were cob webs in the muzzle," he wrote.[79]

As news of the white man's death spread, almost every black man in Laurens County spent the night cowering in the swamps. News accounts listed the white attackers by name, but none were arrested. Instead, police arrested the barely conscious Ashley. The sheriff wanted to move him to another county to avoid a lynching, but Ashley's wounds were too severe. County officials pleaded to Dorsey, who sent in Home Guard troops from Savannah to protect Ashley as he lay unconscious at the county jail. After a week, Ashley died.[80] No one was ever prosecuted.

Southern whites saw black political independence, no matter how limited, as dangerous. In those first weeks of July, J. D. Kirksey, the acting mayor of Hobson City, Alabama, the only all-black municipality in the state, received an unsigned death threat letter—a typical tactic of the Klan. The anonymous correspondents wanted the town to disband because they could not stand the prospect of a black person holding any public office in Alabama, even the mayoralty of a small rural town. Kirksey had just succeeded Mayor Newman O'Neal, who had fled to Ohio after receiving a similar letter, complete with skull and crossbones. Hobson City was founded in 1899 after the white town of Oxford refused them city services.[81] It prospered, but was harassed by whites, who saw the town as a potential political threat. In July 1919, white vigilantes—led by a resurgent Alabama Klan—moved to stamp out the all-black town. In desperation, residents asked nearby Anniston to annex Hobson City to provide police protection. Anniston refused and Hobson City had to fend for itself.[82]

After months of exhausting work, the New York anti-lynching conference and the Cleveland meeting, the NAACP leadership fell into a brief summertime lull in early July. On July 11, likely around the exact time that black defenders gathered around schoolteacher Samuel Jones's home in Longview, almost the whole NAACP board and staff, including Du Bois, Johnson, and White, were back in New York for a short board meeting. The anti-lynching committee announced a modest July effort: they planned to mail a small pamphlet to newspapers.

In personal letters, Johnson complained that he was exhausted from constant travel and talks.[83] Yet within days of the July meeting, the NAACP field secretary was on the road again. There would be much to do in July.

11.

Washington

With your experience in handling Africans in Arkansas, I
think you had better come up here and take charge of the
Police Force.

—FRANKLIN DELANO ROOSEVELT
to a southern friend, July 26, 1919

HOWARD UNIVERSITY PROFESSOR KELLY MILLER WAS SO HORRIFIED
by the East St. Louis riot of 1917 that he published "An Appeal to Conscience." In the pamphlet, which he sold to blacks across the country
through an advertisement in *The Crisis,* Miller wrote that unless the
federal government took swift action to check race riots and lynchings,
such violence could happen "under the dome of the Capitol itself."[1] Most
readers considered such an assertion to be hyperbole, not prophecy.

At the time, Washington was black America's leading cultural and
financial center. More than 110,000 blacks lived there—a fourth of the
city's population. Many held relatively good-paying and steady jobs as
government clerks and workers or as servants for politicians and bureau-
crats. Washington had Howard University, arguably the country's leading institution of black higher education. It had thriving black churches
that dominated social life. It had the nation's first black-owned bank, the
Industrial Savings Bank, founded in 1913.

From the Republic's earliest days, blacks fleeing slavery came to the
District of Columbia.[2] The city had seen racial strife. In 1848, slaves and
free blacks were caught trying to escape north along the Potomac on a
schooner called *The Pearl.* When an abolitionist wrote in favor of the

slaves, whites rioted for three days.[3] In 1910, whites rioted after black heavyweight champ Jack Johnson easily defeated white former champ James Jeffries in a racially charged match billed as "The Fight of the Century."[4]

But despite these episodes, Washington blacks remained deeply patriotic. More than 5,000 African Americans from the District served in various branches of the military during the Great War. In the city's 480-member "First Separate Battalion," 25 soldiers received France's Croix de Guerre.[5] Many more worked in federal departments supporting the war effort.[6]

Blacks in Washington trod more carefully than their counterparts in northern cities, as the District was middle ground between North and South. They endured far more segregation than did blacks in northern states, but they were sheltered from restrictive Jim Crow laws and violence in nearby Virginia and Maryland. Washington's blacks were aware of both their privileged status and the tenuous nature of that privilege.

By 1919, blacks in the capital had developed strong, if relatively conservative, political groups. One organization, the National Race Congress, founded in 1916 and headed by the Reverend William Henry Jernagin of Mount Carmel Church, regularly garnered headlines but did little to mobilize blacks in the city. Washington's NAACP branch grew to be the largest in the country by 1916 and was still vocal and growing three years later (it reached 1,449 members by early July). But it had yet to be tested with a major political issue or crisis. The branch president was Archibald H. Grimké, a Harvard Law School graduate and former United States consul to the Dominican Republic. His family represented the elite of black society; Grimké and his younger brother, the Reverend Francis J. Grimké, helped found the NAACP. Though just about seventy, Archibald still sat on the NAACP national board and battled regularly with Du Bois.[7] Francis Grimké was known in black America as minister of Washington's historic 15th Street Presbyterian Church.

In early July, local NAACP leaders were fighting two bills—introduced by southerners—that would ban interracial marriage in the District. Archibald Grimké also lodged formal complaints that blacks were prohibited from eating in the Senate restaurant.[8] In another case, the NAACP aided the Parents' League of Washington, a black group claiming to represent the 18,000 black children in the school system. The league was working to unseat an assistant school superintendent, Roscoe Conkling Bruce. At the request of the Netherlands embassy, Bruce had given permission to a Dutch anthropologist named H. M. B. Moens to photograph some black schoolchildren without their clothes, supposedly for a comparative racial study. Rumors abounded that the anthropologist's motives were more lascivious than academic.[9] The NAACP helped the group picket and distribute handbills.

And on July 9, NAACP leaders sent letters to the city's four main newspapers, the *Post, Herald, Times,* and *Evening Star,* asking editors to tone down racial aspects of crime coverage. The newspapers, the NAACP argued, were "sowing the seeds of a race riot by their inflammatory headlines, featuring 'Negro' in all sorts of unnecessary ways." Only the *Star* responded, agreeing to tone down coverage.[10] But none of these issues seemed critical enough for Grimké to postpone his annual summer vacation to Boston.

On the sweltering Friday night of July 18, a nineteen-year-old white woman, one of thousands of women office workers brought to the city by the war effort, left her job at the Bureau of Engraving and headed down Ninth Street. Two black men met her coming the other way. The woman alleged the men jostled her and tried to take her umbrella. She said she resisted and the men ran away when whites came to her aid. Through the night, news of the incident spread among groups of white soldiers and sailors in the city on weekend liberty.[11] They learned the woman was married to a Naval Aviation Corps employee and passed the story along, corner by corner. Uniformed men in theaters, brothels, and saloons heard the story, which expanded and distorted with each telling.

Whites did not riot Friday night, probably because police quickly arrested a black man for the attack. A headline in the *Washington Post* announced, "Negroes Attack Girl."[12] Reports of the assault followed a string of similar stories in the preceding month. The competitive Washington newspapers had run large headlines of at least five such attacks.[13]

Rumor inflated the number. One southerner in Washington claimed black men perpetrated "at least a dozen rapes" in the city from mid-June to mid-July. Frank Carter, a Washington correspondent for North Carolina's *Wilmington Dispatch,* declared, "Since about the middle of June Washington has suffered more from Negro criminality than any other American community ever suffered in the same length of time."[14]

On Saturday, police released the man held in Friday's incident due to

lack of evidence. White military men became livid. As dusk arrived—
with temperatures still in the 80s—about a hundred white servicemen
gathered near the Liberty YMCA and started on a rampage. The mob
tried to lynch a black man, but he escaped after being severely beaten.
The mob then milled about downtown in the streets between the White
House, the War Department, the Navy Department, and the Capitol.[15]

During the night, groups of white servicemen attacked blacks, pulling them from streetcars and assaulting them on sidewalks. Shots were
fired. Police and a handful of marines responded to several calls, but
every time they did, the mob dispersed, only to re-form.[16] Ten people—
eight black civilians and two white soldiers—were arrested that Saturday
night, even though all reports stated whites were the ones rioting.[17] News
reports sent across the country Sunday morning assumed the trouble
was over.[18]

NAACP officials urged Navy Secretary Josephus Daniels to act against
sailors involved in the fighting. They reminded him of what had happened
in Charleston—quick action saved lives. Daniels, a North Carolina Democrat and an ardent segregationist, did nothing.[19]

Sunday night, several hundred white sailors and workers marched
from the Washington Navy Yard on the Potomac into the nearby neighborhood, beating any blacks they encountered. They threw stones and
bricks and pulled people from streetcars.[20] Whites packed into cars, drove
into black neighborhoods in northwest Washington, and fired at passersby. These drive-by shootings, known by the slang term "terror cars,"
were a key tactic of urban mobs and gangs in 1919.

Late Sunday, rioting also erupted in the city's retail district as theaters
let out.[21] Under the glare of streetlights and in front of open shops and
restaurants, hundreds of white soldiers, sailors, and marines attacked black
men walking near the White House. A police officer arrested a white soldier on Pennsylvania Avenue near the Mall and was surrounded by an
angry crowd of soldiers demanding the prisoner's release. The officer fired
his revolver in the air to drive the men away. Civilian whites joined the
crowds and incited violence by running up to white servicemen, pointing
at a passing black person, and shouting, "There he goes!"[22]

That night, Carter Godwin Woodson, the dean of Howard University
and a pioneer of African American history, ran into a white mob while
walking home near the Capitol.

Woodson ducked into a store entranceway and watched servicemen
chase a black man who screamed for mercy. As Woodson emerged from

the shadows, he witnessed what he called the "most harrowing spectacle" he had ever seen. The mob caught the black man and hoisted him up "as one would a beef for slaughter" then shot him. Woodson sneaked away, trying not to draw attention to himself.[23]

Riot calls came into police stations in the early morning hours, with mobs roaming from the White House to as far northeast as the Washington Senators' baseball park at Florida and Trinidad avenues. By 2:15 a.m., police reported the city was quieter, but injured blacks streamed into hospitals through the night.[24] Blacks with cuts and bruises showed up at police stations and refused to leave unless an officer escorted them home.[25]

White journalist Chauncey Brainerd of the *Brooklyn Daily Eagle* said the rioting became "infinitely worse" as the weekend wore on. It was obvious, Brainerd said, that the police could not handle the situation.[26]

By Monday morning, the federal government had still taken no action. President Wilson, the man who appointed the District's commissioner and the military's commander-in-chief, was on a weekend vacation to Hampton, Virginia. He left Saturday night, cruising the Potomac on his yacht, *Mayflower*. While on the trip, Wilson suffered an attack of dysentery. He returned on Monday and immediately went to bed.[27]

Until Monday morning, white mobs dominated the rioting with little coordinated resistance from blacks. That changed about 11 a.m., when four black men in a "terror car" sped past the Navy Hospital in southeast Washington. They opened fire on the sentry and patients walking the grounds. The men were arrested, but news spread: blacks were fighting back.[28]

<hr />

District Commissioner Louis "Brownie" Brownlow and District Police Chief Raymond W. Pullman met with Navy Secretary Josephus Daniels, War Secretary Newton Baker, and Army Chief of Staff Peyton March. The military offered four hundred men—cavalry, military police, marines, and others—to support Washington's police officers. Still, officials hesitated with half measures. Military commanders did not cancel leave and Brownlow rejected asking Wilson to declare martial law.[29] Daniels urged sailors to maintain order. Baker agreed to lend military police to the city, but argued that many uniformed rioters were discharged veterans and not under his control.[30] The police warned people off the streets. The Parents' League did the same, distributing 50,000 leaflets urging blacks to stay inside. Brownlow and Pullman issued a statement condemning the attacks on blacks and issued a decree asserting that "the dignity and supremacy of the law must and will be vindicated in the national capital."[31]

By the afternoon, the NAACP leader John Shillady sent a telegram to Wilson, demanding he bring in troops: "The effect of such riots in national capital upon race antagonism will be to increase bitterness and danger of outbreaks elsewhere."[32]

With Archibald Grimké in Boston, other local NAACP leaders, including Neval Hollen Thomas, stepped in to send lawyers to meet with jailed blacks. Volunteers went to hospitals to obtain affidavits about the attacks.[33] NAACP officials urged newspapers to curb inflammatory headlines. They wrote to Daniels at the Navy, imploring him to crack down on the sailors who were causing so much trouble. That evening, local NAACP leaders and black ministers met with Commissioner Brownlow. Ask for troops, the group implored.[34] They complained whites in the District were buying revolvers during the day, but blacks were not allowed to do so.[35] But Brownlow and Chief Pullman insisted they could handle the situation.[36]

"We left saying, 'Very well, if you can't protect us, we will arm and defend ourselves,'" Thomas recalled. "Three hours afterwards Negroes were shooting and beating white people."[37]

Neval Thomas, forty-five, was a quintessential example of the "New Negro." Though combative with Du Bois, he was devoted to the NAACP's Washington branch and Archibald Grimké. He earned a law degree from Howard but had abandoned a legal career to become a history instructor at Washington's Dunbar High School, perhaps the most prestigious black secondary school in the country. Thomas believed he had a duty to educate black students at a black institution. Kelly Miller remarked years later that he considered Thomas to be "the true reformer." He did not join the NAACP to allow white social workers to help him incrementally get ahead. He joined to seize and protect equality for himself and fellow blacks.[38]

Thomas was perpetually active during the Washington riot, urging city officials to act, meeting with lawyers for arrested blacks, contacting the press, printing pamphlets on the riot, and heading out to the streets to see the violence firsthand. His hard work during this crisis led him to be appointed later in 1919 to the NAACP board of directors, overcoming Du Bois's opposition. He was ambitious, eager, and determined—and there were many more black men like him entering the political fray in 1919.

Commissioner Brownlow's reluctance to request aid from President Wilson was strange, considering there were clear signs during two nights of mayhem that more trouble was coming. That morning's *Washington Post* carried a general call for rioters. The article, titled "Mobilization for Tonight," said an unnamed group wanted "every available service man stationed in or near Washington or on leave" to show up downtown on Pennsylvania Avenue at 9 p.m. for "a 'clean-up' that will cause the events of the last two evenings to pale into insignificance."[39] As many as 500 pistols were sold that Monday in stores in the District, almost all to white men.[40] Whites heard rumors that Howard University ROTC officers were giving out guns and ammunition to local blacks.[41]

The District was under direct federal jurisdiction, so troops could have been mobilized immediately, unlike in other cities. Brownlow also could have cited War Secretary Newton Baker's 1917 order that allowed civilian officials to request troops directly from a military garrison, without going through standard channels.[42] Washington was ringed by military installations, so Brownlow could have called up disciplined troops in hours to stop the rioting.

Perhaps the situation overwhelmed Brownlow. A thirty-nine-year-old former newspaperman, his only qualification to run a government overseeing 440,000 residents appeared to be that he was Wilson's friend. Prior to his appointment by Wilson in 1915, Brownlow had been a local reporter for newspapers in Kentucky and Tennessee and then a correspondent in Washington.[43] As commissioner, he had made some accommodations to the city's large black population, but any changes were all within the context of segregated government. The city had a black judge on the municipal court. He allowed some blacks to join the police force. And in January 1919, Brownlow established the District's first all-black platoon in the fire department.[44] Brownlow considered himself an expert on municipal administration and on keeping peace between the races.

Now, faced with his greatest challenge, Brownlow insisted his 700-member police force, plus several hundred loaned troops and 100 auxiliary home guard, could stop the largest race riot in the city's history.[45] His own police chief did not think the city had enough men.

Even as Brownlow tried to calm black leaders in his office at the fortified municipal building, white military men and civilians gathered in mobs across the city. By evening, a throng of sailors gathered at the Peace Monument next to the Capitol. As congressmen and their staff rushed by to head home, they saw a black man surrounded by yelling sailors under the memorial dedicated to Civil War seamen. Police broke up the crowd before anyone was harmed.[46] Again, white crowds swelled along Pennsylvania Avenue near the White House.[47] Black men by the thousands gathered in the streets of their neighborhoods, waiting. Both sides were armed with razors, pistols, clubs, bats, lead pipes, bricks, and knives.[48] Black men set up barricades on streets around Howard University and the LeDroit Park neighborhood. Some black men, a few of them war veterans, manned rooftops with rifles.[49]

"There were at least 2,000 Negroes, many with pistols showing, declaring their purpose to die for their race, and defy the white mob, which was announced as coming to colored sections," Neval Thomas wrote to Archibald Grimké.[50]

As anticipated in that morning's *Post*, at 9 p.m. about 400 men, most of them soldiers in olive green uniforms and sailors in dress whites, gathered at a Knights of Columbus military personnel recreation center on Pennsylvania Avenue.[51]

Rioting and racial attacks were already under way across the city, but this moment set off the full-scale riot downtown. White sailors and soldiers hurled stones and bottles at cars driven by blacks. One rioter crushed a black man's skull with a rifle butt. A group of whites pulled a black seventeen-year-old, Francis Thomas, from a streetcar. Thomas told NAACP investigators his attackers beat him "unmercifully from head to foot, leaving me in such a condition that I could hardly crawl back home."

A *New York Tribune* reporter observed: "Before the very gates of the White House Negroes were dragged from streetcars and beaten up while crowds of soldiers, sailors and marines dashed down Pennsylvania Avenue, the principal thoroughfare in the downtown section, in pursuit of the fleeing Negroes. In one instance a restaurant, crowded with men and women diners, was invaded by a crowd of uniformed soldiers and sailors in search of Negro waiters."[52]

Blacks retaliated, pulling white soldiers and others from streetcars passing through their neighborhoods. Riot calls flooded police stations. Mobs pelted streetcars with bricks. Whites severely beat a black man near the House of Representatives office building after they accused him of trying to steal a bicycle. When the black chauffeur for a white legislator intervened, the mob mauled him too.

Another mob pulled a black veteran off a streetcar and beat him. As he broke free and ran, the streetcar conductor fired a gun at him. Terror cars filled with blacks drove through white areas shooting randomly. Terror cars filled with whites drove through black areas doing the same.

Fear spread in Washington and beyond. In his Baltimore home, eleven-year-old Thurgood Marshall heard how both blacks and whites chased his blue-eyed, light-skinned father, Willie Marshall, a railroad worker who was caught in the Washington fracas.

"He had a hell of a time," recalled Marshall, who long before becoming the first black Supreme Court Justice investigated race riots in the 1940s as head of the NAACP Legal Defense and Educational Fund. "The Negroes would run one place, the white folks were running the other. So he was running back and forth. Wherever he went, he was wrong."[53]

Panic swept through city neighborhoods, even those not consumed by street brawling. Shots echoed in the dark. Police cars and military trucks rushed along barren streets. People scurried home or cowered in their apartments. NAACP publicity director Herbert Seligmann rushed from New York to document the violence. He arrived at 8:30 p.m. just as Monday night's chaos began. Thomas, the local NAACP organizer, met him at Union Station.[54] The two young men, one white, one black, walked out into a city in chaos. They went to a black neighborhood near Howard University. All the shops were closed, some pocked with bullet holes.

Seligmann found a community ready for combat: "There was ominous darkness and silence more menacing than any furious outcry of a crowd, a silence punctuated by an occasional spatter of shots; the streets were filled with sauntering dark men, not a white face among them. Upper windows were lined with watching eyes."[55]

During the night, at least four people were killed and dozens seriously wounded. Hospitals were overwhelmed. Cornered on a streetcar by angry whites, black man Randall Neale opened fire into the crowd, wounding several attackers. Arriving police returned fire, killing Neale.[56]

On G Street, near Union Station, a black teenager, Carrie Minor Johnson, fatally shot twenty-nine-year-old detective sergeant Harry Wilson. Johnson was hiding under her bed when Wilson broke down the door to her second-floor bedroom. Police were responding to reports that a sniper fired from the building into the street. Johnson said she shot Wilson in self-defense. Police called her "a girl sniper."

Police contended they found incriminating evidence in Johnson's house, a seditious publication, *The Boston Age*. This was most likely a detective's conflation of two mainstream black publications, *the Boston Guardian* and the *New York Age*. A news account claimed the publication was dangerous because it discussed "the idea of racial equality between whites and Negroes."[57]

Just east of the Capitol, William Laney, twenty-five, had just taken his girlfriend home from the theater when a white mob set after him. The crowd saw him and yelled, "Catch the nigger!" and "Kill the nigger!" Laney ran down Massachusetts Avenue but was overtaken near Stanton Park. Laney pulled a pistol. The crowd backed off and he ran into a backyard. When Laney reemerged, he saw the mob attacking a house on the other side of the street. Rioters saw him and gave chase. Laney fired three times into the crowd and ran. One of Laney's shots killed a white teenager, Kenneth Crall.

"I fired to protect my life," he said.

Police charged Laney with manslaughter.[58] Initial police accounts claimed he was a black radical. Police said they found letters in Laney's pockets in which he threatened to kill the governors of Mississippi and Georgia if they did not stop lynching.[59] These assertions later were proven false.

Police took many blacks into custody for weapons possession. NAACP lawyers argued, with some success, that blacks traveling that night acted reasonably when carrying weapons and used them only for self-defense.

Fears that a "race war" would spread beyond the District were rampant in the press.[60] Rumors of blacks and whites fighting in the Maryland suburbs reached the city. In Baltimore, the police marshal warned all gun shops to restrict sales until the Washington situation was over.[61]

As the riots consumed Washington, fighting broke out at the naval port of Norfolk, Virginia, after blacks tried to stop white policemen from arresting a black soldier. Norfolk was supposed to be celebrating that day with a parade for black troops returning from France. Instead, police, sailors, and marines patrolled the streets. At least two blacks were killed and two police officers were wounded.[62] That same night two blacks and a white sheriff's son were killed in a "near race riot" in Denmark, South Carolina.[63]

———

In Washington, the streets cleared in the dark hours of Tuesday morning not because of any concerted police action but because the mobs were exhausted. A reporter observed: "A statement issued by the governing authorities denied that the situation had been out of hand at any time last night when riot calls were sounding from half a dozen places at a time."[64] The *Washington Star* declared that the nation's capital "passed through its wildest and bloodiest night since Civil War times."[65] A black newspaper observed, "Hell seems to have broken loose in Washington, D.C."[66]

◇

Despite Monday's chaos, Brownlow's boss seemed to be in even greater denial. President Wilson made no public remarks, though an aide said the president was "alarmed" by the violence.[67] Wilson's seclusion was caused in part by his bout of dysentery. Having returned from months in Europe just two weeks earlier (he was the first president to travel overseas while in office), Wilson's sudden onset of diarrhea that weekend was so serious his doctor worried that he might not be able to make an upcoming national tour to campaign for the League of Nations treaty.[68] The coming political fight was to be the most difficult of Wilson's career.[69]

Wilson had staked his legacy and the reputation of the United States on establishing an international system to mediate disputes and spread democracy. He spent months in Europe hammering out the framework for a League of Nations. He hoped to return a conquering hero. Instead, he returned to meet a hostile, Republican-controlled, isolationist Congress.[70] A race war outside the White House must have humiliated Wilson as he grandly asserted the United States was the world's leading democracy.

A white NAACP supporter wrote to Du Bois that he was horrified that a race riot took place "in the very heart of our capital, where sits our illustrious and humane President, Mr. Woodrow Wilson, who only a few months ago in a speech to the world, said America stood for justice and democracy. . . . Today he sits silent while mob rule sweeps the streets of our capital."[71]

Editors at the leftist black monthly *The Challenge* noted that Wilson "preaches for 'humanity' and sees black men and women shot to pieces under his window."[72] The black weekly *Atlanta Independent* complained, "Our president seems to be in utter ignorance of the conditions obtaining at his door."[73]

Commentators in other countries also ridiculed America's claim as a human rights leader. In Japan, the Osaka newspaper *Maninichi* mocked Wilson: "American statesmen, not to mention Mr. Wilson, should first satisfy the 10,000,000 Negroes in America, before meddling in the affairs of other countries on the plea of justice and humanity."[74]

The German newspaper *Lokal Anzeiger,* in an article titled "The Black Peril," speculated that "the disorders now reported are but a beginning. If the Negroes can find a leader—perhaps already they have one—we may yet experience all sorts of things, perhaps someday a black president."[75]

Du Bois shared this disdain coming from international quarters. In *Darkwater,* his collection of essays completed that summer, Du Bois wrote, "It is curious to see America, the United States, looking on herself, first, as a sort of natural peacemaker, then as a moral protagonist in this terrible time. No nation is less fitted for this role."[76]

Wilson's personal feelings on race also played a part in his inaction. Throughout his life, he demonstrated hypocrisy regarding the treatment of blacks and awkward silence on race relations. Virginia-born and Georgia-raised, the Presbyterian minister's son was a southern white man with all the attendant prejudices. He loved to tell "darky" jokes to dignitaries, politicians, staff, and friends, often with an affected accent.

With blacks, Wilson was often two-faced. He invited Booker T. Washington to his inauguration as president of Princeton University, but then spent his tenure preventing blacks from enrolling.[77] When he ran for the presidency, he actively courted black leaders. The strategy paid off, and Wilson siphoned off some black votes in the North to weaken his two opponents in 1912, Progressive candidate Theodore Roosevelt and Republican incumbent William Howard Taft. When he first took office, Wilson assured black leaders he would listen to their concerns. But his relations with blacks soon soured. African American supporters expected Wilson to give them patronage positions traditionally reserved for blacks. Instead, he gave most to white men. He sanctioned the segregation of large parts of the bureaucracy, infuriating civil rights groups. He held a meeting in 1912 with black leaders about his resegregation of the civil service, a move that countered decades-old policies set in place by President Chester Arthur.[78] When William Monroe Trotter pressed him on the issue, Wilson cut the meeting short, claiming Trotter was impertinent.[79]

As Edmund Wilson once noted, President Wilson had a "self-righteous inability to accept with realistic frankness the fact that he has himself been a practical politician playing the political game."[80] Though he sought black votes from northern cities, much of his support came from white southern segregationists. For every tepid endorsement from someone like Du Bois, Wilson received enthusiastic backing from political leaders like Senator James K. Vardaman of Mississippi, who declared his state's

1898 constitution "was to eliminate the nigger—not the ignorant but the nigger" from voting rolls.[81] This attitude was prevalent among Wilson loyalists.

Wilson also gave blacks many symbolic insults, including appointing a white ambassador to Haiti, a traditionally black post. After the East St. Louis riot of 1917, Wilson asked the Justice Department to investigate, but nothing came of its work and he said nothing publicly. Black leaders complained. A year later, after a spate of lynchings, Wilson issued a public statement in part to appease disgruntled black troops, who War Secretary Baker worried might rebel.[82] Without mentioning race, Wilson condemned "mob spirit," and compared lynchers to the German enemy. It was a bully pulpit scolding, little else. At times, Wilson seemed tortured by racial issues. In a private meeting, he told Oswald Garrison Villard, NAACP board member and liberal editor, that he saw no way around segregation. "It will take a very big man to solve," he said.[83]

He proved during his presidency that he was not that man. By the summer of 1919, many black leaders came to see him as a malign actor. James Weldon Johnson said his feelings for Wilson "came nearer to constituting keen hatred for an individual than anything I have ever felt."[84]

Wilson's repeated dismissal of black entreaties should be understood in the context of an overall lack of black political power at the time. While blacks were securing some elected posts on city councils and legislatures in northern states, no blacks held positions of power in the Wilson administration and no blacks were elected to either house of Congress. George Henry White, the last black Reconstruction congressman, left office in 1901.[85]

The Democrat-controlled House passed a law in 1913, just after Wilson took office, making it a felony for blacks and whites to marry in Washington. Both the House and the Senate chambers were segregated. Even in the midst of the Washington riot, white elevator men at the Senate threatened to strike because a Republican senator arranged for a black man to operate one of the elevators.[86]

Wilson ignored black entreaties for protection and equity without much political fallout, even as chaos reached his own doorstep.[87] Franklin Roosevelt, assistant Navy secretary, seemed more irritated by the riot than frightened. Though his wife, Eleanor, then in Connecticut, was terrified, Roosevelt assured her the "nasty business" did not come to their neighborhood. "I only wish *quicker* action had been taken to stop it," he wrote.[88] Days later, FDR joked with a Harvard classmate who lived in the South: "With your experience in handling Africans in Arkansas, I think you had better come up here and take charge of the Police Force."[89]

By the third day of rioting, ominous developments suggested Tuesday night could be as bad as Monday. A rumor spread that a black man had assaulted a white woman in the Maryland suburb of Capitol Heights.[90] Black agitators distributed the latest editions of *The Afro-American*, Baltimore's black weekly, which carried bold headlines announcing that blacks gained the upper hand in the fighting.[91]

Recovering from his illness, Wilson felt well enough to discuss the crisis with Brownlow. Desperate to save face, Brownlow still rejected an official declaration of martial law. But after Monday night's chaos, he agreed to what amounted to the same thing: a military takeover of the city.

Tuesday afternoon, Wilson summoned War Secretary Baker. In a closed-door meeting, he directed Baker to bring in troops. Though Wilson made no public remarks, his secretary told reporters the president "took cognizance of the situation late today" and "was understood to be greatly concerned."[92]

Baker appointed General William G. Haan to restore order. Haan had a storied career in the military and had seen his share of trouble. The West Point graduate fought the Spanish in Cuba and rebels in the Philippines. He coordinated military relief efforts in San Francisco after the 1906 earthquake. And during the Great War, Haan commanded troops at the second battle of the Marne and led the capture of German defenses at Juvigny. He returned to the United States in April 1919 as a brigadier general.[93]

The hardened soldier blamed the crime-obsessed press for the riot, saying he was fighting "merely a newspaper war."[94] By Tuesday evening, he established a command center at the Municipal Building and dispersed across the city about 2,000 soldiers—many of them disciplined troops with overseas experience. Marines armed with bayonets ordered crowds to break up. Cavalry pushed groups off street corners. Haan restricted auto traffic and threatened to limit gun sales. All theaters were closed. Tanks equipped with machine guns drove in from Fort Meade.[95] By about 9:30, Haan had toured the city again and declared, "I did not find any indication of trouble anywhere."[96] But trouble erupted that night despite the show of force. A black man shot and killed a home guard named Isaac Halbfinger, when the guard tried to search him. Another white home guard also was shot and wounded. Elsewhere, white soldiers shot and wounded a black prisoner.[97] Several white civilians reported being cut by blacks using razor blades.[98]

However, by Wednesday a relieved Baker reported to Wilson in a confidential note that "the City was much quieter than it had been anticipated and no serious disturbances took place." He praised Haan and wrote that black leaders had been helpful in keeping things calm.[99] For the rest of the week, thousands of troops patrolled the streets, with their holsters unfastened and riot sticks ready.[100] By Sunday evening, July 27, the last of the troops were withdrawn to their bases outside Washington.[101]

No one ever determined a final tally of deaths and injuries. Conservative reports listed seven killed: four blacks, three whites (one of them the police detective). Hundreds were injured; an untold number later died.

The federal and District governments never investigated. Some Republicans in Congress declared it a "national scandal" and several presented bills calling for martial law and restricted gun sales in the District.[102] Southern Democrats had their own solutions. Senator Pat Harrison of Mississippi demanded that Washington streetcars be segregated.[103] Representative Frank Clark of Florida drafted a resolution calling for an investigation of why District police could not handle the rioting. He said black criminals assaulting white women had caused the riot.[104] Wilson administration officials were eager to avoid blame. The Washington representative of the Commission on Interracial Cooperation, white educator Thomas Jesse Jones, met with Secretary Baker after the riot and begged him to publicly condemn the white mobs. Baker refused, agreeing only to say that black soldiers did a good job during the war—he did not want to talk about the riot anymore.[105]

Brownlow blamed Bolsheviks, arguing that agitators dressed as soldiers and sailors had started the riot to make the military look bad.[106] The NAACP tried to use the riot as a way to push congressional hearings on lynching and mob violence. Tuesday night, July 22, 1919, James Weldon Johnson arrived in Washington from New York and lobbied for hearings. Both Du Bois and Spingarn volunteered to come, but the board chose to send the diplomatic Johnson. Beginning Wednesday morning, he met with a handful of congressmen and senators allied with the NAACP and urged them to seek public hearings. Senator Charles Curtis, a Kansas Republican, expressed interest in pushing for hearings. Johnson also met with editors of the four major newspapers and discussed their responsibility in the violence.[107] NAACP lawyers met with blacks who were arrested. Others met with Brownlow to discuss allegations of black prisoners being beaten in jail.[108] The national office gathered the signatures of 150 prominent Americans to call on Congress to investigate mob attacks.[109]

White leaders and commentators fumbled to find explanations for the large-scale white rioting and the black response. The influential *New York World*, flagship of the Pulitzer publishing empire, ran a political cartoon of a swarthy brute leaning on the Capitol dome, holding a club. The caption read: "Self-determination in Washington."

The white fundamentalist Baptist pastor John Roach Straton told his large white congregation on the Sunday after the riots: "When we have come to the place in this country where innocent people are dragged from streetcars simply because they are Negroes and shot and beaten and stabbed in the nation's capital, then surely the time has come when we should work with the diseases from which we are suffering."[110]

But many whites blamed blacks for the trouble. Frank Carter at the *Wilmington Dispatch* wrote that black crime had provoked "a comparatively mild outbreak of mob violence," and "straightaway the Negro mob rose and heavily armed bands of Negroes seized automobiles and ripped and snorted and shot and killed through the streets of Washington, while the raping and the robbing went merrily on."[111] Many whites came away from the riots believing the nation needed more segregation. The problem with cities, they argued, was blacks and whites were not kept apart enough. Brainerd, the *Brooklyn Eagle* correspondent, published an essay the Sunday after the riot under the headline, "Race War in Washington Shows Black and White Equality Not Practical." Military service in France made black men more likely to rape white women, he wrote, adding, "It has been a bad and a dangerous experience . . . and it has produced danger for white women in the United States."[112] The *Chicago Tribune*, the Republican newspaper that had championed Lincoln and emancipation during the Civil War, also supported segregation: "If the races cannot get along in certain neighborhoods without fights and brawls and police interference, how long will it be before segregation will be the only means of preventing daily murders and perhaps a recurrence, on a scale vastly enlarged, of the East St. Louis disaster?"[113]

A white reader of the *Atlanta Constitution* who had grown up in the North wrote, "These color distinctions—the 'Jim Crow cars,' the divisions in streetcars, the absolute separation wherever racial contact occurs—must not only be maintained but must be strengthened and emphasized."[114]

While the Washington violence dismayed whites, the black reaction electrified many black leaders. S. M. Kendrick, secretary of the Washington NAACP branch, wrote privately to Archibald Grimké about the "remarkable spirit of unity among colored people" in the city post-riot.[115]

W. E. Hawkins boasted in the leftist black *The Messenger*: "The gaping wounds of would-be lynchers in the city morgue and hospitals speak an eloquent warning that the time of timidity is gone."[116]

Harlem Renaissance writer Jean Toomer, then twenty-four and unknown, focused on the riot in the second piece he ever published, an editorial that ran in the socialist *New York Call* on July 29:

> The outstanding feature remains, not that the Negro will fight, but that he will fight against the American white. It now confronts the nation, so voluble in acclamation of the democratic ideal, so reticent in applying what it professes, to either extend to the Negro (and other workers) the essentials of a democratic commonwealth or else exist from day to day never knowing when a clash may occur in the light of which the Washington riot will diminish and pale.[117]

Chester A. Franklin, editor of *The Call* in Kansas City, declared that Washington proved the era of "THE NEW NEGRO"—printed in bold capital letters—had arrived. "The time for cringing is over," he wrote in his editorial.[118] On July 27, about 2,000 blacks gathered for an Equal Rights League rally at the Palace Casino in Harlem to greet League president William Monroe Trotter on his return from Europe. Trotter went in part to investigate mistreatment of black troops. The United States refused to grant him travel papers so he hid aboard a ship pretending to be a cook.

"We believe that self-preservation is the first law of nature," Trotter shouted as the crowd cheered, clapped, and waved handkerchiefs. "Unless the white American behaves, he will find that in teaching our boys to fight for him he was starting something that he will not be able to stop."[119]

Whites had just learned this lesson in the nation's capital. As the last buck private marched out of Washington on the evening of Sunday, July 27, the same lesson was about to be taught in Chicago.

12.

Chicago Is a Great Foreign City

*Will no action be taken to prevent these law breakers until
further disaster has occurred? An ounce of prevention beats
a pound of cure.*

—IDA WELLS-BARNETT, July 7, 1919

IN MID-JULY, CHICAGO'S TOURISM BOARD LAUNCHED A NATIONAL
advertising campaign with the slogan "Chicago Calls." Billboards her-
alding the Windy City's attractions were put up along highways and on
buildings across the Midwest. One of the most popular was an image of
a white woman in the full-body bathing suit of the time. She was smiling
and splashing at one of the city's many public beaches on Lake Michigan.
"CHICAGO—the summer resort with the cooling lake breeze," the bill-
board proclaimed. The sign promoted more than 30 miles of shoreline
and was signed by "Big Bill" Thompson, the city's flamboyant Republican mayor.[1]

Chicago's leaders loved to boast about the city's beachfront, booming
businesses, and swelling population. The sprawling city epitomized America's powerful industrialism. As the nexus of America's railroads, inland
shipping, and agricultural production, Chicago had grown into the heart-
land's economic capital. In 1919, it was America's second-largest city, with
2.7 million people, up 500,000 in a decade. A modern elevated transit
system, known commonly as the "L," shuttled thousands around Chicago
every day and looped the growing downtown. Wealthy couples strolled
the upscale shopping area of Michigan Avenue. The financial district was

home to institutions like the palatial Chicago First National Bank. The-aters lined State Street. World-class museums, like the Field Museum and the Art Institute of Chicago, drew tourists from around the globe. The skyline included the Woolworth Building, the world's tallest sky-scraper. Industrial barons and financiers built mansions in suburbs north of the city on cliffs overlooking Lake Michigan. In early 1919, Chi-cago was constructing a network of public parks along its lakefront to rival New York's. Most American cities were consumed with civic boost-erism, but Chicago led the pack. The Hearst-owned *Chicago American* published an editorial denouncing "Knockers and Croakers" of the city and demanding, "Take Off Your Hat to the Greatness of Chicago."[2]

But the bluster had a pleading tone. Chicago was notorious for squa-lor. It was the setting of *The Jungle*, Upton Sinclair's 1906 novel of the horrors of the meatpacking industry. Away from the lake, the city became a grid of dirty tenements, sooty factories, foul-smelling slaughterhouses, machine shops, industrial warehouses, coal mounds, and noisy railroad yards. The South Side was dominated by the Union Stock Yards, Chica-go's meatpacking district employing tens of thousands. It was the largest meat-processing operation in the world. The blood, filth, and odor per-vaded a large portion of the city. In *A Farewell to Arms*, Ernest Heming-way compared the carnage on World War One battlefields to "the stockyards at Chicago if nothing was done with the meat except bury it."[3] The killing, carving, processing, and shipping created an insatiable demand for workers.

Immigrants had thronged to the city from all parts of Europe for decades. Irish, Swedes, Germans, Italians, Russians, Jews, Poles, Hungar-ians, Serbs, Croats, Greeks, Czechs, Bohemians, and others transformed Chicago into a network of cramped insular neighborhoods set apart by language and religion. By 1890, more than 40 percent of Chicagoans were foreign-born.[4] By 1919, that percentage dropped to about 30 percent. But many of the native-born population were the children of immigrants and still adhered to their ethnic divisions.[5] Chicago had nearly as many Ger-mans as Dresden, one-third as many Bohemians as Prague, half as many Irish as Belfast, and half as many Scandinavians as Stockholm.[6] Lan-guages, religion, and educational levels divided people. Political fault lines echoed national divisions in Europe. As one social worker summed up in mid-July, "Chicago is a great foreign city."[7]

Each neighborhood had its own political organization. Many also produced their own ethnic gangs, based in "athletic clubs." Young men roamed defined borders of their neighborhood looking for trouble and shaking down small business owners. Sometimes the political organizations and the gangs were one.[8]

The street gangs, made up of young men ages seventeen to twenty-two, often were cozy with police. Ragen's Colts controlled a large neighborhood in the Irish section of the South Side near the stockyards.[9] Other groups, like the Our Flag Club, the Sparkler's Club, the White Club, and the Hamburgers, balkanized the South Side.

Mike Royko, in his political biography of Chicago mayor Richard J. Daley, *Boss*, described the South Side where Daley, a member of the Hamburg Social and Athletic Club, grew up and graduated from high school in June 1919:

> The borders of neighborhoods were the main streets, railroad tracks, branches of the Chicago River, branches of the branches, strips of industry, parks, and anything else that could be glared across. . . . Go that way, past the viaduct, and the wops will jump you, or chase you into Jew town. Go the other way, beyond the park, and the Polacks will stomp you. Cross those streetcar tracks, and the Micks will shower you with Irish confetti from the brickyards. And who can tell what the niggers might do?[10]

In addition to thuggery, other crime—from murder to prostitution to robbery—was rampant in 1919. By April, the police complained openly about being short-staffed and overwhelmed.[11] Organized crime spread. By mid-July, the Chicago Law and Order League, a pro-Prohibition group, estimated the city had more than 1,500 illegal liquor joints.[12] In 1919, a twenty-year-old named Al Capone moved from Brooklyn to Chicago's South Side as Prohibition became national law. Capone fit right in. Chicago was a bustling, sweaty, heaving town. Poet Carl Sandburg, self-appointed chronicler of the metropolis, wrote in 1916 that Chicago was "fierce as a dog with tongue lapping for action."[13]

When the Great War cut off immigration from Europe in 1914, the cutthroat ethnic competition intensified. In 1919, only 3,988 immigrants moved to Chicago, a minuscule amount compared to prewar years. Yet industry still needed a steady influx of cheap menial labor. Business had a ready answer: southern blacks. Companies sent agents to the rural South to recruit black farmers, more than ever before, to move north.

They advertised in southern and black newspapers. Chicago became the center of this movement, a "re-routing point" for blacks heading for Gary, Detroit, Cleveland, and elsewhere.[14] Many never left Chicago. By the start of the war, Chicago had the nation's second-largest black population in the country after Washington. Chicago industries welcomed black workers. In addition to low-cost labor, business owners found a bonus: blacks could be brought in to break strikes, undercut wages, and foment tension among workers in the heavily unionized city. In 1919, companies in the Chicago meatpacking, corn refining, and steel industries all used black workers as strikebreakers.[15]

Black families had good reasons for wanting to leave the South after generations of being denied political rights and living under the threat of violence. The boll weevil had destroyed cotton crops on thousands of black farms. Southern schools for black children were deplorable. In a depressed economy, many southern states passed "Work or Fight" laws that required men of age to work or join the armed forces—and in the South this law weighed heavily on underemployed blacks.[16] Meanwhile, jobs in the North were plentiful. Eager to earn more money and escape Jim Crow restrictions, blacks took free tickets from business agents and saved to buy group fares or full fares to ride the rails north. They saw Chicago as an escape route, much like immigrants who fled economic hardship and political oppression in Europe.

Booker T. Washington, seen for years, at least by whites, as the intellectual leader of black America, had argued against blacks moving to cities. He declared in 1907: "The masses of the colored people are not yet fitted to survive and prosper in the great cities North and South to which many of them are crowding."[17] By 1915, the majority of blacks had stopped listening to Washington and his faction. Thomas Jackson Woofter, a white southern "progressive" eager to keep blacks in the South, bemoaned the economic reality that plantation owners could not compete with the "Eldorado of industry": "The curtailment of European immigration has left the Negro on the southern farm as the largest available group of unskilled laborers in the United States, and this supply is slipping through the fingers of the southern farmer, because the latter is unable to compete with the manufacturer, either in wages paid or living conditions furnished."[18]

Blacks migrated to Chicago for decades, but beginning in 1915, the year Washington died, that steady flow became a flood. Through the war years, railroad cars daily disgorged black southerners into the chaotic bustle of Chicago's Illinois Central Depot. From 1910 to 1920, Chicago's black population soared from 44,103 to 109,458—an increase of 148.2 percent, the largest rate of increase of any ethnic group in the city.[19] In 1915, about 1,100 blacks toiled in Chicago's meatpacking houses.[20] By 1919, more than 10,000 blacks worked there.[21] From 1917 to 1919 alone, an estimated 50,000 blacks migrated to Chicago.[22] In 1917, the *Chicago Tribune* had already identified that a "new problem, demanding early solution, is facing Chicago . . . the sudden and unprecedented influx of southern Negro laborers."[23]

The *Chicago Defender* and its Georgia-born publisher Robert S. Abbott championed this migration, which benefited his publication. In 1905, Abbott founded the newspaper with a run of 300 copies.[24] By 1919, the newspaper sold three-fourths of its 130,000 circulation in the South. Any chance it could, the newspaper urged blacks to move north, especially to Chicago. Thanks to the *Defender*, southern blacks saw the city as the "Top of the World," and many heeded the call.[25] A black man in Hattiesburg, Mississippi, said, "The packing houses in Chicago for a while seemed to be everything." An anonymous black migrant quoted in a study of Chicago's race relations published in 1922 gave as his chief reason for moving north: "Tired of being a flunky."[26] An anonymous poem in the *Defender* in 1917, "Bound for the Promised Land," captured the sentiment:

Why should I remain longer in the South
To be kicked and dogged around?
Crackers shoot me in the mouth
And shoot my brother down,
I would rather the cold to snatch my breath
And die from natural cause
Than to stay down south and be beat to death
Under cracker law.[27]

But instead of arriving in a Promised Land, these migrants found themselves abruptly locked in a fierce ethnic competition for jobs, housing, and political power. Blacks encountered a very different form of racism in Chicago and other northern cities from what they had known. In the South, they were relegated to a subservient status by laws and social codes. In Chicago, they were seen as alien intruders who needed to be contained by groups not faring much better than they were. This prejudice manifested in all forms of interaction. "Notice on a streetcar, or anywhere the funny silly way the poor whites emphasize that they feel themselves too good to sit by a respectable colored person," complained a black doctor in May 1919. "The indignity is not only insulting it is uncalled for. They turn away from you as if you were a bear or a gorilla."[28]

Black relations with organized labor had been tortured and complicated for decades. The overwhelming majority of black workers were not unionized. The majority of white workers—no matter their ethnicity—were. The Chicago situation was an extreme microcosm of labor strife between blacks and whites across the North in 1919. Industry repeatedly brought in black migrants to defeat or weaken unionization efforts.[29]

By 1919, industrial unions based in the North were trying to end this division by lifting color barriers, at least on paper. The American Federation of Labor, at its Atlantic City convention in June, passed a resolution condemning lynching and mob rule, praising black workers, and declaring the AFL "knows no race or creed in its stand for the toiling masses to get justice."[30] The AFL had rejected such a resolution two years earlier.[31] But now, AFL president Samuel Gompers proudly sent the resolution on to President Wilson.[32] Local unions made efforts as well. In early July, Chicago stockyard unions held parades and rallies to recruit black workers.[33]

But nothing much came of these efforts. Union rank and file did not trust blacks. And blacks did not trust the unions.[34] Most of the city's unions had no black members. Those that did had only a handful.[35] On the football field–sized packing complexes and factory floors of the new mechanized America, racial violence flared, day after day. Managers suppressed open fighting, but blacks and white workers seethed, their prejudices reinforced by the union/nonunion split. Blacks responded to the alienation by setting up their own groups to battle with union toughs at the workplace and in the mixed-race bars around the yards. One such group, the "Wilson Efficiency Club," headed by Austin "Heavy" Williams, had five hundred members and got into scuffles with union men in packing houses in June and July.[36]

The fighting in packing plants led to wildcat strikes, where workers walked out without union authorization. Federal labor officials scrambled to arbitrate. Hearings held on June 20, 1919, in the United States Court of Appeals courtroom downtown, shed light on how race, ethnicity, and unionization roiled Chicago's crowded slaughterhouses. The work was grueling and foul. Men toiled as "scraping machine operators" and "hog offal foremen."[37] During the hearing, the judge took testimony on two recent incidents. One was a walkout led by a Polish union man after fights with nonunion black workers. The other involved the stabbing of a black union member by a nonunion black worker at a meat-curing company. Jake Kubek, a Polish worker who spoke at the hearing through a translator, led the walkout. The transcript reveals how race was associated with anti-union activity. Through his interpreter, Kubek said, "I cannot stand working with them. The colored fellows won't obey our orders and they won't get along with us."[38] For the stabbing incident, the arbitrator interviewed Robert Bedford, one of the few black shop stewards for the union. He witnessed the attack and said the assailant shouted, "God damn that union. Anybody that is in that union ain't no good, a lot of bastards. . . . You are nothing but a white folks' nigger." The wounded man was hospitalized for nine weeks.[39]

The general economy exacerbated race and labor tensions. A recession after the war meant that black and white soldiers returning to Chicago found little work. And prices for daily goods shot up during the war and after. A chunk of cheese cost 22 cents in 1913. The price doubled by 1919. Wages increased as well, but if you were unemployed or underemployed, the price increases were brutal.[40] The economic downturn led to waves of strikes across the country. Municipal workers, factory workers, police officers, fire engineers, streetcar operators—anyone and everyone who could organize—struck for better wages and conditions.[41] Management retaliated with strikebreakers, hired thugs, and lockouts. By late July, more than 250,000 workers in Chicago were on strike, threatening to strike, or locked out.[42]

Relations were tense not just at work, but also at home. Aside from a small section of the West Side, blacks were confined to the "Black Belt," a strip of neighborhoods along State Street on the city's South Side. The area—an estimated 27 square miles—roughly corresponded to the boundaries of the city's Second Ward.[43] To the southeast, neighborhoods like Hyde Park, home of the University of Chicago, and nearby Kenwood, were all white and had organized home associations to keep them that way. To the west, Wentworth Avenue formed a sharp dividing line, with Irish, Italian, Polish, and Lithuanian immigrants making sure no blacks moved into their area. The largest public park on the South Side, Washington Park, to the west of the University of Chicago, was a no-man's-land, with gangs of blacks and whites terrorizing people of opposite races and fighting with each other. Fights broke out in the park and in the streets nearby with alarming frequency. Two people were killed in separate incidents.[44]

———————

The Black Belt, with almost 90 percent of all the blacks in the city, had some of Chicago's worst housing.[45] Much of it was dilapidated and overpriced. Disease spread easily in the unsanitary conditions.[46]

Thanks to the economics of scarcity, landlords—most of them white—inflated prices. Realtors in white neighborhoods near the Black Belt used scare tactics to frighten whites into selling low for fear of a black "invasion." Realtors then sold high or rented high to blacks eager to move in. Blocked from renting or buying in most of the city, most blacks had no choice but to pay excessive costs for substandard housing in the Black Belt. British journalist Stephen Graham, who visited black communities across the country in 1919, described Chicago's Black Belt as "appalling," with families living in "filthy, ramshackle frame buildings."[47]

Not all the black areas were run down. The city's de facto segregation forced wealthier blacks to live in the belt, albeit in decent and expensive housing. The area had its own hospital, Provident, as well as social service agencies for the poor and new migrants. The concentration of so many migrants also led to a growth of businesses serving blacks, including a thriving entertainment district. By 1919, a stretch of State Street in the Black Belt nicknamed "The Stroll" hosted numerous cabarets and nightclubs with names like Deluxe, Pekin, Cafe de Champion, and Elite. Joe "King" Oliver moved his band to Chicago from New Orleans and drew large crowds to the Royal Gardens for his style of music, which the black newspapers were alternately spelling as "jazz," "jass," and "jaz."

A young Langston Hughes, visiting The Stroll in 1918, said, "Midnight was like day."[48] But music was not The Stroll's only draw. Brothels, gambling joints, and pool halls also crowded the area. Guide books of Chicago talked about "promiscuous dancing and the intermingling of the races" there.[49] Overcrowding in general and the desire for black families to find decent housing away from the noisy enticements of The Stroll led many to push the boundaries of the Black Belt.

"If the movement of the colored people to the white neighborhoods was an invasion," coroner's jurors wrote after the riot, "it was a necessary invasion because of the deplorable living conditions."[50]

Blacks resented being squeezed in a zone of substandard, overpriced housing. Ethnic whites, who had spent decades carving out their niche in Chicago, felt threatened by the encroachment.

"What of the White Man who is steadily but surely pushing farther and farther away in the matter of homes?" mused Robert Abbott in the *Defender.* "He must stop some time, and when he does we will be right at his side. There is no escape. He wants the best, and so do we."[51]

The situation was untenable, but the federal, state, and local governments did little to ease tensions. Since the black migration to cities began, racial tensions flared in southern and northern cities over where blacks could and could not live. Some cities prosecuted blacks settling in white neighborhoods through ordinances prohibiting such moves. In 1914, Louisville passed an ordinance forbidding home sales from one race to another. The NAACP challenged the law all the way to the Supreme Court; Moorfield Storey presented the arguments. In 1917, the Court ruled in *Buchanan v. Warley* that such laws were a violation of property rights under the Fourteenth Amendment. But the Court stressed the ruling concerned only a white man's ability to sell property, not black civil rights. Regardless, the NAACP hailed the ruling as a victory.[52] The ruling did little to end segregation or ease racial tensions. In Chicago, the city's real estate board met with black leaders and bankers to try to establish a self-segregation system. Blacks rejected it.[53] Individual realtors and property owners developed new tactics—from restrictive covenants on deeds to late-night firebombing—to keep blacks out.[54]

Antiblack violence in Chicago was common since at least the 1890s, when blacks were brought in as strikebreakers. The violence grew with the black population. In the two years leading up to mid-July 1919, whites bombed more than twenty-five homes and properties owned by blacks in white areas.[55] The first bombings came shortly after *Buchanan v. Warley.* Bombs were also thrown at black businesses and at homes of white realtors who sold properties in white neighborhoods to blacks.[56] One bombing killed a little girl. In other incidents, white mobs pelted black homes with bricks and stones. The police never arrested anyone, infuriating blacks.

After *Buchanan v. Warley,* whites formed property associations like the Hyde Park-Kenwood Association to use intimidation and threats to keep white realtors and local politicians in line and keep blacks out. At one Hyde Park-Kenwood Association meeting, a speaker compared blacks moving into the neighborhood to the German invasion of France.

He quoted General Ferdinand Foch's declaration at Verdun: "They shall not pass."[57]

The associations denied any connection to the bombings, but made it clear blacks were not welcome. L. M. Smith, spokesman for the Kenwood Improvement Association, a white realty group, told black leaders, "You people are not admitted to our society."

Smith told a newspaper that more than a hundred blocks in his neighborhood were "tainted" by blacks moving in. Smith said blacks were clean and promptly paid their bills, but "we can't have these people coming over here."

Blacks countered that this de facto ghettoization perpetuated the trouble. Charles S. Duke, a black veteran officer of the war who worked for the city as a civil engineer, told a newspaper: "All attempts at segregation bring only discord and resentful opposition."[58]

Whites, of all ethnic varieties and classes, weren't listening to that message. Irish American writer James T. Farrell captured the assumptive, anxious bigotry of South Side whites in his *Studs Lonigan* novels about the struggles of Irish American poor. As one Irish American character complains in a scene set in July 1919, "Give uh nigger an inch, and dey wants a hull mile."[59] White ethnic groups were committed to making blacks pay for every inch.

———

Chicago's blacks in 1919 faced segregation in housing, second-class status on jobs, and limited access to public services and entertainment. But in one crucial area, they were equals: they could vote.[60]

Corruption pervaded city government, with everyone from beat cops to city planners on the take. Votes equaled power, and the more you could bundle and deliver, the better. By the 1910s, blacks had become a crucial political bloc in the city. This power brought them both suitors and enemies in Chicago's pugilistic politics.

Large ethnic groups like the Irish, Poles, and Italians tended to align with Democrats. Republicans were split between a self-described "progressive" faction led by a coterie of established WASPs and the multiethnic machine of William Hale Thompson. The scion of a wealthy Chicago family, athletic, loud "Big Bill" had aspired to be an actor or a cowboy. Instead, he entered politics at the dawn of the 1900s and built a powerful machine as a city alderman and county commissioner. Germans formed the core of Thompson's coalition. Thompson opposed America's entry into the war, and disparaged the British, which also helped him with Irish voters. His pro-German stance, however, hurt him with other constituencies. Poles, who had been strong Republicans, shifted when Thompson gained German support. Critics labeled Thompson "Kaiser Bill."[61] To bolster his coalition, Thompson aggressively sought the black vote, so much so that opponents called him a "nigger-lover."[62]

In 1915, at the age of forty-five, Thompson was elected mayor, thanks in great part to the support of Oscar Stanton De Priest, elected that same year as the city's first black alderman from the Second Ward. The men shared an aptitude for "pay-to-play" politics. Thompson demanded payments for his campaign war chest from developers, business owners, and anyone else he could shake down.[63] De Priest looked out for the interests of speakeasies, brothels, and gambling joints in his area—for a price. Police were told to look the other way when passing certain establishments in the Black Belt.[64] De Priest was indicted in 1917 for corruption surrounding his affiliations with the black mob. A jury acquitted him, but his reputation stuck. Thompson had strong financial support from The Stroll businesses, legitimate and illegitimate.[65] He rewarded black politicos with city jobs for their friends, so much so that Democratic critics referred to City Hall as "Uncle Tom's Cabin."[66]

In 1919, Thompson faced a fierce reelection fight, since many politicians saw him as vulnerable. He proved them wrong, beating two candidates in the Republican primary in February and then defeating Democrat Robert M. Sweitzer, the Cook County clerk, and Independent Maclay Hoyne, the Cook County state attorney. Large street fights among supporters of Thompson and Sweitzer marred the general election.[67] Thompson won by 28,000 votes citywide, and the black vote proved crucial. He carried the black Second Ward by 14,000 votes. As Walter White noted, "Against the united and bitter opposition of every daily newspaper in Chicago, William Hale Thompson was elected again as mayor, due, as was claimed, to the Negro and German vote."[68]

"We have always stood together and we always will," Thompson told black voters.[69]

Opponents alleged voter fraud.[70] By the summer of 1919, Chicago's politics remained raucous. Much of the city had it in for Thompson, and so did other politicians, including the county clerk and the district attorney. Progressives who backed Hoyne considered Thompson hopelessly crooked.[71] The split caused a rift between Illinois's Republican governor, Frank Lowden, the progressives' darling, and Thompson, the urban roughneck. Both harbored presidential aspirations. When asked about running for the 1920 Republican nomination, Lowden was sheepish. He was reported to have said, "No man who is big enough to be president will aspire to the nomination." Yet at the same time, he was placing essays in magazines about how he planned to deal with the Bolshevik menace. Lowden also promoted organizing efforts on his own behalf across the Midwest.[72]

In June and early July, racial unrest in Chicago began to escalate, even before news of Longview and Washington hit the newspapers. Groups of young men of both races were a menace throughout the South Side. Black women riding streetcars to work carried knives and razors in their shirts and shoes for fear of a riot.[73] In late June, gangs of young white men chased and beat blacks trying to come into Washington Park, the 371-acre public park near the dividing line between the black South Side and the Irish and other ethnic neighborhoods to the west. On June 22, fights broke out at the park's boathouse and other places. A gang of young whites stabbed and shot to death a black veteran of the Army Reserve, Robert Robinson, outside a candy store near the park. The whites were reputed to be members of the Irish gang Ragen's Colts.[74] In a twisted interpretation of patriotism, threatening notes showed up on trees and fences in black neighborhoods in late June: "We will get you July 4."[75]

Despite looming dangers, Chicago's blacks still planned to celebrate Independence Day like everyone else. The Royal Gardens, one of the largest jazz clubs in the Black Belt, advertised a "Patriotic Night" performance by the World's Greatest Jazz Band. With unintentional irony, club owners promised, "Every Night a Big Night—Friday Night a Big Riot."[76] When violence did not erupt in Chicago on the holiday, the editors of the *Chicago Defender* sarcastically expressed shock: "No 'Race Riots' on the Fourth of July, what do you know about that?"[77]

Ida Wells-Barnett, a longtime resident of the Black Belt, champion of black rights, strident opponent of lynching, and perhaps the most famous black woman in America, intuited that the racial situation was unraveling. She had lived on Chicago's South Side for decades and had never been as worried about racial violence. She said the recent attacks by whites reminded her of violence just before the East St. Louis riot of 1917, which she had investigated for the *Chicago Defender*.

"Will the legal, moral, and civic forces of this town stand idly by and take no heed of these preliminary outbreaks?" she asked *Chicago Tribune* readers. "Will no action be taken to prevent these law breakers until further disaster has occurred? An ounce of prevention beats a pound of cure."[78]

In the middle of July, as news from Longview and Washington made it onto front pages, the *Chicago Daily News* ran a series of articles by Carl Sandburg about living and working conditions for Chicago's blacks.[79] Sandburg, forty-one, had already won acclaim for his poetry and prose. His book of poems, *Cornhuskers*, was awarded the Pulitzer Prize in 1919. But Sandburg still liked to report on larger social issues and *Daily News* editors assigned him the project in late June.[80] His "Black Belt" articles, starting on July 14, were eerily prescient; they focused on migration, labor conflict, and housing. He spent ten days speaking with black business owners, black workers, black women, black migrants—people whose voices were rarely heard in major white publications. He also interviewed whites who wanted to keep blacks out of their neighborhoods.[81] Joel Spingarn, the NAACP board member, happened to be visiting Chicago when the series ran, and it so impressed him he brought copies back to New York to show Alfred Harcourt, a friend who had just co-founded the publishing house of Harcourt, Brace & Howe. He urged Harcourt to publish the articles as a book.[82] Back in Chicago, Sandburg was preparing more articles outlining "a program of constructive recommendations" to ease racial tensions in the city. Events, however, overtook his plans. When the riot broke out, Sandburg wrote later, "as usual nearly everybody was more interested in the war than how it got loose."[83]

13.

The Beach

The white man of the North, who might be inclined to lull himself into forgetfulness, wakes at the sound of shooting down his streets.

—HERBERT SELIGMANN, *The Negro Faces America*

TWO DAYS AFTER FEDERAL TROOPS WITHDREW FROM WASHINGTON'S streets, the weather in Chicago was oppressively hot, reaching the upper 90s. On Sunday, July 27, thousands of Chicagoans in stuffy, humid tenements had the same idea: go to the beach. The miles of lakefront provided a respite in a world before air conditioning, and the beach was one of the few cheap leisure options for the city's laborers and their families. Thousands made their way to the beaches, especially on Sundays. On the industrial South Side, the beaches were found behind railroads, amid factories, and in between piles of rocks. They were also segregated. The main white beach on the South Side started at 29th Street, near Michael Reese Hospital, and ran south about 11 miles to Indiana. The smaller "colored beach" was at 25th Street. A rocky, uneven waterfront behind several factories divided the two beaches.

Among the throngs headed to the South Side beach that Sunday were five black teenagers. Two brothers, Charles and Lawrence Williams, Paul Williams, not related to the brothers, and John Turner Harris all lived near 53rd and State. They met up with Eugene Williams (also unrelated). In the early afternoon, the teens jumped on the back of a produce truck and rode east, then ran through an Irish neighborhood. On previous trips, neighborhood gangs had pelted them with stones. The boys weren't supposed to go to the lake on Sundays, but they went off without telling their parents.

The boys—none of whom could swim well—did not head to the black beach, where a lifeguard was on duty. Instead, they headed to a secret beach that they called "hot and cold." The little inlet surrounded by large rocks lay next to the Michael Keeley brewery—which shot hot water into the lake—and the Consumers Ice Company warehouse near 26th Street— which sent freezing cold water into the same inlet.[1]

Only a few black teens knew about this special place to swim. On a previous trip, the boys had lashed together a crude raft from old logs. Around 2 p.m., the five teenagers pushed the raft out onto the lake.

As they bobbed, cool, naked, and refreshed, this is what the boys would have seen of their Chicago: a muddle of light blue sky, blue-green water, and humanity's offering of gray and brown—factories, smoke-stacks, and railroads. To the northwest, they could see the skyscrapers of the Loop. Facing due west were the railroad terminals and junctions of the Illinois Central line, and beyond a horizon of factories and tene-ments. To the south, the shoreline curved toward the steel mills of Gary, Indiana, their smokestacks spewing plumes skyward.

As the boys paddled along, oblivious to anything but their own lazy afternoon, the raft began to drift ever so slowly south toward the white beach at 29th Street, where trouble had broken out. Several black men and women had appeared at the all-white beach and tried to enter the water. They had a legal right to swim there, but the gesture was provoca-tive. A white mob formed and drove the black group off by hurling rocks and curses. The blacks returned with reinforcements, with their own rocks and epithets. Soon the whites rallied with larger numbers and scared the blacks off.

The boys had no idea about the fighting, but did notice a white man standing on some rocks throwing stones at them. The man stood so far away the kids could see the rocks coming, so they dove underwater to make sure they weren't hit. It was a game, as far as it went, and did not concern the teens until Eugene Williams suddenly sank under the water and did not come back up. John Turner Harris, treading water next to him, saw Eugene had been struck by a rock on the forehead. Harris tried to help his bloodied friend, but Eugene "grabbed my right ankle, and hell, I got scared. I shook him off."[2] Eugene disappeared under the water.[3]

Harris and the other teens ran to the 25th Street beach and got the black lifeguard. He and other black men ran over and dove into the water, frantically looking for the young man. Whites joined in. Police arrived and dragged the lake with grappling hooks. Police and lifeguards recovered Eugene Williams's lifeless body and brought it up on the 29th Street white beach.[4] Harris and the other teens told blacks at the 25th Street beach what had happened. Many men, including a black police officer, rushed to the white beach. The boys pointed out a white man named George Stauber as the man who threw the rocks.[5] The white police officer at the beach, Daniel Callahan, refused to arrest Stauber, and did not allow the black officer to arrest him either. Gathered blacks grew furious. Some ran back to the black beach to get more men.[6] Callahan then arrested a black man in the crowd based on a white man's complaint, angering blacks even more. Meanwhile, Stauber hid within a crowd of whites.[7] A photograph taken at the beach that day showed men of both races near the scene where police had brought the body ashore. The afternoon's light cast elongated shadows of men in white dress shirts, wearing caps and straw hats. They stood in clusters around parked Fords. It could be a snapshot of a summer picnic. But if you look carefully, you can see many were talking with one another, grim-faced. And you can see others walking out of the frame, west toward Chicago's neighborhoods. They were hurrying away to spread the news, to spread rumors and demand angry recompense.[8] Chicago's longest and bloodiest race riot was under way.

Two hours after Eugene Williams's body was recovered, about a thousand blacks gathered at the entrance of the white beach at 29th Street by the railroad. They demanded that police turn over Officer Callahan and the alleged rock-thrower Stauber. Police tried to disperse the crowd. About 6 p.m., a thirty-seven-year-old black man, James Crawford, opened fire at the group of officers. A black police officer returned fire and killed him. But the black mob did not disperse. It grew and some of the crowd began attacking white men, who hurriedly left the beach. Four whites were beaten, five stabbed, and one shot. People leaving the beach took with them news of the drowning, the Crawford shooting, and the attacks on whites. Stories were told and retold on stoops, in bars, in shops, on trolleys, and in apartments across the South Side. One such rumor was that blacks drowned a white man.[9] Other rumors claimed blacks were stockpiling weapons and breaking into armories, anticipating a race war. Both stories were false, but it did not matter. As dusk fell, white gangs beyond the western edge of the Black Belt gathered and attacked blacks passing through white neighborhoods. By nightfall, rioting—mostly by white men and boys—broke out over miles of city streets. Writer James Farrell, who was growing up near Washington Park at the time of the riot, captured this frenzied masculinity in his *Studs Lonigan* novels. After Lonigan's fellow thugs hear of the rioting, they arm themselves and head out to hunt blacks:

> Tommy Doyle said the niggers were never going to forget the month of July 1919. Studs said that they ought to hang every nigger in the city to the telephone poles, and let them swing there in the breeze. Benny Taite said that for every white man killed in the riots, ten black apes ought to be massacred.

In the novel, the only black person the gang finds is a ten-year-old boy. They take his clothes and burn them, then burn his feet and bottom with matches. They beat him and urinate on him, and let him run away.[10]

This fictional account echoed reality. From nine o'clock Sunday night till three Monday morning, at least 27 blacks were beaten, 7 were stabbed, and 4 were shot. The South Side's white gangs were on a rampage.

On Monday morning, news of Chicago's riot made headlines across the country. Following the Washington mayhem the week before, the news rattled nerves, but no one seemed to quite understand what was happening. The *Evening Mail* in New York published a skittish editorial titled, "And Now It Is Chicago!" in which it blamed revolutionaries but also anxiously warned that whites, "the pioneers of western civilization," needed to be better stewards of the black race.[11]

In Chicago, the *Tribune* ran a political cartoon showing white bathers pointing to a rope division in the water and threatening a group of black bathers not to cross it. The caption read: "The color line has reached the North."[12] In truth, that line had always been there, but in a congested city of millions, people of both races crossed it regularly for jobs, to see families, to ride a streetcar, to go to the beach. Suddenly all those people were potential victims.

As the sun rose across Lake Michigan, residents headed out of their apartments to work, school, and errands. Racial lines were crossed as they were every day in the congested city. Blacks headed to the stockyards and other menial jobs across the city. Whites came into the Black

Belt to open their shops or to make deliveries. People were doing what they always did. At first, things seemed to have calmed.

Politicians did not seem particularly concerned. Mayor Thompson returned from Cheyenne, Wyoming, where he rode in a parade dressed as a cowboy. As he arrived at City Hall, a reporter asked about the rioting. Thompson said it seemed to be over. Then he went on to talk about a sensational child murder case and a looming transit strike.[13]

But signs indicated trouble was brewing. The heat was punishing and children were out of school, and a reporter sent to the scene of the Eugene Williams drowning found the beach empty. "Not a single swimmer was in the water, and the only persons in evidence were two policemen patrolling the water front," he wrote.[14] Unfounded and dangerous rumors started to appear in major publications. The *Herald-Examiner* on July 28 ran a story titled "Negroes Have Arms," and quoted an anonymous source asserting that blacks had collected more than 2,000 Springfield rifles and a supply of soft-nosed bullets in preparation for an attack on white neighborhoods.[15]

As the day wore on, scattered fighting broke out. Police arrested a black man named Mose Thomas after he fired a revolver at passing white workers.[16] White toughs started jumping black workers who were walking home by themselves or in small groups. In one incident, about twenty white teens attacked Robert Barchton, a black man, at the intersection of Halsted and 51st. Police found him on the ground, bloodied with four teeth knocked out.[17]

The white mobs grew larger, often made up of young men from various ethnic groups, putting aside differences to join together in attacking blacks. In one incident, a white mob chased and beat a black man named Thomas Byrd at 26th and Canal. Police caught three of the mob: a Slav, an Italian, and a German Jew.[18]

Blacks complained for years that white police, many of them Irish Americans, favored neighborhood white gangs. Only 200 of the department's 3,800 cops were black, and were discriminated against in many ways. On this same Monday, three black police officers had gone on trial for insubordination because they objected to being segregated in their sleeping quarters.[19]

On Monday afternoon, a committee of concerned black leaders led by Oscar De Priest met with Police Chief James T. Garrity, who assured the group that blacks would be treated equally and that he had the situation under control. Chief Garrity said he sent 50 mounted police and 100 extra patrolmen to the Black Belt on special duty. He had 500 more police in reserve.

"Everything is ready to meet any emergency," a captain at the Cottage Grove police station told a reporter. "We do not expect any serious trouble, and with the special police that have been assigned to the district any disturbance that might arise would be easily overcome."[20] State officials concurred. State militia units were called up and reported to local armories but were not put into action. The adjutant general in charge of the militia claimed, "The storm has abated."[21] Even as he spoke, the storm worsened.

Racial attacks took place along Wentworth Avenue, which police called the "gang line" or "dead line," dividing the white areas near the stockyards and the Black Belt. Rioting was constant and troublesome. In late afternoon and evening, as black workers from the stockyards and factories headed home, mobs of young whites armed with guns, knives, bats, and razors were waiting. Meanwhile, gangs of armed black men formed to attack whites who strayed into their neighborhoods. Automobiles loaded with armed men, known as "flying squadrons," made runs into black and white areas, opening fire indiscriminately on people walking down the street.[22]

As dusk fell Monday night, white rioters in groups as small as four or five and as large as a thousand patrolled the South Side. The crowds roamed from intersection to intersection and far beyond their own neighborhoods, with no specific objective except to attack blacks. If police dispersed them, they regrouped elsewhere. Gunshots, police sirens, and shouting were heard across the South Side. People barricaded the streets with trash and shot out streetlights for cover. Men shot at each other from rooftops and alleys. Streetcar and elevated train service shut down. Women were reported whacking each other with brooms across yard fences.[23] Police did not have enough men, trucks, or jail space to stem the pandemonium.

The meanderings of one mob showed the fluidity and disorienting persistence of the violence. The group, a loose gathering of white teens, formed after 8 p.m. at 47th Street and the "L." They beat two black passersby, then moved to 51st Street until police drove them away. The crowd re-formed and made its way to the intersection of Indiana Avenue and 43rd Street, where a lone deputy sheriff forced it to turn back. But the group returned later and attacked a streetcar, pummeled a black passenger, and then marched down Indiana Avenue, pulling trolleys off their rails and yanking them from wires. The men and boys attacked any blacks that they met. At 45th Street, a police sergeant fired a warning shot, scattering the mob to 43rd Street and Grand Boulevard, at about 11:30 p.m. There the crowd saw three black men and three black women walking home from the theater. The blacks had no choice but to walk—the rioting had stopped taxi and trolley service.[24]

Rioters shouted, "One, two, three, four, five, six! Everybody, let's get the niggers!" The mob broke into groups in front of and behind the black men, cutting them off about 20 yards from Forrestville Avenue, near the safety of the Black Belt. The whites swarmed on the black men and women. A white seventeen-year-old named Clarence Metz, the son of Jewish immigrants, menaced Louis C. Washington, a black veteran army lieutenant. As Metz lunged with an ax handle, Washington thrust with his pocketknife. Stabbed in the heart, Metz bled to death on the street.[25]

The crowd fled, but Metz's death did not stop the marauding. With the logic of a mob, his death had to be avenged. It regrouped down Grand Boulevard and attacked any blacks it encountered. Finally someone inside a house shot at the crowd, wounding one. The mob fled yet again. Police showed up and arrested the black man who had opened fire.[26]

Scores of such groups repeated this directionless chaos across the South Side and in parts of the West Side. Henry Goodman, a black worker in the stockyards, was riding home through a white neighborhood when a truck pulled up and blocked his streetcar. Three white rioters boarded, threatened the conductor and the motorman, then demanded that blacks disembark. After a brief chase, whites caught Goodman and beat him senseless with a metal pipe. He died later of lockjaw caused by an infection from his head wounds.[27]

At 38th Place and Ashland Avenue, thirty-year-old Nicholas Kleinmark and a gang of other white toughs boarded a streetcar at 7 p.m. and attacked three black stockyard workers with clubs and bricks. One of the blacks, Joseph Scott, pulled a knife and killed Kleinmark.[28]

Black gangs attacked whites trapped in the Black Belt, and whites living on the fringes hid in their homes as blacks sniped at whites in range. Blacks fired at police and firemen as well. One officer on horseback dismounted to use his horse as cover as black snipers opened fire.[29] That evening, four blacks jumped a Greek peddler, Casmere Lazzeroni, sixty, as he sat by his banana cart on South State Street. They stabbed him to death with pocketknives. Minutes later, several black men stabbed and killed Eugene Temple, thirty-five, a Jewish laundry owner, as he stood with his wife outside their State Street business.[30] An unknown black man shot and killed David Marcus, a white shoemaker with a shop on East 37th street. The shoemaker died in a taxi on his way to the hospital.[31]

The worst incident that night stemmed from a false rumor circulating in the black community that a sniper was firing from a white-occupied four-story apartment building, the Angelus, at the edge of the Black Belt. The phantom sniper supposedly shot a black boy near 35th and Wabash. In the late afternoon, about 1,500 black people gathered outside the Angelus and demanded the shooter. One hundred police arrived to protect the inhabitants of the building. Police searched the Angelus, but found no sniper and no weapons. Still, the mob demanded the sniper. About 8 p.m., a brick hit a police officer. Police fired into the crowd, killing three blacks—Joseph Sanford, Hymes Taylor, and John Walter Humphrey. Many others were wounded and the crowd fled.[32]

A fourth black man, Edward Lee, was shot and killed outside a Walgreens drugstore nearby. He had gone to get medicine when a mounted officer shot at the Angelus crowd. When the officer's horse spooked in the chaos, the stray bullet missed the crowd and hit Lee.[33]

At Provident Hospital, in the Black Belt, supplies ran low as staff became overwhelmed with injured. Both black and white mobs attacked the small hospital, trying to get at patients of the opposite race. Many nurses, worn out from the stress, begged to leave but were ordered to stay at their posts without sleep or proper meals. At least 75 riot victims were treated on Monday. Nine of the patients were white. Staff set up cots in the hallways and some wounded slept on the floor.[34]

On Monday night, Joe Crawford, a young black boy living with his parents in a racially mixed apartment building on Wentworth Avenue, heard a knock on the door. A white woman who lived in the building came to warn Crawford's mother that a gang of white teenagers was forming. An hour later, the gang appeared at the front and rear doors of the tenement.

"Niggers, come out and get your ass whipped or stay in there and be barbecued," the leader shouted.

The Crawfords—the parents plus three sons—squeezed out a tiny bathroom window onto the "L" tracks and crept through the darkness until a stranger, a black woman, brought them into her home to hide for the night.

Another black couple, the Grinnells, spent Monday night and Tuesday morning cowering with their eighteen-month-old daughter on their apartment floor to avoid bullets being fired by cars of passing whites.[35]

Black journalist Roi Ottley recounted the story of one anonymous victim, a black Army veteran who served ten months overseas and was a clergyman's son. The man was heading home from a plant on the outskirts of the city, when he stopped at an intersection to transfer to a streetcar bound for the South Side. A group of twenty whites saw him. One yelled, "There's a nigger! Let's get him!"

He jumped onto a trolley, but the mob yanked down the pole from the power line. The motorman opened the rear door and the black man took off, running as fast as he could. He ran for three blocks, and threw away his jacket. Someone tried to trip him. But he jumped into the gutter and got away. He ran into a pharmacy for protection, but a white woman made him leave. He took off running again.

"My strength was fast failing," the black man recalled. "The idea came in my head to stop and give up, or try to fight, but the odds were too great, so I kept running. My legs began to wobble, my breath came harder, and my heart was pounding like a big pump, while they crept up on me."

He outran the mob, but two whites fired guns at him. The man hid for several hours, and for the first time it all sank in.

"The injustice of the whole thing overwhelmed me—and my feelings ran riot," he said. "Had the ten months I spent in France been all in vain? What had I done to deserve such treatment? I lay there trying to imagine how the innocent victim of a southern mob must feel! Must a Negro always suffer because of his skin? 'There's a nigger! Let's get him!'—Those words kept ringing in my ears."

He huddled in a dark alley and prayed to God to get home safely, then loaded his pockets with rocks for ammunition and headed home. When he saw Comiskey Park, where the White Sox played baseball, he knew he was safe. It had taken him five and a half hours to get home. Later, he saw a white heading to work. "My first impulse was to jump on him and beat him up," he said.[36]

In his novel *Behold a Cry*, Alden Bland, who grew up in the Black Belt, summed up the mood that swept the city: "Get them before they get you."[37] By Tuesday morning's light, the social fabric of an American metropolis had unraveled. Seventeen people had been killed or had suffered injuries that later led to their death.[38] At least 172 blacks and 71 whites suffered serious injuries.[39] During the chaos, Cook County coroner Peter Hoffman convened a jury to investigate the riot's homicides—a mammoth task. Jurors went out to riot scenes and swore oaths to do their duty while standing over bloody corpses.[40]

"It's working people killing each other," a black union official moaned to Carl Sandburg.[41]

On Tuesday, the southern half of the city rang out with gunshots and sirens. To make matters worse, transit workers rejected a contract proposal and on Tuesday morning they walked off the job. America's second-largest city became paralyzed. Hundreds of thousands of workers had to find other ways to get to work. Thousands of blacks who took the trolleys to the stockyards did not want to risk walking through white neighborhoods. Armour packing company had 1,500 black employees, but just 19 arrived for work Tuesday.[42] The city government ordered its black employees to stay home. As the rioting shut down the nation's main stockyards and interrupted its main rail interchange, financial markets dropped. Corn and livestock futures plummeted.[43] Daily newspapers, which carried headlines about the Washington riot the week before, now ran headlines about Chicago.

In the Loop and across the city, traffic on this hot summer day was the most chaotic and frenzied it had been since the Great Chicago Fire of 1871. Without trolley service, people were left on their own to get to work. Tens of thousands of sweating commuters tried walking miles to their factories and offices. Those who had cars drove, and the streets became clogged with cars, wagons, and trucks. None of the city's 175 traffic police or 75 mounted police could be found—they were pulled for riot duty.[44] At the height of the rioting, 2,800 of the city's 3,000 police were on duty on the South Side.[45]

In this vacuum, thugs took over the Loop, the business district. White gangs led by soldiers and sailors rampaged throughout the downtown, attacking and robbing blacks. At about 5 a.m., a white mob burst into a diner at Wabash and Adams and stabbed one black man and chased another, Paul Hardwick, into the street where they shot and killed him. Rioters robbed the corpse.

An hour and fifteen minutes later, a mob of 200 white men caught Robert Williams near State and Van Buren. A white man named Frank Biga stabbed him twice. Williams continued to run but then collapsed and died.[46] The city's railroad stations and restaurants were raided by white mobs, who pulled blacks outside and pummeled them. They also assaulted black porters at the rail stations and black barbers at all-night barbershops. A mob chased forty-five-year-old Monroe Gaddy into a lunchroom at East Jackson Boulevard. Gaddy fought off his attackers from behind the counter by hurling cups and plates until they overpowered him. The mob beat him and tried to drown him in the sink. They would have killed him except a policeman arrived and arrested about forty rioters. The luncheon shop was destroyed. Desperate to control the situation, police set up roadblocks to cut off all blacks from entering the Loop. They also set up a cordon around City Hall to protect the government.[47]

By noon, blacks, who made up the majority of the menial workers in the city's financial and entertainment district, were nowhere to be found. Shoeshine men were gone. Restaurant owners had to wait tables themselves or close. The dining room of the famed Palmer House shut down for several days.[48]

Fighting continued on the South Side. At 10:30 a.m., a white man named Harold Brignadello was shot and killed as he joined a crowd stoning a black home on South State Street.[49]

That evening, white mobs killed more black workers venturing home. Samuel Bass was walking five and a half miles from his work to his home when whites caught him near the corner of 22nd and Halsted streets. They knocked him down three times and stomped him so badly that their shoes left gashes in his nose and cheeks. A Jewish peddler took Bass to the Black Belt in his cart, but a doctor refused to treat him when he learned Bass had no money. Police took him to a hospital, which gave him only cursory treatment. Two weeks later, he died of a brain hemorrhage.[50]

Most blacks stayed in their homes Tuesday, while white mobs roamed the Black Belt's margins and black men searched their neighborhoods for stray whites. Those wandering on the wrong side of the racial borders were in mortal danger.

Three young black men—Ben Walker, William Stinson, and Charles Davis—killed two white men, Walter Parejko and Morris I. Perel, early Tuesday morning. The group shot Parejko, a Polish railroad worker, as he walked to work. They stabbed Perel, a Jewish shop owner in the Black Belt, and took his gold watch.[51]

Two black police sergeants were ordered to drive through the Black Belt and urge people to stay off the streets.[52] *Chicago Defender* publisher Robert S. Abbott and two other black businessmen published handbills urging blacks to stay off the streets and to obey police.[53] "This is no time to solve the Race Question," Abbott's handbill declared. As journalist Ottley noted, "The rioters paid little heed."[54]

Bogus rumors spread among black and white communities, fueling anger and more violence. Whites told stories of blacks storing mounds of weapons and ammunition for a race war. Blacks told stories of mass black graves in Bubbly Creek, near the stockyards. Estimates of the number of killed and wounded approached the thousands.

Rumors spilled into print. "Reports of attacks by Negroes on white women, especially in the stockyards district, could not be confirmed," was typical of reporting in the white newspapers.[55] Black newspapers were just as bad when reporting rumors. The *Defender* reported the murder of a black mother and her three-month-old baby, but this story was false and did much to inflame hatred.[56]

City and state officials further inflamed passions. State representative Thomas C. Doyle, a Democrat from the Irish section of the South Side, said blacks in a car tried to shoot him. He urged whites to get guns. "They are all armed and white people are not," he said. "We must defend ourselves, if the city authorities won't protect us."[57] Fire marshal Thomas O'Connor said Tuesday afternoon that blacks were planning to systematically burn down white homes on the South Side. He held all city firemen in reserve, awaiting the onslaught.[58]

Joseph Lovings, a black teen bicycling home from his job through an Italian immigrant neighborhood on the West Side, was killed because of a rumor. Men in the neighborhood heard that a black man shot an Italian immigrant girl. It was not true. However, when a group of men saw Lovings, they gave chase. He ran and hid in a basement at 839 Lytle Street. The mob pulled him out into the street and shot him at least fourteen times. The coroner found at least eight bullets still in his body, as well as stab wounds, contusions, and skull fractures.[59] His death led to further false rumors. Some news accounts reported his corpse was set on fire, which further enraged blacks with echoes of lynching in the South.

Chicago had never seen such widespread mayhem. A *Variety* columnist drove to the Black Belt during the riot to check on cabarets. "This Village is distressingly quiet these days," he wrote, using the pseudonym Swing. "The only things we have to liven up the town are rape, murder, arson, riot, strikes, and pillage. Your correspondent, bound on duty into the riot area, was shot at by some colored gentleman and the fender of his car was dented by a rock hove by a negress whom he has never harmed.

Lew Goldberg, the agent, going about his business in the section, was embarrassed by a Negro who leaped on the running board of his auto and threatened Lew with violence. Lew had to put a revolver against this person's abdomen before he desisted in his attempts to get acquainted."[60]

By Tuesday, the exhausted police department suffered such a manpower shortage that it put out a plea for citizens to work for free as traffic cops to replace officers battling the riots. More than 100 volunteered, half of what the city wanted.[61] The city curtailed services. Road repair stopped. Playgrounds were closed.[62] The post office had troops defend its facilities and mail was delayed as more than 1,000 black postal workers could not get to their jobs. Jails were overwhelmed. The sheriff installed a machine gun at the jail after 150 black men held for rioting broke out of their segregated pen and battled white guards with pieces of a bench, smuggled knives, and razors.[63] Hospitals filled with those suffering gunshot wounds, knife slashes, cracked skulls, and other injuries.[64] Eleven more people, both black and white, were killed in the riots Tuesday, and 139 were severely injured.[65]

Leaders avoided responsibility as the crisis worsened. The game of pass-the-buck was played amid a fog of petty ambitions that clouded government from quickly dispatching enough disciplined troops to quell rioting.

Governor Frank Lowden arrived early Tuesday and set up a command center at the Blackstone Hotel downtown. From his hotel room, he witnessed white mobs chasing blacks.[66] On Monday he heard of the rioting and halted his trip to Nebraska, commissioning a train back home. On Tuesday, he issued a press release, stressing that Mayor Thompson had not asked for state help. He said that he would gladly send in the militia if martial law was formally requested. Thompson, ensconced at his own command post at City Hall blocks away, did not respond directly and the two did not meet. Instead, he told reporters he did not think the militia was necessary and said Lowden, if he wanted, could send in troops on his own authority. It was the same tit-for-tat the two men had played for years, heightened because they saw each other as presidential rivals in 1920, when the GOP expected to retake the White House.

Lowden portrayed himself as a sensible country attorney, pulled into politics out of civic duty, not aspiration. In truth, he studied law in Chicago and became one of the city's most successful corporate lawyers. Born in 1861, he entered politics in his late forties and was elected a congressman twice before becoming governor in 1917.

By 1919, Lowden was positioning himself as the GOP's anti-crime, pro-business candidate. Shortly before the Chicago riot, a supporter praised Lowden in Congress as the heir of Abraham Lincoln.[67] Lowden knew that a race riot in Illinois's largest city, especially following the disaster of East St. Louis in 1917, would harm his chances.[68] Though Lowden evinced calm to the public, his wife's private diary told a different story: "Frank is living through the most anxious days of his life so far," she wrote.[69] Lowden, a former militia lieutenant colonel, had no intention of rushing in state troops, especially into archrival Thompson's jurisdiction, without an explicit request. Thompson, eager to boost his own presidential aspirations, wanted to present himself as the leader of an industrial giant, a man in complete control of a diverse, swelling metropolis. Asking for martial law and state aid would be an admission that his government had failed and Lowden was the better leader.

Neither of the Republicans wanted to ask help from the federal government, run by Woodrow Wilson, the first Democrat in the White House in decades. Also, Major General Leonard Wood, a man considered to be the political heir of Teddy Roosevelt and a leading presidential contender in 1920, was in Chicago as commander of all military installations in the Midwest. He could have promptly mobilized federal troops to aid the city—but he would have been the hero. Neither Thompson nor Lowden wanted that.

Lowden had already started his behind-the-scenes presidential campaigning, including publishing a booklet praising the late president Roosevelt. And Thompson's mayoral victory in the spring of 1919 raised his own hopes of a presidential bid. The two were gearing up to fight for parts of the powerful Illinois delegation at the 1920 Republican Convention.[70] Ultimately, General Wood refused to involve himself in suppressing the riot, though he brought military intelligence agents to bolster the idea that agitators caused all racial and labor strife. Mayor Thompson could have asked Wood for assistance directly following Secretary of War Baker's directive, and Wood could have acted on his own if he determined the situation merited federal troops. Neither man acted.

Meanwhile, people were shot, stabbed, and beaten. As chaos reigned over dozens of square miles, combat-ready troops sat nearby—awaiting orders. A Thompson aide and the commander of the state's reserve militia toured the riot zone Tuesday, but afterward Thompson still made no formal request for aid.[71]

Lowden said, at least for public consumption, that he agreed with Thompson's hesitation because sending in troops might "arouse some antagonism." Flabbergasted *New York Times* editors, who recently had exalted Lowden as presidential timber, opined, "With fusillades over a large part of the city and death roll of two dozen or so, it would seem as if some antagonism had already been aroused."[72]

Thompson said he planned to focus on the transit strike, and deferred riot questions to Chief Garrity, who insisted racial tensions had eased. He ordered all bars and cabarets closed and tried to establish a cordon of police around the Black Belt. He pulled extra officers from all over the city. But that cordon did not help blacks who traveled outside the Black Belt—they were on their own. And police soon ran out of places to house all those arrested. Garrity said state militia might make matters worse, as they had in East St. Louis, by joining white civilians in the mayhem. But his police were not doing much better.[73] Garrity's promises of fair treatment to blacks did not mean much on the street. Most police were white, many of them Irish. They tended to favor whites over blacks when arriving at flare-ups. As one white officer shouted at a black victim of a mob beating, "Where's your gun, you black son of a bitch? You damn niggers are raising hell." Herman M. Adler, the state's criminologist, said that white mobs intimidated police, so they tended to arrest blacks because it was the easiest way to defuse a situation. Police were "taking fewer chances if they 'soaked' a colored man," he said.[74]

Also, many blacks who had to travel into white areas carried weapons to protect themselves. But a city ordinance, in effect earlier in July, outlawed concealed weapons, and blacks unfamiliar with the new law were rounded up.[75] It was a quandary for blacks. If they did not carry weapons, they risked being attacked unarmed by a white mob. If they carried a weapon, they could be arrested. A judge fined an elderly black minister $10 for carrying a loaded revolver. He told the judge he and all his congregants had been threatened and he felt he had no choice.[76] Police arrested another man who claimed to be 102 years old with a loaded revolver. Police also arrested a black woman dressed as a man with a gun. She said she tried to get to the train station and thought being dressed as a man might make her safer.[77]

On Wednesday, five more people were killed as sporadic fighting continued. Some 3,000 blacks tried to return to work at the stockyards Wednesday afternoon, but were met by angry white workers shouting threats and throwing refuse. The NAACP's Walter White, who reached Chicago Wednesday afternoon, changed into work clothes and went to the stockyards pretending to be a worker. He found white workers hooting and threatening blacks throughout the yards.

Racial confusion abounded, muddling the color line whites were so fiercely trying to enforce. Light-skinned blacks walked through the Loop unmolested, but were attacked by blacks as they returned to the Black Belt.[78] Even White claimed that a black man shot at him, mistaking him for a Caucasian.[79] About 5 p.m., on South Ashland Avenue, a white man named Joseph Schoff met a Mexican named Jose Blanco. Schoff kept asking Blanco, "Are you a Negro?" and then slugged Blanco when he did not answer. In self-defense, Blanco stabbed Schoff, killing him.[80]

Black leaders, aided by the NAACP, the Urban League, and other groups, pressed city and state politicians to act. From the riot's start, community leaders had met at the Olivet Baptist Church, the oldest and largest black church in Chicago and a black cultural hub for the city. Olivet was founded in 1850 as the Xenia Baptist Church. By 1919 it had 8,600 members. Beginning Monday, black ministers, social workers, and others led by Olivet's magnetic pastor, Lacey Kirk Williams, met to draw up a position paper, which they gave to Thompson and Lowden on Wednesday. It accused the police of failing to protect black citizens and demanded equal rights. It declared the preceding days were a clear sign that blacks would not meekly submit to violent outbursts.

"The white people do not realize they have in Chicago's colored population a new type to deal with, one that has a distinct race consciousness, that has helped to fight its country's every battle, and that will content itself with nothing less than the full enjoyment of the privileges and rights granted under the law," it stated.[81]

Black leaders called for the militia. F. L. Barnett, prominent black businessman and husband of anti-lynching pioneer Ida Wells-Barnett, led a delegation to meet with Lowden imploring him to intervene.[82] Blacks had been trapped in their apartments for three days. In the first days of the riots, individuals crowded police stations for protection. Now whole families arrived, desperate for food. No shops were open and with work shut down, many were running out of money.[83]

No supplies came into the black neighborhood. Delivery trucks were afraid to enter the area. Ice truck drivers who did brave the Black Belt were mobbed. Unions stopped workers from going into the area.

"My people have no food," declared Jesse Binga, a leading Black Belt realtor and banker.[84]

Loop business owners and newspapers called for martial law. At an emergency meeting of the city council, 20 of 25 councilmen voted to call in the militia. Some wanted as many as 10,000 troops.[85] Police on riot duty begged for troops to relieve them.

Yet despite increasing political pressure and four days of rioting, Thompson and Lowden dithered. Lowden again told reporters that the militia was to march in as soon as the local government requested. Thompson again said the governor could send in troops on his own authority.

Wednesday evening, arson fires broke out across the Black Belt. At about 8:30 p.m., a mob of about 200 Ragen's Colts attacked a black apartment building on 51st Street with bricks and bullets. Police arrested no one. Reports came in that white arsonists systematically were setting fire to black homes.[86]

Blacks set up street barriers and started firing at any whites they saw. Five detectives and a patrolman in a squad car were fired on several times when they tried to drive into a black neighborhood. On Dearborn, near 53rd Street, the car struck telephone wires that had been strung across the road. Once the car stopped, gunmen in nearby homes opened fire. Lieutenant Paul Duffy finally led the police in storming the buildings. Police arrested sixty people and seized guns and ammunition.

Meanwhile, Frank Cole, a black policeman holed up in his apartment, fended off a white mob with an automatic rifle, a pistol, and hundreds of rounds of ammunition. When white police showed, he refused to let them in and exchanged gunfire until they finally captured him.[87]

In the chaos, Mayor Thompson realized he had no choice. At 9:30 Wednesday night he formally asked for state militia. The request, however, was nuanced. Thompson did not call for martial law; he merely asked for military aid. He did not legally acknowledge his government failed, just that it needed assistance. The troops would not supplant local authority, they would supplement it.[88]

Trucks carrying 6,000 white troops of the Illinois reserve militia rumbled into the South Side. Armed with Springfield rifles and Danish-made Krag-Jørgensen carbines, 3,000 troops moved out of armories and took up positions in the Black Belt and to the west in the white areas where the worst fighting had occurred.[89] Another 3,000 troops moved in in reserve, to be rotated in for relief.[90] Lowden ceded authority over the troops to city police. Troops took directions from police precinct captains. Militia staff set up a command center at the Congress Hotel on Michigan Avenue in the South Loop.[91]

Troops were given a simple and clear directive: maintain the peace. They were ordered to use bayonets and rifle butts before shooting, but if needed, they were not to hesitate to open fire. They were to disperse any mobs that formed.[92]

As troops moved in, police reduced their numbers. Machine guns were set up at intersections.[93] "Thank God," an exhausted police officer at Cottage Grove station said. "We can't stand up under this much longer!"[94]

Unlike East St. Louis, the troops were impartial and disciplined. The militia turned over anyone they arrested to the police. With one order, the number of authorities in the riot zone more than doubled, and another group waited in the wings to bring in 3,000 more fresh, disciplined, well-armed troops. A headline in the *Aberdeen Daily American* in South Dakota summed up their arrival: "Riots Quiet in Face of Bayonets."[95]

Most white troops thought blacks were at fault, until they arrived on the scene. "Many went down . . . thinking that Negroes were the most to blame, and it was the intention of the company to clean them up," said Henry McNamer, a militia member from Chicago's North Side.[96] "A change of opinion came as the men got on their job."

Sterling Morton, a militia captain who lived in the all-white suburb of Winnetka, jokingly referred to his assignment as the "African Campaign."[97] He described the eerie experience of his first patrol through a mixed block on South Wells. All the streetlights were shot out. The homes of black families were smoldering. Bits of furniture and shattered telephone coin boxes lay in the streets.

"The houses deserted by Negroes had been looted and in many cases Victrolas [then an evidence of affluence] had been smashed or pulled out to the curb and burned," Morton recalled. Troops found blacks thankful for their arrival: "Generally speaking, the Negroes were orderly after the initial riots, in which they acted largely in self-defense, aggravated by very real fear of a general massacre."

White mobs did not disperse easily. Neighborhood gangs gathered and jeered, as did some army veterans who taunted the guardsmen with chants of "tin soldiers."[98] But the bluster of thugs was empty and short-lived. Violence on the South Side stopped.

"We met with no resistance—but heard many unflattering comments on our appearance and ancestors!" Morton said.

Rain Wednesday and Thursday also helped to keep people off the streets.[99]

On Thursday, the militia worked to get the city back to normal as tension stayed high. The militia presented their weapons as an obvious threat to troublemakers. Machine gun units were set up at intersections and troops in formation had rifles at the ready and bayonets drawn—the riot-control tactics promoted in training manuals.

"Nine-tenths of success or failure in riot duty is determined by the character of the initial attack," author Henry Bellows wrote in 1920, summarizing the tactics used by anti-riot militia in 1919. "If it is prompt, vigorous, completely successful and attended by no unnecessary casualties, the chances are that there will be no more serious trouble; the disorderly element will have learned its lesson and will have acquired an unshakeable respect for military force."[100]

Bellows spelled out the cardinal rule in dealing with mobs: "Never bluff."[101] The Illinois militia did not flinch. And beyond the show of force, they also brought aid. They protected black families as they gathered their belongings and repaired their homes. They befriended black children and helped workers walk safely to their jobs. For the first time since Monday morning, large numbers of black workers returned to the yards. Still, a murder occurred there that morning, when a white worker hit a black worker, William H. Dozier, with a hammer. Whites pursued the wounded man into sheep pens, beating him to death with a shovel and a broom.[102] The militia came to the stockyards and were jeered by white workers. But troops lowered bayonets and white workers backed off.

The guard also kept peace elsewhere. The militia saved a black man from being hanged from a telephone poll near the stockyards.[103] Incidents that could have sparked further rioting were doused by quick action. Lowden ordered militia to protect trucks that brought in food, ice, and supplies to the Black Belt. White truckers drove supplies to the "dead line" border of the neighborhood, and then black drivers took the goods the rest of the way. Meatpackers agreed to pay black workers using banks and other facilities in the Black Belt as distribution centers, allowing black families to buy supplies without risking their lives by walking to the yards.

The unions and the black nonunion groups met with militia to coordinate the return of more than 15,000 blacks to the yards. Signs were posted by the black clubs declaring, "The riot is over. LET'S FORGET IT."[104] White unions called for calm while circulating petitions for the companies to establish strict color lines at work.

———

As Chicago burned, the federal government did nothing. The Army's military intelligence division, based in offices north of the Loop, did an abysmal job of investigating the South Side fighting. Just fourteen agents went down to gather fragmentary reports from questionable sources and mix them with information gleaned from news accounts. They produced a series of ill-informed, vague reports littered with rumor and innuendo for superiors in Washington.[105]

One report claimed blacks broke into armories, which was not true. Yet another claimed: "Radicals reported to be urging Negroes to further violence."[106] This also was untrue.

In the midst of the rioting, the *Chicago Daily News* claimed Wilson was planning to order in troops at any moment: "President Wilson is being informed fully of the Chicago situation. The feeling is general here that unless the president or some other high federal authority takes a strong stand on the race issue soon sporadic outbreaks may be expected from time to time."

The newspaper was wrong; Wilson, gearing up for a national tour to push for ratification of his League of Nations treaty, did nothing about the largest race riot of 1919, even though the violence dominated national headlines for days and came just days after a riot took place right outside the White House.[107]

National coverage, with gory photographs of crumpled corpses lying in alleys and even a sequence of shots showing a black man being stoned to death, alarmed politicians across the Midwest. Blacks and whites fought in Bloomington, Illinois. St. Louis police restricted gun sales. Omaha's police chief stopped all gun sales and its mayor banned a showing of *Birth of a Nation*.[108]

Chicago's black newspapers, all weeklies, had gone to press before the riot erupted, so they did not report on what took place until the militia came in. But when the weekend arrived, they delivered explosive headlines and extensive stories. The normally staid *Broad Ax* carried a breathless headline in its Saturday, August 2, edition: "Bloody Anarchy, Murder, Rapine, Race Riots and All Forms of Lawlessness Have Stalked Broad Cast, Throughout Chicago the Past Week." *Defender* publisher Robert S. Abbott, confronting the biggest story of his career, faced a crisis during the week when his printer, a white newspaper near the stockyards, refused to print the edition for fear of reprisal by white mobs. At the last minute, Abbott found a printer in nearby Gary, Indiana.[109] The August 2 *Defender* headline read: "RIOT SWEEPS CHICAGO." A page-one story blamed Officer Callahan for not arresting Stauber at the beach.

A tough editorial in the same issue, titled "Reaping the Whirlwind," declared: "America is known the world over as the land of the lyncher and of the mobocrat. For years she has been sowing the wind and now she is reaping the whirlwind. The Black worm has turned. A Race that has furnished hundreds of thousands of the best soldiers that the world has ever seen is no longer content to turn the left cheek when smitten upon the right."[110]

Militia leaders were so concerned the *Defender* would spark more violence that they considered censoring it or banning it outright. In the end, the First Amendment prevailed. The militia did not seize the edition, instead they bought large quantities, then dumped them.[111]

A threat of renewed rioting came Saturday morning, when arsonists set fire to 49 houses near the stockyards, leaving 180 Lithuanian and Polish families homeless. Blacks were initially blamed, as were radicals. Various officials later discredited the theory that blacks started the fires.[112] Police never caught anyone for the arson. No rioting ensued.[113]

The Chicago riot stunned the nation. Thirty-eight people—23 blacks and 15 whites—were killed.[114] At least 537 were seriously wounded—342 blacks, 178 whites, and 17 whose race was unknown. (No women were killed but ten were injured.)[115] The *Defender* and other newspapers ran long lists of whites and blacks suffering gunshot wounds, concussions, stabbings, fractures, and eyes gouged out.[116] At least 26 police officers were injured during the riots and one, John Simpson, a black officer who was under suspension when the riot occurred, died from a gunshot wound.[117] More than 2,000 homes and apartments were damaged. Stores were looted, taxis destroyed, and trolleys vandalized. The riots cost millions of dollars. No one ever tallied the full cost. The City of Chicago paid $500,000 to the state for the cost of the state militia and another $100,000 in death claims to the families of riot victims.[118]

A militia officer described conditions on the weekend after the riot as an "armed truce."[119] The *Chicago Tribune* carried photographs of smiling black men and children greeting troops. But the same page also showed troops with their bayonets drawn protecting a cowering black couple, who were so afraid they covered their faces so as not to be identified.[120] The *Variety* columnist wrote: "So now, Chicago is comparatively quiet. But things will probably liven up again. There is talk of a Bolshevik plot to blow up the entire city. Actors who are afflicted with ennui are invited to come to Chicago. After a couple of weeks here they will be thankful to play Germantown, Yonkers and Danville."[121] People weren't in the mood for humor. As in Washington and Longview, the reaction of most whites and most blacks could not have been more different. White commentators were horrified, while black commentators—though disgusted at the violence—were thrilled that blacks fought back. Chicago showed, even more than Washington, that large-scale white violence would be met with large-scale black violence. Black Americans had no intention of abandoning their place in the new, industrial America. A new racial paradigm was established, one that dominated social relations for decades. Herbert Seligmann wrote in *The Negro Faces America*, his book about 1919 racial violence, "The white man of the North, who might be inclined to lull himself into forgetfulness, wakes at the sound of shooting down his streets."[122]

Sunday morning, August 3, after the week of rioting, blacks made their way to church. At the Woodlawn Baptist Church, the Reverend M. P. Boynton delivered a sermon titled "The Devil in Chicago." His message was simple, similar to messages delivered in churches across the city: "The only permanent cure for such social disorder is in the fear of God. He alone can cleanse the human heart, cool the fires of passion and make men of all sorts dwell together in unity."[123]

At Olivet Baptist Church, thousands packed the Sunday service, and as many as two thousand more had to be turned away. The Reverend Lacey Kirk Williams said that reports of blacks crowding rail stations to return south were lies spread by whites hoping that blacks would leave Chicago. If whites thought blacks could be forced out of thriving urban America, then what just happened had shown them otherwise, he said. He told gathered black families, "You would rather die here of hunger than die yonder from other plagues."[124]

Carswell Grove Baptist Church in Jenkins County, Georgia. This church was built on the ashes of the church that a white mob destroyed on April 13, 1919, at the beginning of the Red Summer. The congregation abandoned the second church several years ago because of structural problems.

Photograph by author

The Chicago race riot, the largest of the Red Summer, began on July 27, 1919, after the drowning death of Eugene Williams, an African American teenager. Whites gathered at the 29th Street beach when Williams's body was recovered.

Courtesy of the Chicago History Museum

A white mob hunts for blacks on Chicago's South Side during the July 1919 race riot.

Courtesy of the Chicago History Museum

White rioters beat a black man to death with bricks during the Chicago riot, July 1919.

Courtesy of the Chicago History Museum

White soldiers, men, and boys examine a black home ransacked during the Chicago riot, July 1919.

Courtesy of the Chicago History Museum

"Treat 'em Rough," a political cartoon published after the Washington and Chicago riots.

Courtesy of RedScare, an Image Database by Leo Robert Klein

Features of the News and Personalities

New York Tribune

Magazine and Review

Reactions to the News of the Week

PART VII   TWELVE PAGES

SUNDAY, AUGUST 3, 1919

PART VII   TWELVE PAGES

America's Own Race Problem Blazes Up

Riots Bring Grave Peace Problems

WASHINGTON, August 2.

THE bitter, unfinished truth needs to be told about the recent race riots in Washington.

It needs to be told for the benefit of the entire country, particularly to view of a similar and more serious outbreak in Chicago within a week, actually started there, as in Washington, by whites.

It needs to be told because the old formula for race rioting has been changed by the war, the development of propaganda and the rise of Bolshevism.

The truth strikes both whites and negroes equally.

Race rioting, as defined by the gravest source of disorder last week in the nation's capital meant:

1. Attacks, real and reported, on women by negroes.

2. Roodlumism by men in the uniform of the United States.

3. Insufficient police protection for the national capital.

4. A lack of restrictions upon the sale of firearms, and lax enforcement of the laws against carrying deadly weapons.

5. Secondary press agitation in both white and colored papers.

The ripread among the negro population of this country of dangerous raw propaganda growing out of the war and most commonly based upon the negro soldier's reception in France, the Irish question, Bolshevism and the century-old cry that the white man has oppressed the negro.

Both Sides to Blame

Seven Men Killed

Mob Violence Begins

The Gravest Charge

The CRISIS

Bruising the Hand That Blessed
—From The Richmond (Va.) Planet

(From the cover of the current issue of "The Crisis," the organ of the National Association for the Advancement of Colored People. Drawn by Laura Wheeler.)

(These three drawings, showing the negroes' point of view, are taken from negro publications)

How About Your Own Doorstep, Uncle?
—From The New York Amsterdam News

A Chaos of Opinion

American Press Offers No Solution

IF THERE is any solution of the race riot problem it is difficult to find it in the comment of the American press.

The Southern View

Segregation Suggested

Must We Fight?

The Negro's Question

THE negro papers of the country have spoken plainly of the consequences which they think may result from the race riots. "The New York Age," one of the most important negro papers in the country, commended as follows upon the Washington outbreak:

A Bolshevist Soviet

Fiercely, Relentlessly

YES IT **WAS** STOPPED

A negro journal's view of the Washington riots. From "The Washington Bee."

Willie Brown, chief victim of the Omaha riot, September 28, 1919.

Courtesy of the Nebraska State Historical Society

The burning of Brown's body, September 28, 1919.

Courtesy of the Nebraska State Historical Society

Burning of Omaha police patrol car, September 28, 1919.

Courtesy of the Nebraska State Historical Society

Window in Douglas County Treasurer's office, after the Omaha riot of September 28, 1919.

Courtesy of the Nebraska State Historical Society

Sharecropper shot to death outside Elaine, Arkansas, October 1919.
Courtesy of Arkansas History Commission

Black sharecroppers under arrest outside Elaine, Arkansas, October 1919.
Courtesy of Arkansas History Commission

White posse outside Elaine searching for blacks in the canebrakes.

Courtesy of Arkansas History Commission

Cover of a pro-labor pamphlet issued in the later half of the Red Summer.

Courtesy of the University of Illinois Urbana-Champaign and the Internet Archive

14.

Like a Great Volcano

Your prophecies of serious race conflicts begin to come true.
—H. L. MENCKEN to JAMES WELDON JOHNSON,
July 29, 1919

AFTER THE CHICAGO FIGHTING, BLACKS ACROSS THE COUNTRY WERE aghast that the "Promised Land"—the cultural, economic, and political hub of the New Negro—could be every bit as vicious as backwoods Alabama. Dallas businessman and NAACP member Charles R. Graggs compared the northern cities to Brutus, who betrayed Julius Caesar. "Thou, too, North, an enemy of the Negro," he lamented.[1]

Throughout August, pundits penned angst-ridden treatises on the violence as if they had just discovered racial animosity. Government intelligence officers produced hysterical reports about radicals infiltrating black groups. More people started listening to the NAACP, some out of sympathy and interest and others with fear and anger. The organization became a lodestone for black activism and a target of white suspicion. With Chicago and Washington as rallying cries, the NAACP staff used the riots to promote the organization's political agenda and push politicians to act. Membership soared. Thousands of other Americans turned to fringe political groups ranging from the Ku Klux Klan to the newly formed Communist Labor Party to Garvey's UNIA.

Before August, many dismissed the summer's riots as unconnected flare-ups. But photographs of soldiers with machine guns and bayonets marching down State Street—published in newspapers from New York to California—changed that mindset.

The popular national magazine *Leslie's Illustrated Weekly* was shocked by the scope of the riot in "a distinctly northern metropolis." Blacks must be at fault, *Leslie's* editors assumed, having "mistaken their new-found liberty for license, and, unaccustomed to self-control, indulged in excesses which have gradually irritated their white neighbors to the danger point."[2]

Others saw white prejudice and economic disparity at fault. The Urban League declared Washington and Chicago were "solemn warnings to our country" and "only by improving the housing, health and recreation opportunities of the Negro at the same time that we demand of him the contribution of his hands and brain in industry can we look for fundamental improvement in race relations."[3]

―――――◇―――――

Whites and blacks from all classes and all regions began to realize that this extraordinary summer of troubles was forging a new dynamic in race relations. Race riots—almost every one started by white mobs—were nothing new. They had erupted in every decade since the United States was founded. In most cases, mobs overwhelmed smaller black communities that offered scant resistance or simply fled. To most whites, these riots were caused by "the Negro Problem," as they invariably called it, a national dilemma framed in terms of blacks' behavior, civic engagement, educational levels, or fundamental intelligence. But the true problem that most whites had with blacks was simply their very presence. They did not want blacks living near them. And if blacks did live near them, whites wanted them locked into a clearly defined subservient economic, cultural, and political station. The American Colonization Society, founded by whites in 1816 as a purported philanthropic effort to ship free blacks back to Africa, announced in its sixth annual report in 1824: "It is by colonization, and by this alone, that the mischiefs of slavery, and, what is more to be dreaded than slavery, the living pestilence of a free black population, can be lessened."[4]

The central question festering throughout most of American history was simple: Would free blacks be allowed to live equally with whites? From the American Revolution to the Great War, the answer to this question was overwhelmingly no.

But in 1919, blacks began to broadly challenge the long-held premise that they must exist in this country as inferiors. Led by the NAACP and other groups, they began to assert themselves as equals—many for the first time in their lives. They started fighting in legislatures, courtrooms, and the streets to become full partners in the American democratic experiment.

"There is but one remedy for race riots," declared W. S. Scarborough, president of Wilberforce University, a black college in Ohio, "and that is justice—a willingness to accord to every man his rights—civil and political."[5]

Black response to discrimination and violence took various forms, ranging from lofty oratory to swinging a baseball bat. Some lobbied legislatures. Others made pointed arguments in court. Black newspapers wrote tough editorials. And along Chicago's Wentworth Avenue, young men kept knives and bricks handy.

"We will have riots elsewhere as a result of those here," James Weldon Johnson warned as he met with politicians in Washington. "When they come they will be serious. The colored men will not run away from it and hide as they have done on previous occasions."[6]

Blacks in the Atlanta lodge of the Grand United Order of Odd Fellows set up a committee to draft a report "on the state of the country." Their conclusion: "Thank God, the Negro has awakened a racial consciousness. This spirit, like a great volcano, has been growing for a long time and has now belched forth its eruption."[7]

Other black organizations followed the NAACP's lead. Robert R. Jackson, the head of the Colored Knights of Pythias organization, told thousands at their August convention in Atlantic City: "Let me say to the world that the twelve million people of our race kept the fires of Americanism burning. Let us keep them burning until we burn up every Jim Crow sign and every Jim Crow car in this country."[8]

In late July, James Weldon Johnson wrote to H. L. Mencken, just then approaching his zenith as America's leading cultural critic, and warned him of coming trouble. "Your prophecies of serious race conflicts begin to come true," Mencken wrote back in the midst of the Chicago riot.[9] Mencken wrote with respect to Johnson. But in early August, Mencken wrote a blunt letter to a fellow white journalist, and applied his penchant for racial slurs.

"The race riots in Washington and Chicago have shown a new feature," he wrote. "The coons have fought back—and pretty well beaten the whites. They are armed everywhere and apparently eager for the band to play."[10]

Many whites embraced segregation even more tightly. A Catholic priest in St. Louis urged parishioners to band together to keep blacks from moving into their neighborhood. If blacks tried to buy white homes, he said, "You must slam the door in their faces and tell them, 'You know we don't want you here.'"[11]

Despite prominent examples of strong black resistance, white mob attacks escalated across the country in August. Black men were lynched in Louisiana, South Carolina, Mississippi, Georgia, and elsewhere. In Bogalusa, Louisiana, a black war veteran was accused of attacking a white woman. A mob of 1,000 whites lynched him, tied the corpse to a car, dragged it down the city's main streets, and then burned it outside the alleged victim's home.[12] In Cochran, Georgia, an unidentified black man told other black passengers on a railcar that he came from Chicago to help black Georgians "do what the Negroes of Chicago did." White officials heard of the remark and arrested him. He was found hanging from a tree.[13]

Near Pope City, Georgia, a black veteran named Jim Grant was accused of shooting and wounding two white men. A mob grabbed Grant and dragged his father out to see his doomed son. They beat Grant's father and warned him to leave town for good before lynching his son from a telephone pole.[14]

Near Cadwell, Georgia, twenty white men pulled elderly black farmer Eli Cooper from his home and took him to a black church outside town. The group set the church on fire, then shot Cooper. People living nearby heard more than 50 gunshots. The mob threw Cooper's body into the flames.[15] The mob burned down several black churches and lodges in the area. Cooper's offense? He reportedly remarked that blacks were "run over for fifty years, but this will all change in thirty days."[16] The New York Times reported Cooper was the ringleader of blacks planning to "rise up and wipe out the white people."[17] Some white citizens of Cadwell, led by the local newspaper editor, investigated the rumors and declared the accusations unfounded. What Cooper had said was that farmers, whether black or white, needed to fight for their rights.

"The Negroes around Cadwell are known as some of the most law abiding in the county, and have never given any cause for such outrages as were perpetrated this week," the citizens declared in the local newspaper.[18]

People in cities across the country feared rioting could break out anywhere blacks and whites interacted. In Cleveland, a Packard car full of white men opened fire on a black veteran in early August.

"This looks very much as if there are those in large cities of the North, as well as the South, who are trying to start mob violence thru vicious assaults on our people," warned *Cleveland Gazette* editors.[19]

—⊂⊃—

Strikes and labor clashes broke out throughout the country in record numbers and many involved racial violence. In Chicago, tensions remained high as thousands of white stockyard workers staged wildcat strikes over the return of nonunion blacks. The white unions disrupted business so effectively that the packing companies had to shut down livestock shipments temporarily.[20] White immigrant strikers battled black scabs at an ironworks in Syracuse, New York.

And the Great Steel Strike started to take shape. In June, the AFL–affiliated steelworkers union had authorized a strike against the corporate behemoth U.S. Steel and other steel companies. By August, negotiations broke down and U.S. Steel prepared to bring in more than 30,000 black strikebreakers to keep the mills running if workers struck. The national steel organizing effort was led by the young radical William Z. Foster, who successfully organized white immigrant workers in Chicago packing houses.[21] Foster was acutely aware of racial hatreds between workers. He knew if a labor war came, race would be a large part of it. He blamed capitalists. Company bosses, he remarked after bitter experiences in 1919, "leave no stone unturned to exploit the deep race antagonism between whites and blacks in order to force the Negro to scab."[22]

Woodrow Wilson held an emergency summit with union leaders at the White House on August 28, 1919, in a last effort to stave off the national strike. The meeting produced nothing. Within weeks, the strike—the greatest business-labor clash of a momentous year—would paralyze factories from Buffalo to Gary, Indiana, named in honor of the U.S. Steel's CEO, Elbert "Judge" Gary.

In post-riot Chicago, people cast blame on one another. Desperate to salvage his reputation, Mayor Thompson asked the city council to authorize 2,000 more police officers—a 40 percent increase.[23] But within days, he discounted the riot as an aberration. He was a keynote speaker at "The Race Business Men's Exposition," held in the Black Belt. "The Riot Is Over/Everybody Is Doing Business," the exposition flier declared.[24] In private, Thompson supporters blamed anti-Thompson Democrats and stockyard unions for the trouble.[25]

Thompson's enemies went on the attack in the riot's aftermath. Cook

County state attorney Maclay Hoyne, the progressive trounced by Thompson in the recent mayoral contest, blamed criminal gangs in the Black Belt, a Thompson stronghold. To pressure Thompson, Hoyne ordered "anti-riot" and "anti-vice" raids throughout the Black Belt in late August, netting fifty arrests, guns, and ammunition. Thirty of those arrested were the primary instigators of the riot, Hoyne told reporters. "Negro thugs," using three gambling joints as their bases, orchestrated the riot, he claimed.[26] Hoyne legitimized a widely held view among white Democrats and progressives that blacks had caused the fighting. Black leaders, including Walter White, who spent August in Chicago investigating for the NAACP, were incensed at Hoyne's statements.[27] While organized crime thrived in the Black Belt, Hoyne's claims were never proven.

To restore his presidential aspirations and undermine Thompson's, Governor Frank Lowden created a special race commission to investigate the riot and offer solutions to ease tensions.[28] The commission was made up equally of whites and blacks, including white philanthropist Julius Rosenwald and *Chicago Defender* editor Robert Abbott. Its top staff member was Charles S. Johnson, then a University of Chicago student researcher and destined to become the nation's top black sociologist. Though it took years to complete its report, the Chicago Commission on Race Relations was unique for its exhaustive analysis of an urban riot. The 818-page *The Negro in Chicago: A Study of Race Relations and a Race Riot* was thorough and insightful. But the commission's formation served a more immediate purpose: it allowed Lowden to avoid action while still appearing responsive. It gave him a sheen of authority, and vaguely cast fault on both his Republican rival Thompson and Chicago Democrats.[29]

"To say that we cannot solve this problem is to confess the failure of self-government," Lowden said when appointing the commission. "I offer no solution of the problem."[30]

Many saw Lowden's commission as a disappointment. Editors at the *Chicago Whip*, a black weekly, accused the governor of shirking responsibility. The *Whip* also feared the commission would propose some kind of permanent, quasi-legal segregation, since the *New York Times* erroneously reported the commission had authority to "determine boundary lines for white and Negro activities."[31] In fact, the commission had no such authority and no such intention.

"We need no commission; we need no new law; but what we do need is an executive that has the backbone to enforce the laws already made," the *Whip*'s editors complained.[32]

Chicago aldermen suggested a formal segregation of the city. Supporters of the idea pointed to the creation of Robbins, an all-black city founded in 1917 just south of Chicago. Segregation opponents countered that Chicago's white ethnic groups instigated much of the violence, not blacks.

"Since there were many other races in the riot, and no doubt the cause of this blot on Chicago history, why not let us help to find places of separation for them, if we really intend to separate," wrote one Chicagoan to the *Tribune*. "Separations will never solve anything but, I rather think, will promote further conflicts."[33]

The de jure segregation proposal went nowhere, but a de facto segregation hardened into a block-by-block contest that lasted generations.[34]

The leaders of Chicago's meatpacking unions held meetings and rallies to try to ease racial tensions. They printed a pamphlet, its cover showing a black worker and a white worker squaring off over money, that argued that if blacks joined the unions, the menace of race riots "will become a nightmare of an ignorant, barbaric past."[35]

But it would take far more than pamphlets to soothe Chicagoans after a week of rioting. Chicago's white newspapers urged more police and quick action, but offered little by way of long-term solutions.

"Are not the people of America capable of devising and applying a real solution?" the *Daily News* opined. "From Chicago's terrible outbreak of race hatred must come justice and applied wisdom if the nation is to atone for this disgrace."[36]

Chicago American editors chose denial. They claimed the riot had nothing to do with race at all. "There is very little ill feeling between the white and colored divisions of Chicago's population," they declared. "The rioting is chiefly traceable to gun-toting, knife-packing rowdies who have picked upon an unfortunate incident to run amuck."[37]

Chicago's black press honed in on labor infighting and segregated housing conditions as the causes. "If the reader will take down a map of Chicago he will find that wherever the Colored people have moved in as a rule, that they are the rotten spots of Chicago," complained the *Broad Ax*. "There the saloon flourishes, the questionable hotel, and the buffet flat run by the underworld element of white people. Could you wish this state of affairs to forever continue? And that the present day Negro to be satisfied to rear his dear little children in such polluted stench?"[38]

Several committees and organizations formed that August to ease racial tensions and aid displaced blacks. A joint emergency committee made up of social welfare groups, black uplift organizations, and local clergy formed, but then squabbled. The NAACP, under Walter White's direction, led an effort to raise money for the city's black riot defendants.[39] The Urban League worked with the Red Cross to set up relief centers in the Black Belt and to help people whose homes were burned. Through this work, the NAACP and the Urban League (White nominally worked for both) arose in August as the leading organizations helping blacks in Chicago. They even marginalized Ida Wells-Barnett, the city's most famous agitator against rioting and mob action.[40]

White produced the most thoughtful contemporary analysis of the riot. He spent four weeks in Chicago investigating and produced his analysis in *The Crisis* as "Chicago and Its Eight Reasons."[41] At the time, White's reasons were revelatory:

1. Race Prejudice.
2. Economic competition.
3. Political Corruption and Exploitation of Negro Voters.
4. Police Inefficiency.
5. Newspaper Lies about Negro Crime.
6. Unpunished Crimes Against Negroes.
7. Housing.
8. Reaction of Whites and Negroes from War.

White balanced his criticism of the white press with rebukes of the black press. He criticized political leaders and unions. He produced an analytical critique, one that examined charges and countercharges and incorporated flaws and mistakes on all sides. But the great wrong that White saw as the theme of Chicago was "as is usually the case, the Negro is made to bear the brunt of it all—to be 'the scapegoat.'"[42] In many respects, White's views echoed and elaborated upon Sandburg's *Chicago Daily News* July columns, published that September in book form with an introduction by *The New Republic* cofounder Walter Lippmann.

Lippmann's introduction, written on August 26, 1919, embodied a growing sense among white liberals that legitimate aspirations of blacks to equal rights were multifaceted: political, economic, and social. Lippmann—beginning his decades-long career as America's leading pundit—could not bring himself to embrace the idea of interracial relations or social interaction with blacks. But he did see the need for "our planless, disordered, bedraggled, drifting democracy" to allow for political *and* economic equality for blacks.

"Until we have learned to house everybody, employ everybody at decent wages in a self-respecting status, guarantee his civil liberties, and bring education and play to him, the bulk of our talk about 'the race problem' will remain a sinister mythology," Lippmann wrote. "In a dirty civilization the relations between black men and white men will be a dirty one."[43]

The summer's bloodletting arrived on the tercentennial of the first slaves coming to the American colonies. On August 20, 1619, a Dutch ship from the West Indies sold twenty "Negar" slaves, as one chronicler wrote, to whites at the Jamestown colony in Virginia. Three centuries later, the consequences of that arrival still roiled the continent. *The Crisis* marked the anniversary with a short essay by Du Bois:

> We must remember because if once the world forgets evil, evil is reborn; because if the suffering of the American Negro is once forgotten, then there is no guerdon, down to the last pulse of time, that Devils will not again enslave and maim and murder and oppress the weak and unfortunate.[44]

The NAACP intensified pressure on Congress to hold hearings on anti-lynching legislation, and it also called on the Wilson administration to condemn the riots and take action. Others joined in the call.

"A thousand communities are on edge today, because each furnished the fuel to kindle the fires of riot and bloodshed," declared Sol C. Johnson, editor of the black weekly *Savannah Tribune*.[45]

The New York–based publication *Outlook* pleaded with President Wilson to act: "In times of disorder in a democracy, it is . . . natural for the people to look to their elected leader."[46]

Individuals and groups contacted President Wilson after the Chicago riot, but he politely brushed off calls for a statement. Robert Moton, head of the Tuskegee Institute, pleaded with him to denounce the riots.

"I will take the suggestions you make under very serious consideration, because I realize how critical the situation has become and how important it is to steady affairs in every possible way," Wilson wrote back. But he never issued a public statement.[47]

Wilson saw riot suppression as a state and local responsibility. When leaders of the Southern Sociological Congress wrote to Wilson about their opposition to lynching, Wilson only stated that he read the letter "with the greatest interest." He suggested that they bring their concerns to an upcoming conference of governors to be held in Salt Lake City. In a follow-up letter, the group's secretary implored Wilson to speak:

> Owing to the acuteness of this question of race relations at this hour, it seems to us desirable that every possible influence be brought to bear to get the public to think calmly and justly on this subject. We are aware that you have doubtless been requested repeatedly to make a statement in regard to the recent outbreaks of mob violence.[48]

But the self-proclaimed defender of world democracy, the protector of Europe's ethnic minorities from the Baltic to the Adriatic, had nothing to say after racial violence ravaged his own country.

Others had lots to say. Former president William Howard Taft, in his nationally syndicated column, wrote: "These riots have a lesson which the whites should take to their souls. It is that each one of us has a responsibility to the community in dealing with our Colored fellow citizens. Every time a white man insults a Negro, every time he conveys by his conduct an overweening sense of his race superiority, he contributes to the cause out of which these race riots have come. No race responds so quickly to sympathetic aid as the Negro. No race can be made as easily to forget or forgive past wrongs by sincere cooperation and protection."[49]

Noted American sociologist Frank H. Giddings pleaded for all sides to calm down: "Never mind who began it. Never mind whether an exceptional prevalence of criminality gave provocation for retaliation or not: this is not the time to accuse and certainly not the time to lose control. It is a time for coolness and common sense."[50]

Taft's and Giddings's counsels, however, were largely ignored. Gloating, greed, and fear were more common white reactions to the Chicago riot. Gloating came from the South. Politicians and editorial writers expounded on how they "understood" blacks and how southern white mobs only lynched individual blacks guilty of specific crimes. The *Houston Chronicle* complained that northerners treated blacks too well, and were now reaping what they had sown.

"The immediate cause, like the immediate result, is an old, old story, but both are rooted in a background of silly pampering which leads, and will always lead, to atrocious acts on the one hand and to illogical spasms of temper on the other," the *Chronicle* stated.

The *Vicksburg Herald*, in an editorial titled "Chickens Coming Home to Roost," blamed black newspapers like the *Defender* for stirring up trouble.[51]

Greed also played a role. Business leaders in the South saw the riot as an opportunity to lure back black workers. In August, Kentucky coal mines put out a call for blacks. Even Louisville, where the city's segregated housing laws had led to the Supreme Court's decision in *Buchanan v. Warley* only a few years earlier, now considered building a new swimming pool for blacks.[52] The Coahoma County Chamber of Commerce in Clarksdale, Mississippi, advertised in Chicago newspapers urging blacks to return to the Delta.[53] Even some southern politicians, including Nashville's mayor and Tennessee's governor, urged black workers to return. The NAACP scoffed at the idea.[54] Perhaps the most absurd proposal came from a white real estate developer in Southern California. Hugh E. Macbeth, secretary of the Lower California Mexican Land & Development Company, wrote to Du Bois at *The Crisis* recommending what amounted to a corporate-run reservation for black Americans.

"For the good cause of law and order may I suggest that you quietly refer to us for deportation to Lower California, such rioting Negroes as may be causing the Government trouble in Washington, Chicago and elsewhere," Macbeth wrote from Los Angeles. He thought the land could handle "five million of these Negro malcontents." It's unclear if Macbeth knew to whom he was writing and, sadly for posterity, Du Bois's response, if he sent one, is unrecorded.[55]

Many continued to blame the racial conflict on Communists and anarchists. J. Edgar Hoover, leading the Justice Department's intelligence operations, authorized hiring black undercover agents to spy on black organizations and publications in Harlem.[56] During the Chicago riot, Justice Department officials fed anonymous statements to the press that the International Workers of the World and the Bolsheviks were "spreading propaganda to breed race hatred." Illinois governor Lowden repeated the claim.[57]

Investigators, seeking such a connection, called black leaders to Chicago's federal courthouse for interrogation. The first person called was Ida Wells-Barnett, who ridiculed their questions.[58] The inquiries went nowhere. Army intelligence reports during and after the riot underscored the dearth of government "intelligence." One report offered as strong evidence the claim that "a blind Negro" possibly named Spencer, somewhere in the city, had handed out pamphlets from the socialist *New York Call*. A summary, completed four months after the riot, could only assert vaguely "agitation played an important part."[59] Still, intelligence officers trumpeted this "Red Scare" idea of widespread Bolshevik agitation among blacks.

"The doctrine preached by I.W.W., agitators and radical socialism are daily winning new converts among the Negroes, particularly among the younger and more irresponsible element," one intelligence officer reported to Washington. "The long continued propaganda, as, for example, that carried on by the National Association for the Advancement of Colored People, urging the colored people to insist upon equality with white people and to resort to force, if necessary, in order to establish their rights is not bearing abundant fruit. Beyond a doubt, there is a new Negro to be reckoned with in our political and social life."[60]

Other groups and the press embraced the blacks-and-Bolshevism connection, no matter how feeble. The National Security League, a nationalist, quasi-militaristic organization co-founded by Leonard Wood in 1914, blamed the I.W.W. and Communists for inciting blacks—conveniently avoiding the reality that whites instigated almost all of the violence.[61] The press spread the idea that leftist agitators caused the race rioting and lynching. Again, the fact that white mobs started the overwhelming majority of the violence was ignored.

"Race riots seem to have for their genesis a Bolshevist, a Negro, and a gun," the *Wall Street Journal* declared.[62] The *New York Evening Sun* stated: "That such propaganda has been going on, and doubtless continues, is proven beyond shadow of doubt by the documents now in possession of Federal investigators."[63] The documents then in the possession of federal agents proved no such thing. Evidence seized by investigators showed the opposite. In June 1919, the Socialist Party's Rand School of Social Science in Manhattan had produced a confidential paper, "Socialism Imperiled, or the Negro—A Potential Menace to American Radicalism," which argued that black workers lacked the requisite class consciousness to join such movements.

"If a railroad wreck occurs, or a ship is sunk, the attitude of the average Negro is to scan the death list diligently and if none of his race is among the victims, ejaculate, 'Thank God, they are all white people. There are no colored folk among them,'" the authors complained. "In short, Negroes react to prejudice and discrimination by becoming distinctly race conscious, but so far as their class consciousness is concerned, it is not even as much as scratched." The report denounced black workers as anti-union and the black press as pro-Republican Party.[64]

Stephen Graham, a British journalist touring the United States to research race relations during 1919, wrote: "The Negro is afraid of Bolshevism and Socialism because he knows the common white people, 'those who have nothing and are nothing,' are the last people to give him justice."[65]

The few white radical attempts to recruit blacks in 1919 were unsuccessful. The I.W.W.—the most sympathetic of the radical white groups toward black workers—published a four-page pamphlet titled "Justice for the Negro, How He Can Get It." It was published separately and as part of the August edition of its magazine *One Big Union*. The essay, by Frederick Blossom, gave an obvious suggestion: blacks should join the I.W.W. and shun trade unionism.

"The wrongs of the Negro in the United States are not confined to lynching. . . . When allowed to live and work for the community, he is subjected to constant humiliation, injustice and discrimination," Blossom wrote. "In the cities, he is forced to live in the meanest districts, where his rent is doubled and tripled, while conditions of health and safety are neglected in favor of the white sections. In many states, he is obliged to ride in special 'Jim Crow' cars hardly fit for cattle. Almost everywhere, all semblance of political rights is denied him."[66]

There is no indication that this pamphlet or another I.W.W. pamphlet directed at blacks circulated widely in black areas of any northern city or in the South. The major radical parties had far more involvement with European immigrants. The founding convention of the Communist Labor Party, held from August 3 to September 5, 1919, in Chicago, had no black delegates and few black members.[67] The Communist Party of America, which held its founding convention in the first week of September, also in Chicago, had few black delegates.[68] Both groups had many immigrants.

The writer Claude McKay was one of the few blacks who started to embrace Communism in 1919. Yet he was disappointed that blacks— even left-wing blacks—showed little interest in white radical parties. He lamented in a private letter to Marcus Garvey, "Radical Negroes should be more interested in the white radical movements."[69]

15.

Austin

*I whipped him and ordered him to leave because I thought
it was for the best interests of Austin and the state.*

—TEXAS JUDGE DAVID PICKLE, after leading a mob that
beat John Shillady, August 1919

IN AUGUST 1919, THE NAACP EXPERIENCED UNPRECEDENTED
growth in membership, magazine circulation, and political influence.
James Weldon Johnson, lobbying in Washington, met with several senators and congressmen, some of whom agreed to sponsor legislation and
resolutions backed by the organization.

One supporter wrote to NAACP Secretary John Shillady: "It is very
comforting and reassuring in these days of strife and discord to know
that there is an organization addressing itself to the task of righting these
wrongs."[1]

But growth was met by white hostility. Wherever the NAACP opened
a chapter or held a public rally, white opponents challenged the group.
"The National Association for the Advancement of Colored People
makes a practice of addressing impudent telegrams to southern governors," wrote Harper Leech, a Washington correspondent for the *Dallas
Dispatch*. "Readers might as well be informed that this organization is
largely composed of Socialists, black, white and tan."[2]

Anti-NAACP backlash culminated with two events in late August
that horrified NAACP supporters and solidified the organization's role
as the nation's leading protector of black civil rights. One was a speech
delivered with vituperative bombast on the floor of the United States

House of Representatives. The other was a mob attack on John Shillady on the streets of Austin, Texas.

On August 25, Representative James Francis Byrnes, a South Carolina Democrat, called for a national ban on "incendiary literature" and an extension of the wartime espionage act to limit distribution of black publications. He also demanded that U.S. attorney general Palmer, his close friend, file charges against W. E. B. Du Bois.

Byrnes said that radical remarks in black publications made black neighborhoods from New York to St. Louis "magazines of race-prejudice dynamite, ready to explode at any moment upon putting the flame to the fuse. Riots are imminent—real race riots."

He quoted passages from black publications that, he argued, illustrated a propensity to radicalism and violence. One article in the socialist-leaning *Messenger* praised the I.W.W. for allowing blacks as members. Byrnes said the articles showed "that the Negro leaders had deliberately planned a campaign of violence. . . . Radical leaders of the Negroes are urging their followers to resort to violence in order to secure privileges they believe themselves entitled to, and recent riots indicate that the advice is being taken."

Byrnes read into the *Congressional Record* Du Bois's "Returning Soldiers" essay to prove the violent agenda of the NAACP and other black activists. He declared the article violated the espionage law.[3]

Byrnes, thirty-seven, had been born to a wealthy family in Charleston. As a young prosecutor in Aiken, he gained notice for fighting to secure rights for black crime victims. At the time, black testimony was not allowed in his circuit, so victims had little recourse. Byrnes fought to change that. As a biographer noted: "Winning agreement that black people were, under some circumstances, legally human beings was no small accomplishment at that time and in that section of South Carolina."[4]

But Byrnes's efforts for blacks stopped when he entered politics under the tutelage of South Carolina senator Ben "Pitchfork" Tillman, who had fought for the Confederacy and embraced segregation as divinely imperative. Elected to Congress in 1910, Byrnes developed a reputation as a savvy political boss who lived to secure federal projects in his district and maintain Jim Crow. As he addressed his fellow congressmen, he spoke as the voice of the white South.[5]

A day after Byrnes's speech, an article in the *New York Tribune* quoted unnamed Justice Department officials who said Byrnes's accusations "seemed to be well founded." These officials went on to say black and leftist newspapers were springing up around the country "to spread propaganda and sow discord among the Negroes."[6] Du Bois, directly attacked by Byrnes, ridiculed the widely reported speech, claiming that Byrnes brought free publicity for the NAACP's magazine:

> Mr. Byrnes is alarmed, and so are we. He is alarmed over us and we over him. He accused *The Crisis* and other Negro journals of causing not only the Washington and Chicago riots, but the whole unrest and dissatisfaction of the Negro race. We accuse Mr. Byrnes, and his kind, of being primarily the ones who not only precipitated the riots in Washington, Chicago, Atlanta, Houston, Longview and East St. Louis, but also of encouraging for fifty years the lynching of 4,000 Negroes, the disenfranchisement of a million and a half voters, the enforced ignorance of three million human beings and the theft of hundreds of millions of dollars in wages, but particularly of a freeman—our vote and our self-respect.[7]

Crisis supporters were incensed. A woman in Harlem wrote to Du Bois, "After reading James F. Byrnes's statement in the paper, it has drawn from me more hate toward the white race then [*sic*] what I have in me before."[8]

If Byrnes hoped his reading of Du Bois's essay would shock all whites, he was disappointed. At least one white man wrote to Du Bois that the parts of the *Crisis* editor's essay quoted by Byrnes were "magnificent. It will stir the blood not only of colored men but of every decent white man who hates injustice."[9]

NAACP staffers were in a fighting posture. Only three days before the Byrnes speech, they learned via telegram and newspaper that on August 22 Shillady was beaten in broad daylight outside the ornate Driskill Hotel in downtown Austin. The mob included David Pickle, a county judge, and Charles Hamby, a constable.[10] The fast-growing NAACP worried many whites in Texas. Vigilante committees arose in Dallas and other cities to organize armed white volunteers. In the sawmill town of Leggett, a white council set a curfew for blacks, banned black fraternal and church meetings, and forbade blacks from visiting the railroad station or the post office. White posses drove an NAACP organizer and several black families out of town.[11]

Texas Rangers traveled the state to warn local sheriffs of a pending black uprising. In August, they held an emergency meeting in Houston with law enforcement officials. The goal of the meeting, as one attendee said, was "putting a stop to the Negroes organizing against the white people." A federal official reported to the United States Railroad Administration that the rangers promised they had "positive information that the Negroes are organizing all over the state under the name of the 'National Association for the Advancement of Colored People' and are buying up all the high-powered rifles and ammunition they can possibly buy."[12] In early August, a justice of the peace in Austin summoned the secretary of the local NAACP branch and ordered him to produce all papers and records of the group. Then the state attorney general subpoenaed the Texas NAACP for its financial and membership records. The attorney general claimed that the NAACP could not operate because it had no state charter. He also said the group was violating state law by openly opposing segregation.[13]

The NAACP's fastest-growing state branch was under threat, so board chairwoman Mary Ovington asked John Shillady to visit Austin to try to resolve the charter issue. She knew she was asking a lot. Shillady's wife worried incessantly about threats made against her husband. Worse, the Shilladys had recently lost two children to illness and were grieving.

When Ovington spoke to Shillady about going to Texas, the graying Irish American asked her, "Do you think there is any danger?"[14]

She paused, then said she thought he would be safe: he was white and going to meet leading state leaders, not commoners.[15] Shillady arrived by train in Austin on the evening of August 20.[16] He met with Texas NAACP leaders, and then with an official at the state Capitol. As Shillady walked back to his hotel, eight to ten men stopped him, arrested him, and took him before what they declared to be a "court of inquiry." Judge Pickle headed the inquisition. He berated Shillady and demanded that he leave Texas immediately. Shillady did not. The next morning, Shillady again met with the NAACP. Outside the hotel, the same group of whites accosted him and Pickle accused Shillady of inciting blacks.

"You don't see my point of view," Shillady said.

"I'll fix you so you can't see," Constable Hambry replied. Several men jumped Shillady, beating him to the ground. He suffered a black eye, a split lip, and contusions on his head.[17]

Pickle said they beat Shillady until his face bled and he begged for mercy. Shillady staggered into his hotel and a doctor stitched his face.[18] Austin's mayor provided him with police protection until he could catch the 2:20 p.m. train to St. Louis. Later, Judge Pickle bragged about his participation in the attack.

"I told him our Negroes would cause no trouble if left alone," Pickle told a reporter. "I whipped him and ordered him to leave because I thought it was for the best interests of Austin and the state."[19]

James Weldon Johnson and Ovington met Shillady's train at Pennsylvania Station, where they saw black porters gathered around him, offering to carry his bags for free.

"His face and body were badly bruised; moreover, he was broken in spirit," Johnson recalled. "I don't think he was ever able to realize how such a thing could happen in the United States to an American, free, white and [more than] twenty-one."[20] Ovington sent a telegram to Governor Hobby demanding that Texas prosecute Shillady's attackers. Hobby, who was not in Austin when the attack occurred, was unmoved. "Shillady was the only offender in connection with the matter referred to in your telegram, and he was punished before your inquiry came," he wrote to Ovington. Hobby told her that the NAACP "can contribute more to the advancement of both races by keeping your representatives and their propaganda out of this state."[21]

Hobby was more blunt with a reporter: "I believe in sending any narrow-brained, double-chinned reformer who comes here with the end in view of stirring up racial discontent back to the North where he came from, with a broken jaw if necessary."[22] Back home, a rattled Shillady tried to use the attack to promote the anti-lynching legislation effort, sending out various press releases. He wrote to NAACP stalwart Archibald Grimké, "Anonymous letters of a threatening character have come in, even from New York."[23] He offered some initial bravado, but soon reduced his public role. Shillady was no stranger to angry protest: he had been cursed while representing New York's mayor at unemployment meetings and had often received death threats as the NAACP's top staffer.[24] He used to dismiss those threats. But the Austin attack broke him. Within a year, he would leave his post.

Shillady wrote Grimké with hollow bluster that he felt "this occurrence will be the means of greatly strengthening the Association."[25] In ways Shillady did not envision, the NAACP did gain in strength. With Shillady fading, Johnson and Walter White rose in prominence. Shillady had worked tirelessly, but he focused on publicity and maintaining East Coast white liberal support—the core of the NAACP at its founding. By

1919, such supporters were still vital to the organization's financial well-being, but membership was overwhelmingly black. New chapters more often than not were being set up in black communities of the South and the Midwest, not the East Coast. An organization dedicated to combating antiblack violence and Jim Crow laws sorely needed black leadership to embody its members' bold ambitions. Johnson and White, both black and southern, brought a perspective that Shillady simply did not have. They also brought energy and fearlessness, which Shillady had lost. As Washington and Chicago demonstrated, the hour demanded resolve. After the riot, *Chicago Whip* editors declared in an essay, "The Passing of Uncle Tom," that "the Negro demands new leadership. Calm, intelligent, unswerving leaders. God, give us Men."[26]

In other ways, the Shillady attack sparked an outpouring of support for the NAACP. Lillian Wald, a social worker, feminist, and NAACP board member, wrote to President Wilson, whom she knew, urging him to address the widespread racial violence: "I believe that you can carry comforting balm to the colored people in this time, and the attack upon Mr. Shillady gives you a just and imperative opportunity."[27] Wilson declined, instead asking his secretary to send her a note "in some gentle and kindly way, and express our desire to do everything that is possible to moderate and prevent such outbursts of feeling as she alludes to."[28]

The NAACP was not deterred, rather, it seemed invigorated by the administration's lack of interest. Moorfield Storey pressed Congressman Dallinger to lobby for his anti-lynching bill to get a hearing before the House Judiciary Committee. "Unless lynching of colored people is stopped we are drifting into what may well become a civil war," he told the congressman.[29]

The NAACP asked Wilson, Congress, and New York governor Al Smith to investigate the attack on Shillady. They all declined.[30]

But it did not matter—the point was to present a moral imperative publicly to the nation's leaders. If the politicians did not listen, many citizens, especially black Americans, did. The flood of new members into the NAACP continued. The NAACP board members voted at its August 26 meeting to add 22 new chapters. One of the largest new chapters, with 85 charter members, was in Knoxville, an industrial city in the heart of the East Tennessee mountains.[31]

After the Chicago riot, *Knoxville Journal and Tribune* editors expressed shock that "there are those with white faces and black hearts who would persecute a Negro because he is a Negro."[32]

<hr />

In August Marcus Garvey positioned himself as a new kind of black leader challenging the growing NAACP with his more extreme worldview. Garvey's UNIA was smaller and less organized than the NAACP. But the organization appealed to many blacks frustrated with racial violence and endemic prejudice in white-dominated America.

While the NAACP pushed for equal rights within the United States, Garvey advocated a black empire apart from the white world. Blacks who saw themselves as socialists were drawn to Garvey. Cyril Briggs, editor of the socialist *Crusader*, began to support Garvey. In September, he launched the "African Blood Brotherhood," a paramilitary defense organization aligned with Garvey's UNIA.

"The Irish, the Jew, the Pole—all races are looking towards national existence in a country of their own under government of their own, as the logical solution of their problems," Briggs wrote in the August *Crusader*. "Why should not the Negro also seek such ends?"[33]

Garvey's message appealed to a portion of average blacks, as they watched white mobs form and attack throughout the summer. Percy L. Jones, a Great War veteran living in Chicago's Black Belt, was a likely candidate for UNIA membership. After the Chicago riot, a dejected Jones wrote to Du Bois: "I have been thinking of the situation of the colored people in this Country and it seems that it will never grow any better." The twenty-eight-year-old former sergeant wanted to form "an exploring party" of about 2,000 black men to travel to Africa and "start a Government of our own."[34]

Garvey's message attracted men like Jones. Garvey preached apartness, the foil to the Ku Klux Klan. If whites did not want blacks as equals in their world, he said, then blacks must create their own. The race riots only enhanced his appeal.

In August, Garvey told a large rally at Carnegie Hall that the days of the "Uncle Tom cringing Negro" were over. "They say to us in Chicago, 'We don't want you here,'" he said to cheering crowds. "They say to us in Washington, 'We do not want you here,' in America. . . . The audacity of the white man after keeping the Negro in America in slavery for 250 years! That Negro, through his sacrifice, through his blood, has made America what it is today."[35]

Garvey called for a world revolution not for the proletariat, but for the black race: "We are not Bolshevik, I.W.W., Democratic, Republican, or Socialists, we are pro-Negro and our fight is for the new Negro race, that is to be."[36]

Both the NAACP and the UNIA advocated self-defense and political activism, but the messages were diametrically opposed. The NAACP saw its efforts as asserting blacks' rights within American democracy. The UNIA focused on setting up a separate black nation. The NAACP saw justice as a color-blind legal system. For the UNIA, justice was a Hammurabi-style retribution and separation of the races into opposing camps.

"Within the next few months our organization will be in such condition," Garvey promised at Carnegie Hall, "that if there is a lynching in the South and a white man cannot be held to account down there, the button will be pushed here and a white man in New York will be lynched."

Thousands of blacks—sick of years as second-class citizens—listened intently to Garvey. Federal and New York state intelligence agents listened, too. They brought stenographers to the gathering and took copious notes.[37]

UNIA chapters organized across the country. Chicago opened a chapter. The UNIA and its publication *The Negro World* railed against the riots and used them for recruiting. But the UNIA had no clear political plan to better black life in the United States. In the end, the UNIA did not pressure politicians, help many victims, or take legal action in response to the riots. That difficult work was left to the NAACP.

NAACP leaders viewed Garvey's grandiose histrionics and business schemes with disdain. Du Bois and others were already contacting federal agents to investigate the finances of Garvey's Black Star shipping line, just then purchasing its first ship. Asked about the venture, Du Bois warned a relative, "Don't under any circumstances invest any money in the Black Star Line."[38]

16.

Knoxville

Of all the things that ought to shake our optimism it is this
Knoxville riot.

—Edwin Mims, September 17, 1919

"Sober Knoxville," as civic leaders called it, had a tradition of decent, even enlightened, race relations. Founded in 1786 at a broad bend of the Tennessee River, this mountain outpost grew into an important transportation hub for East Tennessee. When the railroad came, the city became a commercial center. With the approach of the Civil War, most of Knoxville's whites favored secession because of strong ties with southern trade, but most people in the surrounding area opposed it. Some helped the Underground Railroad smuggle slaves to freedom. During the war, Union forces took over Knoxville and made it a supply depot. After the war, ex-slaves from across East Tennessee and western North Carolina made their way to the city. A relatively large black population developed as Knoxville became an industrial powerhouse, with factories and mills producing shoes, clothes, foodstuffs, and other goods. Railroad operations, ironworks, and cement companies hired thousands of blacks, and by 1880 almost a third of the city was African American. Confederate veterans founded the first Ku Klux Klan in central Tennessee, and it thrived across the state during the fight against Reconstruction, but Knoxville stayed free of major racial clashes and lynchings. Blacks were segregated and did not have all rights afforded whites, but within the framework of Jim Crow, they did well. Blacks who paid a poll tax could vote, they could serve on the police force and, in theory, could hold office.[1]

A black middle class developed its own businesses, restaurants, educational institutions, newspaper, and library. In 1875, the Presbyterian Church founded Knoxville College, and by the 1910s the college was one of the nation's leading black institutions of higher learning. The black population was considered stable, safe, and well-off; that is, until massive demographic changes hit Knoxville during the war.

During the 1910s, Knoxville's population more than doubled as factories ginned up to meet the demands of a growing nation and the railroads hired more workers. Many of the city's skilled black laborers left for better-paying jobs up north. Many more rural whites flooded into Knoxville to make more money than they could eke out of small farms in Appalachia. As a result, Knoxville's black population grew during the war, but its overall percentage of the city's population shrank. By 1919, Knoxville's African Americans were more of a minority than they had been in decades. And many of its whites came from remote areas where they knew little of black people beyond prevalent stereotypes.[2]

Writer James Agee was raised in Knoxville. His memoir-novel, *A Death in the Family*, set in 1915, captured the crowded, grimy nature of the city, as well as its racism. The book's main character, six-year-old Rufus Follett, is picked on by older white boys, who claim he has a "nigger" name. His mother warns her son never to use that word, but her opinion is presented as rare among whites. The boys continue to harass Rufus and call out, "Rufus Rastus Johnson Brown! What are you gonna do when the rent comes roun'?"[3]

Knoxville leaders, however, viewed their city as modern and relatively free of racial animosity. Near the war's end, Charles Warner Cansler, black principal of Knoxville Colored High School, wrote to then-governor Tom Rye that "in no place in the world can there be found better relations existing between the races than here in our own county of Knox. No race riot has ever vented its fury here upon any Negro victim."[4]

In August 1919, a business group launched a campaign called "Let's Make Greater Knoxville Greater."[5] British journalist Stephen Graham visited Knoxville in 1919 and was impressed with the bustling, clean city, calling it "one of the most responsible of southern cities."[6] Everyday, both races traveled through the city to their jobs in cotton mills, ironworks, and railroads without incident. In August 1919, the city's black community established its first NAACP branch, but leaders thought the focus of its work would be in rural Tennessee, where the KKK was organizing.

Knoxville was not without problems. Food price increases and wage freezes caused labor strife. City streetcar operators demanded higher wages to meet higher costs. White workers in several industries joined unions but, like in other cities, blacks were reluctant to sign up. Those who joined met prejudice.

In politics, Mayor John E. McMillan, a first-term Democrat, faced a tight reelection against challenger E. W. Neal. Just hitting fifty in 1919, the pudgy, balding McMillan, a bank cashier, spent the summer trying to secure every vote he could, including black support. He campaigned in black areas and openly criticized the resurgent KKK when it set up a branch in Knoxville.[7] White opponents derided him as the "black" candidate.[8]

Knoxville had a crime problem, trumpeted daily in the press. That August, the sensation was the hunt for a serial rapist. During the summer, a criminal described by victims as a light-skinned black man broke into homes and assaulted white women. Alarmed whites blamed Mayor McMillan for what they considered a feeble police response.

But at the close of August, as stifling temperatures relented and the Labor Day weekend arrived, people seemed to put aside these worries and plan for fun. Though black and white workers planned separate festivities in two city parks, free movies, baseball games, fireworks, and a combined parade were all set for Monday. McMillan and Neal planned to deliver speeches.

On Friday, August 29, Governor Albert Roberts was nearby, visiting the Tennessee National Guard's 4th Infantry Regiment, which held its annual two-week training at a rifle range in Fountain City, a Knoxville suburb.[9] A unique brand of progressive, Roberts was both a strong opponent of lynching and a strong supporter of the death penalty, which was banned in Tennessee.

Roberts argued unsuccessfully for anti-lynching legislation in the Tennessee general assembly earlier in the year.[10] He also wanted to restore capital punishment. He believed lynchings were committed by those who were angry that murderers could not be executed by the state. "While I am governor of Tennessee I shall use every means and power at my command to prevent the crime of lynching," Roberts declared after an attempted lynching in January.[11]

Roberts was pro-labor, supported black rights, and was eager to avoid the clashes occurring elsewhere. So far in 1919, Tennessee had been spared a major race or labor confrontation. Riots in Memphis were averted (by luck more than design) and the state only suffered a few lynchings. But Roberts was worried. If something did happen, he feared the state would not be able to intervene. During the war, the state's 3rd Infantry Regiment had been called to fight in France, leaving Tennessee without any infantry. The 4th Regiment was hastily created to fill the gap, but was composed mostly of middle-aged men and boys as young as fifteen. They had completed only a handful of training sessions.

"The State Guard is the only weapon Tennessee has to put down uprising and disorders, and it must be a very efficient organization," Roberts said after seeing the troops at shooting practice.[12] That night, the regiment held a banquet at the park where the white Labor Day festivities were to be held. Roberts and local war heroes were the honored guests. These troops were then allowed weekend liberty. By Saturday, many expected to be heading back to their homes across the state.

But Saturday morning, August 30, about 2:30 a.m., Bertie Lindsey and her cousin, Ora Smyth, awakened to a noise in Lindsey's home.[13] The two white women were terrified. Lindsey's husband was out of town, trying to find work up north in Akron. Smyth told police she saw a black man at the end of the bed. He was holding a gun and a flashlight. She said the man ordered Lindsey to lie on the floor. She did, but then resisted when he tried to molest her. She scrambled for the door. The man shot her once, and she fell dead. He then turned to Smyth and threatened to rape her. She begged him to take her money instead. He grabbed her purse and fled.[14] Police arrived, then put out a call to patrol cars. A patrol car with one white officer, Andy White, and one black, non-officer driver, Jim Smith, was sent to investigate. Smith said later that White told him, "God damned Maurice Mays killed that woman." White denied making such a remark.[15] Ten days before, police picked up Mays on suspicion of prowling outside a white woman's house, but he was released.[16]

White and Mays had had several run-ins in the previous months. At least once, White threatened to break Mays's skull "if he did not quit his ways."[17] According to one historian, Mays, then about thirty, was "one of the most flamboyant and controversial figures in Knoxville. A handsome, debonair black man with skin so light he resembled an Indian."[18] Mays, a notoriously dapper dresser often sporting a bowler hat and a cane, had operated a saloon called the Stroller's Cafe in Knoxville's black neighborhood, known as the Bowery. The saloon allowed blacks and whites to dance together. But by August, Mays had fallen on hard times. The city shut his saloon down months earlier for code violations and arrested him several times for petty crimes.

Mays had spent Friday campaigning for McMillan. Perhaps he wanted the mayor to help him in licensing a new saloon, but rumors abounded that Mays was McMillan's bastard son.[19] At about 3:30 a.m. Saturday, the police officers found Mays in his house a mile from the murder scene. Mays reluctantly answered their repeated knocks. Police said his pants, folded on his bed, were damp. His pistol appeared to have been fired recently and replaced with a fresh cartridge. Mays said he had last fired the gun at a rat four months earlier. The police took him to the murder scene to see if Ora Smyth could identify him. Mays agreed to stand under a bright streetlight. The distraught woman said he was the attacker. He protested three times, and each time she insisted he was the killer. She added that she could identify him by his soft voice.[20] Mays was taken downtown to the small Knoxville jail.[21]

News that an "unnamed Negro" had killed Lindsey made the morning edition of the *Knoxville Journal and Tribune*, and white crowds gathered outside the jail as well as at the funeral home where Lindsey's corpse lay. Police chief Edward M. Haynes was anxious, having read about the riots in Chicago and Washington. He had only 75 to 100 officers on duty at any one time in his city of 77,000. At 8:30 a.m., the chief moved Mays to the Knox County Jail, an imposing brick Victorian building near the county courthouse. The newly elected county sheriff, William T. Cate, lived next to the jail. When a mob formed outside, the anxious Cate sent his wife and children out of town. In the early afternoon, with a judge's permission, he and a railroad agent sneaked Mays out of jail and boarded a Chattanooga-bound train. The sheriff left his nephew, J. Carroll Cate, the chief deputy, as well as his son, R. Austin Cate, in charge of a small group of deputies to defend the jail. With Mays in another city, Cate figured, the angry crowd would disperse.

The mob grew. By midafternoon, several hundred people gathered outside the jail, and thousands more milled about at nearby Market Square, in the heart of the city.[22] When the afternoon edition of the *Knoxville Sentinel* came out with more details of the murder, it sold out in minutes. False rumors swept through the crowd that Lindsey was pregnant and had been raped before she was murdered.

By 6 p.m., the downtown crowd, strengthened by Labor Day weekend loafers, swelled to more than 5,000. Many were drinking moonshine. Eventually, the mob at Market Square marched military-style to the jail. Deputies cowering inside told mob leaders Mays was in Chattanooga. A drunken man in the crowd demanded that a committee be allowed to search the building.

"That nigger is down there and I know it!" he shouted.[23]

The deputies on duty let three different groups to search the jail, but the gestures did not appease the crowd.[24]

Sometime before 8 p.m., Chief Deputy Cate came out of the jail, pulled his revolver, and threatened to shoot anyone who attacked the building. Members of the mob shouted, "Tear down the jail!" Others threw stones at the deputy. Cate hesitated. "He's afraid to shoot!" someone shouted. "Let's go get him, too."

Cate fired a shot, and a dozen in the crowd fired back. Cate ran inside and bolted the jail's heavy riot doors. The deputies killed the lights as stones and bullets shattered every window. Men from the mob ran to the Tennessee River and tore a large piece of timber from a barge and used it to batter the steel door. Others shot at the locks.[25]

For forty-five minutes, the doors held. The deputies repeatedly called city police for help, but no one arrived. The mob looted dynamite from a hardware store and used it to blow the bars off a window. Within minutes, rioters pushed past the deputies, opened the front doors, and hundreds rushed inside.

"I was cuffed about and overpowered, helpless to do anything," said one deputy.

The mob ransacked the building, stealing guns, ammunition, confiscated whisky, and more than $3,000 in cash from a safe. Rioters made off with food, medicine, bedding—anything they could. They cut telephone lines, destroyed furniture, smashed lights. One deputy stood in front of the cellblock for black inmates with his gun drawn and warned no one to enter. The mob backed off, but destroyed much of the rest of the building, tearing out water pipes and releasing every white prisoner, including a murder suspect.[26] When one prisoner refused to leave, a member of the mob shouted, "Get out of here or we'll kill you." Within a half hour, most of the rooms of the jail were burned, defaced, and piled with smashed furniture. All the light fixtures were shattered and the toilets broken. Amid the confusion, Deputy Hall escaped and got to a telephone. He called the mayor, who immediately summoned the Tennessee 4th

Infantry Regiment to come into the city. Most troops were on weekend leave, but at 10 p.m., sixty troops in two squads arrived. The ill-prepared soldiers were overwhelmed, and their weapons taken. Then the mob beat the soldiers and took their uniforms.[27]

Later, Adjutant General Edward Baxter Sweeney, commander of the 4th Infantry, arrived with three companies—about 150 armed men. Sweeney, from the small town of Paris, Tennessee, had served with distinction in France, fighting at Saint-Mihiel and the Argonne forest. He was made an adjutant general of the militia only days after mustering out of the regular army in April 1919.[28] He had been commander of the 4th for only four months, and the two weeks of training just finished was the first chance he had had to lead the men for any length of time.

The Knoxville mob heckled General Sweeney when he arrived, and it appeared as though the emboldened mob might attack his troops as well. But Sweeney addressed the crowd and announced he was sympathetic. He promised Mays would be executed, but urged rioters to disperse.

The crowds refused to leave, but they held off attacking Sweeney and his men. More troops arrived as soldiers on weekend leave were mustered for the emergency. The mob kept pillaging the courthouse, but did not attack the growing contingent of militia.

"The Negro is not here. . . . Go find him, wherever he is . . . . I am not trying to defend any Negro," Sweeney pleaded. "I would like to see the Negro punished as much as you do."

A veteran in the mob then stood up and shouted, "I believe that the Negro is in there, and we are going to get him."[29] The crowd made another demand. They wanted to inspect Sheriff Cate's home, adjacent to the jail. They were convinced Mays was hiding there. Sweeney allowed three groups of twenty-five people to search the house. They found nothing. But after fruitless searches, the mob overwhelmed guards and ransacked the place, smashing furniture, kitchen plates, and beds. They stole anything of value, even the young Cate children's clothing.

As this chaos unfolded, blacks in their neighborhood a few blocks away prepared defenses. Blacks visited hardware stores all day to buy ammunition. So many came to Sam Bower's store that he finally stopped selling bullets to blacks. The move infuriated Joe Etter, a black Spanish-

American War veteran. He threatened the clerk before he stormed out. Earlier in the day, Etter told his wife, "If they're going to have a race riot, I'll be killed in it."[30]

Blacks set up a rough perimeter at the entrance to their area, just northwest of downtown. They shot out streetlights and overturned a gravel truck to strengthen their defensive position.

Dr. Joseph E. Carty, the white owner of the Economy Drug Company near the Bowery entrance at Vine and Central, was closing up his store at 11 p.m. when he noticed about a hundred blacks on the corner, looking anxiously toward the courthouse. Many were armed. At 11:30, a group of armed white men appeared and the two sides exchanged gunfire. The whites ran back to the jail. Carty did not know who started the shooting, but he knew he had to get out of there.

"I said to the boy helping me in the store that it was time we were getting out of the place," he said later. "I had about $3,000 in the cash drawer and safe. I grabbed that, started my car and wheeled off. . . . In a brief interval I heard general firing begin."[31]

The white group rushed back to the mob at the jail and urged the militia to return with them. They claimed blacks had shot two militiamen on Vine Street. This was not true, but Sweeney sent troops to investigate, with a horde of rioters following. The mob now had official sanction.[32]

White rioters broke into hardware stores and took pistols, rifles, and bullets, and anything that could be used as a weapon: pokers, razors, axes, meat cleavers.[33] The riot had been expanding downtown for six hours. Now it degenerated into a full-fledged battle. Vine Street became a no-man's-land and steady gunfire echoed through Knoxville for the first time since the Civil War.

Jim Henson, a black man, was the first to die, firing at the mob as it moved to attack Vine and Central.

Soon two militia machine gun units arrived. Sweeney was the commanding officer, but it is unclear if he was at the scene and ordered them to take position. The two teams set up their guns on large tripods at Vine and State as the gun battle raged between the militia and whites on one side and black defenders of the Bowery on the other.[34] The guns were the most powerful weapons in the militia's arsenal short of artillery and could fire at least 450 rounds per minute. Clear command and control when using these guns were vital.

The next year, riot expert Henry Bellows warned against using

machine guns for riot control, because a slight misfire could lead to dozens killed or injured: "The machine gun has been more talked about than
any other weapon in connection with riot duty, and yet, in the United
States at least, it has practically never been used. The reason is obvious: all
the objections that apply to the use of rifle fire against crowds and mobs
apply with multiple force to the employment of machine guns." If such
guns were to be used, he argued, officers must be certain of a clear field
of fire.[35] This was not done in Knoxville.

The machine gun units set up and joined the gun battle on the side of
the white rioters. Gun smoke clouded the street, making it hard to see.
Lieutenant James W. Payne, a regular army officer from Kentucky attached
to the Tennessee guard as an instructor, took two men and moved down
the street shortly before 1:40 a.m. What the men were doing was not
clear. Some witnesses reported they were trying on their own to pinpoint
the positions of black snipers. Others said they were ordered forward by
the machine gunners.[36] After Payne and his men advanced about 200
yards, black defenders with rifles opened fire from a second-story window. Whites returned fire.

One reporter noted: "Several [white] civilians were handling the firearms carelessly and endangering the lives of the soldiers by shooting at
every moving object. Some of them were drunk."[37]

Someone behind the machine guns shouted, "Let them have it!" and
the guns opened up down the street.[38] The gunners could not see their
targets but kept firing anyway, because white mob members behind them
claimed a contingent of armed black men was bearing down on their position. The guns were in fact trained on Payne and his men. The lieutenant
scrambled behind a telephone pole, but his body was riddled. A private
was also hit. For at least three minutes, machine gunnery crews sprayed
enfilading fire up and down the street. Because of the noise, their crews
could not hear pleas from other troops to stop shooting. A reporter at the
scene described Payne's body as "folded up like a crumpled dollar bill."
The private begged the reporter to call an ambulance. "I am shot through
and through," he said before passing out.[39]

The frantic commander of the machine guns finally stopped the firing,
but not until the entire area was sprayed. Large-caliber bullets from the
Brownings punched holes in Carty's store windows "as easily and smoothly
as punching holes through a sheet of paper with a pencil," a reporter
wrote. The store was destroyed. A nearby soda shack was also hit, with
stick candy and soda sprayed all over the sidewalk.[40]

The black fighters were driven down the street, but kept up sporadic fire. Several times they regrouped and tried to capture the machine gun emplacements. Joe Etter, who had predicted his own death earlier in the day, was shot and killed near the machine guns. Gunfire spread, as groups of whites and blacks maneuvered in nearby alleys and side streets. Prostitutes and johns ran out of buildings; patrons fled illegal saloons.

Residents cowered in their homes. Knoxville General Hospital filled to capacity. Blacks fled their neighborhood and hid in nearby forests, churches, cemeteries, and boxcars. A young white girl recalled seeing blacks running down the street "like rabbits."[41]

The militia spent hours battling black defenders, but did nothing to disperse the white mob that had destroyed the county's jail and was now serving as the militia's riffraff auxiliary. Finally, at 3:15 a.m., the regiment's full contingent, about 1,100 men, arrived and deployed in the downtown area. It drove the remaining black defenders from their makeshift barricades. The ebullient white mob rushed to attack the black neighborhood, but the militia abruptly stopped them, presumably under orders from Sweeney. Perhaps Sweeney felt he could impose order because he finally had enough troops and the rioters were running out of energy by early morning. Troops armed with machine guns set up a cordon around the Bowery. Whites were not allowed in and blacks were not allowed out.

The Knoxville riot was over. But for roughly six hours, a white mob numbering in the thousands destroyed a jail, plundered a sheriff's home, and assaulted law officers, state militia, and innocent civilians. They instigated a gun battle with defenders of Knoxville's black neighborhood and were joined by state militia in the effort. In that running battle, stores were destroyed and other buildings were riddled with bullets.[42] "The miracle of the whole thing is, the police say, that more persons were not killed," a reporter noted.[43]

The riot set off a panic among blacks throughout East Tennessee. A reporter witnessed "a hegira of Negroes" walking out of the city, fleeing in cars and crowding at train depots. "Many of them carried their worldly possessions in suitcases, trunks and other containers," the man wrote. "It was a pathetic sight."[44]

⊂⊃

The night of rioting transformed Knoxville into an armed camp. In addition to the 1,100 state militiamen, the city's 75 police, plus an emergency auxiliary of 200 special officers and 75 deputy sheriffs, patrolled the city. They responded to riot calls all day Sunday. The mayor imposed a 10 p.m. curfew. There was sporadic shooting, mostly by jumpy militia firing at black civilians. Hundreds of weapons were confiscated. Fearful blacks did not go to work at restaurants and hotels.[45]

Mayor McMillan met with General Sweeney, then traveled the city urging people to disarm.[46]

White ministers preached about the riot. "Even the Negro under arrest should have a chance to prove his case," the Reverend Len G. Boughton, pastor of the First Baptist Church, told his congregation.[47]

Black churches did not meet that Sunday for fear of inciting white mobs. Blacks objected to being searched by soldiers, especially since troops sided with the white mob during the riot and harassed blacks afterward. One black man working for an undertaker even had his hearse searched for weapons.[48]

"There is very little difference in being mobbed by lawless citizens and being victims of a mob of soldiers," said Charles Cansler, a school principal who was also an activist and leader in black Knoxville.[49]

Harlem radical Cyril Briggs saw Knoxville as another example of white military and police favoring whites over blacks: "And once again it has been made but too apparent that not only have the authorities no intention of protecting the Negro in his rights but that when he beats back the wanton aggression of white mobs these are usually reinforced, aided and abetted by the white militia and regulars called out to preserve 'law and order.' "[50]

Rumors spread among whites and blacks that as many as fifty people had been killed. But the coroner refused to conduct an inquest, so no one ever knew. Dozens were seriously injured. People were so desperate for information that newspaper carriers were mugged for their editions.[51]

On Labor Day, union leaders called off a parade and politicians cancelled their speeches, though blacks and whites held subdued festivals in separate parks as planned.[52] An advertisement announced amnesty would be granted to those who returned guns stolen from the jail or the hardware stores. About 250 were returned, though many more had been stolen. By Tuesday, most of the troops withdrew, though special police stayed at the courthouse, just in case.[53]

The riot crushed McMillan's reelection chances. His political posters were defaced, and black voters, whose support he courted, were afraid to go to the polls. He was roundly defeated on September 6.[54]

The riot worried blacks throughout the region. At one point in the riot, five trucks of white rioters headed off for Chattanooga, intent on lynching Mays. Though they never showed up, the news panicked blacks there.[55] When Stephen Graham visited Chattanooga months later, he found them still frightened. White toughs had been starting fights with blacks on trolleys, promising Chattanooga was next.

Graham found blacks "were ready to seize the first opportunity to go northward. Mr. T——said, 'They might kill us all.' Mrs. W——said: 'All who have children want to go away. There'll be no chance for our children here. Before the war it was much better, but they seem to dislike us more now.' "[56]

The Knoxville riot had occurred in a supposedly "modern" city in a southern state led by a progressive governor. The violence—complete with drunken whites destroying a county jail, ransacking the sheriff's home, and looting downtown businesses—exploded southerners' smug view that they only lynched guilty individuals, whereas northerners attacked blacks solely because of their skin color. The *Knoxville Journal and Tribune*, while stressing Mays should be executed, was stunned by the chaos.

"Knoxville for more than 48 hours has stood in the presence of a crisis which demands the thoughtful and prayerful consideration of every good man and good woman irrespective of race and color," the editors wrote.[57]

In September, members of the Commission on Interracial Cooperation, progressive James Hardy Dillard's group that was trying to quietly improve race relations in the South, met in Atlanta with the YMCA and others. Dillard tried to sound optimistic and told the group that in the South, "I see on all sides a feeling of good fellowship developing in a nice way." But the bad news of Knoxville was clear.

Edwin Mims, a prominent literature professor from Vanderbilt University in Nashville, told the group that Knoxville was a frightening warning to the South: "Of all the things that ought to shake our optimism it is this Knoxville riot. It is the last place a thing like this should have been expected to happen."[58]

The loose-knit group, dominated by white southerners, took no immediate action. In fact, it would not hold another meeting until 1920.

But James Weldon Johnson, a black southerner, was quick to use Knoxville for political effect. He wrote to Senator Charles Curtis of Kansas, whom he met after the Washington riot. Johnson urged Curtis to call for congressional hearings on the violence. It was an ambitious idea, one that underscored both the urgency of the situation and the political will of Johnson and other NAACP leaders. Congress had not conducted hearings on racial violence since the 1870s. Johnson gambled, however, that with the right support on the Hill and national alarm, he could make it happen. He would make his push in September.

Johnson had a lot of work to do, but he was confident he had a unified and growing political movement behind him. In the *New York Age*, Johnson wrote of white rioters: "The poor fools! Can't they understand that the more Negroes they outrage, the more determined the whole race becomes to secure the full rights and privileges of freemen? And this determination cannot be destroyed by lynching a dozen Negroes a day."[59]

17.

A New Negro

*Brothers we are on the Great Deep. We have cast off on
the vast voyage which will lead to Freedom or Death.*
— W. E. B. Du Bois, *The Crisis*, September 1919

BY EARLY SEPTEMBER, RACIAL HOSTILITY WAS PANDEMIC. IN SAN
Francisco, soldiers and sailors from the Presidio attacked a black neighborhood after blacks beat a drunken sailor for insulting them. More than
a thousand servicemen, armed with weapons stolen from shooting galleries, vowed to clean out the Barbary Coast. Police and Navy provost
guards had to quell the fighting.[1]

In Harlem, a black mob scuffled with a plainclothes police officer
after he shot and killed a black man. Other whites gathered to defend the
officer and more shots were fired. Some in the crowd shouted, "Lynch
him!" as other police came to whisk away the injured officer. Police went
through the neighborhood wielding billy clubs on those who would not
disperse.[2]

Lynchings continued in the South, including in places like Monroe,
Louisiana; Jacksonville, Florida; and Oglethorpe County, Georgia. In
Memphis, a white mob tried to lynch Henry Johnson, a black driver who
struck and slightly injured some white children with his car. The mob
placed a noose around Johnson's neck when a white man, Jack Stewart,
intervened, telling the mob to let police handle the matter. Instead, the
crowd tried to hang him as well. Police rescued the two just in time.[3]
Other minorities became victims. In Pueblo, Colorado, a mob seized two
Mexican immigrants accused of killing a police officer and hanged them

from a bridge. Police and volunteers were put on duty during the night and the next day to stop any further trouble as hundreds of Mexican immigrants filed through the morgue to view the bodies. No one was arrested for the lynchings.[4]

Police across the country conducted riot drills and stockpiled riot equipment. In September, Savannah police said they did not expect trouble in their city, yet they purchased pump-action shotguns, bayonets, riot guns, and 10,000 rounds of ammunition.[5] State militias were put on alert.

Pundits and politicians offered up analysis of and solutions for the escalating "Negro problem." William Monroe Trotter's National Equal Rights League pushed for the United States to take over some or all of Imperial Germany's African colonies and encourage black Americans to colonize them.[6] A black mailman from New Orleans wrote Woodrow Wilson outlining a plan for a government loan program to keep black farmers in the South. The plan required blacks to pay into a fund that then would invest in property and aid black agriculture. "There must be a complete revolution in sentiment as to the status of the Negro," W. W. Kerr wrote. Wilson did not respond.[7]

On the bucolic campus of Alabama's Tuskegee Institute, that bastion of racial acquiescence, Booker T. Washington's political heir Robert Moton watched the unfolding crisis with astonishment. Washington had promised a segregated but prosperous South, where the social role of African Americans would be secondary but secure. This concept of a benevolent, segregated society, embodied in Washington's 1895 speech to the Cotton States and International Exposition in Atlanta, guided political thinking for decades, despite dissenters like Du Bois. Now this idea was evaporating. Blacks balked at being second-class. Many whites, in the North and the South, rejected blacks getting secure positions in society whether they were subservient or not. On September 4, Moton told the press: "I hope our leaders in every community, white and black, will get together and smooth out matters that are misunderstood, so that America can teach the world that black people and white people can live peacefully and harmoniously in our great country."[8]

When his mentor Washington issued such pronouncements, they had the impact of papal bulls among blacks. Now Moton's words were barely acknowledged. The mantle of black political leadership clearly had been passed to the NAACP. William Scarborough, the sixty-seven-year-old president of Wilberforce University in Ohio, spent decades battling against segregation laws and for educational improvements for blacks. The longtime NAACP supporter was thrilled by what he was seeing.

"The spirit of the Negro who went across the seas—who was in action, and who went 'over the top'—is by no means the spirit of the Negro before the war," he declared. "It is a new Negro that we have with us now, and may we not hope also that we have a new white man?"[9]

Postwar inflation, commonly called "HCL" for high cost of living, hit everyone, and strikes abounded. On September 9, Boston police struck, plunging the city into chaos until Governor Calvin Coolidge, a Republican, sent in Massachusetts militia to restore order and break the strike.[10] Later that month, the American Federation of Labor ignored pleas from Woodrow Wilson and launched a coordinated strike of 400,000 steel workers across the country. It was the largest strike up to that point in American history.[11] Steel operations from Colorado to Pennsylvania shut down. The effort, led in part by future American Communist leader William Z. Foster, stalled as the steel companies brought in tens of thousands of strikebreakers.[12] Strikers were killed and wounded in clashes with police.[13] Corporate publicity agents and journalists stoked fears that the nation stood on the brink of revolution.[14] Hopeful leftists believed it, too. Eugene Debs, the sixty-three-year-old Socialist Party leader then in federal prison for a sedition conviction, saw the labor situation unraveling: "The fight is on and I can foresee a possible revolution as the outcome of the present struggle."[15]

Riot insurance tripled in areas around steel plants and heavily industrialized cities. In one ten-day period in September, brokers wrote between $100 million and $200 million in riot policies—an enormous amount at the time.[16]

Race was enmeshed in the labor crisis.[17] Steel corporations hired as many as 40,000 southern blacks as strikebreakers. They transported the black workers, and housed them in barracks to keep them from angry union members.[18] The move helped disrupt the strike's momentum in major steel areas like Pittsburgh, Chicago, and Gary, Indiana.

"The colored man is not very responsive to trade unionism, he seems to feel he can best solve his problem by breaking down the white working man," Foster said.

White workers attacked blacks at picket lines in Indiana, Illinois, Pennsylvania, and Ohio. Black strikebreakers armed themselves. The cynical motives in using black workers were transparent. Months later, when the strike collapsed, company officials told a church group investigating what happened: "Niggers did it."[19]

Amid the labor clashes, many white workers turned to extremist groups. The newly formed Communist and Communist Labor parties sapped supporters from the more traditional Socialist Party. In late September, the Socialist Party tried to expand its shrinking base by passing a resolution to send organizers among black workers. In the middle of September, a radical black union called the National Brotherhood of Workers of America held a convention in Washington. The group allowed the I.W.W. to have three seats, but barred the AFL.[20]

Black recruitment to the white leftist parties remained insignificant, though blacks joined the NAACP and Marcus Garvey's UNIA in droves in response to the riots.

In September, Garvey spoke in various cities, and UNIA chapters formed across the country. Appealing to "All Thoughtful Negroes Who Desire to Prepare Against the Future," he collected tens of thousands of dollars for his Black Star shipping line.[21] By September 14, he purchased his first ship, the *Yarmouth*, and docked the boat off Harlem, with fanfare. He rechristened it the *Frederick Douglass*. The publicity brought in more money. The UNIA also formed the African Blood Brotherhood, a self-described defense organization to protect blacks from riots and lynching. The small group accomplished little, but it did alarm federal agents, just then planning a nationwide roundup of Marxists and anarchists. Du Bois considered Garvey a charlatan, but could not ignore the man's growing appeal.

The Ku Klux Klan, presenting itself as a defender of Anglo-Saxon civilization, also found broad appeal. It set up chapters across the South and launched chapters in the Midwest. Money for memberships, uniforms, booklets, and other material poured into the KKK's Atlanta headquarters. The organization railed against blacks, Catholics, immigrants, Communists, socialists, and unions.

Pundits fretted. Syndicated columnist Newell Dwight Hillis wrote: "Enemies are abroad in the land, lighting the flames of class hatred and organizing their forces for revolution." He quoted a radical pamphlet: "Once black men waited to be emancipated; now white men wait for Trotzky [*sic*]. Our slavery in the American factory is worse than that of Uncle Tom." Hillis titled his essay, for the popular *McClure's Magazine*, "What Is the Matter with the United States?"[22]

Political leaders jockeyed for position, as the country's domestic relations unraveled and the 1920 presidential contest loomed. The public was riveted by the showdown between majority Republicans in the Senate, the elected body responsible for approving all treaties, and Woodrow Wilson, who staked his presidential legacy on passage of the Versailles Peace Treaty. Republicans argued the treaty would surrender American sovereignty and tie the country to European intrigue. Wilson, who had spent months in France negotiating the agreement, considered it the key to lasting world peace. He bent his waning energies to one purpose: the treaty's passage.[23]

In September, Wilson struck out on a 10,000-mile whistle-stop tour to rally public support. He met enthusiastic crowds, but the political tide was against him. In Seattle, he implored the GOP to "forget there is an election in 1920," as if such a thing were possible.[24]

On the stump, Wilson made his only recorded public utterance about the Red Summer violence. It was one sentence. In Helena, Montana, he said as an aside to the crowd, "And I hope you will not think it inappropriate if I stop here to express my shame as an American citizen at the race riots that have occurred in some places in this country where men have forgotten humanity and justice and ordered society and have run amuck."[25]

On the trip, Wilson's health flagged severely. After delivering a speech in Pueblo, Colorado, on September 25, Wilson suffered what his doctor suspected was a minor stroke. Wilson wept to his personal secretary, "I seem to have gone to pieces."[26] The tour was cancelled and the train rushed back to Washington. He suffered a much more serious stroke October 2 that left him paralyzed.

Wilson would remain in office for another year and a half, but his presidency was effectively over. In late September, black ministers delivered 30,000 signatures to the White House asking for clemency for Washington blacks charged with petty crimes in the riot. The incapacitated Wilson never responded.[27]

Organizations like the NAACP did not mourn Wilson's exit from the political arena.[28] Wilson's illness allowed the NAACP to more aggressively press Republicans in Congress, who felt emboldened by the president's

decline. James Weldon Johnson found it easier to forge a small but growing coalition of those sympathetic to the NAACP.

But Wilson's illness created a power vacuum. The lack of presidential
direction left attorney general A. Mitchell Palmer and his Justice Department staff to their own devices in cracking down on subversives. Palmer
was under intense public pressure to strike at radicals. He prepared a
national sweep to round up many and deport them. His assistant J. Edgar
Hoover was convinced that black organizations were involved and had
sparked many racial clashes.

Following the Knoxville riot, the NAACP went into action on a scale
never seen before, not only in the history of the organization but in the
history of any American black rights organization. It added more branches
and members. It petitioned politicians, met with the media, and raised
money for court battles. Other groups like the UNIA followed suit but
on a much smaller scale.

Writing in *The Crisis*, Du Bois seemed particularly attuned to this
general shift in black awareness.[29] "Brothers we are on the Great Deep," he
wrote. "We have cast off on the vast voyage which will lead to Freedom or
Death. For three centuries we have suffered and cowered. No race ever
gave Passive Resistance and Submission to Evil longer, more piteous trial.
Today we raise the terrible weapon of Self-Defense. When the armed
lynchers gather, we too must gather armed. When the mob moves, we propose to meet it with bricks and clubs and guns."[30]

Du Bois kept articulating the group's views in *The Crisis*, but cut back
on public events. His nerves were shot from too much work. James Weldon Johnson took up more responsibilities, with Walter White's assistance. In September, Johnson, the former diplomat, marshaled the group's
members to cajole and prod the small but growing coalition of congressmen sympathetic to the NAACP. September 1919 would be a high point
of Johnson's political efforts, and his hard work would pay off.

Since the Washington riot in July, Johnson had gone several times
from New York to the capital to meet with elected officials. Starting in
September, he focused much of his energy on Senator Charles Curtis of
Kansas. On September 3, right after Knoxville, Johnson sent Curtis a note
urging him to make good on a tentative promise to call for a hearing on
the racial violence. Johnson told him at least four other Republican senators supported the measure.

"Since I talked to you last, we have had another race riot—the one in Knoxville, Tenn., which, although not so great in extent as the Washington and Chicago riots, is, nevertheless, fully as serious and as ominous," he wrote.[31] He also enclosed a report outlining why a federal investigation of lynching was needed. Johnson highlighted the racial violence so far in 1919 and determined, as best as possible, that 43 black men and four white men had been lynched. Also eight black men had been burned at the stake. Some of the numbers and dates of incidents in Johnson's report were inaccurate, largely because the NAACP gathered information piecemeal from members and from clippings in the New York newspapers. Often the number of victims was undercounted because New York newspapers usually stopped covering an incident after a day or two. But the portrait Johnson painted of American race relations was gruesome enough. Johnson used a range of arguments in the brief, including the legal, political, economic, and even psychological impact of lynching on society. He quoted a New York neurologist who declared lynching was "an act of perversion only found in those suffering from extreme forms of sexual perversion."[32]

Johnson did not mention black equal rights guaranteed under the Constitution. He knew such an argument held no sway in the all-white Congress.[33]

Curtis used the brief, as well as the NAACP pamphlet *Thirty Years of Lynching in the United States, 1889–1918,* as the basis for his resolution, which he submitted on September 22.[34]

Once Curtis made his request, Johnson telegrammed all NAACP state branches. He wanted 100,000 telegrams and letters sent to senators to press the Judiciary committee to take up the matter. The telegram stated: "STRONG PUSH NOW WILL PUT IT OVER. . . . CALL MASS MEETING. EXPLAIN MEASURE AND SPUR PEOPLE TO ACTION."[35]

Johnson knew there was little chance to pass anti-lynching legislation that session. But he thought the racial violence of 1919, combined with an emboldened Republican Congress, meant national hearings on the matter were possible. Enlisting Curtis, the Republican minority whip in the Senate, was a shrewd move. Curtis was no flighty do-gooder. Instead, he was the ultimate insider, a "whisperer" on the Senate floor who made things happen.[36] "You boys tell me what you want, and I'll get it through," he once told fellow Republicans.[37]

With the Republican takeover of the Senate in 1918, he became one of the most powerful men in American government.[38] But Curtis also had a unique story that made him amenable to the NAACP's mission. "Indian

Charley" was half Native American and spent much of his childhood on a Kaw reservation. The short, heavy man spoke Kansa before he spoke English. He rode ponies bareback and could hunt with a bow and arrow. He had fought to secure Indian rights and knew how to battle from a position of weakness within a legislative body.

Johnson's efforts excited the NAACP's rank and file, and members sent in petitions, money, and suggestions. One supporter recommended that black churches and social groups be sent form letters for members to sign and then send to Congress. NAACP supporters learned that mere altruism did not move politicians. The game was about power. On September 23, Johnson held meetings all day with politicians and black leaders in Washington. Then he returned to New York "to start the whole machinery of the Association on the Curtis Resolution."[39]

The NAACP national office worked at a frenzied pace. At its monthly meeting, the board discussed sending out a flurry of press releases and pamphlets. In a five-week period, the board accepted 27 new chapters. They came from all over: Keokuk, Iowa; San Bernardino, California; Saginaw, Michigan; and anywhere blacks felt compelled to organize to protect their community.

The board reviewed reports from its legal committee. By fall 1919, the courts were becoming a main avenue for the association to pursue its agenda and defend black citizens on multiple fronts. In Chicago, the association raised thousands of dollars for the legal defense of blacks arrested in the riot. In Texas, it explored hiring lawyers to sue the state of Texas for the attack on John Shillady. The group also aided those arrested in Washington. The NAACP also fought discrimination, from inadequate schools for black children to the treatment of black travelers on railroads.

The organization's $2,000 legal budget for 1919 had been spent, and as the fall began new cases piled up. The board planned to approach wealthy donors by the end of the year.

Though it was the most active and visible, the NAACP was not the only black organization launching legal challenges to unequal application of the laws and antiblack violence. From Memphis to Washington, blacks by themselves and in groups were organizing, filing lawsuits, and hiring lawyers.[40]

In east Georgia, Joe Ruffin's white lawyer, Archibald Blackshear, pressed a Jenkins County judge to move Ruffin's coming murder trial out of the county. Although Ruffin sold his land to raise money for Blackshear's services, the prominent white lawyer's motivations certainly went beyond financial recompense. He was taking the case of a black man charged with murdering two white law officers in a rural county near his home in Augusta. It was dangerous work. All over America in 1919, whites and blacks were taking such risks to counter lawlessness.

On September 6, Blackshear filed his motion with Judge Archibald B. Lovett of the Jenkins County Superior Court. Blackshear's argument was simple: Joe Ruffin could not expect a fair trial with an impartial jury and the county sheriff could not protect him from getting lynched. The minds of Jenkins County residents "have been poisoned against him," Blackshear argued.[41]

The judge ordered a hearing. Blackshear drove down to Jenkins County to argue his request at the county courthouse. The transcripts of that hearing have been lost, but Blackshear won the motion when a prosecution witness testified he could not say what would happen if Ruffin was tried and acquitted. It was clear any trial in Jenkins County would be a farce.

The judge ruled that if a mob would just lynch Ruffin in the case of acquittal, then "the trial would amount to no trial at all. It would be merely a lynching under the forms of law."

On September 26, Judge Lovett ordered the trial moved to the coastal city of Savannah, 70 miles south of Millen. Lovett ordered the change, he said, "in the interest of justice to this darkey."[42]

18.

Omaha

While his feet were still dancing in the air, they riddled his
body with bullets. It was the most horrendous sight.

—HENRY FONDA, fourteen, witness to the Omaha riot

IN 1919, NEBRASKA SEEMED AN ODD SPOT FOR A RACE RIOT. THE
state was less than 1 percent black, with an economy powered by small
farmers, almost all of them native-born.[1] But Omaha, Nebraska's largest
city with 191,000 residents, was different from the rest of the state. Set on
the western bank of the Missouri River on the edge of the central Great
Plains, the city grew as a staging area for settlers seeking land claims to
the West. With the railroad, Omaha became a center for getting goods to
farmers and for shipping farm products east. Thanks to railroads and the
proximity to large cattle ranches, the city became the nation's third-
largest meatpacking center, hiring thousands of workers to slaughter cattle, dress the meat, and ship it. Thousands of other unskilled laborers
worked for the railroads.[2]

The white population of Omaha was a conglomeration of immigrants, including Czechs, Germans, Russian Jews, Swedes, Italians, and
Poles. Blacks lived north of downtown.[3] Though Nebraska's black population was small, it doubled during World War One and almost all of that
growth was in Omaha, where 78 percent of the state's blacks lived. More
than half of Omaha's black laborers worked in the stockyards. Most
migrated from the South.[4]

To outsiders, Omaha looked like an American success story of peace
and prosperity, where capital, labor, and agriculture worked in harmony.

Carl Ackerman, the nationally syndicated conservative columnist for the *Philadelphia Public Ledger,* visited Omaha in late August 1919 and bragged about skyscrapers and factories rising across the city. He saw a smiling police officer directing traffic and declared the sight to be "not only an example but a sermon in civic democracy." Unlike elsewhere in America, "The city had forgotten strikes existed."[5]

But Ackerman's serene assessment of Omaha was wrong. In truth, Omaha's workers were seething over job losses and the rising cost of living. That summer, boilermakers, bricklayers, tailors, telegraphers, teamsters, truck drivers, newspaper reporters, butchers, stockyard workers, and even downtown cooks struck. Police and firefighters threatened to walk out as well if they did not get pay increases.

Race became a factor in these disputes, with companies using non-union blacks as scabs. During the summer, Omaha newspapers reported trainloads of black strikebreakers arriving in the city—raising racial tensions.[6]

Omaha politics were in turmoil. A year earlier, reform candidate Edward Parsons Smith, backed by the churches and the county dry league, defeated the three-term pro-saloon Mayor "Cowboy" Jim Dahlman. Born on a farm in Iowa, Smith moved to Nebraska in 1890, and built a successful law practice. Though he served as Nebraska's assistant attorney general for two years and campaigned for populist presidential candidate William Jennings Bryan, he never sought elected office prior to running as a progressive coalition's mayoral candidate in 1918. To the stupefaction of Omaha's corrupt political establishment, he won.[7]

Smith defeated the machine of Tom Dennison, a Dahlman supporter who ran his operations out of the back of a bar. Dennison was a behind-the-scenes politico tied to bars, gambling operations, and brothels.[8] After Dahlman's defeat, Dennison teamed up with *Omaha Bee* publisher Edward Rosewater to attack the Smith administration and to undercut the reformists. The *Bee* reported an alleged crime wave involving black criminals. Police commissioner John Dean Ringer, a progressive attorney and Smith ally, was a focus of the newspaper's diatribes.

Smith and Ringer created a special morals squad, fulfilling a campaign promise. On Labor Day, a black bellhop was killed in a vice raid on a hotel, infuriating blacks and whites. The ongoing strikes and unpopular vice squad hurt Smith's popularity. In the summer of 1919, opponents launched a petition drive to recall Smith. The effort fell short of forcing a special election, but the group gathered 5,000 signatures.[9]

Rosewater's *Bee* stepped up stories about "Negro" attacks and the administration's failure to make arrests. Smith's law firm once defended a black man accused of raping white women, a point often repeated by critics.[10] Between June 7 and September 27, 21 women in Omaha reported they were assaulted, 16 by black men.[11] Antiblack sentiment had a long tradition in the city. In 1891, a white mob took a black man accused of rape from the jail and hanged him from a lamppost. Officials trying to stop the lynching had been shouted down. Firefighting crews who responded to the riot had their fire hoses cut.[12]

Omaha's black community, meanwhile, was highly politicized and well organized. As early as 1917, George Wells Parker, a Harvard-educated community leader, formed the Hamitic League of the World in Omaha and began giving speeches on black contributions to early civilizations.[13] By 1919, the NAACP had a strong Omaha branch with hundreds of members. Harrison J. Pinkett, the state's first university-educated black attorney and a veteran who served as a first lieutenant in France, was one of its founders.[14] Du Bois even visited in the spring of 1919 and spoke to a packed lecture hall. The branch led campaigns against discrimination and unfair press coverage. In April, 600 blacks came to an NAACP-led meeting to lodge complaints to the police chief concerning insensitive remarks by Omaha police about blacks arrested for various crimes. The NAACP also complained the *Bee* was fomenting trouble between the races.[15] Omaha's other major newspapers were more subdued, but the *Bee* paid no heed to black complaints—it was out to unseat Smith.

⟜⟝

On Thursday night, September 25, a white couple, Agnes Loebeck, nineteen, and her disabled boyfriend, Millard Hoffman, twenty-three, were walking home in South Omaha.[16] At 11:45 p.m., according to the two, a black man with a pistol knocked Hoffman to the ground, then dragged Loebeck by her hair into underbrush and raped her. The attack lasted about 15 minutes.[17]

The Friday edition of the *Bee* reported the attack by a "Black Beast."[18] On Saturday, police arrested Willie Brown, a forty-one-year-old packing house worker who suffered from acute rheumatism. Brown, arrested at his apartment on the south side of the city, had moved to Omaha just months earlier, possibly from Tennessee.[19] A photograph purportedly of

Brown shows a man with a dark complexion wearing a workman's hat and staring mournfully past the camera.[20]

The police brought Brown to Loebeck's home where both Loebeck and Hoffman identified him as the assailant.[21] A crowd of 250 angry whites gathered around the home, and police were only able to get Brown to jail after reinforcements and an hour of negotiation. Commissioner Ringer put extra officers on duty all night in case of trouble.[22]

That night and Sunday morning were calm. But at 1 p.m. Sunday, about 50 to 60 white men and teens met at a school near Loebeck's home.[23] Loebeck had recently graduated from the school, and many of those gathered were her old classmates. Hoffman, Loebeck's disabled boyfriend, led the call for Brown's lynching. An hour later, the group marched to the courthouse, where Brown was being held. By then the mob had grown to 600.

The six-story Douglas County Courthouse cost $1.5 million to build when it opened in 1912. The Renaissance Revival building was a downtown landmark.[24] The building had several entrances so it was difficult for a small group to defend its lower floors. The jail cells, however, were on upper floors and access could be cut off by a few defenders at the stairwells.

When the crowd first arrived, two dozen police and county deputies were on duty. Two hours later, the mob had swelled to an estimated 4,000, while the force of police and deputies had grown to only about 100.[25]

In a standoff that lasted into the evening, the mob milled around the courthouse, calling for Brown's death. Outnumbered police stood guard at the building. Chief Marshal Eberstein decided the situation would not escalate. He sent 50 policemen home.

After they left, a school friend of Loebeck's, William Francis, rode across the courthouse lawn on a white horse, exhorting the crowd with a rope dangling from his saddle.

Around 5:15 p.m., the rowdy crowd surged forward. Officers countered by spraying rioters with a hose, which only made them angrier.[26] Chief Eberstein ordered people to leave. The crowd jeered him. A black police officer, William Ransom, pulled his revolver, which infuriated the mob. He was ordered inside. Authorities allowed two groups from the mob to search the jail, while the police hid Brown upstairs. The crowd was not placated.[27]

The throng swelled with angry rioters and onlookers. Estimates ranged from 5,000 to as many as 15,000 people crowding downtown by Sunday evening.[28] Any black men walking nearby were chased and beaten. Two small girls with pails full of stones walked through the crowd handing them out.[29] The mob broke into two gun stores, stealing weapons and ammunition. Soon men with shotguns stood at each courthouse entrance so Brown could not escape. Shots rang out. A white man climbed on a truck and shouted, "We'll get the nigger if we have to burn the whole shack down." Rioters set gasoline fires at the doorways as the crowd cheered. Some onlookers waved American flags.[30]

When the crowd learned Mayor Smith was upstairs with police, another shouted, "He's a Negro lover. They elected him. He's no better than they are!"

To this point, troops could have dispersed the crowd. Allan Tukey, the American Legion post commander in Omaha, estimated that "a squad [about ten soldiers and an officer] could have stopped everything."[31]

Federal officials were aware of the courthouse trouble from the start. Several federal prisoners were housed there, giving them legal justification to intervene. Under Secretary of War Newton Baker's 1917 authorization, federal troops could act without a formal request from local officials to the president or the secretary.[32] Lieutenant Colonel Jacob Wuest, commander at Fort Omaha, refused to act, however, convinced he could not unless directed by President Wilson or Baker.[33] Wuest's hesitation may have stemmed from fear. Most of the men in his garrison were green recruits training how to operate observation balloons.[34] In the coming hours, local police, elected officials, and even the federal marshal in Omaha called Wuest for help. He turned them all down, claiming it was beyond his authority. He did order troops to prepare for action. The soldiers took machine guns out of storage.[35]

After 5:30 p.m., the crowd—thousands of men, women, and children— rushed the courthouse's large oak doors, cracking one that led to the basement. "Hang the nigger!" a rioter shouted. "And if you can't get him, get someone else!"[36]

Douglas County sheriff Michael Clark, his deputies, and police retreated. To try to scare the crowd, police fired shots into an elevator shaft. This riled the mob even further.[37]

At 7 p.m., Clark, Eberstein, and their men fled to higher floors with 121 prisoners. Rioters and police exchanged gunfire. A member of the mob, sixteen-year-old Louis Young, was killed as he led rioters to attack the fourth floor. Two blocks away, a thirty-four-year-old businessman,

James Hykell, who was not involved in the riot, was struck by stray bullets. He later died.[38]

Using cans of stolen gasoline, the mob destroyed the lower floors of the courthouse, setting fire to the walls and furniture. Smoke billowed out windows as fire spread. Bullets whizzed above the crowd. Inside the building, the blaze reduced thousands of court and property records to ashes. The mob demolished a judge's private office, the records office, the building's Red Cross office, and its law library.[39]

Prisoners and deputies screamed from the upper windows for help. Firefighters arrived, but the mob cut their hoses. Rioters took a cannon, captured from Austria in the war and donated to the city, wrapped it in pieces of fire hose, then used it as a battering ram. Police reinforcements arrived, but rioters overwhelmed them and took their guns. At some point, the deputies released 15 panic-stricken women prisoners, letting them disappear into the crowd. The male prisoners—about 60—were moved to the roof as the flames and heat intensified. The fires made it difficult to breathe. The rooftop scorched their feet, while rioters fired at them from other buildings.

"I thought sure I'd be saying hello to the devil," said one officer.[40]

The deputies and prisoners retreated through the smoke back to the upper floors.[41] Mayor Smith called Fort Omaha for help several times. Wuest still refused. Police asked for officers from Council Bluffs, Iowa, across the Missouri River, but the neighboring town refused.[42]

At 8:20 p.m., Nebraska lieutenant governor Pelham Barrows sent a telegram to Baker in Washington: "RACE RIOT IN OMAHA COURT HOUSE BEING TORN DOWN POLICE FORCE INADEQUATE NO STATE TROOPS GOVERNOR CAN BE REACHED ORDER OUT FEDERAL TROOPS AT FORT CROOK RUSH."[43] Baker's office received the wire at 9:40 p.m.

About an hour later, Mayor Smith, horrified by what he was seeing and with no help arriving, felt he had no choice but to appeal to the mob directly. He came downstairs with several staffers. Smith, two days from his fifty-ninth birthday, was not a robust man. He had suffered an accident years earlier and had a metal plate in his skull. He made his way through the crowd and stood on a police car.

"If you take [Brown] from this courthouse it will be over my dead body," Smith shouted.[44]

Rioters knocked him down.[45] Barely conscious, he was dragged down Harney Street. A rope was cut from a trolley pole and a noose was put around his neck. Someone shouted, "String the mayor up." A few protested that Smith should be released.[46]

The mob tried to hoist Smith from a trolley pole, then a lamppost. As the noose tightened, Smith blacked out. A young man named Russell Norgaard appears to have prevented Smith from being lynched by repeatedly taking off the noose. Either police arrived in time to save the mayor, or Norgaard convinced the mob to release the unconscious Smith, who had blood streaming from his head. An ambulance arrived and rushed Smith to the hospital.[47] His injuries were so severe that newspapers reported he died. After he regained consciousness at the hospital, Smith's first question was, "What did they do with the colored man?"[48]

———

Back at the riot, the mob torched a police squad car after an ambulance took Smith away. A photograph taken of the burning shell of the car showed a mob of white men, most of them young, smiling and waving. One was dressed in a soldier's uniform.[49] The rioters continued their courthouse siege, with police and prisoners still trapped upstairs and overcome by stifling heat and blinding smoke.[50] Rioters fired from nearby rooftops. Sheriff Clark tried to move the men downstairs, but rioters blocked the stairwells.[51] According to some accounts, Brown became hysterical.[52] Others reported he was the calmest of the trapped prisoners.[53] Sheriff Clark gave yet another version of Brown's composure. Clark said Brown sobbed to him on the roof, "I never did it, my God, I am innocent."[54]

Trapped in the burning building, some prisoners prayed, others cursed. Some demanded that Brown be turned over.[55] Sheriff Clark reported that white deputies stopped black prisoners from throwing Brown off the roof to the waiting crowd.

About 11 p.m., nine hours after the mob first formed, it achieved its objective.[56] As rioters made their way onto the smoky upper floors, "somebody handed the nigger to us," one told a reporter. "We tied a rope around his neck and dragged him to the south side of the building." Investigators later believed Clark handed him over, though he denied it.[57]

Before they brought him to the mob, rioters beat him senseless and tore off his clothes. "Here he is!" rioters cheered as they dragged him outside.[58]

Fourteen-year-old Henry Fonda saw the lynching from the second floor of his father's printing shop across from the courthouse. His father felt it was important for his son to witness the savagery. Fonda recalled looking down on the mob "choking the courthouse square, cursing, waving guns and clubs." Fonda saw Brown dragged from the jail by a group of armed men.

"A great huzzah went up when they saw the poor fellow," he recalled. "They took him, strung him up to the end of a lamppost, and while his feet were still dancing in the air, they riddled his body with bullets. It was the most horrendous sight. Then they cut down the body, tied it to an auto, and dragged it through the streets of Omaha."

Fonda's father did not say a word as they drove home.

"My hands were wet and there were tears in my eyes," Fonda wrote later in his autobiography. "All I could think of was that young black man dangling at the end of the lamppost, the shots, and the revulsion I felt."[59]

Omaha's black weekly, *The Monitor*, reported, "Mothers with babes in arms pushed forward to see the body. A few women fainted, but more shouted with glee."[60]

The corpse was driven several blocks away, then soaked in gasoline, piled with debris, and set aflame. A photographer recorded the gruesome event. In one photo, Brown's body roasted in flames, his melted, empty skull facing the dark sky. The charred torso, the limbs burned away, lay on burning planks. Satisfied rioters stood around the dead man and mugged for the camera. A young boy smiled over a shoulder to stare down at the remains. A workman with a derby leaned smiling toward the fire.[61] After the fire died down, people kicked the torso down the street.[62]

Rioters looted more hardware stores for weapons and ammunition, then went to the city jail to look for black prisoners, but the police captain on duty had already let them all go. He let a committee of rioters inspect the jail. They eventually left.[63]

———

Some of the mob started to march on the city's black neighborhood. But before it reached the area, numbers dwindled and the effort fell away. Maybe it was fear. Recent events in Knoxville, Chicago, and Washington showed there was a good chance they would meet armed resistance. "Practically every one of the 10,000 Negroes in Omaha was armed and is ready to fight for his life and home. Last night the Negroes looted several hardware stores in the north end of the city and obtained additional weapons," the *New York Times* reported.[64] Maybe the mob was tired. After killing Brown, many exhausted rioters headed home. Also, word had spread that troops from Fort Omaha were finally going to show up.

⸺◇⸺

As lynchers booted Brown's remains down the street, federal troops drove toward downtown Omaha. After hours of delay, they had obtained directives from superiors to act. In the words of historian Clayton Laurie: "The army intervention was both overwhelming and late."[65]

Military officers later claimed in an official report that commanding officers decided as early as 9:30 p.m. to send in troops, but could not secure transportation. Yet in the same report, officers also said they sent in troops only after commanders received authorization from War Secretary Baker via telegram.

At 10:45 p.m., 73 troops at nearby Fort Crook commandeered streetcars and rode into the city. At the same time Wuest sent about 250 men from Fort Omaha.[66] They established a command center at police headquarters and took control of intersections. The troops encountered no resistance and the mob melted away. By 1:50 a.m., Wuest reported order restored.[67] All day more troops arrived, eventually reaching a total of 1,600. They set up checkpoints, including machine-gun nests, throughout downtown. Three hundred troops were sent to protect Omaha's black neighborhood.

An observation balloon hovered over downtown looking for outbreaks of rioting or arson. Police also were out in force, and about 400 American Legion members, both black and white, joined them.[68]

Wuest issued a proclamation announcing: "Rioting in the streets of Omaha has been suppressed and the situation is well in hand." He demanded firearms be handed over to military authorities, who told the NAACP to warn blacks to stay home Monday.[69]

Governor Samuel McKelvie arrived and examined the damage. His postmortem: "One who is acquainted with conditions in Omaha during the last few months could not be very much surprised at what has happened."[70]

Costs for the destroyed courthouse ranged from $750,000 to $1.1 million. Vandalism, looting, and arson had damaged other downtown buildings. Omaha's blacks fumed.

"I am humiliated almost beyond expression," wrote the Reverend John Albert Williams, editor of *The Monitor* and local NAACP president.[71] "The wolf-pack has slunk away. It murdered and robbed and burned and destroyed, and now, it has slunk away, and real Omaha must assert herself and redeem herself."[72]

But while Omaha's politicians, business leaders, and black people abhorred what had occurred, many working-class whites were proud. The *New York Times* reported that many women working in downtown shops declared it a good thing.[73]

Even though military officials in Omaha announced the trouble was over early Monday morning, Major General Leonard Wood, head of the Army's Central Department, commandeered a train to rush to Omaha. His telegram to Washington read that he was abandoning an inspection tour in South Dakota to "INVESTIGATE THE SITUATION ON THE GROUND."[74]

Wood saw 1920 as his chance to take the presidency as the law-and-order candidate. The presidency would end years of career frustration for the fifty-eight-year-old military man. Born at the dawn of the Civil War, Wood believed himself to be destined for greatness early on. Though a Harvard Medical School graduate, he eschewed a comfortable medical career and joined the military. In 1885, he battled Geronimo in Arizona and was awarded the Congressional Medal of Honor for that campaign. During the Spanish-American War in 1898, Wood led the famous cavalry regiment known as the Rough Riders. Teddy Roosevelt was his second in command. In 1910, President Taft appointed Wood his Army chief of staff. As the prospects for a European war increased, Wood became a vocal proponent of an American military buildup and helped organize a military preparedness movement. He published books on the subject, and his speeches drew thousands. Journalists talked about Wood as a presidential prospect. A man of boundless ego and machismo, Wood responded to such talk by writing more books about the importance of serving one's country. Standing 5 feet, 11 inches tall and weighing 195 pounds with a 44-inch chest, Wood saw himself as the embodiment of America's Manifest Destiny.

But with the election of Democrat Woodrow Wilson, Wood's career trajectory arced downward. Wilson distrusted the self-aggrandizing Wood, in part because of Wood's close ties to Teddy Roosevelt and William Howard Taft. He also disliked Wood's campaign for military preparedness, since Wilson had been elected on promises he would keep America out of a European war. When the United States did enter the war, many saw it as a vindication for Wood and assumed he would be made commander of American forces. Instead, Secretary of War Baker chose John Pershing, and kept Wood stateside commanding training facilities. Wood and his supporters were apoplectic.

As the Great War raged, Wood found himself doing what one biographer described as "deadly dull, swivel-chair work."[75] He saw it as downright unpatriotic. Others saw it as wise to keep Wood subdued. "The energies of Leonard Wood are fiercer than his intellectual equipment can employ or control," Walter Lippmann wrote.[76]

But by spring 1919, Republican leaders were pushing Wood on the public, commissioning books and articles, and having him give speeches around the country. Though he did not make a formal announcement in 1919, he was considered the GOP front-runner. All he needed was some action to prove his mettle.[77]

Though he was stationed in Chicago, Wood did not get involved in the riot there. Perhaps it was so large he did not want to risk failing to suppress it. Perhaps he wanted two potential rivals, Governor Lowden and Mayor Thompson, to fail. Whatever the reason, Wood did nothing. But that did not prevent him from giving his opinion on the riot: "It was indeed an ugly blot on American history, as humiliating to the nation as it was to the city in which it occurred."[78]

With the war over, Wood switched from calls for military preparedness to demands that America root out subversives. Labor strife and racial violence, he asserted, were caused by outside agitators. "My motto for the Reds is 'S.O.S.'—ship or shoot," he told a New York audience in late 1919. "I believe we should place them all on a ship of stone, with sails of lead and that their first stopping place should be Hell."[79]

Wood's message was extremely popular with the nervous public. To bolster his presidential chances, he also needed to show he was a man of action. Omaha—with the trouble already over by the time he arrived—was his chance. The reason for the riot, in Wood's mind, could not be racial tensions. It had to be agitators. From his first arrival, he said the I.W.W. caused the riot.[80]

The general mobilized the local American Legion for auxiliary patrols and praised their cooperation. He knew such praise would please veterans, a key constituency in his presidential bid. He imposed partial martial law, ordered a curfew, and suppressed newspaper stories he considered inflammatory. He even prohibited Major League Baseball scores from being posted at an intersection downtown to avoid drawing crowds.[81] These moves brought publicity that reinforced Wood's image as a tough leader.

His name ran in headlines in all the major cities, and he was portrayed as the muscular adherent of law and order—perfect for a presidential candidate in 1920.[82]

In early October, Wood told a gathering at Omaha's University Club that the antiblack riot was "unquestionably fathered by the I.W.W."[83] It was an odd claim, considering Wood also asserted that the I.W.W. was recruiting black workers in Omaha. If they did, they certainly were not effective. Regardless, any agitation among black workers was irrelevant in Omaha because—and this point was lost on Wood, federal investigators, and the press—blacks in Omaha never rioted, only whites did. No evidence was found to substantiate Wood's claim.

The I.W.W. mocked Wood. *One Big Union*, its monthly magazine, ran a political cartoon of a towering Wood looking down at a rabble of Ku Klux Klan members and Loyalty League members with knives, guns, and nooses. Wood pointed to a quiet worker reading an I.W.W. newspaper.

"It was the I.W.W. that incited you to riot," Wood declared.[84]

W. A. Domingo, a black Jamaican immigrant and socialist who edited a small New York weekly, *The Emancipator*, commented: "When we shoot down the mobbist that would burn our properties and destroy our lives, they shout 'Bolshevist.' When a white man comes to our side armed with the sword of righteousness and square dealing, they howl 'Nigger lover and bastard.'"[85]

While General Wood sought the spotlight, Mayor Smith ran from it. After his near-murder at the hands of rioters, he was praised as a hero across the country. The *New York Evening Mail* called Smith "an example of courageous devotion to duty that is as timely as it is inspiring."[86]

But when the NAACP tried to bestow on Smith the honor of being the main speaker at its 1920 annual meeting in New York, he firmly declined. "I have received a great deal more commendation than I was entitled to because of my actions on the night of the riot here in Omaha. I cannot conceive how any public officials who had a due sense of appreciation of his duties and responsibilities, would have done differently under the same circumstances." Of course, most politicians in 1919 faced with similar circumstances did not put their lives at risk.[87]

Smith's political enemies in Omaha heaped scorn upon his administration, though Smith himself was temporarily beyond reproach as he recovered from his injuries in the hospital. Rumors circulated that Tom Dennison, the machine boss, fomented the riot. A grand jury investigation—though it would issue no specific indictments—cited as the main cause of the riot "a concerted effort on the part of certain citizens, officials, and part of the press to discredit the police force."[88]

A Dennison ally denied that assertion years later, but added, "I don't say he didn't get a kick out of it."[89] Regardless of whether Dennison was involved, the riot was a political defeat from which Smith and the progressives never recovered. After being released from the hospital, Smith traveled to Missouri and Florida to recuperate. When he returned, Smith served out his term, but declined to seek reelection.[90]

———◇———

The *Omaha Bee*'s reporting of crime and race before the riot was singled out for sharp criticism from General Wood. "With the exception of a few men and one paper, you have a good city," he said in one speech.[91]

Police Chief Ringer and others in the Smith administration condemned the newspaper. In early November, the newspaper was indicted on charges that it and one of its reporters incited rioting and arson.[92] The NAACP and other black groups joined in blasting the *Bee*.

"We, ourselves, do not know whether Brown was guilty or innocent of the terrible crime charged against him," wrote C. Valentine (likely a pseudonym for Cyril Briggs, whose middle name was Valentine) in *The Crusader*. "We do know that, innocent or not, he was entitled to a fair trial under the Constitution and laws of the United States. . . . 'Brown willingly went to his death,' says the white press. So did Jesus Christ."[93]

Though the *Bee*'s inflammatory stories helped ignite the mob, other Omaha newspapers distinguished themselves. Harvey Newbranch of the *Evening World Herald* wrote an editorial, "Law and the Jungle," that condemned the mob so roundly he won the Pulitzer Prize for editorial writing in 1920. Newbranch had harsh words for the city government for not rushing Brown out of town and not vigorously dispersing the mob when it started.

Of Omaha's blacks Newbranch wrote:

> They naturally and properly resent having been confined to their homes, in trembling fear of their lives, while red riot ran the streets of the city. But their duty as good citizens is precisely the same as that of the rest of us, all of whom have been outraged and shamed as citizens.

It is to look to the law for their protection, for their vindication, and to give the law every possible support as it moves in its course. The law is their only shield, as it is the only shield of every white man, no matter how lowly or how great.[94]

On the national stage, whites were unnerved by the violence, though many assumed—as usual—that black crime was the root cause. Even a children's magazine, *The Youth's Companion*, felt compelled to remark that Brown "probably deserved death, though we should have been surer of it if he had been convicted in open court." But the editors condemned the mob attacking police, the court, and the mayor. "In every part of the country men are drifting further and further from sanity and self-control and orderly behavior," they wrote. "The 'lid is off.'"[95]

The NAACP wasted no time in using the Omaha violence to again press for congressional hearings. On September 30, Shillady issued a statement titled "Shall the Mob Govern?" that called for hearings "in the name of civilization."[96]

Johnson, by this time the lead voice of the NAACP, praised Mayor Smith for his bravery but condemned police "assininity" for their slow response. "The fire of the mob spirit began to kindle and blaze and spread for several days before it became a great conflagration; and all the while the police were busy squirting on it through atomizers," he wrote.[97]

News of Omaha led to a sharp exchange in Congress, echoing the famous pro- and anti-slavery arguments from six decades earlier. It came amid prolonged and heated debate over passage of Wilson's League of Nations treaty. Republican senators opposed the treaty. Southern Democrats supported it.

Senator John Sharp Williams, Democrat from Mississippi and perhaps Woodrow Wilson's staunchest supporter, stood up on the Senate floor and condemned Republican senator William Borah of Idaho, a strong opponent of the treaty.[98] Borah had criticized the Wilson administration's handling of race riots, lynching, and the recent labor strife.

"The Senator from Idaho has been preaching peace, peace when it comes to 'niggers,' when capital and labor are involved," Williams declared. "And yet when he comes to international affairs he is standing in the pathway of the very thing to which he has paid so high an oratorical tribute."

Williams did not excuse lynching; he heartily endorsed it: "The conduct of the criminal at Omaha deprives me of all inclination and power to say one word against the crowd that captured the criminal and punished the crime. Race is greater than law now and then and protection of women transcends all law, human and divine."

It was an amazing declaration: the accusation of rape was more important than the execution of the law. This statement was not delivered by a boisterous speaker to a street rabble. It came from a United States senator, sworn to uphold the Constitution, as he stood in Congress. That this came during a debate about the Versailles Peace Treaty underscored how much race had permeated political discourse.

Senator Borah stood up and fired back: "I want to say considering the ultimate welfare of the human family, there can be no justification for the lynching of any person, and the man who preaches it is sowing the wind that reaps the whirlwind, no matter how black the skin of the victim may be. If the republic does not protect the lives of its people the seeds are planted that ultimately will lead to its disintegration."[99]

The exchange garnered widespread newspaper coverage, and was presented as a clash of the two prevailing views on racial violence. But though Borah opposed lynching, he was no ardent supporter of black rights. Like many so-called progressives at the time, he supported strict adherence to the law, but wanted the country to remain dominated by white Anglo-Saxon Protestants. He rejected NAACP efforts to enlist his support for federal anti-lynching legislation, contending such laws would be struck down as unconstitutional. His motives may have been less than legalistic. Borah, who was toying with a presidential run in 1920, was one of the few Republicans to strongly support the South's right to disenfranchise voters using property ownership and education levels as restrictions.[100] He considered blacks being given the right to vote "a stupendous error."[101]

Williams's attack on Borah was well received below the Mason-Dixon Line. Politicians and editorial writers yet again trumpeted northern violence as an absolution for southern misdeeds against blacks.

For southern progressives, however, Williams's open support for lynching tore down a new image they were trying to construct. "It is no time for lunatics to be abroad," declared C. B. Wilmer, a white pastor of St. Luke's Episcopal Church in Atlanta and an activist working to improve race relations. "One must therefore deplore the reported utterances of Senator Williams of Mississippi. . . . I cannot conceive of a more pernicious doctrine to spread abroad than that we can protect our women by the course recommended."[102]

And whatever happened in the North, antiblack violence in the South continued. On September 30, vigilantes in Montgomery, Alabama, killed three black men and wounded another after a white police officer died in a shootout. The posse killed two of the black men, Miles Phifer and Robert Crosky, in the street. The men were told to run and then were shot down for fleeing. In the middle of the night, mob members broke into a hospital where John Temple, the man accused of killing Officer John Barbare, lay wounded in police custody. The men overpowered hospital guards and shot Temple to death in his bed. The vigilantes also tried to kill another black man, a war veteran, but he was only wounded in the attack.[103]

19.

Phillips County

All this journalistic diarrhea about "radical Negro editors"
and "race uplifters inciting Negroes to revolt against the
white man," etc. is unadulterated and unsophisticated
bosh, buncome, "bull" and "bull-sheviki."

—HOUSTON INFORMER, November 1, 1919

IN SEPTEMBER 1919, HERBERT SELIGMANN PUBLISHED AN ESSAY
about the race riots in the popular news monthly *Current Opinion.* Like
other NAACP staffers, Seligmann called for congressional hearings. He
recounted the violence in Washington, Chicago, and elsewhere, and laid
blame on local governments and the Wilson administration for feeble
responses to the disorders. He also argued any violence by blacks was
self-defense.

But editors gave the essay a headline that underscored how many
white Americans viewed the violence. The headline asked: "What Is
Behind the Negro Uprisings?"

William T. Francis, a prominent black lawyer in St. Paul, Minnesota,
wrote to *Current Opinion* editor Edward Wheeler: "The Negro has never
indulged in 'Uprisings' in this country. Every race riot that this country
has had has been started by the whites. And it was only in the Washington and Chicago riots that the blacks have even struck back."[1]

In fact, blacks had risen up against slavery numerous times, and many
fought back against white mobs since the earliest days of the Republic.
But Francis was right regarding 1919: whites started almost all of the

mass violence that year. Wheeler replied that Francis was hypercritical, saying, "The difference between an uprising and striking back seems to be a pretty fine one."[2]

But Francis's complaint got to the heart of the matter: Many whites—from liberals like Wheeler to conservatives like J. Edgar Hoover—equated black self-defense and self-assertion with revolution.

Nowhere would this false logic play out more tragically than in Phillips County in the Delta flatlands of east Arkansas. Beginning at a little black church in a sharecropper community on the night of September 30, it would be the last major racial clash of 1919, and probably the bloodiest. What whites insisted was a black insurrection would prove to be a massacre of black innocents.

⊂⊃

The region's landscape and history laid the groundwork for the slaughter. With the silty, serpentine Mississippi River forming its eastern border, Phillips County had some of Arkansas's richest soil. When levees were built to reduce flooding and lowlands were drained, the area became ideal for cotton production. The county also developed a healthy timber industry. Both industries required cheap manual labor, so plantation owners brought in so many slaves that by 1860, blacks made up 60 percent of the county's population. The county had far more slaves—about 9,000—than any other in the state.[3] The county seat of Helena, set on the river, shipped bales of cotton and cottonwood timber north to Memphis and south to New Orleans, and by the outbreak of the Civil War it was the largest Arkansas city on the Mississippi. Phillips County whites enthusiastically endorsed secession and enlisted in the Confederate army in large numbers.[4] But Union forces seized Helena in 1862 and used it as a supply base for the siege of nearby Vicksburg. When Abraham Lincoln issued the Emancipation Proclamation, many former slaves in the county joined the Union Army.

Like other southern states, Arkansas experienced black political activity during Reconstruction, but white Democrats reasserted control afterward. Despite white political and economic domination, many blacks saw Arkansas as a better place to farm than other southern states. Moderate governors allowed some blacks to vote, and black representatives served in the state legislature until 1893. The state Republican Party embraced black voters and allowed them into its leadership.[5] Not only did many blacks stay in Arkansas after the war (living in counties along the river and in the southern part of the state), but others moved in from neighboring Mississippi and Louisiana. The majority of these blacks were poor sharecroppers who could no longer tolerate the oppressive conditions on plantations east of the Mississippi.[6] Word of better conditions in Arkansas drew a steady stream of black migrants for decades. Eventually, blacks made up about a quarter of Arkansas's population. Several counties became majority black, with Phillips being the largest such county.[7]

Starting in the 1890s, Jim Crow crept across Arkansas, disenfranchising blacks, sapping their economic power, and constraining their movements and social interactions. In the first decades of the twentieth century, black land ownership fell; segregation became pervasive; nightriders attacked black farmers; and the Democratic Party cut blacks from voter rolls. Elements of the Republican Party launched efforts to set up an all-white party. More blacks than ever were sharecropping, most of them trapped in a cycle of debt bondage not far removed from slavery.[8]

Like elsewhere across the South, cotton prices rose sharply in Arkansas during the Great War, but profits did not transfer to sharecroppers. White landlords and shop owners set the rates, and they often shortchanged black farmers. White attorney Ulysses S. Bratton in Little Rock represented black sharecroppers in legal cases against landlords.[9] Blacks, however, rarely won in a state where whites wrote laws and cases were presented before white judges and juries. As Bratton wrote, "The system that prevails in the dealing of the landlords with the Negroes in the large majority of the cases prevents the Negro from ever reaching the point that he had any money turned over to him that he can call his own."[10]

Violence against blacks was less than in other southern states, but conditions were still abysmal. From 1889 to 1918, 182 blacks were lynched in Arkansas, according to NAACP records.[11] Riots and lynchings in some counties established "sundown towns" and even two "sundown" counties in the state where blacks could not reside.[12]

Despite these restrictions, Arkansas's elite blacks generally accepted segregation and other indignities in exchange for relative peace and a chance to accumulate wealth and preserve some rights. When the Great War came, black leaders, including Scipio Africanus Jones, a prominent Little Rock attorney, businessman, and Republican, endorsed the segregation of troops at Camp Pike, the 6,000-acre base near the state capital where army recruits trained for combat. The state government enlisted dozens of black speakers around the state to sell millions in government bonds at black churches and community groups.[13] Thousands of black Arkansans enlisted.[14]

Despite the strictures of Jim Crow, life for blacks in Phillips County improved during the war. Cotton prices were so good that no matter how white landlords tried to rig the system, blacks made money. Cotton that sold for 11 cents a pound in 1915 went for 40 cents in 1919. Acreage owned by blacks in Phillips increased 40 percent from 1910 to 1920.[15] And Phillips sharecroppers worked larger tracts than those in other parts of the Delta. With more blacks leaving for industrial jobs in the North, black farmers who remained found themselves in greater demand. Delta factories and businesses also suffered a shortage of cheap black labor. In 1917, the U.S. Department of Labor hired several hundred blacks to build Camp Pike, the military base near Little Rock. Phillips County's white business league filed a complaint, arguing the project caused a labor shortage, especially in lumber mills. The department agreed to release its black workers.[16] The *Helena World*, the main white newspaper in the county, acknowledged in May 1919 that the black worker "is an asset which the community can ill afford to lose or abuse or neglect."[17]

Phillips County was one of the most populous in the rural state. Despite the Great Migration, blacks still made up almost 75 percent of its 44,530 people. By comparison, blacks made up 27 percent of Arkansas's total population of 1.75 million.[18] The county had an active black middle class, made up of clergy, doctors, lawyers, and teachers. Black fraternal organizations, like the Colored Knights of Pythias, thrived. Black church congregations swelled and their ministers, such as Reverend Elias Camp Morris, rose to national prominence. Born a slave in Georgia, Morris became pastor of the Centennial Baptist Church in Helena in 1879, and over the next thirty years built it into one of the largest black congregations in the South.[19] He also ran several businesses and co-founded the Helena Negro Business League. As head of the National Baptist Convention, Morris was one of the most influential black religious leaders in the country.

Helena and other towns nearby like Elaine supported numerous black businesses and institutions. Author Richard Wright was eight in 1916 when his family moved from Mississippi to live with relatives in Elaine, a town 17 miles south of Helena. Phillips County blacks were the most well-to-do Wright had ever seen. His aunt's bungalow, garden, and yard impressed him. "It looked like home and I was glad," he wrote in his autobiographical novel *Black Boy*.[20] His uncle, who owned a saloon, could afford a horse and buggy and let Richard eat his fill at dinner.[21] But Wright also saw the perplexing aspects of being black in the South. He saw robust black soldiers in uniform marching off to fight Germans, when he had no idea who Germans were. He also saw his first chain gang of black prisoners, and wondered why they did not overpower their white guards.[22] Wright lived in Elaine in 1917 when white men murdered his uncle under murky circumstances, a horror he described as "my first baptism of racial emotion."[23]

Other black men reported deep prejudice in Phillips County. One veteran, James Campbell, who served as a private and was gassed on the front lines, was sent home to Arkansas to recuperate. When doctors released him, he went home to Helena and "met nothing but sneers from the whites." One white man, seeing his service stripes, said aloud: "There is another overseas nigger. I guess he knows it all." Campbell left the South for St. Louis, and told the *Cleveland Gazette*, "I felt safer in the trenches than in Arkansas."[24]

Campbell wrote about his experiences just months before the Arkansas Delta was to suffer its worst outbreak of violence since the Civil War. From October 1 to October 4, 1919, the canebrakes, cotton fields, and forests of southern Phillips County saw untold black deaths, so many that most historians no longer refer to what happened in and around Elaine in 1919 as a "riot." They call it a massacre.

In ways, the rampage echoed the Jenkins County, Georgia, riot that launched the Red Summer six and a half months earlier. Like in Jenkins County, the trouble broke out in a southern area where blacks were the majority, but whites controlled politics, economics, and the law. Phillips County also was cotton country, where the sharecropping system dominated. Like Jenkins County, the violence started after white lawmen were shot outside a black meeting held at a church. In confused circumstances, white officers were shot, sparking violence. Then for days, white mobs roamed the countryside attacking blacks. Like Jenkins County, black men were forced to fight for their lives in hostile courts.

But sharp differences existed as well, differences that illustrated how much race relations had changed over the chaotic months. During a summer of race riots and lynchings across the country, blacks had shown that they would fight for their rights and were organizing to do so at every turn.

The Crusader, the monthly black magazine, displayed a two-frame political cartoon that captured this transformation. In the first frame, a southern colonel stood on a black corpse while behind him another dead black man swung from a tree.

"We want no interference in our affairs," the defiant colonel announced. "We can settle this nigger problem ourselves."

In the next frame, an armed black man pursued the now terrified colonel, who bolted up a hill toward Congress.

"Help! Help!" the colonel exclaimed. "This nigger problem has changed."[25]

On the evening of September 30, 1919, Ed Ware, a successful, forty-eight-year-old sharecropper, left his farm northwest of the tiny community of Hoop Spur and drove to a country church just off the main dirt road linking Elaine, the largest town in southern Phillips County, with 400 residents, and Helena, the county seat with 9,000.[26] Hoop Spur was little more than a crossroads, and the biggest attraction in the area aside from the church was a nameless honky-tonk.[27]

Ware came to attend a meeting of the Progressive Farmers and Household Union of America, a black fraternal self-help organization that had sprung up in the county a few months earlier. Despite its majestic name, the union was loosely organized and limited to a few small communities in Arkansas.

A year earlier, four black men incorporated the union in Drew County, south of Phillips, "to advance the interests of the Negro morally and intellectually and to make him a better citizen and a better farmer."[28] They proclaimed in a brochure: "WE BATTLE FOR THE RIGHTS OF OUR RACE." Yet they did not specify how.[29] In the bylaws, the group defined itself as a quasi-Masonic, joint-stock company that required members to purchase at least one share for $5, similar to the schemes of Garvey's UNIA. The union's leaders controlled funds to finance construction of a grand lodge and to buy other land. The bylaws held that any members who revealed any "secrets of this order" would face fines and expulsion. The group declared itself dedicated to the United States Constitution and ordered that a chaplain open and close its meeting.[30]

One of the original organizers, Robert Hill, had served in the Army, and when he was discharged, he settled with his family in nearby Ratio.[31] In April, he helped establish lodges in Phillips County, including one among poor farmers in his tiny plantation community.[32] In September, share-croppers there decided to meet with Ulysses Bratton, the white Little Rock attorney who specialized in representing blacks and suing white landlords to get fair, published contracts for their cotton, hogs, and corn.

The charismatic, twenty-seven-year-old Hill organized seven lodges that summer, pulling together black farmers tired of getting ripped off by white cotton merchants. Many were unsure how the union would work, or what it could accomplish, but they were willing to give it a try. Hill and other union leaders urged the farmers to refrain from selling cotton until at least mid-October if they could not get a fair price.[33]

Ware joined the union in late August and had attended just two meet-ings of the newly formed Hoop Spur lodge.[34] Perhaps because he was good with numbers and a successful farmer, lodge members appointed him secretary. He said later he did not know much about the group when he took the job.[35] Once asked to explain the group's goals, Ware said, "The main object, it was explained to me, was for the purpose of cooperating the Negroes, to care for one another, take care of the sick ones and all alike, and make better progressive farmers."[36]

Like other sharecroppers, Ware had done well during the war, thanks to the dramatic rise in cotton prices. The Louisiana migrant built up a farm using money earned from a taxi service. He and his wife, Lulu, suf-fered personal loss—all four of their children died from illness—but materially, they prospered.[37] By September 1919, the Wares were renting 121 acres (and subletting some of that land) for cotton and corn. Ware owned two mules, a horse, a Jersey cow, a farm wagon, tools, 8 hogs, 135 chickens, and a Ford. Within the economic strictures of the sharecrop-ping system, Ware was succeeding.[38]

But like other sharecroppers, Ware was thwarted by an economic sys-tem where white businessmen set prices and controlled accounts. For years, black farmers felt white merchants shortchanged them when times were bad. Now blacks saw that even in good times, they were being held back.

Planters and merchants often did not provide black sharecroppers with written contracts, and often loaned farming material and other goods at exorbitant interest rates. The loose system provided "plenty of room for misunderstanding and for outright fraud on the part of plant-ers," one historian noted.[39]

In 1919, with costs rising, black sharecroppers and workers in Phillips County objected and took action. Sawmill workers in Elaine refused to let their women pick cotton. Some refused to pick cotton unless they set their own price.[40] Ware himself described how on September 26, two white merchants tried to pay him 24 cents a pound for his ginned cotton. When he balked, they offered 33 cents.

"I refused to take it," he said later. "And they said they were going to take the cotton at that price. I rejected their offer and said I'd take my cotton to Helena to sell."

On September 29, Ware hired an attorney in Helena "so I would not have to deal" with white gougers. While in Helena, Ware checked other white merchants' cotton prices. They were paying 44½ cents a pound.[41] The union, Ware and others hoped, would change the situation by fighting in court for written, signed contracts and fair prices at the beginning of a growing season.

These economic strains exacerbated racial tensions in a county where blacks far outnumbered whites, but whites controlled everything. White business owners became acutely aware of their weakened economic position. As early as 1917, the *Helena World* ran stories of labor unrest around the United States and warned local businesses about I.W.W. agitators infiltrating their businesses.[42]

Keeping black farmers' income down became anxious work. The county's white business owners heard about black farmers forming a secretive farmers' organization. Their fears melded with the national Red Scare panic. In early September, Helena merchant Sebastian Straub hired a black detective from Chicago to infiltrate the union. The detective reported hearing rumors that union leaders were formulating a plot to kill white plantation owners.[43] E. M. "Mort" Allen, president of the Helena Business Men's League, said later, "The I.W.W. has been feeding their sort of stuff to all the Negroes of the South for the past year, and a lot of harm has been done."[44] As it had in the months of violence, age-old southern fears of a Nat Turner–style revolt of blacks fused with apprehension over the rise of ideologies that called for capitalism's overthrow. In truth, the I.W.W. did little in the state.[45]

On September 25, Ware left the Elaine post office and ran into Will McCullough, a white man he had known for years since they both lived in Louisiana.[46] McCullough grilled Ware about the new black union. Was it planning a cotton strike? Ware assured him no.

"You get out of that thing," McCullough warned, "because it is going to cause trouble here."[47]

Five days later, Ware arrived at the Hoop Spur church at nine on a dark, moonless night. The surrounding fields were full of cotton plants bursting with bolls. A clump of cottonwood trees and underbrush obscured the view of the main road. The meeting had been going about two hours when he arrived. About a hundred men, women, and some children had packed in the church to sing songs and hear speeches.[48] Ware set up a table and set out the group's literature. Organizers planned to discuss how to increase membership and ways to secure fair crop contracts.[49]

In response to weeks of threats, lodge president Jim Miller stationed armed guards outside, and many farmers brought shotguns to the meeting. The guns were stacked in the corner.[50]

Two hours later, a car driving south from Helena stopped on the road, about 40 yards west of the church. The car's lights went out. Two white men—county deputy Charles Pratt and railroad detective Will Adkins—got out. A third man, a black jail trusty named "Kidd" Collins, stayed in the backseat. Pratt and Adkins were armed. The white men had brought Collins along to change a tire or walk for help if needed. Pratt later said the officers stopped only to urinate by the side of the road before driving on to Elaine, where they were looking for a white bootlegger who had threatened members of his family.[51] They stopped near the church meeting by chance, Pratt said later. He said armed black men approached the two whites and, without provocation, opened fire.

"I did not know they were holding a meeting in the church," Pratt said. "It was very dark there, and I could see only the forms of the Negroes."[52]

According to black testimony, the men in the car fired on the church.

"The first shooting occurred at the end of the automobile, the end towards Helena," said John Ratcliff, a guard outside the meeting. "I saw the flashes, but don't know who fired them."[53]

All those at the meeting said they were fired upon. Ware said he had just finished his membership books when he stood up and bullets flew through the church from the direction of the road.

"Two volleys came in at the window and knocked glass all over the house," Ware said. "I don't know whether it was glass come by my face or a bullet."

People dove to the floor, overturning benches, snuffing out lamps, and strewing pamphlets all over. When the shooting ceased, people bolted through church windows and doors. Ware scrambled out of the building and hid in an alfalfa patch. Then he ran to a friend's cabin.[54]

Detective Adkins was killed, and Deputy Pratt was wounded in the knee. No blacks were seriously injured. Pratt and Collins fled. A few minutes later, another white man drove up and was fired upon. The man was shot, but he was able to drive for help. Blacks fled the scene. Whites who arrived half an hour after the shooting found Adkins's corpse in the road with a shotgun blast to the stomach and a rifle shot in the neck.[55] His car was riddled with bullets.[56] Though some whites later claimed the church was not hit, blacks and other whites said the church was peppered with gunfire, its windows shattered. Inside, benches were overturned and clothes and hats were strewn about the floor.[57] Within days, however, white men torched the church—and whatever evidence it held.

<hr/>

After the shooting, Kidd Collins, the trusty, ran to a railroad station and called the sheriff. Despite a shattered knee, Charles Pratt crawled several hundred yards to the railroad and hours later flagged down a freight train, which took him to a hospital.

The shooting set off panic among whites, and Arkansas newspapers carried stories of a "Negro plot to rise against the white residents of the southern part of Phillips County."[58] By daybreak, the mayors of Helena and Elaine issued calls for posses to hunt down those who shot Adkins and Pratt.

The all-white American Legion post in Helena told its members to show up with guns. Rumors abounded that black insurrectionists were encircling Elaine. Phillips County sheriff Fred Kitchens and Mayor J. C. Knight of Helena closed public venues and ordered civilians to stay in their homes. White and black ministers met in Helena to try to defuse the crisis, but it was too late.

"The situation was reported to be critical at Elaine last night, the Negroes greatly outnumbering the whites, and an urgent call was issued for additional assistance from adjoining counties and the military authorities," the *Arkansas Gazette* reported.[59]

<hr/>

Groups of armed whites poured into the county from other parts of Arkansas, as well as from neighboring Mississippi and Tennessee.[60] John

Miller, the white prosecuting attorney, told a historian decades after the riot that the Mississippi posse members arrived "with blood in their eye."[61]

Ed Coleman, seventy-nine, a sharecropper leasing 18 acres, slept in his bed two and a half miles from the Hoop Spur church when the shooting occurred. He awoke as blacks from the meeting ran past his house.

"When the morning had come, I saw about 200 white men in cars shooting down the Negroes and sent us word that they were going to 'kill every nigger' they could find in the county," Coleman said. "And at 11:30 that day we saw near 300 armed white men coming and we all ran back of the field. . . . We was still running and made it to the woods, where we were hid all night and all the next day."[62]

Ed Ware made it back to his farm by late morning, but then a white posse showed up and started shooting. He fled into the woods. The posse, he said, "began to shoot down everything they saw like a Negro." Later, Ware was questioned about running from his home when the white posse showed up. "Why did you run?" a prosecutor asked. "So I could get to doing what I am doing now, talk again," Ware replied.[63]

All of the shooting panicked whites in nearby Elaine.

"A pitched battle was in progress in the streets of Elaine and the Sheriff's posse was outnumbered," the *Helena World* reported incorrectly. "The men opposing the posse are believed to be Negroes affiliated with a bootlegger gang."[64]

Authorities made matters worse. Sheriff Kitchens went home ill that morning and businessman Sebastian Straub was made acting sheriff for the rest of the day.[65] Straub had hired the black detective from Chicago and was convinced of a black plot to rise up and kill whites. For Straub and others, the trouble at Hoop Spur signaled a black revolt—engineered by white labor radicals—had begun.

By midmorning Wednesday, white men in Phillips County formed posses and combined with hundreds of incensed white men from surrounding areas. Discipline was loose. Without clear orders, groups ranged the countryside looking to kill any blacks they found. H. F. Smiddy, a white railroad detective, later signed an affidavit that said several hundred whites came at Elaine from Helena and elsewhere "and began to hunt Negroes."[66]

Smiddy, who joined a posse, said he shot and wounded an unarmed black man. He then arrested the man and charged him with being involved in the alleged rebellion. White reporters in Elaine described black corpses being shot multiple times.

Black sharecroppers near Hoop Spur fled into the woods as white posses ransacked their homes. Some black men, including war veterans, banded together to briefly repel attacks. They were outnumbered and outgunned by whites, many of whom were members of the local American Legion post. It is unclear how many blacks were killed, but two whites died. Clinton Lee was shot while sitting in his car. Another white man, John Tappan, had his jaw shot off and later died. Smiddy later said other posse members had shot Tappan by accident.[67] Four black men—adult brothers from a prominent Helena black family—were shot to death on a nearby road. The Johnston brothers (including one who was a doctor visiting from Oklahoma) were taken into custody as they returned from a squirrel-hunting trip. The posse confiscated their rifles, took them off a train, and drove them to a waiting group of armed whites along a road near Elaine. An altercation ensued, and a guard, O. R. Lilly, an Elaine alderman, was shot to death. The other guards opened fire on the brothers, who were all bound together. Their bodies were left in a heap in the road.[68] "All four of the Negroes were so shot to pieces that their bodies were unrecognizable," *Crisis* editor W. E. B. Du Bois wrote in an angry letter about biased coverage of the Elaine violence.[69]

During the next three days, white posses gunned down black sharecroppers throughout southeastern Phillips County. Posse members later said they saw black men shot while surrendering with their hands in the air. Others were hanged from a bridge.[70] Posses rounded up hundreds of black farmers into a makeshift jail in Elaine. Whites west of Elaine gathered white women and children into a farmhouse and guarded it for fear of an attack that never came.

Local political and business leaders sent urgent telegrams to Arkansas governor Charles Hillman Brough, begging for soldiers.[71] Rather than instill calm, Brough raised the alarm. He called Secretary of War Newton Baker and asked for troops from Camp Pike to be sent to Phillips County. He followed up his telephone conversation with a telegram: "RACE RIOT AT ELAINE PHILLIPS COUNTY THIS STATE FOUR WHITE SAID TO BE KILLED NEGROES SAID TO BE MASSING FOR ATTACK REQUEST COMMANDING GENERAL CAMP PIKE BE AUTHORIZED TO SEND SUCH UNITED STATES TROOPS AS MAY BE NECESSARY."[72] Baker approved the request in the afternoon, but because of delays in orders and preparation, troops did not head out from Camp Pike until about midnight. Four hundred soldiers from the Army's Third Division and 150 soldiers from the Fifth Infantry Division left Little Rock on a train commandeered by Colonel Isaac Jenks. The men brought along six trucks, two ambulances, twelve machine guns, and "a sufficient supply of ammunition to quiet the situation no matter how serious." Many of the troops had seen combat in France at the bloody Second Battle of the Marne. Like federal troops mobilized in Charleston, Washington, and Omaha and state militia mobilized in Longview, Chicago, and Knoxville, all the soldiers were white. Governor Brough rode on the train with the men. He told reporters he wanted to see what was happening firsthand.[73]

⎯⎯◦⎯⎯

Charles Brough, first elected governor in 1916, saw himself as an Arkansas version of Woodrow Wilson, a public intellectual turned progressive leader. Like Lowden, Dorsey, and other governors of the time, Brough considered himself as both forward-thinking and a defender of the social order. He supported a woman's right to vote, praised education, backed big business, and advocated Prohibition.[74]

The son of a Union Civil War veteran, he retained none of his father's northern sympathies. His views on race were a muddle of paternal interest in black improvement and profound fear of black advancement. Brough grew up and attended college in Mississippi; he earned his PhD in history at Johns Hopkins University in Baltimore. As a history professor back in Mississippi, he published a paper about the 1875 race riot in Clinton, Mississippi, in which he condemned the pro-black Reconstruction government.[75]

However, Brough did back modest black uplift in the vein of Booker T. Washington. While teaching economics at the University of Arkansas at Fayetteville, Brough joined the Commission of Southern Universities on the Race Question and helped organize the Southern Sociological Congress. As a proponent of the "New South," he became a leading advocate for improvements in black education and black health.

"In this substantial progress of our glorious Southland, the Negro has had a distinct and commendable share," he wrote in a 1913 essay. Yet even when speaking of black education, Brough stressed his view that blacks were morally and intellectually inferior to whites: "As the sons of proud Anglo-Saxon sires, we of the South doubt seriously the wisdom of the enfranchisement of an inferior race. We believe that reconstruction rule was 'a reign of ignorance, mongrelism and depravity,' that the Negro is the cheapest voter and the greatest Bourbon in American politics, North and South alike, and that as a political factor he had been a disturbing factor in our civic life."[76]

Brough began his governorship in 1917, after defeating two opponents who were anti-intellectual and flagrant racists. He instituted progressive policies and spoke out against lynching. During the Great War, he became an avid promoter of the draft and the public sale of savings bonds.[77] With the rise of the Bolsheviks in Russia, he became fiercely anti-radical.[78] Brough looked forward to meeting Wilson, his political paragon, in Little Rock on September 27, 1919, when the president was to address the Arkansas legislature on his national tour. To Brough's disappointment, Wilson's health collapse scrapped the speech.[79] Instead of the political boost from a presidential visit, Brough continued legislative wrangling, until four days later when he received frantic telegrams from Elaine and Helena. In the middle of the night, the forty-three-year-old Brough, a jowly man with a bald pate, tired eyes, and a large nose, found himself on a military train heading toward what he believed was a black rebellion.

The military train pulled into Elaine at 8:45 a.m., Thursday, October 2. Colonel Jenks's adjutant reported seeing "small groups of white people armed with shotguns, pistols and rifles. They appeared tired and very much excited."[80] Brough walked side by side with Jenks during most of the operation.[81] The governor also took time to speak with white constituents. He delivered a reassuring speech to a crowd on the steps of the Elaine Mercantile Company.

Jenks declared martial law and dispersed his men to search for "Negro insurrectionists" that white civilians assured him were gathering in the forests west of town. The blacks were getting ready to attack, whites said. The colonel left a small contingent in Elaine and ordered them to disarm everyone, black or white. He headed out into the fields. Jenks ordered his troops to shoot any blacks who did not surrender promptly.

Later that day, a skirmish took place near a thick canebrake west of Elaine. A soldier was killed and another wounded. The exchange sparked troops to open fire on blacks in the area for the next 36 hours. Military reports about the Elaine fighting never mentioned soldiers killing or even wounding blacks. First-person and second- and third-hand accounts, however, indicate the soldiers killed many black civilians.

John Elvis Miller, the white lawyer who later prosecuted the indicted blacks, said soldiers killed at least a hundred blacks in one incident. He did not say where. Gerald Lambert, owner of a plantation near Elaine, later recounted how troopers brought a prisoner to his company store for interrogation and tied him to a column. Lambert described the black man as "extremely insolent." The soldiers soaked him in kerosene and set him on fire. When the engulfed man broke free of his bonds, the soldiers riddled him with bullets.[82]

Despite statements that white farmers and their families in the outlying areas around Elaine were being fired upon, no incident was confirmed.[83] The troops spread out from Elaine.[84] At one point, gunshots went off near where Brough and Jenks were driving at the rear of a company of men. No one was hurt, but journalists telegraphed that blacks fired on the two men, which raised Brough's status as a defender of law and order.[85]

On Thursday and Friday, troops roamed the countryside, using machine guns liberally. They took blacks into custody and seized shotguns, pistols, and rifles.[86] No "rebellion" ever materialized. The soldiers, who called themselves the Phillips County Expeditionary Forces, a play on the American Expeditionary Forces in Europe, took complete control of the area by Friday morning.[87] Posses from other counties and states returned to their homes.

More than 400 black men—and several women—were taken into custody by the posses and held at a schoolhouse in Elaine. About 60 blacks were taken into custody in Helena.[88] White deputies also arrested a white man, Ocier Bratton, the son of attorney Ulysses Bratton, and accused him of conspiring with blacks to revolt. Deputies charged him with the murder of Adkins at Hoop Spur, though about a month later, thanks largely to the efforts of his father, prosecutors dropped all charges.[89] He had to be smuggled out of town in the back of a car to escape lynching.[90] Black prisoners were not so lucky. They were taken to the city telephone building for questioning. No attorneys were present as the prisoners were interrogated. Many prisoners later said they were systematically and severely beaten. The *Arkansas Gazette* mentioned the mass interrogations only in passing: "Some of them confessed, while others would only admit that they 'belonged to de union.'"[91]

Brough and a contingent of soldiers traveled on to Helena. Brough met at the Phillips County Courthouse with seven local white political and business leaders, including Mort Allen, head of the Helena Business Men's League; H. D. Moore, the county judge; J. C. Knight, Helena's mayor; and Sheriff Fred Kitchens. The Committee of Seven also included Sebastian Straub, the businessman who had hired the black detective to infiltrate the farmers' union. It was hardly an impartial panel, but Brough appointed the men, under questionable authority, as a de facto oligarchy to rule the county and investigate the alleged black plot.[92]

On October 4, 1919, Brough returned to Little Rock and declared peace restored. He seemed thrilled by the turn of events, and brought back souvenirs: a bullet and forms from the farmers' union. "The white citizens of the county deserve unstinted praise for their action in preventing mob violence," he said.[93]

The front page of the October 3, 1919, *Helena World* carried the banner headline: "Elaine Insurrection is Over; Committee of 7 in Charge."[94] The committee, along with posse members, sheriffs, and soldiers, continued their mass interrogation of black prisoners. Within days, committee members dictated to eager reporters "confessions" they had extracted.

Their tale was harrowing. In reports that were published in newspapers from coast to coast, unnamed investigators "definitely revealed" that "organized Negroes . . . had planned a general slaughter of white people." The union leaders planned to kill twenty-one prominent white men, which would bring about a general uprising to kill all whites in the area. Black "Paul Reveres" were to carry the news to blacks in the area with the password, "We've just begun." Committee members said a handful of white and black leaders had tricked the farmers by telling them Washington officials were ordering them to revolt and kill whites. They offered no evidence to support the story.[95] The Hoop Spur shooting, they said, exposed the planned revolt before the systematic killing started.

"The present trouble with the Negroes in Phillips County is not a race riot," the committee pronounced. "It is a deliberately planned insurrection of the Negroes against the whites."[96]

In a search of Bratton's satellite law office in Helena, authorities found socialist pamphlets and contracts to represent black farmers. This "evidence" enforced the story that radical shysters misled Phillips County's simple black farmers.[97] "The Negroes at Hoop Spur have been under the influence of a few rascally white men and designing leaders of their own race who have been exploiting them for personal gain," authorities said.[98]

Phillips County's white leaders—like their counterparts in places as urban as Chicago or as rural as Jenkins County—were eager to forget about racial violence as soon as they could, to explain it away and get back to business. In Chicago, that meant getting cheap, unorganized black workers back in the stockyards and slaughterhouses. In Phillips County, it meant getting farm laborers back in the fields to pick the cotton crop, just set to be harvested.

On October 7, 1919, the Committee of Seven distributed a circular "to the Negroes of Phillips County," which declared: "No innocent Negro has been arrested, and those of you who are at home and at work have no occasion to worry. All you have to do is to remain at work just as if nothing had happened." It ended with the Orwellian admonitions:

STOP TALKING
STAY AT HOME
GO TO WORK
DON'T WORRY.[99]

For days, the Committee of Seven presented its harrowing story to white reporters, who transmitted it across the United States to tens of millions of readers. "Big Uprising Was Plotted" ran part of a headline in the *Washington Post*. "Negroes Plot White Massacre" was a headline in the *Los Angeles Times*.[100] The army embraced this story as well. "It is the same old story of a bad leader, exploiting and hookwinking the Negro race for mercenary purposes," an infantry officer at Camp Pike wrote in an intelligence report.[101] The narrative meshed with nationwide white fears of racial violence and radicalism: stored ammunition, passwords, "Paul Reveres" riding into the night, and a white socialist lawyer as a mastermind. But the cinematic story was completely contrived.

Instead, what took place was nothing less than an antiblack massacre. To this day, no one has any idea just how deadly it was. Grif Stockley and Robert Whitaker, two authors of books on the Elaine incident, both estimated hundreds of blacks were killed. In the 1920s, estimates of the number of blacks killed varied widely. In 1927, a student at an Arkansas teachers' college, Bessie Ferguson, wrote her history thesis on the Elaine riot using interviews with anonymous white witnesses. She claimed people told her of ears being cut off black corpses and blacks being dragged through the streets. She wrote that an estimate of 25 blacks killed was conservative.[102] James Weldon Johnson put the death toll at 200 to 400.[103] White Arkansas journalist L. Sharpe Dunaway claimed in 1925 that 856 blacks were killed, most by federal troops. Though he was himself a racist, Dunaway was appalled.

"The fact that certain Federal soldiers were sent over to the scene of the trouble for the purpose of 'quelling a riot' and ended up by starting a crusade of death that claimed the lives of nearly a thousand innocent victims of their uncontrollable wrath, justifies the scathing criticism and righteous condemnation heaped upon them by the better class of white citizens," he wrote.[104]

An official of the black Pythian and Masonic lodges in Arkansas claimed in 1920 that his lodge paid for 103 burials after Elaine, and that he knew of another 73 other blacks who were killed.[105] In the vacuum of a thorough investigation of the death toll, the national media fudged the numbers. A *New York Times* account from October 4, 1919, put the death toll at 24—5 whites and 19 blacks. "The bodies of other Negroes probably will be found in the woods by searching parties," the story stated.[106] Later stories from the *Times* and other publications reported "a score" or so. No forensic accounting of what happened in Elaine was ever conducted.

At first, this information was suppressed. The Committee of Seven bolstered its version of events with forced confessions gleaned from the accused.[107] The prisoners, crammed into the jail and wearing the same dirty clothes they wore when they were captured, were not allowed to see family or friends.[108] Months later, when they finally secured legal defense they could trust, the black men gave hair-raising accounts of posses slaughtering farmers and families. They told of being beaten until they signed confessions.

One defendant, William Wordlow, twenty-two, attended the Hoop Spur church on the night of the shooting. He said white men in four or five cars drove up to the church and started shooting. A sharecropper who worked 14 acres of cotton, Wordlow lost everything in the riot and was sentenced to death. He signed a sworn statement that he hid in the forest with his wife and children after a white posse shot at them and chased them. Later, he surrendered to soldiers, who put his family in with others at the schoolhouse in Elaine. Posse members held him for five days, then took him to the jail in Helena. He said there he was "whipped nearly to death to make me tell stories on the others, to say we killed the white people and colored people when at the church that night I did not have a gun whatever. The white people want to say that union was the cause of the trouble. It's not so. . . . The Phillips County people know they started this trouble and they only got the army there to cover what they had done." He said his interrogators blindfolded him, covered up his nose and mouth, and gave him electric shocks during his "confession."[109]

Other defendants told similar stories of torture. Walter Ward, thirty-five, claimed white interrogators beat him with a metal-studded rubber strap that sliced through his skin with each beating. "I do not know how many licks I was hit, but I know that they nearly killed me," he said later.[110]

After days of such interrogation, a handful of men—some beaten and some not—agreed to testify for the prosecution about an alleged plot. The Committee of Seven turned them over to prosecutor Miller. The politically ambitious Miller had Phillips County as part of his circuit. From the beginning, Miller had reservations about the "evidence" from the interrogations. He knew, however, that he had to prosecute a substantial portion of the hundreds of black farmers in custody.[111] He could not launch a political career by alienating leading white constituents, let alone the powerful white governor who sanctioned what they had just done.[112] He had to deliver convictions.

After releasing 150 black men and all female prisoners, Miller moved quickly to prosecute the remaining suspects.[113] On October 27, he impaneled a grand jury of white men in the overwhelmingly black county. Two grand jury members, Sebastian Straub and T. W. Keese, also served on the Committee of Seven. After four days of deliberations, the grand jury indicted 122 blacks on charges relating to the "insurrection," 73 of them with murder.[114] No whites were indicted.[115]

Several black men involved with the union, including Robert Hill and Ed Ware, fled the state to escape warrants. Hill made his way to Kansas, while Ware fled to Louisiana. Their flight fueled fears among whites across Arkansas that a broad conspiracy was afoot. Whites surmised members of the black union must be sheltering the fugitives.[116]

The sharecroppers in jail lost what little property they had. Many of those Miller released also lost their rented land and had to move away. Ida Wells-Barnett, who took up the cause of the black defendants, wrote later: "If this is democracy, what is bolshevism?"[117]

On November 2, trials began—and they were quick. All the blacks were assigned white defense attorneys from Phillips County. Not one lawyer filed a motion for continuance, even though they had only days to prepare a defense against charges as serious as murder. No lawyers asked for a change of venue. No lawyers asked that all-white juries be disqualified. Thirty-six men pleaded guilty to lesser charges, but the rest who stood trial were all found guilty. With at least two cases, jurors deliberated for no more than six minutes before reaching a verdict.[118] In high-stakes murder trials, the defense called no witnesses. Within days, 11 men were sentenced to death by electric chair. Authorities arrested Ed Ware in New Orleans and brought him back for a quick trial. A jury found him guilty and he joined the other 11 on death row. Other black defendants were convicted and sentenced to long terms in prison. A reporter described the speed of the trials as "rapid progress."[119] Brough believed the quick actions of Phillips County officials and his own heroic arrival with soldiers averted a disaster. As his private secretary noted at the time, if Brough had not taken decisive action, "the Negroes would have wiped out three or four of those little towns down there in the southern end of Phillips County."[120]

To many white Americans, the ready solution to racial violence was just such a legal crackdown on blacks. On October 4, 1919, a jury deliberated eight minutes before finding Maurice Mays, the man who was at the center of the Knoxville riots in September, guilty. He received the death penalty.[121]

The official Arkansas story of a Negro plot proved what many whites long feared. A month later, this belief received the imprimatur of a federal Justice Department report to Congress that linked revolutionary conspiracies with black publications.

But the official narrative of the Arkansas riot soon met a powerful antithesis. In the aftermath of Phillips County, black organizations, led by the NAACP, launched a sustained effort to dismantle the dominant narrative that blacks were conspiring with radicals.

On October 3, with Elaine still on front pages across the country,

James Weldon Johnson took the train from New York to Washington and met again with Senator Charles Curtis of Kansas, the sponsor of the Senate resolution calling for congressional hearings on race riots and lynchings. Johnson attacked the Committee of Seven story and told Curtis that the arrested blacks were being railroaded. Curtis was not completely convinced. A few days later, Curtis wrote to Johnson asking for information about the I.W.W.'s role in Arkansas and elsewhere. Like many white politicians, he accepted much of what he read in the newspapers about radical connections.[122]

But Curtis and others were also learning to respect the NAACP's political muscle. It had grown to become the largest African American uplift organization in history. Curtis told Johnson he had received "an avalanche" of positive letters and telegrams from NAACP supporters urging him to press for a hearing on mob attacks.

The group's expansion gave it power and reach. When the NAACP board met in the association's New York offices on October 13, Shillady reported a record 83,509 members and 293 branches. The NAACP's income grew with more members. But growth also meant the association's expenditures grew exponentially. The board estimated it needed to raise an extra $25,000 to $50,000 for a special legal defense fund and another $30,000 to $60,000 for a special fund to respond to all the Red Summer crises. But as of September 30, its general fund had only $8,016.56; its legal fund had only $92.50.[123] The NAACP launched an intense fund-raising effort even as it began a publicity campaign to pressure Congress and an unprecedented legal defense effort to help those charged in Phillips County. The association worked to keep the money it was raising for legal defense quiet. The board feared that if Arkansas whites knew the NAACP was paying for the men's legal defense, the information would destroy the defendants' chances in court. "It would queer the case if a northern organization was known to be financing it," Ovington wrote to one contributor.[124] It was a charade. Everyone knew the NAACP was involved. Representative Thaddeus Caraway, a segregationist Arkansan, was livid that the organization, which he said should be called "an association for the promotion of revolution and inciting to riots," was interjecting itself in Arkansas's affairs. The NAACP, he declared on the House floor, "thrives financially by falsehoods and antagonisms."[125]

Walter White traveled to Arkansas within weeks of the outbreak. The trip earned the NAACP, and White himself, great renown and offered a spirited alternative to the official narrative of the violence. With his light complexion and credentials from the *Chicago Daily News*, White passed himself off as a white reporter. Governor Brough even met with him and provided him with a letter of introduction to Phillips County officials.

Prominent black lawyer Scipio Jones urged White not to go to Phillips County, since it would endanger any blacks who spoke with him. But White chose not to follow Jones's advice:

> As I stepped from the train ... I was closely watched by a crowd of men. Within half an hour of my arrival I had been asked by two sharecroppers, a restaurant waiter, and a ticket agent why I had come to Elaine, what my business was, and what I thought of the recent riot. The tension relaxed somewhat when I implied I was in sympathy with the mob. Little by little suspicion was lessened and then, the people being eager to have a metropolitan newspaper give their side of the story, I was shown "evidence" that the story of the massacre plot was well founded, and not very clever attempts were made to guide me away from the truth.[126]

In his investigation, White determined the real cause of the violence was white backlash against black sharecroppers' efforts to organize "a cooperative society to combat their economic exploitations by landlords, merchants, and bankers, many of whom openly practiced peonage." He published an article in the *Chicago Daily News*, concluding the planned insurrection was "a figment of the imagination of Arkansas whites."[127] Though he had some facts wrong (including the name of the town he was in—he thought it was Elaine when it was in fact Helena), the account was an important challenge to the conspiracy story, because it appeared in a large-circulation, white daily newspaper in a major city. White followed up with similar stories in other publications, including *The Nation* and *The Crisis*.

White declared in *The Nation* that unless the twelve condemned men had their sentences commuted, they would be "additional victims of America's denial of rudimentary justice to 12,000,000 of its citizens because of their color."[128] White later claimed that after a few days in Phillips County, he left not a moment too soon:

I walked down West Cherry Street . . . one day on my way to the jail, where I had an appointment with the sheriff, who was going to permit me to interview some of the Negro prisoners who were charged with being implicated in the alleged plot. A tall, heavy-set Negro passed me and, *sotto voce*, told me as he passed that he had something important to tell me, and that I should turn to the right at the next corner and follow him. Some inner sense bade me obey. When we had got out of sight of other persons the Negro told me not to go to the jail, that there was great hostility in the town against me and that they planned harming me. In the man's manner there was something which made me certain he was telling the truth. Making my way to the railroad station, since my interview with the prisoners (the sheriff and the jailer being present) was unlikely to add anything to my story, I was able to board one of the two trains a day out of Elaine. When I explained to the conductor—he looked at me so inquiringly—that I had no ticket because delays in Elaine had given me no time to purchase one, he exclaimed, "Why, Mister, you're leaving just when the fun is going to start! There's a damn yaller nigger down here passing for white and the boys are going to have some fun with him."

I asked him the nature of the fun.

"Wal, when they get through with him," he explained grimly, "he won't pass for white anymore."[129]

The day he returned to New York, White wrote to Archibald Grimké in Washington, saying, "I secured some information which I believe will do much toward clearing up that much-clouded situation there. All talk about a 'massacre of whites' is absurd."[130]

Grimké wrote to Secretary Baker asking if the federal troops treated blacks fairly. Baker responded with a brief, imperious rebuff: "I have no hesitancy in stating that the policy of the War Department, in the matter of disarming persons engaged in uprisings against the constituted authorities, would make no differentiation on the basis of race."[131]

Other black leaders and groups joined the NAACP to come to the defense of the twelve hapless farmers—including Ed Ware—now on death row and to expose what really happened in Phillips County. Ida Wells-Barnett's Negro Fellowship League, William Monroe Trotter's National Equal Rights League, and Chicago black politician Oscar De Priest all raised legal defense funds. Barnett and others deluged Brough with telegrams demanding he stay any executions.[132] Wells-Barnett visited the men in jail and published a booklet and articles calling for a reprieve. The Urban League, holding its annual conference in Detroit two weeks after Elaine, issued resolutions "that the Negro will be given fair treatment, and be protected in buying and selling" and "that the life and property of every Negro will be protected against all lawless assaults."[133]

Du Bois took up the fight for the condemned. Though exhausted by the summer of violence, editorial work, public speaking, and completion of his book *Darkwater*, Du Bois revived by the end of September. When the Elaine massacres occurred, he wrote numerous letters to white publishers and editors attacking the "insurrection" narrative. Du Bois wrote the editor of the *New York World* telling him the notion that whites had suppressed a black insurrection was ridiculous. The trials of the black defendants, he wrote, were "a most outrageous farce."[134]

In *The Crisis*, Du Bois skewered Brough, who once defended blacks, but sacrificed them in Elaine for political gain: "When the 'uprising' occurred in Phillips County, he let slave barons make their own investigation, murder the innocent, and railroad ignorant, honest laborers to imprisonment and death in droves; contrast this with the actions of Governor Lowden of Illinois and Mayor Smith of Omaha!"[135]

The black press and uplift groups across the country joined in a chorus condemning the Phillips County violence. "It does not take an I.W.W. to clinch the argument that the majority of the Negroes in the United States cannot vote," declared the *Black Dispatch* in Oklahoma City. "It does not take a Bolshevist to inform us that freedom of movement is restricted to us and that, under the guise of law a separate status as citizens, is designed for the black man."[136]

An editor at the black *Houston Informer* declared: "All this journalistic diarrhea about 'radical Negro editors' and 'race uplifters inciting Negroes to revolt against the white man,' etc. is unadulterated and unsophisticated bosh, buncome, 'bull' and 'bull-sheviki.'"[137]

The National Race Congress met and passed resolutions calling for the federal government to stop the violence. A group of ministers representing major black churches sent appeals for clemency to President Wilson, attorney general Palmer, and Governor Brough. Both groups were ignored.[138]

———

Marcus Garvey pointed to the violence as proof that blacks should separate from whites and establish their own empire. When the violence broke out, he was on a speaking tour in the Midwest, setting up new UNIA chapters. On October 1, he delivered two speeches in Chicago's Black Belt.

"We do not want to start any riots, but we say this: before any one moves to get me I am going to get him first," he told the hundreds gathered. Justice Department spies recorded his statements.[139]

Garvey's message had broad appeal and many blacks signed on with the UNIA. Back in Harlem on October 14, a disgruntled black man named George Tyler, a part-time vendor for Garvey's newspaper who claimed Garvey owed him money, went to the UNIA offices on 135th Street and shot Garvey four times.[140] Garvey survived the attack, which won him more prestige. Sales of his booklets and newspaper soared. A rally at Madison Square Garden on October 30 drew 6,000 people. Rally handbills showed a black woman kneeling with her arms outstretched, her children cowering next to her, as their home burned.

"Negroes Awake!" the bills announced. "The hour has come to save your Race from the burning stake. Invest in the Black Star Line."[141]

Key players in the white press began to voice some support for black civil rights and federal protections. The *New York Times* ran a long article on October 5, 1919, based upon—but not attributing—the position paper that James Weldon Johnson had given Senator Curtis. The paper argued that the federal government needed to intervene to stop the violence—a key NAACP position:

"So far this problem, in some respects the most grave now facing the country, has been allowed to drift. The States have done nothing. The Federal Government has done nothing. The only move made at Washington is the introduction by Senator Charles Curtis of Kansas of a resolution."[142]

If amelioration of America's racial divide remained beyond reach, a short-term answer to the racial violence arrived, spontaneously, in much of the country that October: prompt, forceful, and unbiased government enforcement of law and order. It had worked well in Charleston in May and in some instances during the following months. Whenever disciplined police or troops enforced law and order, rioting stopped. But far too often during the Red Summer, governments had been too slow to respond, or leaders delayed for political reasons or personal bias. That began to change in October, at least in urban areas.

Throughout the month, white mobs attacked blacks, but local government leaders started responding rapidly and forcefully to shut down violence. Politicians had too many recent examples of what could go wrong and no one wanted to become the next headline.

On the night of October 2, about a hundred white soldiers from Camp Meade rioted in a black neighborhood in East Baltimore after someone threw a bottle at them. Soldiers started shooting at blacks until police rushed to the area. Several soldiers were arrested. When more enraged soldiers showed up to fight, they "were met by the police with heavy clubs," the *Washington Post* reported. Order was quickly restored.[143]

On October 3, the Universal Portland Cement plant in Indiana Harbor, Indiana, reopened for the first time since the national steel strike began. Strikers manhandled two black strikebreakers, who pulled revolvers and fired, wounding a striker. The local sheriff immediately sent in 500 deputies to keep the peace.[144]

On October 11, in Chester, Pennsylvania, Charles Neely, a twenty-seven-year-old black man, was ejected from a saloon for being drunk. He opened fire on a crowd, killing one white and wounding five others. Police arrested Neely while a large mob formed outside the bar. The mayor ordered the defendant driven to another town. He then deputized hundreds of supporters to patrol the streets to keep peace. All bars were shut down.[145] Such actions saved lives.

In the rural South, however, lynchings continued. In Lincolnton, Georgia, a mob of 1,000 whites grabbed Jack Gordon, accused of killing a white officer and wounding another white. The mob also abducted another black for allegedly misdirecting their hunt for Gordon. The two were hung from a tree and shot to death at 4 a.m., October 6. Their riddled bodies were then thrown on a bonfire of pine. Other blacks in the area were whipped.[146]

On October 7, a mob lynched twenty-nine-year-old Eugene Hamilton in Georgia's Jasper County after an all-white jury convicted him of attempting to shoot a white farmer. The case was before the Georgia Court of Appeals when Hamilton was moved to a jail in nearby Jones County. The sheriff heard a mob was coming to the jail so he headed out with three deputies to drive Hamilton to a jail in Macon, the nearest large city. In the early morning hours, sixty armed men stopped them on the road. The mob took Hamilton, drove him to a bridge in Jasper County, and shot him to death.[147] John Cooper, a prominent white attorney from

Macon who defended many blacks, wrote an angry letter to Governor Hugh Dorsey: "I firmly believe in the absolute innocence of Eugene Hamilton. He was convicted on the color of his skin."

Yet unlike the response of many government officials in preceding months, Dorsey wrote back embarrassed and livid about what had happened.

"I am thoroughly indignant and ready to do anything I can," he wrote, adding, "I shall leave no stone unturned to bring the guilty parties to punishment."

He quickly asked the local sheriff for an explanation and offered a reward for information leading to the arrest of those involved. Cooper offered to be the state prosecutor.[148] Dorsey's reaction showed that a new day was coming, even in the rural South where such extrajudicial killings were rampant. In the fall of 1919, Dorsey increased his public calls for harsher anti-lynching laws, calls that he amplified in coming years.

As October came to a close, the town of Corbin in central Kentucky evicted almost its entire black population in one night. After a white man there was robbed and stabbed, rumors spread that the assailants were black, though it was later shown the attackers were white men in blackface. Three hundred whites rounded up as many as 200 black railroad workers, waking many from their beds at gunpoint. The mob forced the workers into a boxcar, and sent it south to Knoxville in the middle of the night.[149] In a few hours the town lost most of its black population. The black workers had been brought to Corbin to expand a yard of the Louisville & Nashville Railroad. The influx of black workers—hired by the railroad because of the war labor shortage—increased racial tensions in town. Corbin's white citizens blamed many crimes on the black workers.[150]

"Corbin must hang her head in shame," one woman wrote to the local newspaper.[151]

By October's close, many Americans were mortified by all of these antiblack outbursts. America's leaders wanted solutions. Some thought the nation needed to crack down on vice. In late October, both houses of Congress overrode Wilson's veto of the National Prohibition Act, known as the Volstead Act after its chief sponsor, Republican Representative Andrew John Volstead of Minnesota. Under the law, the nation was set to go "dry" by July 1920.

Others clamored for a federal crackdown on leftist agitators and an investigation of their links to the racial unrest.

And all the while, the NAACP and others amplified calls for federal anti-lynching legislation.

Staid editors of the *North American Review* announced the United States was "suffering a race war," and if such strife erupted in a small European country, Americans would demand intervention.

"It might be well for such altruistic propagandists to consider the ancient adjuration, 'Physician, heal thyself,'" they wrote to the nation.[152]

20.

Let the Nation See Itself

There's no managing the neegahs now, they's got so big-gety since the war.

—WHITE WOMAN IN SHADY DALE, Georgia, late 1919

BY NOVEMBER, THE "RACE WAR" OF 1919 THAT HAD ROCKED THE nation arrived at an unsettled and incomplete truce—and no one was quite sure why. Everyone welcomed the respite, but people remained uneasy.

Why were there less riots and lynchings? Several factors played a role. Many were exhausted from all the chaos, and were less likely to take to the streets. Also, local governments, now painfully aware of the consequences of inaction, swiftly responded.[1]

Whites inclined to form a mob had learned, at least in large cities, that they would meet armed resistance. And blacks knew their safety came in organized and rapid response to violence. Local newspapers, seeing the carnage and bad publicity heaped on cities hit by riots, urged politicians to crack down at the first sign of trouble.

The NAACP used the Red Summer to try to shame government—local, state, and federal—into action. Since Shillady's beating in Texas, James Weldon Johnson had taken over as the organization's public face, delivering speeches, organizing chapters, raising money, and lobbying Congress. At the May anti-lynching conference in New York, Johnson had emerged as a new black voice. By November, he arrived as black America's ambassador to its white government.

Johnson's message was clear and his logic concise. On November 9, he joined other activists at the Tremont Temple in Boston and delivered a speech that foreshadowed arguments pushed decades later by black leaders not yet born.

On self-defense, he spoke much as Malcolm X would one day:

> I know we can't settle this race trouble by taking a shotgun and going out and shooting up people, but I will say it will go a long way toward settling this thing if we shoot back when we are shot at.

On race relations, his remarks anticipated the strategy and the philosophy of the Reverend Martin Luther King Jr.:

> We've got to wake up the conscience of the American people, to hold the mirror before the people and let the Nation see itself—a sinning Nation—for the American spirit is not dead.
>
> We need an organization of the white people and the black people to save America from mob violence. We must have organization, a militant organization. Patience is a virtue, but not always. I want to see the Negro patient, but I want to see him fight incessantly for what he believes is his right. No one is more confident than the American Negro, for he knows he is right and has God Almighty on his side and can't lose.[2]

Other black leaders took up the messianic tone. In a sermon that November, Charles Spencer Smith, bishop of Detroit's Bethel African Methodist Episcopal Church, accused Moses of committing the first "race riot" in history.

"Moses killed an Egyptian [Exodus 2:11–12], after he saw him beating a Jew. Because he hid the Egyptian's body in the sand, Moses was a coward. Still, he was better than the white rioters of 1919 who kill and then justify the act by claiming racial superiority," Smith declared. "Let the bloodthirsty lynchers in this country take warning lest their sins be visited on their children and their children's children."

Smith had seen the full arc of the black experience from the Civil War to the Great War. Born in 1852, he rose from slavery and poverty to teach school for the Freedmen's Bureau, serve in the Alabama legislature during Reconstruction, and earn a medical degree. As a bishop in the AME Church, he traveled to Africa and wrote about his experiences. He was a success, yet at the same time he saw the setbacks for his race in the South, black difficulties in the North, and the bloodshed of the Red Summer. He remained hopeful about the future of a multiracial America and scoffed at calls for blacks and whites to separate.

"There is far more to be gained by our walking together in agreement than by our walking apart in disagreement," he told his congregation. "The three most potent agencies which can act in its defense are the press, the pulpit and the bar."[3]

Opponents of blacks rights were horrified by this new attitude. Stephen Graham, a British journalist who toured the country in the fall of 1919, met a despondent white woman in Shady Dale, Georgia.

"There's no managing the neegahs now," she told him. "They's got so biggety since the war."[4]

On November 10, the NAACP board met in Manhattan to review recent triumphs, pressing business, and future plans. Johnson rushed back from his Boston rally. Du Bois and Walter White attended, as did Shillady. The board learned it had not reached its ambitious goal of 100,000 members set in May, but it had come close. A group that had fewer than 10,000 members at the start of 1918 now had 84,877 members and 299 branches across the country. *The Crisis* continued to sell about 100,000 copies a month, making it one of the largest black publications in the country.[5]

Much of the meeting centered on efforts to push anti-lynching bills and resolutions in Congress. Johnson told board members he had made headway. Even stray Democrats in the North began to offer support. Herbert Claiborne Pell Jr., a Democratic congressman from New York who had just taken office in 1919, wrote to the NAACP on November 6 offering full support: "I do not regard lynching as being exclusively or even in the greatest degree harmful to the colored race, because I feel sure that in the long run the white people who tolerate them will suffer more severely than any one else."[6]

The NAACP special anti-lynching committee held its meeting on November 14 at Moorfield Storey's home in Boston. The group drew up two lists, one of possible speakers if Congress held a hearing on the Red Summer violence, and the other of potential donors to the NAACP's depleted anti-lynching fund. After the May conference, the committee raised more than $9,300. By November, it had only $1,300 left. Storey and another board member each agreed to donate $1,000.[7] The committee readied itself for efforts in 1920—and it was already seeing results from 1919. Within days of the meeting, Kentucky voters overwhelmingly passed a constitutional amendment allowing peace officers to be fired if they let mobs take prisoners.[8]

———

Several trials stemming from the Red Summer concluded that November. In Arkansas, a dozen black men were sent to death row.[9] In Chicago, blacks and whites were convicted in a slew of cases. Despite one judge's call in August to "hang the rioters," many were released for lack of evidence. A handful received lengthy prison sentences.[10] The NAACP was convinced blacks had been mistreated by police in initial arrests and battled hard for courts to release black defendants unless compelling evidence existed. Throughout the summer, far more blacks faced trial than whites in riot-related cases.[11] In Savannah, Joe Ruffin, who survived the Carswell Grove shootings in April, was found guilty of murder after a one-day trial. The judge set execution by hanging for January 9, 1920. Ruffin begged the judge for mercy, crying and screaming in the courtroom.[12]

———

The narrative that agitators were swaying blacks—a story promoted by white newspapers and politicians and bolstered by military intelligence and the Justice Department—became the official position of the federal government on November 17. Attorney general A. Mitchell Palmer submitted a 187-page report to the Senate Judiciary Committee. In October, the administration's Senate critics passed a resolution demanding to know what Palmer was doing about subversives. The report was Palmer's answer, and it painted an ominous picture: Bolsheviks and anarchists were working to destroy the Republic.

On November 7, the second anniversary of the Bolshevik Revolution, federal agents began long-awaited raids on Palmer's orders. Palmer claimed the Justice Department had amassed the names of 60,000 Marxists and anarchists—most of them European immigrants. The report's first hundred pages focused on white radicals, especially Russian-born anarchists Emma Goldman and Alexander Berkman. Justice had begun deportation proceedings against several hundred radicals, including Goldman and Berkman.[13]

Palmer's letter served as an answer to critics who had attacked him for being inactive in the face of a perceived national threat. Other motivations

for his reports may have included money and power. Palmer was pushing Congress for increased funds to investigate radicals, and Republican
legislators had balked. Also, Palmer was jockeying to win the 1920 Democratic nomination for president.[14]

But the report's focus shifted from immigrant subversives with
Exhibit 10 of the report, beginning on page 101. The next 86 pages were a
collection of quotations from black publications about resisting white
violence.[15]

The author, presumably Hoover, saw the writings as evidence of anti-
American rebellion by blacks. He wrote, "Since the first report was prepared there have occurred the several race riots in Washington, Knoxville,
Chicago, Omaha, and Arkansas and the more radical Negro publications
have been quick to avail themselves of the situation as cause for the utterance of inflammatory sentiment—utterances which in some cases have
reached the limit of open defiance and a counsel of retaliation."[16]

The report castigated black leaders for their "ill-governed reaction
toward race rioting. . . . In all the discussions of the recent race riots
there is reflected the note of pride that the Negro has found himself, that
he has 'fought back,' that never again will he tamely submit to violence
and intimidation."[17]

The report, without ever establishing a proven link, equated black
self-defense to anarchistic plots to overthrow capitalism: "If this report
serves to give a substantial appreciation of the dangerous spirit of defiance
and vengeance at work among the Negro leaders, and, to an ever-increasing
extent, among their followers, it shall have accomplished its purpose."[18]

Once again, the white press embraced this story line. The *New York
Times* published a selection from the report under the heading, "Radicalism and Sedition Among the Negroes, as Reflected in Their Publications."[19]

James Weldon Johnson attacked the report in the *New York Age*,
claiming he would "eat a bundle of these reports without taking water"
if anyone could show how black newspapers and magazines could logi-
cally be grouped with anarchist publications.

"What do all of these extracts amount to when boiled down?" he
asked. "They amount to a demand not for anarchy, not for the overthrow
of the Government, but to a demand for the strict and impartial enforcement of law, and to an expression of the determination of the Negro to
defend himself when and where the law refuses or fails to protect him
against the mob. . . . Let those who are holding up their hands in holy
horror at the mere thought of lawlessness on the part of the Negroes stop

and consider that in not one of these outbreaks were Negroes the original aggressors. All of the 'race riots' which occurred last summer were
started by lawless white men."[20]

Although the report devoted many pages to supposed radical statements in black publications, the Justice Department did not indict one
major black leader or editor.[21]

So why did the report take aim at black publications? Perhaps it was
Palmer's inherent distrust of blacks. Perhaps friends or staff influenced him.
He was close with Representative James Byrnes of South Carolina, who rose
in Congress and denounced Du Bois's essay on returning soldiers. Perhaps
Mitchell thought that including the section would engender support from
southern senators and congressmen, whom he needed for delegate votes
at the Democratic convention in San Francisco the following year.[22]

Some whites, moderates, and progressives in each party mocked Palmer's fears of imminent revolution. They argued that 1919 showed America's real problem was mob violence. "The real peril as distinguished from
the bogey is that the difficult readjustments just ahead of us will be accom-
panied by nerve-wracking and distracting disorder," Walter Lippmann
wrote. "Revolution there will not be, but a great deal of rioting there
may be."[23]

———

Though racial violence lessened substantially in November, residual
trouble continued. On November 3, four hundred whites gathered near
Macon in search of Paul Booker, a black man accused of attacking a fifty-
year-old white woman. The mob cornered Booker in a boxcar. Sheriff's
deputies tried to negotiate with the mob, but when the woman identified
the man as her attacker, they dragged Booker away, soaked him in gasoline, then shot him to death as he writhed in flames.[24] On November 11,
Jordan Jameson, charged with killing a sheriff, was yanked from jail and
burned to death in the public square in Magnolia, Arkansas. The same
day, a marshal in Stonewall, Mississippi, had to drive full-speed with his
prisoner to escape two carloads of lynchers.[25]

On November 13, in Wilmington, Delaware, whites rioted after black
men were accused of shooting and killing a white police officer and
wounding another when police searched their home for guns. White mobs
roamed the streets attacking blacks. Three hundred whites cornered four
blacks at one point, but the black men were armed and a gun battle ensued.
Police arrived and drove back the mob as the blacks escaped. Officials

moved fast to defuse the situation. The three black men charged were sent under guard to a jail in Philadelphia, and blacks were ordered to stay off the streets while police patrolled in full force. The Delaware attorney general promised speedy, fair trials and the mob dispersed.[26]

No one was under the delusions that racial violence, let alone racism and segregation, would soon vanish. Yet among blacks and their supporters, hope abounded.

"Spasmodic and ungodly actions will yet mark the temper of many belated individuals, and great wrongs will have to be endured yet a while longer," J. Stanley Durkee, the last white president of Howard University, told a November 13 gathering at the school. "But the flood tide of democracy and righteousness has now definitely set in."[27]

⸺

Late in November, a bloody shootout in Louisiana's pine country pointed to a new way for American race relations. In a sawmill company town, whites died defending a black man.

As many as seven white union members holed up in a garage to fend off a posse from seizing Sol Dacus, the president of the local black timber union. In a pitched gun battle, Dacus escaped, but four of his white defenders were killed.[28] Bogalusa, in the east section of the state on the Mississippi border, was fraught with tension as unions attempted to organize lumber workers. The town was created and owned by the Great Southern Lumber Company, founded by magnates from Buffalo, New York, who were attracted to Louisiana's virgin forests of longleaf yellow pine.

The company founded Bogalusa in 1906, hewing it out of the forests and calling it "the Magic City of the Pinelands." The town's sawmill became the busiest in the world. Company officials ran Bogalusa with paternalism and intimidation. They built parks, schools, homes, and hospitals—all company owned. They set up a YMCA and organized parades and festivals. By 1915, the mill alone employed more than 3,000 people—half of them black. Before the war, union efforts failed. Workers showed little interest in offending their bosses.[29]

The war changed that. The military placed large orders at the mill, and also enlisted many area workers while industrial jobs lured blacks north. Labor shortages became common.[30]

The company raised pay, but also charged more for rent, hospital visits, and other services to offset losses. After the war, demand for lumber fluctuated, and the company laid off workers. In town, workers joined the local AFL unions, the Union of Timber Workers and the United Brotherhood of Carpenters and Joiners, which in early 1919 launched a drive to unionize the mill.[31] Whites joined and formed local white chapters. The company responded by firing white union members and replacing them with nonunion blacks—by now a common industry tactic.[32]

But in Bogalusa, something new happened: whites met with blacks and persuaded them to set up their own local. Sol Dacus, a longtime lumber worker in his midfifties, became the group's president.

To combat the unions, the Great Southern Lumber Company hired a large private army to battle and intimidate organizers. The workers, tough southern woodsmen, responded in kind. L. E. Williams, the union head, was an amateur champion wrestler. He was not going to back down.

The company organized the Self-Preservation and Loyalty League, composed of white army veterans and company men, to intimidate workers and break up union efforts. Both company and union groups began carrying weapons. When the League threatened to break up a black union meeting, armed white union men vowed to defend their comrades and marched through the black neighborhood.

Blacks and whites began fraternizing at the mill and in the town. League members and supporters, including the town's company-owned newspaper, attacked union members as Bolsheviks, condemning their "utter disregard for the time-honored practice of segregation."[33]

An anti-union company brochure ran a photograph of black and white unionists, warning: "The South'll get it if it don't watch out. Get what? Social equality, niggers and whites, men and women, all mixed up together like potatoes in one bin."[34]

Street fights became commonplace. In late August, hundreds of whites lynched a black veteran accused of assaulting a white woman and dragged his corpse through the town's main streets. A white union leader was hauled from a meeting and beaten. League members attacked Dacus's home several times, once killing his dog.[35]

On November 21, a merchant who was also a volunteer police officer swore out a warrant for Dacus's arrest, claiming he was "a dangerous and suspicious character."[36] A posse came to Dacus's home but he fled into the nearby swamp. He spent the night there while the men destroyed his house. That same night, 500 League members stopped a train coming to town to search it for "undesirables."[37]

The next morning, Dacus emerged from the woods and found two members of the carpenters' union, J. P. Bouchillon and Stanley O'Rourke, returning from a hunting trip with shotguns. They agreed to take him to L. E. Williams's garage, where they could figure out what to do. As they walked, a town policeman saw them and alerted the police chief, who organized a posse.

Williams met the men just as the posse surrounded the building. They demanded Dacus, as well as Bouchillon and O'Rourke for harboring a fugitive. The union men refused to give the men up and shooting broke out. The union men were outgunned.[38] Bouchillon, O'Rourke, Williams, and a man named Thomas Gaines were killed. One League member was wounded. In the smoke and confusion, Dacus escaped the garage. He and his wife fled to New Orleans leaving everything behind. On November 25, the army sent in 105 soldiers to patrol Bogalusa.[39]

The shootout killed the union effort. With Williams dead and Dacus gone, other leaders scattered. The state American Federation of Labor demanded arrests, and in December, thirteen men were taken into custody.[40] But Washington Parish grand juries refused to indict.[41] Despite pleas from state union leaders, Louisiana governor Ruffin Pleasant refused to investigate. Sol Dacus and Williams's widow separately sued the Great Southern Lumber Company for damages. They lost.

Disappointment was nothing new. But hope was. The story of whites defending a black man to the death made national news. Black newspapers heralded the men as heroes. The *New York Times* ran a headline: "Unionists Shielded Negro."[42]

The stunning news came after a year of strife where black and white workers were so often at odds. Historian Stephen H. Norwood described the Bogalusa gun battle as "probably the most dramatic display of interracial labor solidarity in the Deep South during the first half of the twentieth century."[43]

◁▷

As Thanksgiving approached, President Wilson, now an invalid ensconced in the White House, issued a holiday proclamation filled with platitudes: "Our democracy remains unshaken in a world torn with political and social unrest," it read.[44] It made no reference to America's own racial and labor strife.

Yet despite the bloodshed, blacks were thankful for the collective courage they had shown during the year. On November 27, the Reverend Francis Grimké delivered a sermon on "The Race Problem . . . in light of the developments of the last year" to a packed Plymouth Congregational Church in the heart of black Washington. The sixty-seven-year-old Grimké, born into slavery, had seen Washington's black community rebound from the July riot and felt blacks had won a great victory.

"There are more colored people thinking about their rights today than ever before," he said in the sermon. "They are alive, wide awake, as never before . . . but back of their interest there is a purpose, a resolute determination that is also new, and that will someday have to be reckoned with."[45]

Through the tribulations of the Red Summer, a triumphant spirit had taken root among black Americans. Still, this élan was freighted with pain and loss. The day after Grimké's sermon, a black man named Sam Mosely, accused of assaulting a white woman, was lynched outside of Lake City, Florida. Passersby found his body, riddled with bullets, hanging from a roadside tree.[46]

At least five more black men would be lynched before the year was out.

21.

Capitol Hill

Pessimism is cowardice.

—W. E. B. Du Bois, *Darkwater*, 1920

ON JANUARY 29, 1920, THE HOUSE JUDICIARY COMMITTEE CONVENED a hearing to review three federal anti-lynching bills. It was the lengthiest discussion about the Red Summer violence ever held before a federal body.

The meeting, called by one of Congress's most powerful committees, was not important for its immediate result: none of the bills passed. But the occasion gave a coalition of black leaders and white allies, led by the NAACP, a government forum to outline their grievances about 1919 and present solutions to stop such mass antiblack violence from ever occurring again. The hearing was a beginning, albeit a modest one, of a political effort that would one day result in the Civil Rights Act of 1964.

The committee that convened that chilly Thursday morning was made up entirely of white men. Some were sympathetic to racial equality; many opposed it. Others believed ensuring racial equality was not the federal government's business.

The black and white speakers before the committee, however, were of one voice in calling for federal intervention to end racial violence. Citing the Fourteenth Amendment's guarantee of equal protection under the law, they urged Congress to punish rioters, lynchers, and local government officials who let such violence take place.

At 10:30 a.m., the committee's chair, Representative Andrew Volstead, the austere Minnesota Republican with a walrus mustache who had led the victorious fight for national prohibition, was about to start the hearing when fellow Republican and committee member Leonidas Dyer interrupted.[1]

Dyer had authored the leading anti-lynching bill. It proposed fines and prison terms for local officials who did not stop rioting and lynching. His bill was a revised version of the legislation he submitted after the devastating 1917 race riot in East St. Louis. But at the hearing, Dyer asked Volstead if two other congressmen with similar bills, Frederick Dallinger of Boston and Merrill Moores of Indianapolis, could address the committee instead. Volstead agreed and Dallinger, a longtime NAACP supporter, went first.

Dallinger's bill required that the federal government ensure equal protection under the law. If rioters or lynchers killed a person, black or white, the local government that allowed it to happen should be held responsible.

"If a community where those things are occurring does not give to the sheriff and the officers of the law the protection which they should have for the enforcement of the law," Dallinger told the committee, "I do not consider that there is the equal protection to which every citizen is entitled."

Congressmen pressed him. Should local governments be held accountable even if they tried to stop a lynching or a riot but it happened anyway? Yes, he said.[2]

Several congressmen, led by Arkansan Thaddeus Caraway, balked, questioning the bill's constitutionality on the grounds of states' rights. The Constitution's authors carefully proscribed federal intervention in local and state affairs, they argued. Dallinger, Moores, and Dyer disagreed, claiming not only was federal intervention allowable, but the Constitution required it if people's safety and equal rights were not being protected. Moores also submitted a position paper of support from former president William Howard Taft.[3]

"If we could bring it home by making the taxpayers of the community interested in not lynching men, white, black, or yellow, it will be more wholesome for the whole country," Moores said.[4]

Arthur Spingarn, representing the NAACP's legal committee, dismissed any constitutional questions raised by the bills' opponents.

"Here is the greatest cancer eating at the vitals of American civilization, which makes America sneered at all over the world," said Spingarn, who along with his brother Joel had served the NAACP since its founding and were leading white advocates for racial equality.[5]

"You have two horns of the dilemma," he said. "The States are either powerless to prevent lynchings or they do not choose to prevent lynchings. If they are powerless to prevent lynchings, then we have mob rule in the states, 'mobocracy,' and the violation of the Constitution itself. If they can do it and they do not prevent it, you have a violation of the Fourteenth Amendment in that we do not give equal protection."[6]

The last five speakers at the hearing were all black men affiliated with the NAACP. The five—James Weldon Johnson, Archibald Grimké, William Wilson, Neval Thomas, and George William Cook—each appealed to justice and American principles of equality in seeking protection for black citizens. And they all delivered a warning to white America: change your ways.

Johnson, already well known to the committee, spoke briefly to give others time to expound. He provided the committee with the NAACP's data about lynching and riots from the past few years and flayed attorney general Palmer's report to Congress that linked the riots and lynching to radical agitation among blacks.[7]

Next came Archibald Grimké, snow-haired head of the NAACP's Washington branch, prominent lawyer and a doyen of the equal rights movement. Though by no means a literal New Negro, the elder brother of famed minister Francis Grimké argued with as much energy as anyone else that day. In what can only be characterized as a jeremiad he scolded the House committee to pass the bills:

Now, what we want, we want you to look at our case, just look at our case as you would look at it as American citizens. Here we are, a part of the United States; we have been here 250 to 300 years, with our never having done anything to it but on the good side and never having gotten anything out of it but on the bad side. . . . The rights which we ask here are the simple rights of American citizens. Can not we live in this country at peace with ourselves and at peace with our neighbors? If we walk upon the street and happen to jostle a belligerent white man in the South, it is a signal for what? For a lynching bee. It is an impudent Negro. That is the cry. . . . If you could really put yourselves in our places and just reverse the whole thing, suppose that a lot of colored people were lynching white people, men, women and sometimes children, as it has occurred, do you think that you would find a way, a committee like this, Constitution or no Constitution, that you would find a way to reach those colored people who were doing it, and save the honor of the country and protect the white men and women and children in peace and in safety. Can we not get the same protection?[8]

Howard University professor George William Cook spoke last, telling the committee he had testified on the Hill for twenty years, but none of those hearings were as important as this one. He said whites attacked his only son during the Washington riot, and afterward the young man had gone off to Canada, with no intention of returning. Cook knew of blacks who now refused to sing the national anthem, he said, but he still sang it.

"I sing it," Cook told the committee. "Why? It is my country. Born here, my mother and father before me and my grandmother and grandfather, and what they added in honest industry went to help build up this Nation and to make it strong. It is my country. I will not forsake it. Why? I treat it very much as I will a leaking house. I will repair the roof. I will not abandon it."[9]

It had taken months of terrifying newspaper headlines coupled with intense lobbying by James Weldon Johnson and others to secure this hearing. During the Red Summer, Congress had largely followed President Wilson's lead, talking little about the racial mayhem.[10] It appeared as though the Republic's legislative body planned to ignore all the deaths, injuries, destroyed homes, and businesses.

But then came the January 29 hearing. In his remarks to the committee, Professor Cook said, "When we come to you, in behalf of twelve million American Negroes, you tell us there is no redress for our wrongs. . . . What are we to hope for?"[11]

Herbert Seligmann, the NAACP's publicity director who risked his life by traveling to Vicksburg and other riot scenes in 1919, published a book in early 1920 called *The Negro Faces America*, which discussed the Red Summer violence. He was at the hearing and heard Cook's remarks. To Seligmann, the entire Red Summer posed a looming question for America's future: Where and how would blacks fit in? Or, as Cook put it, what could blacks hope for?

"No intelligent answer to the question put by that colored leader has yet been attempted," Seligmann wrote.[12]

Seligmann knew the popular notion of removing all blacks from the

United States—whether proposed by the KKK or by Marcus Garvey—
was absurd. The only resolution to racial strife had to be political and
social equality, enshrined in law and enforced by government:

> Race relations constitute democracy's most essential problem, a prob-
> lem compounded of all the other adjustments which free men are
> called upon to make in forming and maintaining social relations.
> Shameful as was the year 1919, with bloodshed, lynching, and race riot
> in the United States, its function was still to bring before the attention
> of all the nation that a national problem, long unsolved, demanded
> serious attention. A condition which had been glossed over, the illegal
> disfranchisement by methods of terrorism of millions of colored Amer-
> icans, was brought boldly to light.[13]

The Red Summer, as Seligmann put it, "accomplished anxious heart-
searchings that were long overdue."[14] Bloody 1919 made clear that black
Americans had to be afforded their rights if the Republic's core principles
were not to be confounded by terminal hypocrisy.

Black sociologist Charles S. Johnson, chief author of the Chicago
Race Commission's report, wrote, "Both races need to understand that
their rights and duties are mutual and equal, and that their interests in
the common good are identical."[15]

Though the Red Summer crystallized America's race issues for the coming century, white America by no means accepted a quick end to segregation or antiblack violence.

In the Red Summer's immediate aftermath, whites in political power
forgot 1919 or misremembered it as a time of radical agitation among
blacks, not as a time when white mobs attacked in record numbers. Southern politicians heaped ire on the NAACP. When the NAACP submitted a
report in support of Representative Dyer's revamped anti-lynching bill in
1920, Representative Caraway of Arkansas attached a two-page rebuttal,
calling it "merely a reprint of a brief filed with the committee by a society
domiciled in New York which has for its sole object, not the securing of
justice for Negroes charged with crime, but immunity from punishment
for their crimes."[16]

Because of such opposition, Dyer's bill failed as did Curtis's resolution. Versions of Dyer's bill failed in 1921 and 1922 as well.[17]

The battle to end racial inequality in America was joined, but average Americans, black and white, continued to see society primarily through the lens of race.

And though 1919 was a high-water mark of race riots and lynchings, such mass violence continued for years afterward. In 1921, mobs in Tulsa, Oklahoma, destroyed the black Greenwood section of the city. To this day, no one knows how many blacks died, though estimates run into the hundreds. In 1923, white vigilantes destroyed the mostly black town of Rosewood, Florida. At least six blacks and two whites were killed.

During World War Two, labor pressures again overwhelmed cities and tensions arose over the role of black soldiers and workers. Rioting and fighting erupted in several cities, an echo of 1919. The worst riot came on the hot Sunday evening of June 20, 1943, in Detroit. Thirty-four people—25 black, 9 white—died in rioting. Police arrested 1,800. President Franklin Roosevelt sent in 5,000 soldiers when the city's crucial war industry ground to a halt.[18] In 1951, thousands of whites rioted in Cicero, Illinois, to keep blacks from moving in.

White mobs were not finished, though they were on the wane. In one of the most famous events of the civil rights era, whites gathered at Little Rock Central High School in 1957 to block black children from going to the all-white school. But President Dwight Eisenhower sent in thousands of federal troops and federalized the state militia to stop trouble. Eisenhower's action worked.

Lynchings also lessened dramatically after 1919. In that year, the Tuskegee Institute recorded eighty-three documented lynchings, all of black men except for a handful of whites and two Mexicans. That number was the highest since 1904 and stayed the highest ever after. A key reason for the decrease was quick action by local and state government, something sorely lacking in 1919.

In February 1920, a black man named Will Lockett was arrested in Lexington, Kentucky, and charged with killing a white woman. Outside his trial, thousands gathered, threatening to storm the building. The governor dispatched the Kentucky militia, giving soldiers orders to shoot if necessary. They did, killing six in the mob. The national press praised the action. One headline read, "Lynchers Don't Like Lead."[19] Lockett later was convicted and executed.

A decade later, the annual number of lynchings dropped to the low teens. By the 1950s, the annual number dropped to single digits and when lynchings did occur, they were front-page news. When a pack of whites murdered Emmett Till in Money, Mississippi, in 1955, they did so in the dark of the night and swore themselves to secrecy. The fourteen-year-old's death made national headlines for months and activists pursued his murderers for decades. Thirty-six years earlier in Ellisville, Mississippi, thousands of "respectable" people—including politicians, reporters, and town leaders—gathered in broad daylight to watch as John Hartfield was tortured, shot to pieces, and burned. People collected his body parts as souvenirs. No one was ever prosecuted.

Jim Crow was put on the defensive after 1919, but it was by no means swept aside. The NAACP branches in the South came under intense pressure in the 1920s, and many folded. In the North, unofficial segregation in the workplace, in schools, and in neighborhoods was often as fierce as anything south of the Mason-Dixon Line. Government prejudice hardened, with segregation in the military and other branches firmly entrenched and black political representation limited. Victory finally came, but did so after many setbacks. It came in installments and over decades.

The year 1919's historic importance was that it was the start of a process—a great dismantling of institutional prejudice and inequity that marred American society. In military terms, the Red Summer was more akin to Lexington and Concord than to Yorktown.

In August 1919, amid the height of the race riots, merchants in Atlanta held a fund-raiser to collect $60,000 for an aging Confederate veterans home. Contributions poured in from whites across the South. But several blacks gave, too. One elderly black woman showed up at fund-raising headquarters to donate a precious dime from her purse.

"If it hadn't been for President Jefferson Davis us niggers still wouldn't be free," the impoverished woman told surprised white men gathered there.[20]

A reporter wrote down her remarks as proof of the simplicity and docility of blacks. He assumed she confused Lincoln with Davis. There is another way to read what she said. Without the Civil War, precipitated by the Davis-led secession, black Americans may never have been released from their bondage. History is the complex story of causation. So it was in 1919. White mobs formed, believing they were putting blacks down. In truth, they strengthened black political resolve and awakened the nation to the racial inequities that were poisoning it.

In 1963, Martin Luther King Jr. stood at the Lincoln Memorial and delivered his "I Have a Dream" speech to hundreds of thousands—and, via television, to millions. The groundwork for that speech was laid by James Weldon Johnson and other NAACP members in Washington in 1919, even as the Lincoln Memorial was still under construction. As ugly and costly as the Red Summer was, it helped birth the movement that culminated in the Civil Rights Act of 1964 and the Voting Rights Act of 1965. It sparked a long effort that led to the integration and participation of black Americans in every aspect of our society and government even to the presidency.

———

Yet despite the Red Summer's importance, most Americans have no idea of the crucible of 1919, despite its importance in shaping modern race relations. When Americans picture race riots today, they recall Watts in 1964, Detroit and Newark in 1967, dozens of riots after Martin Luther King Jr.'s assassination in 1968, or the Los Angeles riot of 1992. Our nation is covered with plaques and monuments marking battles, inventions, constitutional conventions, and other important events. But no plaque or cenotaph marks the racial violence of 1919. It may be an intentional cultural amnesia. The human compulsion is to avoid history we find too ugly or complex. Seligmann called this impulse the "ostrich habit."

But even if 1919 was hushed up and forgotten by generations, the Red Summer's legacy has pervaded race relations to the present day. Much of that legacy had been positive. Black America awakened politically, socially, and artistically like never before. Blacks were emboldened by the Red Summer, not diminished by it. They joined political organizations. They campaigned for politicians. They registered to vote where they could. They lobbied the government with an energy and frequency not seen since at least the 1870s. Tens of thousands joined the NAACP. Though the organization's membership and finances fluctuated in the 1920s—largely because of the crackdown on its southern branches—it remained the leading civil rights group for decades.

The three top black NAACP leaders—James Weldon Johnson, Walter White, and W. E. B. Du Bois—were scarred and drained by the Red Summer. Johnson was exhausted. White took an extended vacation. Du Bois cancelled lectures and saw doctors for headaches and nerves.[21] But they also were emboldened by the black awakening they witnessed. Johnson and White each later headed the NAACP. Du Bois championed black equality for decades.

James Weldon Johnson described the Red Summer fourteen years later as "that summer when the stoutest-hearted Negroes felt terror and dismay."[22]

Yet Johnson, who took over as the NAACP's executive secretary in December 1920 and held the post for a decade, learned a vital lesson from 1919: blacks had to organize and push for change themselves. As he told a black audience in New York in December 1919, "The Negro must discover the elements of force within himself."[23]

Walter White, who devoted himself to the NAACP and served as head of the organization from Johnson's departure to 1955, regaled audiences for the rest of his life with stories of his 1919 adventures.

Twenty years after the riots, Du Bois wrote of the Red Summer: "Never since the red days of Reconstruction did Negroes suffer in the United States as they suffered in these days."[24]

And yet Du Bois recorded his most important lesson from 1919, even as riots were still erupting. "Pessimism is cowardice," he wrote in *Darkwater*.[25]

The NAACP's platform, spelled out in its Tenth Annual Report in 1920, was not escapist or defeatist—it was triumphant and brimming with energy:

> The Negro everywhere is determined to press his right to the citizenship guaranteed him by the federal constitution and to resent as un-American all discriminations against him as a United States citizen. In this spirit he is realizing increasingly that organization for his citizenship advancement is essential. He cannot depend upon others to secure his rights, nor can he consent to be the ward of a favored class of citizens.[26]

During the unprecedented violence, the group's growth was astounding. At the end of 1918, it had 43,994 members. By the end of 1919 it had 91,203. It had branches in 42 states, as well as Canada, Panama, and the Philippines.[27] James Weldon Johnson and Walter White had played a major role in the effort, crossing the country to deliver dozens of speeches. Johnson delivered 76 and White delivered 86 in 1919, far more than their white colleagues.[28]

In its 1920 report, the organization outlined goals that set a course for the civil rights movement for decades to come. It called for:

—Equal voting rights for all black men and women
—Equal educational opportunities for blacks

—Fair trials for blacks

—Protections against lynchings and mobs

—Equal access to public services, including libraries and public parks

"Lynching can be stopped when we can reach the heart and conscience of the American people," the report stated.[29]

For the 1920 presidential election, *The Crisis* sent candidates a seven-part questionnaire, demanding to know their public positions on lynching and segregation.[30]

The admission ticket to the NAACP's annual meeting in New York for January 2, 1920, carried the slogan: "Down with lynching. We've just begun to fight."[31]

Separatism, the idea that blacks should split with the white-dominated United States, continued as a political notion, and Du Bois even embraced it when in his later years he moved to Ghana. But separatism—as opposed to the NAACP's belief in equality in the United States—never gained much credence with most African Americans, in 1919 or afterward. Garvey's UNIA, the largest black organization ever to espouse this proposal, came apart in 1923, after the charismatic leader was sentenced to prison for tax evasion, mail fraud, and perjury. However, it played a vital role in arousing black political awareness.

The Red Summer did not just mobilize blacks and energize black leaders, it also changed the attitudes of many white leaders. Republican Party leaders spoke out against lynching more firmly. In Chicago, Mayor "Big Bill" Thompson brought more blacks into his administration and supported black candidates in local races. Like in many other industrial cities, blacks had become a voting bloc too powerful to ignore. In 1922, when Governor Lowden's race commission finally issued its report, few of its suggestions for defusing tensions were implemented. But it was praised by politicians and became a model for later efforts into the 1960s.[32]

In the South, segregation reigned but it was now perpetually on the defensive. In 1921, newly elected President Warren Harding, an Ohio Republican, visited Birmingham, Alabama, and in a speech before tens of thousands urged southern whites to give blacks the right to vote.

Though southern whites condemned his speech as pro-black, Harding stressed he opposed social equality and praised Lothrop Stoddard's *The Rising Tide of Color*. He urged equal rights and education, but hoped a "natural segregation" would evolve.

"Unless our democracy is a lie, you must stand for that equality," he said, looking at the white audience.

Whites were silent. Blacks cheered from their section of the park.[33]

But not all southern whites were blind to the need to change. The Commission on Interracial Cooperation set up new chapters in all southern states. Several white politicians in the South stood publicly and persistently against lynching, even if they supported segregation.

Georgia's Governor Dorsey, who pressed for tough anti-lynching legislation during the Red Summer, set up his own commission on race relations and published a blistering pamphlet attacking lynching and mistreatment of blacks in the state.

"To me it seems that we stand indicted as a people before the world," he wrote. "If the conditions indicated by these charges [of specific lynchings] should continue, both God and man would justly condemn Georgia more severely than man and God have condemned Belgium and Leopold for the Congo atrocities."[34]

After listing all of the lynchings in Georgia during his term as governor, Dorsey called on new legislation to give his office more authority to punish lynchers and officials who did little to stop them.

Even Governor Brough of Arkansas, who marched with the troops in Phillips County, seemed chastened by the poor publicity that 1919 brought. When a race fight broke out in Dumas, Arkansas, in January 1920, Brough sent in 130 federal troops, who stopped trouble in hours.[35]

Brough made pleading speeches about Elaine, defending his actions but also stressing to those outside Arkansas that he supported equal rights for blacks, stating, "None but the most prejudiced Negro hater, who oftentimes goes to the extreme of denying that any black man can have a white soul, would controvert the proposition that in the administration of quasi public utilities and courts of justice the Negro is entitled to the fair and equal protection of the law."[36]

This from the governor who oversaw the Elaine massacre. Sincere or not, he felt obliged to make these assertions publicly. The national discussion of race had shifted. And though many did not realize it, it had shifted for good.

America's legal system began an incremental transformation after the Red Summer. Where prosecutors had the will and the evidence to make cases, rioters—from both races—were punished. In Charleston, some sailors were drummed out of the service. In Chicago, juries convicted a handful of black and white rioters of serious crimes. Several served long sentences for murder and manslaughter. In Washington, the courts punished whites and blacks.

But most who committed criminal acts during the riots and lynchings in 1919 escaped any punishment or even arrest, especially in the rural South. The men who killed Joe Ruffin's two sons and threw them into the fire at Carswell Grove were never charged with a crime. The men who killed John Hartfield or Lloyd Clay in Mississippi were never charged. Thousands who rioted in Charleston, Longview, Washington, Chicago, Omaha, Elaine, Knoxville, and elsewhere did so with impunity. Many who were arrested and charged were later released because the state could not prove its case or all-white juries would not indict or convict. Some received minor fines or sentences.

Yet along with these travesties, 1919 delivered clear signs that the nation's legal system—in its creaky, delayed fashion—started to afford black defendants protections approximating equal justice.

In Washington, Carrie Minor Johnson, the black teen who shot police detective Harry Wilson, had been charged with first-degree murder. She was later convicted of manslaughter, but the verdict was overturned. In 1921, prosecutors declined a new trial, and released her.

After the Chicago riot, Maclay Hoyne, the Cook County state's attorney, rounded up men in the Black Belt he believed had conspired to launch a revolt. Underworld black gangsters and radicals caused the riot, he claimed. At trial in the fall, he presented days of testimony involving dozens of witnesses, all of which Hoyne made sure was played up in the newspapers. But the trials were flops. Four defendants were acquitted and two more were each fined $1. Similar cases against blacks arrested in the riot fell apart as well.[37]

Blacks began to assert their rights in the courts. Even Maurice Mays, the defendant at the center of the Knoxville riot, was granted a retrial after being convicted of murder. Though he was later executed, the lengthy retrial showed signs of due process.

By far the most important legal ruling to come out of the Red Summer stemmed from the Arkansas violence. After the rapid county trials and cursory plea agreements in October and early November, juries convicted 67 black men of various charges and another 36 pleaded guilty to second-degree murder. Twelve men were sentenced to death for first-degree murder.

The trials came after confessions were obtained through abusive interrogation and were conducted with armed mobs gathered outside the courthouse. They were only held after public assurances from local leaders, two who sat on the grand jury, that those arrested would be severely punished. The all-white juries delivered rapid verdicts with little opposition from local white attorneys appointed as defense counsel. The twelve men were set to be executed by electric chair in December.

Without the help from the NAACP and other groups raising funds and supporting legal efforts, these men certainly would have been executed. But thanks to those efforts, the condemned secured better legal counsel for their appeals, including Little Rock attorneys Ulysses Bratton and Scipio Jones. The men were granted stays of execution. By year's end, however, their situation still seemed hopeless, as the higher courts in Arkansas were poised to uphold the death sentences.

Ed Ware, the farmers union member and one of those on death row, wrote a blues song while in jail during what would become years of court proceedings and legal appeals. The song's chorus went:

And I just stand and wring my hands and cry,
And I just stand and wring my hands and cry, Oh Lord!
Sometimes I feel like I ain't got no friends at all,
And I just stand and wring my hands and cry.[38]

The executions were postponed repeatedly, through the persistence of Bratton, Jones, and Moorfield Storey, as well as the NAACP and other black organizations. The lawyers pleaded to the Supreme Court, arguing that threat of mob violence, forced testimony, and rapid trials irrevocably prejudiced the court against the defendants. The trials had been shams, they contended in a writ of habeas corpus.[39] In January 1923, the three attorneys argued before the nation's highest court that the defendants' rights under the Fourteenth Amendment—which guaranteed that no state could "deprive any person of life, liberty, or property, without due process of law; nor deny to any person within its jurisdiction the equal protection of the laws"—were violated in Phillips County. In February

1923, the court ruled in *Moore v. Dempsey* that the defendants had been unjustly convicted. Writing for the majority, Justice Oliver Wendell Holmes found "if in fact a trial is dominated by a mob so that there is an actual interference with the course of justice, there is a departure from due process of law." Holmes cited statements by members of the Committee of Seven that they had stopped lynchings only by promising the mob that justice would be "carried out":

> According to the allegations and the affidavits there never was a chance for the petitioners to be acquitted; no juryman could have voted for an acquittal and continued to live in Phillips County and if any prisoner by any chance had been acquitted by a jury he could not have escaped the mob.

Six of the death row convictions were vacated and six others were ordered for retrial. The high court required any retrials would require constitutionally guaranteed protections for defendants.[40]

The six were later convicted of lesser charges and each sentenced to twelve years in prison. The NAACP aided their defense the whole way. Scipio Jones secreted the first six men out of Arkansas as soon as their cases were dropped. Later he got the others released and spirited them out of the state as well. By the end of 1923, the Arkansas 12, who in November 1919 were as good as dead, all left Arkansas free men. And *Moore v. Dempsey* still stands as a buttress of the American legal system and a powerful antipode to lynch law. The ruling established legal precedent that death penalty defendants, whatever their race, could seek redress in federal court if they believed they had not received a fair trial in a state court.

On a Sunday in the winter of 1923, a young man knocked on Ida Wells-Barnett's door in Chicago. He asked if she recognized him, but she did not. He was one of the twelve men who had been on death row, he told her. He came to thank her for her fund-raising and publicity, and for visiting them in jail. In her memoirs, she did not record which man it was. The man told her family that Wells-Barnett had bolstered the men's flagging spirits and urged them to have faith. "We never talked about dying anymore, but did as she told us," he said, "and now every last one of us is out and enjoying his freedom."[41]

And what of Joe Ruffin, the Georgia farmer almost lynched in Jenkins County on April 13 at the start of the Red Summer? He spent most of 1919 in jail mourning his dead sons and awaiting trial for murder. He lived for months in the Chatham County jail in Savannah, where he was so well behaved that jailers made him a trusty. The 1920 census records him in jail, and all the Ruffins who had lived on his farm in Jenkins County were no longer there. His white lawyer, Archibald Blackshear, moved the trial away from Jenkins County, but it hadn't mattered—an all-white jury in Chatham County found Ruffin guilty of killing one of the law officers.[42]

But as in the Arkansas cases, something extraordinary happened. Ruffin was saved from death on the very day he was to be executed. Blackshear and a prominent Savannah attorney with whom he partnered, Alexander Lawrence, sought a new trial, and on the day in January 1920, the judge granted a stay. After a hearing later in the year the judge threw out the verdict and ordered a retrial. It is not clear from the existing court records why he granted a new trial, but the move gave the doomed Ruffin a chance.[43] When the second trial was held in Savannah in November 1920, the jury acquitted him. But the prosecutor did not give up. Next a Jenkins County grand jury indicted Ruffin for murder of the other officer, but a jury acquitted him again.[44]

These legal victories for a black man in the heart of the Jim Crow South did not go unchallenged. Whites in Jenkins County impaneled yet another grand jury which in 1921 indicted Ruffin for the murder of his friend Edmund Scott, who was killed in the Carswell Grove shootout. The prosecution argued Ruffin shot Scott while firing at the other two white officers. Ruffin's lawyers sought to retry the case in Savannah, where previous cases against their client had failed. But after a jurisdictional battle, the state Court of Appeals ruled the Jenkins County Court could decide where the case would be tried. The Jenkins judge decided the trial would be held in rural Effingham County, not Savannah.[45]

In Effingham County, not far from Jenkins County, a jury found Ruffin guilty of manslaughter, and sentenced him to fifteen years in prison.[46] Blackshear and Lawrence, however, argued to the Georgia Court of Appeals (the Georgia Supreme Court refused jurisdiction) that the conviction was a clear example of double jeopardy—being tried for a crime for which a defendant had already been acquitted. Since Ruffin was found not guilty of killing the two white officers, they asked, how could he be convicted of shooting his friend in the same incident? The court of appeals agreed and overturned Ruffin's conviction, so the county dropped the case. In a final act, a Jenkins County jury indicted Ruffin for embezzlement, arguing that when he had offered to pay his friend Scott's bond, he presented a checkbook of the church where he was treasurer. Even though he never even wrote the check, he was convicted and fined $500.

Ruffin paid the fine and on May 30, 1923, a black man who for years expected to be lynched or executed after a perfunctory trial walked out of jail a free man.[47]

Ruffin had lost two sons, four years, and his farm. He could never return to his home county. As he declared at trial in 1919, "There has been nobody suffered in this matter like I have."[48]

Yet to his own astonishment, he was alive. The American legal system delivered some kind of justice. Ruffin said nothing to the press on his release and disappeared from public view.

"He left the jail quietly last night," one reporter wrote. "No one there knows his destination, but it is thought he has left this part of the country."[49]

Who did start the shooting at Carswell Grove? No court ever determined. Some reports sent to the NAACP stated Ruffin's son Louis, the other chief suspect, escaped to Atlanta, then fled to Detroit to live under an assumed name. He was never found. The prosecutor dropped the case.

Joe Ruffin's freedom, the *Savannah Tribune* declared, gave blacks promise of a better future: "We are glad for our courts that this man, already having suffered passing description, could be cleared and freed." "It is one of the few cases that offers hope."[50]

———

Black political awakening and legal victories paralleled a remarkable cultural expansion in 1919 that carried through the 1920s. Jazz, already popular among blacks and whites, spread throughout the country, thanks in large part to the spread of radio. A black literary movement began to flourish, centered in Harlem and informed by the Red Summer. Among its offerings was Jean Toomer's *Cane*, a novel about race and violence in rural and urban America, which appeared in 1922. Other novels, plays, poems, short stories, and serious nonfiction by black writers found publishers throughout the 1920s. Lynching and racial violence were common themes. James Weldon Johnson, the writer-turned-activist, played a major role in promoting black literature. By 1929, V. F. Calverton found enough writing to edit a Modern Library *Anthology of American Negro Literature*. Calverton included Walter White's essay, "I Investigate

Lynchings," as well as landmark works by W. E. B. Du Bois, James Weldon Johnson, and Kelly Miller. Calverton dedicated his book to Walter White "in admiration of his courage in the cause of his people."[51] One of the first black films, *Within Our Gates*, by director Oscar Micheaux, was filmed in 1919 in Chicago, in response to the riot there. The Red Summer also launched an infectious artistic energy among younger black Americans. Teenager Langston Hughes kept a notebook in 1919 to sketch or write down his musings, including these undated lines:

> If you strike a thorn or rose
> > Keep a-goin!
> If it hails or if it snows,
> > Keep a-goin!
> 'Taint no use to sit and whine,
> When the fish ain't on your line,
> Bait your hook an keep
> > On tryin—
> > Keep a-goin![52]

The year 1919 also spawned the nation's purblind movements. The KKK gained chapters and membership all over the United States in the early 1920s, largely in response to 1919's mayhem. Though the organization collapsed into factions by the mid-1920s, groups with similar agendas continued for decades, sowing hate.[53] After 1919, Jim Crow was put on the defensive, but its political supporters waged a prolonged and spirited defense. Southern politicians fought tenaciously for its preservation. Economic oppression of blacks continued for decades, with peonage and misuse of the legal system securing cheap black labor throughout the South.

An unofficial segregation hardened in America's growing cities. Months after the Chicago riot, a white homeowners group in Hyde Park and Kenwood near the Black Belt said in a newsletter, "As the Negro has increased his invasion and is looking for the opportunity to deliver the final paralyzing blows at property values, he is attempting to justify his actions by vague phrases, placed in his mouth by cheap politicians . . . and, as a result, Negroes, whose knowledge of the Constitution is about as comprehensive as their understanding of the fourth dimension, are shouting, 'constitutional rights!' "[54]

This prejudice continued to permeate the federal government. In the executive branch, especially the Justice Department, officials assumed for decades that black political activism was linked with Communist or anarchist subversion. This canard was constantly forwarded by the man who wrote most of Palmer's November 1919 report to Congress: J. Edgar Hoover. Hoover went on to head the Federal Bureau of Investigation from 1924 until his death in 1972.

The ugliest legacy of the Red Summer was the toll on those caught in the violence. Many carried scars from beatings, stabbings, and gunshots. Families, both black and white, lost loved ones. Today the Red Summer dead lie in cemeteries from Texas to Chicago to Washington, with only an occasional death date to reveal them as mob victims. Other dead, like the two Ruffin boys killed at Carswell Grove or John Hartfield in Mississippi or Eli Cooper in Cadwell, Georgia, never were afforded proper graves.

The riots and chaos traumatized tens of thousands. Some were emotionally crushed. Two public examples: John Shillady, the NAACP's white executive secretary who was beaten in Austin, and Omaha mayor Edward Smith, almost killed by the mob outside his city's courthouse. Both drifted out of public life. Many others—politicians, businesspeople, workers— also withdrew, from fear or shame or disappointment. Others grew strident and angry after the violence.

The Red Summer forced millions to examine America's ugly race relations and their individual role in those relations. The gulf between the races, Du Bois's "veil," was laid bare. In the fall of 1919, Claude McKay, author of the poem "If We Must Die," was living in Harlem. He had befriended a white pickpocket, whom he identified only by the first name Michael.[55]

One day Michael visited McKay's apartment and noticed a revolver on the table. McKay explained that he and other black railroad workers carried weapons as protection from white mobs. The exchange with Michael haunted McKay for years. McKay recalled in a memoir published in 1937:

> There had been bloody outbreak after outbreak in Omaha, Chicago, and Washington, and any crazy bomb might blow up in New York even. I walked over to a window and looked out on the backyard.
>
> Michael said: "And if a riot broke in Harlem and I got caught up here, I guess I'd be killed maybe."
>
> "And if I were downtown and I was caught in it?" said I, turning round.

Michael said: "And if there were trouble here like that in Chicago between colored and white, I on my side and you on yours, we might both be shooting at one another, eh?"

"It was like that during the war that's just ended," I said, "brother against brother and friend against friend. They were all trapped in it and they were all helpless."

I turned my back again and leaned out of the window, thinking how in times of acute crisis the finest individual thoughts and feelings may be reduced to nothing before the blind brute forces of tigerish tribalism which remain at the core of civilized society.[56]

The two men did not speak for months, until shortly before McKay sailed for London. The black poet, at least for the time being, was sick of America.[57]

The impulse to run away from the ugly violence was natural and, in many cases, logical: thousands did it. Some, like C. L. Davis and Sam Jones of Longview, Texas, fled to northern cities to join hundreds of thousands of other blacks in ghettoes. Eventually millions of whites—in one of the largest movements of self-segregation in history—fled American cities for the suburbs, in part to escape conflict with blacks. Many blacks also retreated into the safer confines of segregation.

In July 1921, *Chicago Defender* publisher Robert S. Abbott complained, "Less than a dozen of our group were to be seen on the beaches Friday, when the whites were out by the thousands. And why? Surely the 29th Street episode some two years ago has not frightened them away. If so they are out of place in a northern city. Chicago especially has no room for quitters or spineless individuals."[58]

Coda: Carswell Grove

Do not be afraid or lose heart because of these riots.

—R. R. WRIGHT, 1919

THAT JOE RUFFIN WOULD WANT TO FLEE GEORGIA SEEMED OBVIOUS to me as I researched this book. He had lost his farm and his family had scattered. I assumed he joined the Great Migration to live out his life in anonymity in a city like Chicago, Detroit, or Cleveland. My efforts to track down his whereabouts and surviving relatives came up empty. I could not find a death certificate or a mention of him in other public records or newspapers. Then I got lucky.

In 2008, Bill Rankin, courts reporter for the *Atlanta Journal-Constitution*, interviewed the first African American chief judge of the Georgia Court of Appeals. The judge was retiring from the bench and Bill thought it would make a good profile story. Bill asked what the retiring judge would do with his free time. The judge, John H. "Jack" Ruffin Jr., said he wanted to look into a matter in his family's history. He was reluctant to discuss it. Bill pressed him. The judge tried to change the subject, but Bill asked again. The judge finally said he wanted to find out what happened to his grandfather and great-grandfather at a church in Jenkins County. Judge Ruffin said he grew up in Waynesboro, Burke County, but his family used to live over the county line in Jenkins. He did not know much about what happened because his parents would never speak about it.

Bill, a good friend who had read a draft of the first section of my manuscript, made the connection. "Was it Carswell Grove?" he asked.

The judge's mouth fell open.

I first met Jack Ruffin, then seventy-three, a few days later as he cleared out his state office. I showed him the trial records from the 1919 case.

"You've shown me more in five minutes than I learned my whole life," he said quietly.

The judge filled in what he could about his family. His grandfather, J. Holiday Ruffin, had been lynched at Carswell Grove, but his father, then three years old, was whisked away by family members. The family talked about how Joe Ruffin lost all of his land defending himself in a trial. Joe Ruffin had lived out his last years over the border, somewhere in South Carolina.

Several weeks after our first meeting, the judge and I met again for lunch. He chose a quiet corner of the staid Commerce Club in downtown Atlanta, a refuge for Georgia's powerful. Beneath prints of fox hunts and portraits of white captains of antebellum industry, this short bald man with a sonorous voice and burnt sienna skin told me his own extraordinary story, and how the Carswell Grove lynching remained a hushed mystery throughout his life.

Jack Ruffin grew up a twenty-minute drive from Carswell Grove, yet his mother never allowed him to visit the place. His mother rarely mentioned it, he said, and then only as an oblique warning in the segregated rural South: "Don't get in trouble with white folk." His mother worked as a laundress, and told stories of Klansmen bringing in robes to her store to be cleaned. She constantly feared for her son's safety.

When Jack Ruffin was very young, his parents divorced, and for years he was estranged from his father. When Jack reunited with his father as a teenager, he asked about the lynching. His father refused to discuss it. Once, an aunt whispered to him an outline of what happened: White mobs tried to kill all the male Ruffins, she told him. The family fled to nearby counties.

Jack's mother and other relatives scrimped to send her bright son to Morehouse College in Atlanta. His mother had dreams of him becoming a teacher—a prestigious and safe profession. But as Ruffin entered freshman year in 1954, momentous events began to take place. The U.S. Supreme Court handed down its landmark decision in *Brown v. Board of Education*. The next year, America was talking about a Morehouse alum, the young Reverend Martin Luther King Jr., who was leading a bus boycott in Montgomery, Alabama.[1]

By junior year, Ruffin told his mother he wanted to go to law school and practice civil rights law in east Georgia. She was furious.

"It's going to resurrect the Carswell Grove mess," she moaned.

Ruffin attended Howard University Law School in Washington. He graduated in 1960 and set up a private practice in Augusta in 1961. Julian Bond, then working for the NAACP and later a founder of the Student Nonviolent Coordinating Committee, asked him to handle civil rights cases for the NAACP in the area. Ruffin readily agreed. In the ensuing years, he had numerous run-ins with sheriffs and courts. When he won an acquittal for a black man accused of the rape and murder of a white woman in a rural county, the judge ordered a deputy to escort the two safely over the county line. When he sued to demand the desegregation of Richmond County schools in Augusta, whites made violent threats. It took years to win the case, but the schools were finally desegregated. Later, he filed a similar case in Burke County, where he grew up.

Jack Ruffin broke down numerous racial barriers in Georgia. He became the first black member of the Augusta Bar Association, even though the association waited a decade before giving him the honor. In 1986, he became the first black superior court judge in Augusta. In 1994, he joined the Georgia Court of Appeals. And in 2005, he became the first black chief judge of that court. It was the same court to which his great-grandfather's lawyers had appealed to save their client's life. Judge Ruffin was well known among blacks in east Georgia, and was often invited to speak at their churches. Once, a congregant at Carswell Grove asked him to come and speak. He agreed, telling the man that he always wanted to learn more about what had happened to his family there. There was an awkward silence. The church member called back a few days later and cancelled the visit without explanation. Ruffin always regretted not visiting the church.

As we left the lunch, I promised Judge Ruffin that I would take him to Carswell Grove one day. During the next year we spoke on the telephone and exchanged e-mails as I worked on this book. But we never got the chance to go to Carswell Grove. On January 29, 2010, Jack Ruffin died of complications from heart disease. He was seventy-five.

―――◦――――

After the judge died, his widow put me in touch with Judge Ruffin's father, John H. Ruffin Sr. After decades of living around the country, he was now in an assisted-living home back in Waynesboro, where he had grown up after his family fled Jenkins County. In his midnineties, he had been reluctant to talk at first, and he said his memory was poor. He recalled he was a toddler when his mother told him that whites killed his father and his grandfather was in prison. He said what happened at Carswell Grove was "all hush, hush" when he was a boy. When his mother would take him in a buggy to Millen to shop, she would tell him not to look any whites in the eye, and never to say his name was Ruffin. He never visited Carswell Grove, though he had lived only a few minutes from the church much of his life. He heard his grandfather was in jail, and later released, but he never saw him. He heard he died in South Carolina, but he wasn't sure where or when.[2]

"People was quiet about it. They didn't talk about it," he said. "People don't talk about it now."

On February 5, 2010, I drove to Judge Ruffin's wake at the Tabernacle Baptist Church in Augusta. The enormous brick edifice towers over a poor black section of the city. A heavy rain fell, but hundreds of people came to pay their respects. Inside, blacks and whites—many of them powerful politicians—lined up. Resolutions from various governments and courts were posted near the judge's open casket.

Afterward, I walked into the wet winter night thinking of the lives of two Ruffins, Joe and Jack, and how the tragedy of one bent the trajectory of the other.

Joe Ruffin was almost lynched and two of his sons were murdered at the country church at the start of the Red Summer in 1919. He spent years in jail and had to sell his land to pay for his defense in multiple court proceedings. Through tenacity, luck, and some justice provided in a Jim Crow court system, he survived. His great-grandson was never able to ask about the lynching, but ended up dedicating his life to the law and civil rights. Most of his career was spent fighting racial barriers in and around the city where his great-grandfather once sat in jail fearing the arrival of a lynch mob.

Even a skeptic must conclude that American history, with all its violence and contingency, has progressed in extraordinary ways regarding race relations. The Red Summer was a spasm of brutality, but from that violence came something vital and, ultimately, unstoppable—black Americans' collective will to reach true equality. Jack Ruffin's story could never be told without Joe's.

The night of the funeral I decided on impulse that instead of driving straight home to Atlanta I would visit Carswell Grove once again. I drove through the rain along Highway 25, going in reverse the route that Joe Ruffin had traveled while crouching in a county commissioner's car that fateful April night in 1919.

In the gloom, I passed barns of warped clapboard, untilled fields, and barren trees.[3] Driving down Big Buckhead Church Road, the forest thickened and made the night seem even darker. Then, the white-gray shadow of the Carswell Grove Baptist Church loomed abruptly in a clearing. The country church was desolate.

This was the church black farmers built in the fall of 1919 amid the ashes of what the white mob had destroyed in the spring. Now the replacement building was a ruin, unsafe for services for a diminished congregation. At the time of the killings, news reports said Carswell Grove church had 1,000 members. By 2009, it had about 30, most living miles away in Millen, the county seat. They met every other Sunday in a one-room cinderblock building just down the road. The congregation could no longer afford to repair the 1919 church, nor could they afford to tear it down. So it sat. Chunks of wood, bits of glass and bricks lay scattered beside the building. Vines crept along its foundation.

I got out of my car and stepped into the night. Frogs croaking in the surrounding swamps created an eerie cacophony. I circled the church, walking among toppled, worn grave markers in the sandy cemetery. It was a sharecroppers' graveyard, the kind that dot the landscape of the rural South. You can tell by the quality of the markers. Most were made of concrete. Arrayed loosely like broken teeth, many of the graves were unmarked, the stones bleached by time. Some were only rusting metal signs with faded paper labels attached.

The place seemed simultaneously cursed and sacred. Something horrible happened here, but also something vitally important to understanding our collective history. Here began the bloody phenomenon that James Weldon Johnson would call the Red Summer. But there is no historical marker—just a collapsing, forgotten church.

Ralph Ellison, author of *Invisible Man*, noted in 1959 in the midst of the civil rights movement, "At best Americans give but a limited attention to history. Too much happens too rapidly, and before we can evaluate it, or exhaust its meaning or pleasure, there is something new to concern us. Ours is the tempo of the motion picture, not that of the still camera, and we waste experience as we wasted the forest."[4]

The 1919 riots do not comport with America's standard view of its racial history, in which the South played villain to the North's hero. In truth, both North and South were bad on race, in their own way, and the Red Summer laid the flaws of both regions bare. Many did not want to look at it. Most wasted the experience. As Herbert Seligmann observed, the Red Summer violence "was so terrible a commentary on our civilization as to be forgotten almost as it was past."[5]

⸺◇⸺

The first time I visited Carswell Grove, I met a deacon, Irvin Williams, who drove up from Millen to show me around. A sixty-seven-year-old retired big rig equipment driver, he was short, muscular and trim. One of seventeen children of a cotton and peanut sharecropper, Williams had attended the church since boyhood. He remembered Big Buckhead Road when it was dirt.

That day I asked Williams about 1919. What he knew was hearsay, from an uncle. The story was vague and brief. It went like this: trouble started when a church member named Joe Ruffin tied up his mule at the post of the nearby white folks' church. When they told him to move his mule, he refused. Then shooting erupted. I asked Williams what he knew about Ruffin. He did not know much more than the man's name.

In the 1940s and 1950s, Williams said, no black adult would tell him anything about what happened. And he never dared ask a white person.

"When I was a kid, they did everything to smother the story," he said, looking at his work boots. "Now nobody alive really knows about it. I've heard a bunch of stories, but I'd like to know what really happened. Whites did not want to remember it and most black people tried to forget about it too."

It had all been kept in the dark, he told me, then gave me a sideways glance. "Maybe we ought to turn the lights on," he said.

⸺◇⸺

It is time to turn the lights on and see the importance of the Red Summer. The story of American race relations is often presented as an unredeemable blight that descended upon this nation—history as chronic illness. The Red Summer can be viewed in this context as a painful rheumatic flare-up striking the body politic. But I found that if you explore the whole story of those troubled months, you are not left thinking of America's bald and cruel failings, but of its astounding and elastic resilience. The Red Summer is a story of destruction, but it is also a story of the beginning of a freedom movement.

In my readings of 1919, I continually was struck by how optimistic many of the black writers were, despite uncertainty and strife. Richard R. Wright, a minister and editor of a black church newspaper in Philadelphia, wrote one of the most hopeful passages I have ever read, one that summarized not only black struggles in 1919, but those spanning the twentieth century:

> Do not be afraid or lose heart because of these riots. They are merely symptoms of the protest of your entrance into a higher sphere of American citizenship. They are the dark hours before morning which have always come just before the burst of a new civil light. Some people see this light and they provoke these riots, endeavoring to stop it from coming. But God is working. Things will be better for the Negro. We want full citizenship ballot, equal school facilities and everything else. We fought for them. We will have them: we must not yield.[6]

Acknowledgments

Many authors mention a spouse or partner at the end of their acknowledgments. This practice has always struck me as burying the lede. So I will start with my wife. Thanks foremost to Ramsay for putting up with so many nights of me at the keyboard and so many days of me in libraries, and for repeatedly reading drafts of this book. Thanks to my children, Blythe and Finn, for being understanding about their dad working so many weekends. Thanks to my parents. Thanks to the Ruffin family, especially to the late Judge Jack Ruffin and his wife, Judith.

Ninety years ago, Robert Kerlin, a white advocate for black rights, wrote in a preface to his book *The Voice of The Negro, 1919*: "When I told a publisher that I was making this compilation he remarked that my book would make disagreeable reading. There are worse things than disagreeable reading." Two people, my agent Geri Thoma and my editor Jack Macrae, committed to this disagreeable book when it was just an idea. Thanks to Geri, who took a chance on my proposal after we drank tea together in New Haven. Thanks to Jack, Henry Holt's distinguished editor, who shaped what you have just read. Thanks also to Kirsten Reach, his organized assistant editor, and Rita Quintas, Henry Holt's senior production editor.

Many people aided me in writing this book. Chief among them is *Atlanta Journal-Constitution* colleague Bill Rankin, a man of infinite patience, who read draft after draft of my manuscript and offered vital criticism. Former pugilist and South Sider Bill Torpy aided with sharp editing. Others who critiqued all or portions of this book and offered valuable advice include Dexter Filkins, Hank Klibanoff, Andrew McWhirter, James Scott, Mae Gentry, Darci McConnell, Tom Andersen, Goldie Taylor, and Tia Cudahy. William Tuttle, professor emeritus at the

University of Kansas and the nation's leading scholar on the racial violence of 1919, generously gave me time and encouragement. He also provided his extensive files. Thanks to you all.

Thanks to the Nieman Foundation for Journalism at Harvard University for granting me a fellowship. It gave me access to incredible resources and allowed me to meet and interact with amazing, intelligent people, including the class of 2007 fellows. Thanks to Harvard University professors Evelyn Brooks Higginbotham and Henry Louis Gates Jr., for allowing a Nieman fellow to intrude on their graduate seminars and receive their insights on African American history and literature. Thanks to authors Justin Kaplan and Anne Bernays for early encouragement.

Thanks to librarians throughout the country for their hard work in helping befuddled people like me find the arcane items for which we are searching. Thanks finally to fellow journalists across this planet who work tirelessly to keep people informed.

Notes

ABBREVIATIONS

AC   *Atlanta Constitution*
BG   *Boston Globe*
BWGM   *Black Workers in the Era of the Great Migration, 1916–1929* [microfilm].
            Edited by James R. Grossman. Frederick, Md.: University Publications of
            America, 1985.
C   *The Crisis*
CD   *Chicago Defender*
CDJ   *Chicago Daily Journal*
CDN   *Chicago Daily News*
CSM   *Christian Science Monitor*
CT   *Chicago Tribune*
DP   Papers of W. E. B. Du Bois 1803 (1877–1965). Sanford, N.C.: Microfilming
            Corporation of America, 1980–1981.
AGHU   Papers of Archibald Henry Grimké, ca. 1868–1930. Howard University,
            Moorland-Spingarn Research Center, Manuscript Division. Washington,
            D.C.
JNH   *Journal of Negro History*
JWJY   James Weldon Johnson and Grace Nail Johnson Papers. New Haven: Yale
            Collection of American Literature, Beinecke Rare Book and Manuscript
            Library.
KJT   *Knoxville Journal and Tribune*
KS   *Knoxville Sentinel*
LAT   *Los Angeles Times*
MKS   W. Mosley F. Kirk Scrapbooks, South Carolina Historical Society.
NAACPM   Papers of the NAACP [microfilm]. Frederick, Md.: University Publications
            of America, 1986.
NAACPAL   NAACP Anti-Lynching Files [microfilm]. Frederick, Md.: University Pub-
            lications of America, 1985.
NIC   Chicago Commission on Race Relations. *The Negro in Chicago: A Study
            of Race Relations and a Race Riot.* Chicago: University of Chicago Press,
            1922.
NYT   *New York Times*
NYTrib   *New York Tribune*

SvR   Records relating to *State of Georgia v. Joe Ruffin* and *Joe Ruffin v. the State*. Existing court records including filings, appeals, transcripts, most of which are held by the Superior Court Clerk of Effingham County, Georgia. Others gathered from the State Court of Appeals and the State Supreme Court. Files in author's possession. Documents include the Brief of the Evidence in the first murder case against Ruffin, comprising testimony of Ruffin and others, from the November 1919 trial in Chatham County Superior Court, Savannah.

WP   *Washington Post*

WD   Collection of primary source documents posted by author Robert Whitaker. Accessed July 11, 2010, http://robertwhitaker.org/robertwhitaker.org/Laps%20Documents.html.

WTP   William Tuttle Personal Papers. Lawrence, Kansas.

1. Carswell Grove

1. Sadie Ruffin, probably Joe Ruffin's mother or maybe his older sister, sold him the property in 1908. She bought the land from the estate of J. H. Daniel in 1907 for $190.34, as stipulated in Daniel's will.
2. The 1910 census records indicate that Ruffin could not read or write; however, the 1920 census reports that he could.
3. In 1910, Joe Ruffin took out a ten-month, $350 loan from the Bank of Millen, putting up two black horse mules and one bay horse as collateral. In 1914, he took out a six-month loan from the bank for $50, putting up two bay horses as collateral, according to Jenkins County records.
4. Census reports and news accounts report his name as Louis, though in some court records it was spelled Lewis.
5. P. B. Haney, W. J. Lewis, and W. R. Lambert, "Cotton Production and the Boll Weevil in Georgia: History, Cost of Control, and Benefits of Eradication," *Research Bulletin*, no. 428 (November 1996), of the Georgia Agricultural Experiment Stations, College of Agricultural and Environmental Sciences, University of Georgia, 31.
6. Ibid., 10.
7. In the 1920 census, Georgia reported 1,689,114 whites and 1,206,385 blacks. Though the number of blacks increased from the 1910 census, the percentage of blacks as a part of the total population dropped from 45.1 percent in 1910 to 41.7 percent in 1920, due to migration to northern cities.
8. In Georgia, for example, blacks in 1899 owned 1,062,223 acres. By 1919, that number rose to 1,839,129 acres—an increase of 73 percent. See Federal Writers' Project, *Georgia: A Guide to Its Towns and Countryside,* American Guide Series (Athens: University of Georgia Press, 1940), 83. According to census data, total land ownership by blacks peaked in the South in the 1910 census at about 15 million acres, then declined slightly in 1920. After that, black ownership of Southern farmland plummeted.
9. SvR.
10. The reconstruction of the events at Carswell Grove on April 13, 1919, is pieced together from news accounts and the testimony of witnesses and the defendant delivered at the murder trial of Joe Ruffin held November 19, 1919, in Chatham County Superior Court, as well as an interview by the author with John Holiday Ruffin Sr., the grandson of Joe Ruffin, on July 20, 2010.
11. The Prince Hall Masonic Order, founded in the late eighteenth century, exclusively for black men, saw dramatic growth in membership following World War One.
12. Today known as Billy Branch.
13. The church was organized in 1778 and the current edifice, near Big Buckhead Creek,

was built about 1800. See Federal Writers' Project, *Georgia: A Guide to Its Towns and Countryside*, 402.

14. William Tecumseh Sherman, *Memoirs of General William Tecumseh Sherman* (New York: Penguin, 2000), 555.

15. See http://www.nps.gov/hps/abpp/battles/ga026.htm. Days later, Union forces occupied Millen, burning down the railroad depot and other important buildings. In the 1950s, the Georgia Historical Commission placed a marker at the spot of the cavalry action, but declined to label the fight as a federal victory or note Confederate losses.

16. SvR.

17. SvR.

18. In other areas of the South and the North, they were known as "Blind Pigs."

19. The law went into effect in January 1908.

20. "Jenkins Is Quiet Again; 7 Are Dead," *Macon Telegraph*, April 15, 1919, 1.

21. SvR.

22. "Ruffin Is Moved from Augusta Jail," *Augusta Chronicle*, April 15, 1919, 1.

23. SvR.

24. SvR.

25. SvR.

26. *The 145th Anniversary of Carswell Grove Baptist Church, April 13, 2008, History of Carswell Grove Baptist Church, 1867–2008*, 2. Pamphlet in author's possession.

27. "Louis Ruffin Sought in Three Counties," AC, April 15, 1919, 1.

28. "Gives Millen Account of Recent Disorders," AC, April 17, 1919, 5.

29. "Jenkins Is Quiet Again; 7 Are Dead."

30. "Millen Lodge Asks Help," *Atlanta Independent*, May 3, 1919, 10.

31. The census estimated about 85 percent of the black population lived in the South. That was the lowest percentage since the government began taking the census in 1790. Reynolds Farley, "The Urbanization of Negroes in the United States," *Journal of Social History* 1/3 (Spring 1968): 245, Table 1. The size of the African American population at the time was debated. The 1920 census, conducted in 1919, put the black population at 10,463,131, or 9.8 percent of the total U.S. population of 106 million. However, Howard University professor Kelly Miller and others challenged the count as defective. Miller, who taught mathematics, argued the government underestimated the black population in large part because of the dislocation of tens of thousands of black families moving off farms to cities. Census officials countered that the relatively low rate of increase in the black population was the result of the influenza epidemic. Le Verne Beales, "The Negro Enumeration of 1920: A Reply to Dr. Kelly Miller," *Scientific Monthly* 14/4 (April 1922): 352–60.

32. Throughout this book, I have used the term black or African American. Many sources quoted used the term Negro. At the time, there was little consensus regarding the capitalization of the word. I have decided to capitalize Negro when used in quotations in this book for the sake of uniformity.

33. "Race Riots at Millen, Ga.," *Washington Bee*, May 31, 1919, 1.

34. "The Jenkins County Murderers," *Savannah Tribune*, April 19, 1919, 4.

35. See National Association for the Advancement of Colored People, *Thirty Years of Lynching in the United States, 1889–1913* (New York: Negro Universities Press, 1969).

36. "Jenkins Is Quiet Again; 7 Are Dead," *Macon Telegraph*.

37. SvR.

2. Things Fall Apart

1. "The Wonderful Year," *NYT*, January 1, 1919, 16.

2. "Negro Praised for His Work Overseas," *CSM*, January 29, 1919, 12.

3. John Hope Franklin, *From Slavery to Freedom, A History of Negro America*, 3rd ed. (New York: Knopf, 1967), 480.

4. See 66th Congress, 2nd Session, Report No. 1027, *Anti-Lynching Bill Report*, filed May 22, 1920, by Rep. Leonidas Dyer.

5. George Haynes, *Function and Work of the Division of Negro Economics in the Office of the Secretary of Labor*, BWGM, Reel 21, Record Group 165, War Dept. General Staff, 391, corrected March 15, 1919.

6. Richard Slotkin, *Lost Battalions: The Great War and the Crisis of American Nationality* (New York: Henry Holt, 2005), 41.

7. Ibid., 399.

8. "The Plea of the Colored Soldiers." DP, Reel 7, 566.

9. W. E. B. Du Bois, "Returning Soldiers," *C*, May 1919, 14.

10. William Allison Sweeney, *History of the American Negro in the Great World War* (Chicago: G. G. Sapp, 1919), 304.

11. Ibid.

12. Stanley B. Norvell to *Daily News* editor Victor Lawson, August 22, 1919, The Papers of Julius Rosenwald, University of Chicago Library, Box VI, Folders 3 and 4.

13. Advertisement: "Colored Dolls for Your Children," *C*, April 1919, 309.

14. Jean Toomer, "Reflections on the Race Riots," *New York Call*, August 1, 1919.

15. M. L. Rosenthal, ed., *Selected Poems and Two Plays of William Butler Yeats* (New York: Macmillan, 1962), 91.

16. Newspapers were the main source of information at the time. Commercial radio broadcasting would not begin until 1920.

17. Kelly Miller, *The Everlasting Stain* (Washington, D.C.: Associated Publishers, 1924), 6–7.

3. The World Is on Fire

1. "White Men Kidnap Baptist Preacher," *CD*, April 19, 1919, 17.

2. The mob attacked the church because Tom Griffin, who worked on the plantation, was accused of killing white police officer George Dorminey who had stopped a group of blacks from throwing dice. Gower to Dorsey, May 20, 1919, Governor's Subject Files, 1917–1921, Record Group 001-01-005, Georgia Archives.

3. "Attack by Negroes on Military Guards," *AC*, April 22, 1919, 3.

4. "Mob's Third Drive Fatal to the Negro," *AC*, April 30, 1919, 11.

5. "Growing Black Belt Causes Race Riot," *AC*, April 24, 1919, 17.

6. William M. Tuttle Jr., *Race Riot: Chicago in the Red Summer of 1919* (New York: Atheneum, 1970), 201.

7. Document from the United States Employment Service of the Department of Labor, April 19, 1919, BWGM, Reel 21, Record Group 165, 378.

8. U.S. Department of Labor, U.S. Employment Service, Washington, April 19, 1919, BWGM, Reel 21, Record Group 165, War Dept. General Staff, 378.

9. John D. Baker, Jacksonville Chamber of Commerce, to Col. Arthur Wood, April 22, 1919, BWGM, Reel 21, Record Group 165, 357.

10. Emmett J. Scott, private report to Grosvenor B. Clarkson, director of National Council of Defense, March 26, 1919, WTP.

11. Harper Barnes, *Never Been a Time: The 1917 Race Riot That Sparked the Civil Rights Movement* (New York: Walker & Company, 2008), 59.

12. Ibid., 144.

13. Lindsey Cooper, "The Congressional Investigation of East St. Louis," *C*, January 1918, 117.

14. Elliott Rudwick, *Race Riot at East St. Louis, July 2, 1917* (Urbana: University of Illinois Press, 1982), 133. Though Wilson would take no action, several commissions investigated the riot. The first was a union committee, which found the unions were

not to blame. The second was a military board of inquiry appointed by Illinois Governor Lowden. It found the military was not at fault. However, a follow-up congressional committee found both the unions and militia were at fault. The federal and state Governments did nothing with any of the commissions' recommendations. David John Olson, "Racial Violence and City Politics: The Political Response to Civil Disorders in Three American Cities" (PhD diss., University of Wisconsin, 1971).

15. Rudwick, *Race Riot at East St. Louis*, 61.

16. Barnes, *Never Been a Time*, 191. The NAACP's support soured later, however, after leaders squabbled with the argumentative Bundy over his financial demands. The NAACP also was embarrassed over Bundy's signed affidavit in which he acknowledged that for years he had been paid by East St. Louis's white political bosses to deliver black votes. Before Bundy's trial got under way in 1919, the NAACP declared it was no longer involved in his defense. Other black groups and leading black newspapers stepped in to raise money.

17. Bundy sat out the violent Red Summer in prison. Less than a month after his conviction, the forty-six-year-old began serving his sentence at a prison in Chester, Illinois. The Illinois Supreme Court eventually overturned his conviction, discrediting key testimony. He was freed after a year in jail and returned to Cleveland.

18. "Dr. Bundy in Penitentiary," *CD*, May 3, 1919, 1; "Dr. Bundy Guilty; Gets Life Sentence," *CD*, April 5, 1919, 20.

19. "Life for Bundy," *CD*, April 5, 1919, 20.

20. William J. Maxwell, ed., *Complete Poems: Claude McKay* (Chicago: University of Illinois Press, 2004), 134–35. "The Dominant White" was first published in *The Liberator*, April 1919.

21. Mark Robert Schneider, *"We Return Fighting": The Civil Rights Movement in the Jazz Age* (Boston: Northeastern University Press, 2002), 15. Storey to Shillady, January 10, 1919.

22. James Dillard, "After-the-War South," *NYT*, letter to the editor, April 13, 1919, 38.

23. Benjamin Brawley, *Doctor Dillard of the Jeanes Fund* (New York: Fleming H. Revell Co., 1930), 6.

24. The John F. Slater Fund was founded in 1882 to support rural black education. The Negro Rural School Fund was created in 1907 by the bequest of Quaker Anna Jeanes. Both organizations combined with two other groups in 1937 to form the Southern Education Fund.

25. In 1914, Dillard joined the leadership of the Phelps Stokes Fund, which sponsored research on African American education.

26. James Dillard, "After-the-War South," *NYT*, April 13, 1919, 38.

27. NAACPAL, Reel 2, 70.

28. The group disbanded after the Red Summer. It never issued another proclamation.

29. Isaac F. Marcosson, *The War after the War* (New York: John Lane Company, 1917), 7.

30. John Dos Passos, *1919, U.S.A. Trilogy* (New York: Modern Library, 1937), 16.

31. George Jean Nathan and H. L. Mencken, *Vade mecum, The American Credo, A Contribution Toward the Interpretation of the National Mind* (New York: Knopf, 1920), 32.

32. Carl Grayson, *Woodrow Wilson: An Intimate Memoir* (New York: Holt, Rinehart and Winston, 1960), 85.

33. Untitled entry on editorial page, *Cleveland Gazette*, April 19, 1919, 2. At the time, "pumpkins" was black slang, roughly corresponding to the term "big shot."

4. The NAACP

1. Kelly Miller, *An Appeal to Conscience: America's Code of Caste, A Disgrace to Democracy* (New York: Arno Press, 1918), 15.

2. George S. Schuyler, *Black No More* (New York: Modern Library, 1999), 65.

3. Du Bois to Spingarn, October 28, 1914, Joel E. Spingarn Collection. Yale Collection of American Literature, Beinecke Rare Book and Manuscript Library.

4. Du Bois wrote: "Mr. Washington represents in Negro thought the old attitude of adjustment and submission." W. E. B. Du Bois, *Souls of Black Folk* (New York: Dover, 1994), 30.

5. The magazine was paying for itself by 1916. In 1919, circulation skyrocketed. In January 1919, the magazine earned $323. By June, it brought in $1,078. DP, Reel 8, 879.

6. Du Bois's letter to Joel Spingarn, October 28, 1914, quoted in Stephen R. Fox, *The Guardian of Boston: William Monroe Trotter* (New York: Atheneum, 1970), 143–44. Modern readers will note Du Bois did not mention black women.

7. Du Bois to Johnson, November 1, 1916, JWJY.

8. Johnson to William C. Graves, May 24, 1919, JWJY.

9. Today it is known as Clark Atlanta University.

10. Johnson to Walter White, December 15, 1917, JWJY.

11. V. F. Calverton, ed., *Anthology of American Negro Literature* (New York: Modern Library, 1929), 390.

12. Kenneth Robert Janken, *White: The Biography of Walter White, Mr. NAACP* (New York: New Press, 2003), 2. Another biographer noted "Walter was no scholar," certainly compared to Du Bois and Johnson. See Thomas Dyja, *Walter White* (Chicago: Ivan R. Dee, 2008), 27.

13. Shillady's speech to the conference, NAACPM, Part 1, Reel 8, Group 1, Series B, Box 6, 499.

14. Another member, not at the April meeting, was Oswald Garrison Villard, grandson of famed abolitionist William Lloyd Garrison and editor of *The Nation* and the then-liberal *New York Evening Post*.

15. Mary White Ovington, *The Walls Came Tumbling Down* (New York: Arno Press, 1969), 153.

16. Telegram from Shillady to Bilbo, March 8, 1919, NAACPAL, Reel 13, 458.

17. A few months earlier Bilbo told a reporter that the NAACP could "go to hell" and he did not "relish any organization in New York making any demands whatsoever upon him nor will anybody else in Mississippi." *Summary of Important Editorials on Lynching, January 1–March 1, 1919*, NAACPAL, Reel 2, 3–6.

18. NAACPAL, Reel 13, 471.

19. Southern white politicians were not the only ones critical of the NAACP. So were black political opponents. That April, the black weekly *Cleveland Gazette* condemned the NAACP as "white-men controlled" and blasted "Dr. 'Alphabetical' DuBois" as a sell-out. "Bundy Given Life Sentence," *Cleveland Gazette*, April 5, 1919, 1.

20. Herbert Aptheker, ed., *Writings in Periodicals Edited by W. E. B. Du Bois: Selections from* The Crisis, *1911–1925*, vol. 1 (Millwood, N.Y.: Kraus-Thomson Organization, 1983), 180.

21. Raymond Wolters, *Du Bois and His Rivals* (Columbia: University of Missouri Press, 2002), 114; Emmett J. Scott, *Scott's Official History of the American Negro in the World War* (self-published by Scott, 1919), 458.

22. "With This Black Man's Army," *Independent*, March 15, 1919, 385.

23. Francis Grimké, "Address . . . Men's Progressive Club of the Fifteenth Street Presbyterian Church," April 24, 1919, NAACPAL, Reel 2, 318–19.

24. Maurice Davie, *Negroes in American Society* (New York: McGraw-Hill, 1949), 315.

25. Roi Ottley, *New World A-Coming: Inside Black America* (Cleveland: World Publishing Company, 1943), 317.

26. "Returning Soldiers," *C*, May 1919, 13–14.

5. National Conference on Lynching

1. "Hughes Condemns Lynching of Negro," *NYT*, May 6, 1919, 15.
2. *The Centenary of the Birth of Ralph Waldo Emerson, as observed in Concord May 25, 1903, Under the Direction of the Social Circle of Concord* (Cambridge, Mass.: Riverside Press, 1903), 104.
3. William B. Hixson Jr., "Moorfield Storey and the Defense of the Dyer Anti-Lynching Bill," *New England Quarterly* 42/1 (March 1969): 69.
4. Mark Robert Schneider, *"We Return Fighting": The Civil Rights Movement in the Jazz Age* (Boston: Northeastern University Press, 2002), 14. The national conference came about after the first proposed southern regional conference failed to attract enough southern political leaders. See B. Joyce Ross, *J. E. Spingarn and the Rise of the NAACP, 1911–1939* (New York: Atheneum, 1972), 46.
5. *Houston Chronicle*, December 31, 1919, NAACPAL, Reel 1, 1272.
6. NAACPAL, Reel 1, 1340.
7. Nannie Helen Burroughs to Shillady, February 6, 1919, NAACPAL, Reel 1, 1323.
8. Anti-lynching files, NAACP, Reel 2, 7–11.
9. Board meeting notes, NAACP, March 10, 1919; "The Lynching Evil," *The New Republic*, May 3, 1919, 3.
10. Schneider, *"We Return Fighting,"* 15. She died twenty days after the conference opened, at age fifty-one.
11. Board meeting notes, May 5, 1919, NAACP.
12. NAACPAL, Reel 1, 1092.
13. Ibid., 1094.
14. Ibid., 1209.
15. Ibid., 1201.
16. "The Lynching Evil," 8.
17. "A Bad Record," *AC*, May 3, 1919, 8.
18. Dorsey: "I believe that if the Negroes would exert their ultimate influence with the criminal element of their race and stop rapes that it would go a long way towards stopping lynching." Hugh Dorsey to John Shillady, November 30, 1918, Governor's Subject Files, 1917–1921, Record Group 001-01-005, Georgia Archives.
19. "National Conference on Lynching Opens With Large Audience," *CD*, May 10, 1919, 5.
20. James Weldon Johnson, *Along This Way* (1933; repr. New York: Penguin, 2008), 78.
21. Ibid., 157–58.
22. Johnson was a longtime friend of Washington, who died in 1915.
23. Walter White, *A Man Called White* (New York: Viking, 1948), 34.
24. "National Conference on Lynching Opens With Large Audience," *CD*, May 10, 1919, 5.
25. Charles Flint Kellogg, *NAACP: A History of the National Association for the Advancement of Colored People, 1909–1920*, vol. 1 (Baltimore: Johns Hopkins University Press, 1967), 234.
26. "Federal Law Urged Against Lynching," *AC*, May 7, 1919, 18.
27. "Negroes Ask Vote and Equal Rights," *WP*, May 14, 1919, 4.
28. "America's Shame," *Independent*, May 24, 1919, 277.
29. "Fund Raised to Oppose Lynching," *CSM*, May 9, 1919, 1.
30. Anonymous to Du Bois, May 28, 1919, DP, Reel 8, 1080.
31. James Hardy Dillard presided over the convention. "Sociology Congress Condemns Lynching," *AC*, May 13, 1919, 20.
32. "Anti-Lynching Drive Announced," *CSM*, July 3, 1919, 14.
33. "Return of Negro to South Urged," *CSM*, June 13, 1919, 15; "Negroes Consider Problems in South," *CSM*, June 10, 1919, 13.

34. "Lynching Conference of the N.A.A.C.P. The First of the Week—Prominent Speakers of Both Races," *Cleveland Gazette*, May 10, 1919, 1.

35. Schneider, *"We Return Fighting,"* 15.

36. Fred W. Thompson and Patrick Murfin, *The I.W.W.: Its First Seventy Years, 1905–1976* (Chicago: Industrial Workers of the World, 1976), 129.

37. Even people's understanding of time and space was coming undone. Late in May a British astronomer, observing an eclipse off the coast of Africa, found the trajectory of starlight being bent by the mass of the Sun. It was the first scientific confirmation of Albert Einstein's theory of relativity.

38. "Mob Enters Court and Hangs a Life Convict Sentenced Under Law Barring Death Penalty," *NYT*, May 29, 1919, 1. A handful of other whites—as well as two Mexicans—were lynched in 1919.

39. "Editorially Speaking," *Independent*, June 7, 1919, 353.

40. NAACPAL, Reel 1, 346–58.

41. NAACPAL, Reel 13, 405.

42. In 1921, Pace founded Black Swan Records, the first major record company owned by a black person.

43. The 1920 conference was held in Atlanta, the first time such a meeting was held in the South.

44. Pace to Shillady, May 31, 1919, NAACPAL, Reel 2, 141.

45. Jones to Shillady, May 28, 1919, NAACPAL, Reel 2, 122–23.

6. Charleston

1. Lee E. Williams, "The Charleston, South Carolina, Riot of 1919," in *Southern Miscellany: Essays in History in Honor of Glover Moore,* ed. Frank Allen Dennis (Jackson: University of Mississippi Press, 1981), 155, 164, 170.

2. Untitled, *CD*, May 24, 1919, 1.

3. Williams, "The Charleston, South Carolina, Riot of 1919," 1.

4. *Record of Proceedings of a Court of Inquiry Convened at the Navy Yard, Charleston, S.C., by Order of the Commandant, Sixth Naval Dist.*, 235, File #26283-2588 relating to a riot in Charleston involving U.S. Navy personnel. Department of the Navy, 1798–1947, Record Group 80, National Archives, College Park, Md.

5. Williams, "The Charleston, South Carolina, Riot of 1919," 156–57.

6. "Affidavit of Augustus Bonaparte; Resolutions presented by the Negro Citizens of Charleston, S.C., Concerning a riot by enlisted men in Charleston, May 10, 1919," WTP.

7. "Six Men Killed in Race Battle at Charleston," *AC*, May 11, 1919, 1.

8. *Record of Proceedings of a Court of Inquiry Convened at the Navy Yard, Charleston, S.C.*, 258–61.

9. Cyril Burton, statement to Mayor Tristram Hyde, Secretary of the Navy: General Correspondence, 1916–1926; Entry 19-B, File #26283-2588 relating to a riot in Charleston involving U.S. Navy personnel. Department of the Navy, 1798–1947, National Archives.

10. NAACP board meeting notes, May 12, 1919.

11. Edward Ball, *The Sweet Hell Inside* (New York: William Morrow, 2001), 156.

12. "Commandant's Orders 10," Records of 6th Naval District, General Correspondence by Subject, 1917–39, Box 7; Records from Naval Districts and Shore Establishments, 1784–1981, Record Group 181, National Archives, Southeast Region, Ellenwood, Ga.

13. "Commandant's Order No. 9, Sept. 17, 1918," ibid.

14. Beatty to Commanding Officer, Training Camp Extension, January 11, 1919, "Three Plain Clothes Men Added to Force," Box 9, File 63-1 Guards—General, Records of 6th

Naval District; Records from Naval Districts and Shore Establishments, 1784–1981, Record Group 181, National Archives, Southeast Region, Ellenwood, Ga.

15. Memo from Beatty, April 24, 1919, Records of the 6th Naval District, Box 9, File 63-1 Guards—General.

16. At least one person was killed in election violence.

17. "Hyde People Go to Supreme Court," MKS, May 14, 1919.

18. George W. Hopkins, "From Naval Pauper to Naval Power: The Development of Charleston's Metropolitan-Military Complex," in *The Martial Metropolis: U.S. Cities in War and Peace*, ed. Roger W. Lotchin (New York: Praeger, 1989), 7.

19. Williams, "The Charleston, South Carolina, Riot of 1919," 167.

20. MKS, May 12, 1919.

21. Ibid.

22. Williams, "The Charleston, South Carolina, Riot of 1919," 158–59.

23. *Record of Proceedings of a Court of Inquiry Convened at the Navy Yard, Charleston, S.C.*, 251–52.

24. MKS, May 11, 1919.

25. Williams, "The Charleston, South Carolina, Riot of 1919," 161.

26. MKS, May 12, 1919.

27. "Commandant's Order #73, Issued May 17, 1919," Records of 6th Naval District, Box 7, Record Group 181.

28. "Commandant's Order #74, May 20, 1919," ibid.

29. Henry A. Bellows, *A Treatise on Riot Duty for the National Guard* (Washington: Government Printing Office, 1920), 96.

30. Ibid., 97.

31. Clayton Laurie, "The U.S. Army and the Omaha Race Riot of 1919," *Nebraska History* 72/3 (Autumn 1991): 136.

32. Williams, "The Charleston, South Carolina, Riot of 1919," 165–67.

33. MKS, May 16, 1919.

34. Williams, "The Charleston, South Carolina, Riot of 1919," 175.

35. "Endorsements, July 14, July 22, August 28, 1919, Judge Advocate General; Secretary of the Navy: General Correspondence, 1916–1926; Entry 19-B, File #26283-2588 relating to a riot in Charleston involving U.S. Navy personnel. Department of the Navy, 1798–1947, Record Group 80, National Archives, College Park, Md.

36. Journal of the City Council, Charleston, S.C., 1915–1919, May 1919, Proceeding of Council, May 27, 1919, 838.

37. "Resolutions presented by the Negro Citizens of Charleston, S.C., Concerning a riot by enlisted men in Charleston, May 10, 1919," WTP.

38. Mrs. Emma Dawson, letter regarding Peter Irving, September 18, 1920, Secretary of the Navy: General Correspondence.

39. Theodore Roosevelt, Assistant Secretary of the Navy, March 18, 1921, Secretary of the Navy, General Correspondence. Roosevelt was the late president's son.

40. Beatty, who would have two ships named after him, died in 1926.

41. Williams, "The Charleston, South Carolina, Riot of 1919," 165–67, 169.

42. "Report—Six Killed in Sailor-Negro Riot," *NYT*, May 11, 1919, 3.

43. Even Du Bois planned one, and the NAACP board initially funded the project. Du Bois, however, never completed it.

44. After much debate, blacks were allowed to join, but only in all-black, segregated chapters. In Arkansas, black members were not allowed to attend the state convention. An editorial in a black weekly, *The Hot Springs Echo*, declared: "For valor displayed in the recent war, it seems that the Negro's particular decoration is to be the 'double cross.'" Robert T. Kerlin, *The Voice of the Negro, 1919* (New York: E. P. Dutton, 1920), 73.

45. "Our AEF Contemporaries," *Stars and Stripes*, May 2, 1919, 5.

46. John Hope Franklin and Isidore Starr, eds., *The Negro in Twentieth Century America: A Reader on the Struggle for Civil Rights* (New York: Vintage, 1967), part 6, selection 39.

47. "Baker to Reply to Charges of Army Severity," *CT*, February 19, 1919, 4.

48. Letter from S. D. Redmond to Du Bois, DP, Reel 8, 171. See also Craig Lloyd, *Eugene Bullard, Black Expatriate in Jazz-Age Paris* (Athens: University of Georgia Press, 2000), 69.

49. Barnes to Du Bois, May 16, 1919, DP, Reel 8, 435. Many white authorities saw Du Bois's essay as sedition. The U.S. Post Office's translation bureau cited a portion of the Espionage Act to hold up distribution of the May *Crisis*. A postal official charged Du Bois's essay was "seditious, insolently abusive to the country," and a "not too veiled threat." More than 150 NAACP supporters sent telegrams complaining to the postmaster. The postal solicitor relented and sent the magazine out after six days. Theodore Kornweibel Jr., *"Seeing Red": Federal Campaigns Against Black Militancy, 1919–1925* (Bloomington: Indiana University Press, 1998), 57.

50. "Four Are Slain in Riot," *CD*, May 17, 1919, 1.

51. "Reactions," *C*, May 1919, 29.

52. "Stop Whites with Guns in Philadelphia Riot," *CD*, May 10, 1919, 10.

53. "Whites and Negroes Riot at New London," *BG*, May 30, 1919, 16; "Negro Sailors Attack White at New London," *Hartford Courant*, May 30, 1919, 1.

54. "Negro Kills One; Shoots Up Five, Fighting Posse," *AC*, May 2, 1919, 1.

55. "Mob in Mississippi, Lynches Two Negroes," *AC*, May 9, 1919, 1; Anti-Lynching Bill, 66th Congress, 2nd Session, Report No. 1027, submitted by Mr. Dyer, May 22, 1920, 14.

56. "Mob Uses Rope, Fire and Bullets to Lynch Negro," *AC*, May 15, 1919, 1.

57. 1919 Annual Conference, NAACPM, Part 1, Reel 8, Series B, Box 2, 505.

58. Report of the Secretary, June 1919, NAACP.

59. Horace Jones to Shillady, May 26, 1919, NAACPAL, Reel 2, 124.

60. Walter White to Judith McAdams, July 17, 1919, NAACPAL, Reel 2, 342, and Reel 2, 117–18.

61. Milan, in the central part of Georgia, is not to be confused with Millen, the seat of Jenkins County, where the Carswell Grove incident took place.

62. Richard Knott to Hugh Dorsey, July 21, 1919, Governor's Subject Files, 1917–1921, Record Group SG-S: 001-01-005, Georgia Archives.

63. "Rewards Offered in Lynching Case," *AC*, July 27, 1919, 1.

64. "Johnson County Mob Shoots Negro Dead," *AC*, May 16, 1919, 16.

65. "Negro Churches Burned This Week," *Eatonton Messenger*, Friday, May 30, 1919, 1; "Firebugs Burn Down Churches in Putnam," *AC*, May 29, 1919, 13; "Pulling Together," *AC*, August 5, 1919, 8. Eatonton was the boyhood home of Joel Chandler Harris, the author of the Uncle Remus stories. Black novelist Alice Walker, the daughter of sharecroppers, was born in Eatonton in 1944.

66. Martin to Du Bois, May 30, 1919, DP, Reel 7, 1081.

67. Ibid.

68. "Mob Is Induced to Thrash Negro," *AC*, June 2, 1919, 1; "Making Progress," *AC*, June 3, 1919, 10.

69. "Ceremonial Is Held by the Ku Klux Klan," *AC*, May 18, 1919, 9.

70. "Negroes Alarmed at False Reports of Race Trouble," *AC*, May 21, 1919, 22. As early as February 1919, the NAACP was looking into challenging the legality of the reborn KKK. NAACPAL, Reel 1, 1329–32.

71. "Memphis Sheriff Stops Big Riot," *CD*, June 7, 1919, 17.

72. NAACPAL, Reel 2, 467.

7. Bombs and the Decline of the West

1. William Klingaman, *1919: The Year Our World Began* (New York: HarperCollins, 1989), 352–53.
2. Roosevelt contracted crippling polio in 1921.
3. Geoffrey Ward, *A First-Class Temperament: The Emergence of Franklin Roosevelt* (New York: Harper & Row, 1989), 456.
4. Alice Roosevelt Longworth, *Crowded Hours* (New York: Scribner, 1933), 282–83.
5. Klingaman, *1919*, 353.
6. Ibid., 354.
7. The only casualty of the first wave of bombings was Ethel Williams, the black housemaid of Thomas Williams Hardwick, the just retired U.S. senator from Georgia. She opened a package when it exploded, ripping off her arms.
8. Though they did little about it by early 1919, Communists had discussed bringing blacks into the fold. As early as 1915, Lenin argued that blacks in the American South—like serfs in Russia—were an obvious group for Communists to recruit.
9. Arthur S. Link et al., eds., *The Papers of Woodrow Wilson* (Princeton, N.J.: Princeton University Press, 1986), 61:471. From the diary of Dr. Cary T. Grayson, Sunday, March 9, 1919.
10. The man who became Wilson's Secretary of War, Newton Baker, was also a Quaker.
11. Stanley Coben, *A. Mitchell Palmer, Politician* (New York: Columbia University Press, 1963), 199.
12. Ibid., 206.
13. U.S. Department of Justice, *Report Submitted to Congress by Attorney General A. Mitchell Palmer, Nov. 15, 1919. A Report on the Activities of the Bureau of Investigation of the Department of Justice Against Persons Advising Anarchy, Sedition, and the Forcible Overthrow of the Government* (Washington: Government Printing Office, 1919), 8.
14. Ibid.
15. Coben, *A. Mitchell Palmer*, 237.
16. It could be argued that the violence of 1919 drove more blacks to such parties.
17. Portia James, "Hubert H. Harrison and the New Negro Movement," *Western Journal of Black Studies* 13/2 (1989): 87.
18. David P. Berenberg to Francis Peregino, May 16, 1919, *New York Legislative Documents, One Hundred and Forty-Fourth Session, 1921, Vol. 18, No. 50—Part 2, Revolutionary Radicalism: Its History, Purpose and Tactics. Report of the Joint Legislative Committee Investigating Activities, filed April 24, 1920, in the Senate of the State of New York* (Albany: J. B. Lyon Company, 1920), 1511.
19. "And is there no hope that the Negro race may be truly free! Decidedly there is a way out of their degradation and poverty, and but one way—by educating and organizing on the job in the One Big Union of the workers—the 'Industrial Workers of the World.'" *Weekly Industrial Worker*, July 9, 1919, *New York Legislative Documents*, 1210.
20. "I.W.W.," *C*, June 1919, 60.
21. David Levering Lewis, *W. E. B. Du Bois, The Fight for Equality and the American Century, 1919–1963* (New York: Henry Holt, 2000), 4.
22. Moorfield Storey, *Obedience to the Law, An Address at the Opening of Black Petigru College in Columbia, South Carolina. June 9, 1919* (Boston: Press of George H. Ellis Co., 1919), 18.
23. R. W. Shufeldt, *The Negro: A Menace to American Civilization* (Boston: Gorham Press, 1907), 13.
24. Ibid., 145.
25. Charles H. McCord, *The American Negro as a Dependent, Defective and Deliquent* (Nashville: Benson Printing, 1914).

26. Ibid., 13–14, 25.
27. John Ambrose Price, *The Negro: Past, Present, and Future* (New York: Neale Publishing Company, 1907), 166, 185.
28. The book was published posthumously. Chesterton joined the British Army in the Great War and was killed in 1918.
29. Cecil Chesterton, *A History of the United States* (New York: George H. Doran Company, 1919), 298–99.
30. W. E. B. Du Bois, *Darkwater: Voices From Within the Veil* (New York: Harcourt, Brace and Howe, 1920), 94.
31. Ella Barksdale Brown to Johnson, September 19, 1919, JWJY.
32. "Hymn of Hate," *Cleveland Gazette*, June 14, 1919, 2.
33. Reuter would go on to teach for years at Fisk University.
34. Edward Byron Reuter, *The Mulatto in the United States, Including a Study of the Role of Mixed-Blood Races Throughout the World* (Boston: Gorham Press, 1918), 395.
35. In 1919, Japan pressed for equal status with white nations in peace negotiations in Europe.
36. This racial view of history found its full expression in the platform of a small German workers' party formed in Munich. In the fall of 1919, army veteran Adolf Hitler joined the group and became one of its leaders. In 1920, the party renamed itself the Nationalsozialistische Deutsche Arbeiterpartei, known as the Nazis. Hitler made numerous disparaging remarks about blacks and black advancement in *Mein Kampf* (1925), including: "From time to time illustrated papers bring it to the attention of the German petty-bourgeois that some place or other a Negro has for the first time become a lawyer, teacher, even a pastor, in fact a heroic tenor, or something of the sort. While the idiotic bourgeoisie looks with amazement at such miracles of education, full of respect for this marvelous result of modern educational skill, the Jew shrewdly draws from it new proof of the soundness of this theory about the equality of men that he is trying to funnel into the minds of the nations." Adolf Hitler, *Mein Kampf*, trans. Ralph Manheim (New York: Houghton Mifflin, 1971), 430.
37. Oswald Spengler, *The Hour of Decision* (New York: Knopf, 1934), 11.
38. Madison Grant, *The Passing of the Great Race or the Racial Basis of European History* (New York: Scribner, 1916), 69.
39. Ibid., 73.
40. Lothrop Stoddard, *The Rising Tide of Color Against White World-Supremacy* (New York: Scribner, 1920), xxix.
41. Ibid., xxxii.
42. George Edmund Haynes, *The Trend of the Races* (New York: Council of Women for Home Missions and Missionary Education Movement of the United States and Canada, 1922), 151.
43. Thomas Dixon, *The Fall of a Nation* (Chicago: M. A. Donohue & Company, 1916).
44. Dixon's 1919 novel *The Way of a Man* (New York: D. Appleton, 1919) attacked feminism.
45. Vachel Lindsay, *A Handy Guide for Beggars* (New York: Macmillan, 1916), 23–24.
46. Herbert J. Seligmann, *The Negro Faces America* (New York: Harper & Brothers, 1920), 257.
47. Simmons was not the first one to have the idea. As early as 1906, after the Atlanta race riot, an *Atlanta Evening News* editorial had called for a resurrection of the Klan. See Mark Bauerlein, *Negrophobia: A Race Riot in Atlanta, 1906* (San Francisco: Encounter Books, 2001), 286.
48. Ralph McGill, *The South and the Southerner* (Boston: Little, Brown, 1963), 130.
49. William Joseph Simmons, *America's Menace or the Enemy Within* (Atlanta: Bureau of Patriotic Books, 1926), 66.

50. Winfield Jones, *The Story of the Ku Klux Klan* (Washington, D.C.: American Newspaper Syndicate, 1921), 59.

51. *Atlanta Constitution* editor Ralph McGill later recounted a possibly apocryphal story told to him by one of the men asked to come to Stone Mountain that night. "Jesus, Doc," the man said. "I can't even climb Stone Mountain in the daytime. Can't you revive the ancient glories in the flatlands?" McGill, *The South and the Southerner*, 132.

52. Simmons, *America's Menace*, 1.

53. William J. Simmons, *ABC of the Invisible Empire, Knights of the Ku Klux Klan* (Atlanta: Ku Klux Press, 1917), unnumbered pamphlet.

54. Simmons, *America's Menace*, 37, 56.

55. A 1921 exposé in the *New York World* labeled them "Nightie Knights." Wyn Craig Wade, *The Fiery Cross: The Ku Klux Klan in America* (New York: Simon and Schuster, 1987), 160.

56. Carl Carmer, *Stars Fell on Alabama* (New York: Literary Guild, 1934), 28.

57. H. L. Mencken, *The American Scene: A Reader* (New York: Vintage, 1982), 38.

58. "The Ku Klux Are Riding Again!," *C*, March 1919, 231.

59. Kenneth T. Jackson, *The Ku Klux Klan in the City, 1915–1930* (New York: Oxford University Press, 1967), xi–xii.

60. Newell Dwight Hillis, "Bolshevism as a Conspiracy of Thieves," *AC*, July 13, 1919, D4.

61. Oswald Spengler, *The Decline of the West*, vol. 1, *Form and Actuality*, trans. Charles Francis Atkinson (New York: Knopf, 1939), 104.

62. The *Titanic* had been part of the White Star Line fleet.

63. Melvin Drimmer, ed., *Black History, A Reappraisal* (Garden City, N.Y.: Anchor Books, 1969), 398.

64. Stephen Graham, *The Soul of John Brown* (New York: Macmillan, 1920), 73.

65. Ibid., 72.

8. Ellisville

1. July Report of the NAACP Secretary to the Board, DP, Reel 7, 1215. House Committee on the Judiciary, *Segregation, Part II, Anti-Lynching Hearings*, 66th Cong., 2nd sess., January 15 and 29, 1920, 59.

2. "The Hartfield Killing," *Jones County News*, July 3, 1919, 4.

3. Ibid.

4. "Lynch Negro Who Confessed Crime," *NYT*, June 27, 1919, 17.

5. Federal Writers' Project, *Mississippi: A Guide to the Magnolia State* (New York: Hastings House, 1938), 427–28.

6. "Utterly Powerless," *AC*, June 28, 1919, 8.

7. "Hang Wounded Negro," *WP*, June 27, 1919, 3.

8. "Lynch Law in Action," *The New Republic* 67 (July 22, 1931): 256.

9. "Lynching Inevitable, Governor Declares," *LAT*, June 27, 1919, 15; "Hang Wounded Negro."

10. "Lynch Law in Action," *The New Republic* 67 (July 22, 1931): 256–57. Stephen Graham, in his tour of the South in 1919, also encountered this commerce in grotesque memorabilia. He wrote: "I met many Whites who boasted of having taken part in a lynching, and I have met those who possessed gruesome mementoes of the shape of charred bones and gray, dry, Negro skin. I said they were fools. . . . They were proud of their 'quick way with niggers,' they justified it, they felt the wisdom of lynching could never be disproved." Stephen Graham, *The Soul of John Brown* (New York: Macmillan, 1920), 225.

11. "Angered by Lynching, Negroes Ask Troops," *AC*, June 27, 1919, 2.

12. Herbert J. Seligmann, *The Negro Faces America* (New York: Harper & Brothers, 1920), 28–29.

13. "Gov. Bilbo Blames French Reception and Negro Press, Admits It Is Practically Impossible to Prevent Rapists' Lynching," *Jones County News*, July 8, 1919, 1.

14. Seligmann, *The Negro Faces America*, 260.

15. "Mississippi Savages' Call to Negroes to Organize for Protection," *Baltimore Daily Herald*, May 16, 1919, NAACPAL, Reel 13, 423.

16. Everett Dean Martin, *The Mob Mind vs. Civil Liberty* (New York: American Civil Liberties Union, 1920), 14. Selections from Martin's *The Behavior of Crowds*.

17. Grimké to Shillady, July 12, 1919, NAACPAL, Reel 2, 317.

18. "Order of Klansmen Scored by Governor," *AC*, June 30, 1919, 2.

19. "Gov. Pickett Denounces Order of Klansmen," *Savannah Tribune*, July 12, 1919.

20. "The Governor's Message," *AC*, June 29, 1919, D4.

21. Redmond to Du Bois, June 10, 1919, DP, Reel 8, 171, S.D.

22. NAACP July Board Meeting notes, DP, Reel 7, 1215.

23. "Troops in Street Fight," *NYTrib*, June 6, 1919, 6; "Southern Soldiers Ejected," *CD*, June 14, 1919, 9.

24. "Fifteenth Infantry Mobilizes," *CD*, June 28, 1919, 5.

25. "Negroes in Riot Turn Upon Police," *San Francisco Chronicle*, July 1, 1919, 6.

26. Editorial selection, *Baltimore Sun*, June 28, 1919, NAACP-2, WTP.

27. Lucy Bland, "White Women and Men of Colour: Miscegenation Fears in Britain After the Great War," *Gender & History* 17/1 (April 2005): 34.

28. "Colour Riots in Liverpool," *Manchester Guardian*, June 7, 1919, 11; "The Racial Trouble in Liverpool," *Manchester Guardian*, June 12, 1919, 5.

29. "The Riots Renewed. Another White Man Killed," *Manchester Guardian*, June 13, 1919, 7.

30. "Serious Racial Riots at Cardiff," *Manchester Guardian*, June 13, 1919, 7.

31. "Repatriating the Negroes," *London Observer*, June 29, 1919, 12.

32. William W. Giffin, *African Americans and the Color Line in Ohio, 1915–1930* (Columbus: Ohio State University Press, 2005), 47.

33. Statement of Pullman Conductor N. W. Narrimore, June 6, 1919, BWGM, Reel 6, 444.

34. Seligmann, *The Negro Faces America*, 23.

35. Mark Robert Schneider, *"We Return Fighting": The Civil War Movement in the Jazz Age* (Boston: Northeastern University Press, 2002), 35, quoting from *New York Age*, June 4, 1919, 4.

36. Lucian Lamar Knight, *A Standard History of Georgia and Georgians*, vol. 6 (Chicago: Lewis Publishing, 1917), 3275–76.

9. Cleveland

1. See Sheila Tully Boyle and Andrew Bunie, *Paul Robeson: The Years of Promise and Achievement* (Amherst: University of Massachusetts Press, 2001).

2. Paul Robeson, "The New Idealism," Rutgers College Valedictory Address, June 10, 1919, *The Targum* 50 (1918–1919): 571.

3. C. H. Duvall, *The Building of a Race* (Boston: Everett Print, 1919), 6.

4. See John Hosher, *God in a Rolls Royce, The Rise of Father Divine, Madman, Menace, or Messiah* (New York: Hillman-Curl, 1936).

5. Johnson to Grace Nail Johnson, May 16, 1919, JWJY.

6. "Taft Talks on Negro Problem," *LAT*, June 4, 1919, II4.

7. "The Tenth Anniversary Conference," *C*, June 1919, 88.

8. Annual Conferences, NAACPM, Part 1, Reel 8, Record Group 1, Series B, Box 2, 489.

9. "National Association for the Advancement of Colored People, the Tenth Anniversary," *C*, August 1919, 189.

10. Ohio had the most delegates with 57, and Georgia had the most of any southern state with 15.
11. "National Association for the Advancement of Colored People," 191.
12. Emmett J. Scott, speech delivered in Cleveland, June 22, 1919, "Did the Negro Soldier Get a Square Deal?" NAACPM, Part 1, Reel 8, 478.
13. Annual Conferences, NAACPM, Part 1, Reel 8, 828.
14. Board minutes, July 11, 1919, NAACP.
15. Report of branches, June 28, 1919, NAACPM, Part 1, Reel 8, 742.
16. Rev. G. W. Williams, speech in Cleveland, "Rural Conditions of Labor," NAACPM, Part 1, Reel 8, 579–80.
17. B. Harrison Fisher, speech in Cleveland, June 26, 1919, NAACPM, Part 1, Reel 8, 652.
18. Ibid., 653.
19. G. A. Gregg, speech in Cleveland, "Estrangement of the Races," June 28, 1919, NAACPM, Part 1. Reel 8, 709.
20. Mary White Ovington, *The Walls Came Tumbling Down* (New York: Arno, 1969), 167.
21. Annual Conferences, NAACPM, Part 1, Reel 8, Group 1, Series B, Box 2, 501–2.
22. Ibid., 625.
23. "National Association for the Advancement of Colored People," 190.
24. NAACPM, Part 1, Reel 8, 832–33.
25. "National Association for the Advancement of Colored People," 193.

10. Longview

1. Kenneth R. Durham Jr., "The Longview Race Riot of 1919," *East Texas Historical Journal* 18/2 (1980): 5. Reprinted as an e-book by the Texas Ranger Hall of Fame and Museum.
2. Shillady interview with S. L. Jones and C. P. Davis, Olivet Church, Chicago, August 18, 1919, WTP. The *Chicago Defender* was not the only black publication to publish this assertion. The *New York Commoner*, edited by black veteran Osceola McKaine, also published an item on Walters's death, probably cribbing the item from the *Defender*. The *Commoner* had a small circulation, primarily in the New York area.
3. Shillady interview with Jones and Davis. An official Texas Ranger report on the riot stated that the county sheriff admitted handing Walters to the white mob, but that the men told him they were just going to beat him. Another account by the sheriff's son was that he secreted Walters on a train out of town, but lynchers intercepted him. Durham, "Longview Race Riot," 3.
4. Shillady interview with Jones and Davis.
5. No newspapers, including the *Chicago Defender*, mentioned the woman's name in print except for the *Los Angeles Times*, which identified her as the daughter of J. S. King of Kilgore. See "Negro Trouble Believed Dead," *LAT*, July 18, 1919, IV12.
6. Ibid.
7. Robert T. Kerlin, *The Voice of the Negro, 1919* (New York: E. P. Dutton & Company, 1920), 75–76. William Tuttle, "Violence in a 'Heathen' Land: The Longview Race Riot of 1919," *Phylon* 33/4 (1972): 327.
8. Shillady interview with Jones and Davis.
9. At the time, 16 percent of the Texas population was black.
10. Tuttle, "Violence in a 'Heathen' Land," 327.
11. Francis White Johnson and Ernest William Winkler, *A History of Texas and Texans*, vol. 3 (Chicago: American Historical Society, 1914), 1075.
12. Durham, "Longview Race Riot," 4.
13. Shillady interview with Jones and Davis.

14. Durham, "Longview Race Riot," 5.
15. Theodore Kornweibel Jr., *"Seeing Red": Federal Campaigns against Black Militancy, 1919–1925* (Bloomington: Indiana University Press, 1998), 83.
16. "Treat the Black Man White," *Broad Ax*, July 12, 1919, 8.
17. George Edmund Haynes, *The Trend of the Races* (New York: Council of Women for Home Missions and Missionary Education Movement of the United States and Canada, 1922), 17.
18. Claude McKay, *A Long Way from Home* (New York: Harcourt, Brace, 1970), 31.
19. Claude McKay, "If We Must Die," in *Anthology of American Negro Literature*, ed. V. F. Calverton (New York: Modern Library, 1929), 203–4.
20. McKay, *A Long Way from Home*, 31.
21. Some scholars have stated that Winston Churchill quoted the poem in a speech during the Battle of Britain. There is no evidence Churchill ever did, or was even aware of the poem's existence, according to Richard Langworth, editor of the Churchill Centre website (www.winstonchurchill.org) and noted Churchill scholar.
22. Shillady interview with Jones and Davis.
23. Durham, "Longview Race Riot," 6.
24. Shillady interview with Jones and Davis.
25. "Longview Is Quiet After Race Rioting," *Dallas Morning News*, July 12, 1919, 2.
26. "Negro Trouble Believed Dead," *LAT*, July 18, 1919.
27. Shillady interview with Jones and Davis.
28. Tuttle, "Violence in a 'Heathen' Land," 329.
29. Durham, "Longview Race Riot," 6.
30. Sarah Davis Elias, *Recalling Longview: An Account of the Longview, Texas Riot, July 11, 1919* (Baltimore: C. H. Fairfax, 2004), 46; Tuttle, "Violence in a 'Heathen' Land," 329; Durham, "Longview Race Riot," 4.
31. Durham, "Longview Race Riot," 6.
32. Tuttle, "Violence in a 'Heathen' Land," 329.
33. Elias, *Recalling Longview*, 46–47.
34. Tuttle, "Violence in a 'Heathen' Land," 329.
35. Durham, "Longview Race Riot," 7.
36. Ibid.
37. Shillady interview with Jones and Davis.
38. Davis told NAACP investigators that he got the uniform from a neighbor. His wife said years later he got the uniform from her sister. See personal correspondence by Sarah Davis Elias, Davis's daughter, to Bill Tuttle, November 4, 1968, WTP.
39. Shillady interview with Jones and Davis.
40. Elias, *Recalling Longview*, 46.
41. Durham, "Longview Race Riot," 7.
42. Ibid., 8.
43. Ibid., 8.
44. Lewis L. Gould, *Progressives and Prohibitionists: Texas Democrats in the Wilson Era* (Austin: University of Texas Press, 1979), 255–56.
45. NAACPAL, Anti-Lynching Investigative Files, Reel 1, 1292–301.
46. Not only did Texas add branches, its branches swelled with members. In March 1918, the San Antonio branch was founded with 52 people; by the summer of 1919, it had more than 1,700 members. Steven A. Reich, "Soldiers of Democracy: Black Texans and the Fight for Citizenship, 1917–1921," *Journal of American History* 82/4 (March 1996): 1490.
47. Durham, "Longview Race Riot," 7, 9.
48. "Hobby Proclaims Martial Law in Gregg County," *Dallas Morning News*, July 14, 1919, 2.

49. Durham, "Longview Race Riot," 10–11.

50. Ibid., 15.

51. Ibid., 14.

52. "Call Guard to Curb Race Riot," *Idaho Statesman,* July 12, 1919; "Four Whites Wounded in Texas Race Riot," *Philadelphia Inquirer,* July 12, 1919.

53. "Negro Trouble Believed Dead," *LAT,* July 18, 1919.

54. "The Riot at Longview, Texas," *C,* October 1919, 18, 297–98.

55. "Race Clash at Port Arthur," *AC,* July 15, 1919, 11.

56. "Our Own Amendments," *Life,* July 17, 1919, 119.

57. On July 5, 1852, Frederick Douglass, in a speech in Rochester, New York, declared that black slaves saw July 4th as "a day that reveals to him, more than all other days in the year, the gross injustice and cruelty to which he is the constant victim."

58. For Bisbee riot, see http://www.library.arizona.edu/exhibits/bisbee/ (accessed July 9, 2009).

59. "U.S. Cavalry Goes to Bisbee to Quell Negro Troops' Riot," *Tucson Citizen,* July 4, 1919, 1.

60. Ibid.

61. Fort Huachuca was a supply base for the expedition of United States forces into Mexico in 1916 and 1917.

62. "Colonel Defends Negroes; Commander of 10th Cavalry Denies His Troopers Began Bisbee Riot," *NYT,* July 22, 1919, 2.

63. "U.S. Cavalry Goes to Bisbee," *Tucson Citizen.*

64. "14 Negro Soldiers Held as Result of Clash at El Paso," *Forth Worth Star-Telegram,* July 4, 1919, 1.

65. "Bisbee Quiet After Negro Troops Riot," *San Francisco Chronicle,* July 5, 1919, 4.

66. "General Pershing Presents Trophies to Allied Winners," *AC,* July 7, 1919, 10. Edward Solomon Butler went on to participate in the 1920 summer Olympics and become one of the first blacks to play college and professional football.

67. Kerlin, *The Voice of the Negro, 1919,* 38–39.

68. Ibid.

69. "Negroes Cause Riot in Arizona," *Lexington Herald,* July 5, 1919.

70. David Levering Lewis, *W. E. B. Du Bois: Biography of a Race, 1868–1919* (New York: Henry Holt, 1993), 426.

71. See Eric Goldman, "Summer Sunday," *American Heritage,* http://www.american heritage.com/articles/magazine/ah/1964/4/1964_4_50.shtml (accessed September 20, 2009).

72. The United States Department of Labor investigated the deportation of black workers from Coatesville. "Industry," *C,* June 1919, 102.

73. "Negroes Accused of Inciting Riot," *Philadelphia Inquirer,* July 10, 1919. The NAACP later reported to Congress and the *New York Times* that a race riot erupted on July 5 in Scranton, Pennsylvania. However, no evidence of such an incident exists.

74. "Southern Pig Iron Is Marked Up $1 a Ton," *Wall Street Journal,* July 12, 1919, 7.

75. See Douglas Blackmon, *Slavery by Another Name: The Re-Enslavement of Black Americans from the Civil War to World War II* (New York: Doubleday, 2008).

76. "Negro Leadership," *Montgomery Advertiser,* July 3, 1919, editorial page.

77. "Governor Addresses Big Negro Audience," *AC,* July 8, 1919, 15.

78. "Race Trouble Stirs Dublin," *AC,* July 12, 1919, 1.

79. "One Dead, Two Hurt in Battle Between Negro and Whites," *Macon Telegraph,* July 8, 1919, 1.

80. "Dublin Home Guard Withdrawn Sunday; Negro Still Alive," *AC,* July 14, 1919, 7; "1 Dead, 2 Wounded in Affray at Dublin," *AC,* July 8, 1919, 4. See also *Courier-Herald* website, http://www.courier-herald.com/blog/2877045/Pieces+of+Our+Past (accessed September 14, 2009).

81. A handful of all-black towns existed in the South in 1919. The federal government even created some, to provide housing for black workers in key war industries while also maintaining segregation. For example, the United States Housing Corporation built Truxton, Virginia, next to the naval port at Portsmouth.
82. "Black Hand Letter Threatens Mayor of Colored Town," *AC*, July 18, 1919, 3; "Town Exclusively for Negroes Wants to Join Anniston," *AC*, July 27, 1919, 6.
83. Johnson to Anne Spencer, May 20, 1919, JWJP.

11. Washington
1. Kelly Miller, *An Appeal to Conscience: America's Code of Caste, A Disgrace to Democracy* (New York: Macmillan, 1918), 36.
2. A black man, Benjamin Banneker, was one of the principal surveyors for architect Pierre Charles L'Enfant when he laid out the city's broad avenues. Federal Writers' Project, *Washington: City and Capital*, American Guide Series (Washington: Government Printing Office, 1937), 68, 75.
3. See Stanley C. Harrold Jr., "The Pearl Affair: The Washington Riot of 1848," *Records of the Columbia Historical Society of Washington D.C.* 50 (1980): 140–60.
4. Film screenings of the fight caused riots across the country, and some cities banned them. Johnson was the first black heavyweight champion, but by 1919 he was washed up. The "Galveston Giant" was reduced to boxing in exhibition matches in Cuba and Mexico. See Geoffrey C. Ward, *Unforgivable Blackness: The Rise and Fall of Jack Johnson* (New York: Borzoi, 2004).
5. Constance McLaughlin Green, *The Secret City: A History of Race Relations in the Nation's Capital* (Princeton, N.J.: Princeton University Press, 1967), 187.
6. Federal Writers' Project, *Washington: City and Capital*, 81.
7. The NAACP awarded Grimké its Spingarn Medal at the June conference in Cleveland. Du Bois had already won the award. Grimké and Du Bois battled over various issues, and Grimké tendered his resignation from the national board in the summer of 1919 over its decision to pay Du Bois's expenses for his trip to Europe. He remained on the national board throughout the year, but then left. See Dickson D. Bruce Jr., *Archibald Grimké: Portrait of a Black Independent* (Baton Rouge: Louisiana State University Press, 1993).
8. Shillady to Grimké, July 12, 1919; Grimké to Sen. Henry Cabot Lodge, July 15, 1919, AGHU.
9. Green, *The Secret City*, 189; DP, Reel 8, 271–72.
10. NAACP pamphlet of events of Washington riot, published July 23, 1919, AGHU.
11. Arthur I. Waskow, *From Race Riot to Sit-In, 1919 and the 1960s* (Garden City, N.Y.: Doubleday, 1966), 23; "Service Men Beat Negroes in Race Riot at Capital," *NYT*, July 21, 1919, 1.
12. Waskow, *From Race Riot to Sit-In*, 23.
13. Kevin Conley Ruffner, *Terror in Washington: The Race Riots of 1919* (Washington Historical Society), unpublished, April 6, 1981, 4.
14. Frank Carter, "The Southerner's View," *NYTrib*, August 4, 1919, 8.
15. "Troops Check Race Rioting at Washington," *CT*, July 20, 1919, 2.
16. "Race Riot at Capital," *NYT*, July 20, 1919, 14.
17. "Service Men Beat Negroes in Race Riot at Capital," *NYT*, July 21, 1919, 1.
18. "Troops Check Race Rioting at Washington." *CT*, July 20, 1919, 2. Similar racial flare-ups broke out in other cities, though many flamed out as quickly as they started. That same night, a brief riot broke out in Harlem, but police stopped it within an hour.
19. NAACP pamphlet of events of Washington riot.
20. Ruffner, *Terror in Washington*, 2.

21. "Efforts to Check Capital Rioting," *CSM*, July 22, 1919, 4.
22. "Service Men Beat Negroes in Race Riot at Capital," *NYT*, July 21, 1919, 1.
23. Jacqueline Goggin, *Carter G. Woodson: A Life in Black History* (Baton Rouge: Louisiana State University Press, 1993), 147–48; "Soldiers Try to Terrorize Colored Folk," *Baltimore African American*, July 28, 1919, 1–4.
24. Ruffner, *Terror in Washington*, 2.
25. "Service Men Beat Negroes in Race Riot at Capital," *NYT*, July 21, 1919, 1.
26. "Race War in Washington Shows Black and White Equality Not Practical," *Brooklyn Daily Eagle*, July 27, 1919, 4.
27. "Wilson Ill in Bed; Parleys Called Off," *CDN*, July 21, 1919, 1.
28. "Efforts to Check Capital Rioting," *CSM*, July 22, 1919, 4.
29. Waskow, *From Race Riot to Sit-In*, 26–28.
30. "Efforts to Check Capital Rioting," *CSM*, July 22, 1919, 4. Congressmen received assurances from military branches that soldiers and sailors would not participate in further violence. Waskow, *From Race Riot to Sit-In*, 26.
31. Ruffner, *Terror in Washington*, 10.
32. John R. Shillady to Wilson, July 21, 1919. In Arthur S. Link et al., eds., *The Papers of Woodrow Wilson* (Princeton, N.J.: Princeton University Press, 1986), 61:576.
33. Woodson, a founding member of the NAACP branch, submitted an affidavit.
34. NAACP publication of events of riot, July 23, 1919, AGHU.
35. Ruffner, *Terror in Washington*, 9.
36. "Washington Calm Following Riots," *CSM*, July 23, 1919, 2.
37. Neval Thomas to Grimké, July 28, 1919, AGHU.
38. Michael Hyatt, "The Political Ideologue," *Western Journal of Black Studies* 2/13 (Summer 1989): 92–102.
39. Federal Writers' Project, *Washington: City and Capital*, 82; Chalmers Roberts, *The Washington Post, The First 100 Years* (Boston: Houghton Mifflin, 1977), 151.
40. "National Capital Depends on Army to Stop Race Riots," *AC*, July 28, 1919, 2.
41. Waskow, *From Race Riot to Sit-In*, 27.
42. Clayton D. Laurie, "The U.S. Army and the Omaha Race Riot of 1919," *Nebraska History* 58/3 (Fall 1997): 136.
43. See John F. Kennedy Presidential Library Archives, http://www.jfklibrary.org/Historical+Resources/Archives/Archives+and+Manuscripts/fa_brownlow.htm (accessed January 10, 2010). Brownlow's handling of the riot seemed to tarnish his reputation in the capital. He left his post in 1920 to become city manager of Petersburg, Virginia.
44. Green, *The Secret City*, 187.
45. "Efforts to Check Capital Rioting," *CSM*, July 22, 1919, 4.
46. "Bloody Race War at Washington," *AC*, July 22, 1919, 1.
47. "Ten Casualties in a Race War," *LAT*, July 22, 1919, 1.
48. Ruffner, *Terror in Washington*, 3.
49. Thomas lived in this area.
50. Neval Thomas to Grimké, July 28, 1919, AGHU.
51. Roberts, *The Washington Post*, 151.
52. "Washington Is Swept by Race Riots; Many Shot," *NYTrib*, July 22, 1919, 4.
53. Juan Williams, *Thurgood Marshall: American Revolutionary* (New York: Times Books, 1998), 32–33.
54. Neval Thomas to Grimké, July 28, 1919, AGHU.
55. Herbert Seligmann, "The Menace of Race Hatred," *Harper's*, March 1920, 537–38.
56. "Four Dead in Race Riots," *BG*, July 22, 119, 1.
57. "American's Own Race Problem Blazes Up," *NYTrib*, August 3, 1919. Johnson was charged with Wilson's murder but a jury acquitted her of manslaughter. Delia Mellis,

"'Literally Devoured': Washington, D.C., 1919," *Studies in Literary Imagination* 40/2 (Fall 2007): 1, 22 n. 3.

58. Laney argued self-defense, but his conviction for manslaughter was upheld on appeal in 1923. See *Laney v. United States*, No. 4000, Court of Appeals of the District of Columbia, 54, App. D.C. 56, 294 E 412 (1923); reprinted in *Encyclopedia of American Race Riots*, Walter Rucker et al., eds. (Westport, Conn.: Greenwood, 2006), 775–76.

59. "Police Think Negro Killed Washington Boy," *BG*, July 24, 1919, 3.

60. "Bloody Race War at Washington," *AC*, July 22, 1919, 1.

61. "Renew Capital Riot, 2 Die," *CT*, July 23, 1919, 1.

62. "Ten Casualties in a Race War in the Capital," *LAT*, July 22, 1919, 1; "Rioting Breaks Out at Norfolk," *NYTrib*, July 22, 1919, 2; "Six Persons Shot in Norfolk Riot," *AC*, July 22, 1919, 2.

63. "Three Men Killed in a Racial Fight," *AC*, July 21, 1919, 5.

64. "Renew Washington Race Riots," *LAT*, July 23, 1919, 11; "Washington Calm Following Riots," *CSM*, July 23, 1919, 2.

65. Ruffner, *Terror in Washington*, 3.

66. Robert T. Kerlin, *The Voice of the Negro, 1919* (New York: E. P. Dutton & Company, 1920), 77.

67. "Renew Capital Riot, 2 Die," *CT*, July 23, 1919, 1.

68. Wilson returned to the United States on July 8, 1919. On July 14 he received a delegation from Ethiopia, one of only two independent African nations at the time, at the White House.

69. Roosevelt to Ogden Mills Reid, January 1, 1919, in Elting Morison, ed., *The Letters of Theodore Roosevelt* (Cambridge, Mass.: Harvard University Press, 1954), 1420. Roosevelt died on January 6, 1919.

70. In the 1918 congressional elections Democrats lost control of the Senate. Democrats had lost control of the House in 1916.

71. Mr. L. Cook to Du Bois, July 23, 1919, DP, Reel 8, 520–21.

72. U.S. Department of Justice, *Report Submitted to Congress by Attorney General A. Mitchell Palmer, November 15, 1919. A Report on the Activities of the Bureau of Investigation of the Department of Justice Against Persons Advising Anarchy, Sedition, and the Forcible Overthrow of the Government* (Washington: Government Printing Office, 1919), 171.

73. "He Fought for a Democracy Denied Him," *Atlanta Independent*, July 25, 1919, 4.

74. "The Japanese Press on Our Race Riots," *NYTrib*, September 21, 1919, C9.

75. Cyril Brown, "Germans Watching Japan and America," *BG*, July 28, 1919, 3. Brown was a *New York World* correspondent in Berlin.

76. W. E. B. Du Bois, *Darkwater: Voices from Within the Veil* (New York: Harcourt, Brace and Company, 1920), 50.

77. Kenneth O'Reilly, "The Jim Crow Policies of Woodrow Wilson," *Journal of Blacks in Higher Education* 17 (Autumn 1997): 117–18.

78. Nicholas Patler, *Jim Crow and the Wilson Administration* (Boulder: University Press of Colorado, 2004), 10.

79. In June, Trotter sent a telegram to Wilson asking him to aid in presenting a petition on black rights to negotiators at Versailles. Wilson never replied. Link, *The Papers of Woodrow Wilson*, 27.

80. Edmund Wilson, *The Shores of Light: A Literary Chronicle of the Twenties and Thirties* (New York: Vintage, 1952), 304.

81. Patler, *Jim Crow*, 13.

82. Henry Blumenthal, "Woodrow Wilson and the Race Question," *JNH* 48/1 (January 1963): 1–21.

83. O'Reilly, "Jim Crow Policies," 118.

84. Ibid., 229.

85. The North Carolinian lived out the rest of his life in Philadelphia. He died in December 1918.

86. "White Elevator Men Employed by the Senate to Strike Against Negro," *AC*, July 26, 1919, 10.

87. Wilson's cabinet members also ignored the riot. Navy Secretary Josephus Daniels barely mentioned it in his diary. Sunday night Daniels wrote only: "Riot—race—following Negro assaults on white women." The next day he wrote about the shooting at the Navy hospital. Ruffner, *Terror in Washington*, 12; Waskow, *From Race Riot to Sit-In*, 24. Daniels's 638-page memoir, *The Wilson Era, Years of War and After, 1917–1923* (Chapel Hill: University of North Carolina Press, 1946) makes no mention of the riot.

88. Geoffrey Ward, *A First-Class Temperament: The Emergence of Franklin Roosevelt* (New York: Harper & Row, 1989), 459–60.

89. FDR to Joseph R. Hamlen, July 26, 1919, in Frank Freidel, ed., *Franklin D. Roosevelt: The Ordeal* (Boston: Little, Brown, 1954), 30; Elliot Roosevelt, ed., *FDR: His Personal Letters, 1905–1928* (New York: Duell, Sloan and Pearce, 1948), 479–80.

90. "Victim Describes Assault by Negro," *WP*, July 23, 1919, 3.

91. "Capital Quiet After Rioting," *BG*, July 24, 1919, 1.

92. "Home Guard Killed in Capital Riots," *BG*, July 23, 1919, 1.

93. "Capital Kept Calm by Federal Troops," *NYT*, July 24, 1919, 7.

94. Waskow, *From Race Riot to Sit-In*, 29.

95. "Race Riots in the Nation's Capital," *NYTrib*, July 27, 1919, E11.

96. "Capital Kept Calm by Federal Troops," *NYT*, July 24, 1919, 7; "Washington Calm Following Riots," *CSM*, July 23, 1919, 2; "2,000 Troops in Washington; Rioters Quiet," *NYTrib*, July 24, 1919, 3.

97. Waskow, *From Race Riot to Sit-In*, 31.

98. "Home Guard Killed in Capital Riots," *BG*, July 23, 1919, 1.

99. Link, *The Papers of Woodrow Wilson*, 610.

100. "Regulars Leave Capital," *NYT*, July 28, 1919, 4.

101. Ibid.; "Troops Withdrawn From Capitol as Rioting Ends," *NYTrib*, July 28, 1919, 1.

102. "Renew Capital Riot, 2 Die," *CT*, July 23, 1919, 1; "National Capital Depends on Army to Stop Race Riots,"*AC*, July 28, 1919, 2.

103. "Renew Washington Race Riots," *LAT*, July 23, 1919, 11. Harrison was a Wilson ally who later became a supporter of Franklin Roosevelt.

104. "Washington Calm Following Riots," *CSM*, July 23, 1919, 2.

105. Atlanta meeting, July 24, 1919, Robert W. Woodruff Library, Atlanta University Center, Commission on Interracial Cooperation Papers, 1919, 1944, Series II, Folder I, Reel 20, 24–25.

106. Green, *The Secret City*, 191.

107. NAACP board meeting minutes, September 8, 1919.

108. NAACP publication of events of Washington riot, July 23, 1919, AGHU.

109. NAACP press release, "Hughes, Taft, Root, A. Mitchell Palmer Sign Address to the Nation Demanding Congress Investigate Lynching," July 25, 1919, AGHU.

110. "Pastor Protests Killings of Negroes in Washington," *NYTrib*, July 28, 1919, 2.

111. "The Southerner's View," *NYTrib*, August 4, 1919, 8. *New York Times* editors, too, felt black criminals were a primary cause of the strife. They regretted the new attitude among blacks moving into Washington and declared "as a matter of fact practically all the crimes of violence in Washington were committed by Negroes." See "Race War in Washington," *NYT*, July 23, 1919, 8.

112. "Race War in Washington Shows Black and White Equality Not Practical," *Brooklyn Daily Eagle*, July 27, 1919, 4.

113. The *New York Tribune* devoted the front page of its opinion section to the riots on August 3 with a banner headline: "America's Own Race Problem Blazes Up."

114. "Northern-Born Writer Gives Interesting View on the Race Problem," *AC*, July 25, 1919, 6. The writer, James A. Metcalf, sent the letter to the newspaper on July 22, 1919.

115. Kendrick to Grimké, July 25, 1919, AGHU.

116. U.S. Department of Justice, *Report Submitted to Congress by Attorney General A. Mitchell Palmer, Nov. 15, 1919. A Report on the Activities of the Bureau of Investigation of the Department of Justice Against Persons Advising Anarchy, Sedition, and the Forcible Overthrow of the Government* (Washington: Government Printing Office, 1919), 171.

117. Jean Toomer, "Reflections on the Race Riots," *New York Call*, July 29, 1919.

118. Kerlin, *The Voice of the Negro, 1919*, 77.

119. "Urge Negroes to Use Force to Get Rights," *NYT*, July 28, 1919, 4.

12. Chicago Is a Great Foreign City

1. "Poster Calling Attention to Chicago's Qualities," *CDN*, July 15, 1919, 4.

2. "Take Your Hat Off to the Greatness of Chicago," *Chicago American*, April 11, 1919, editorial page.

3. Ernest Hemingway, *A Farewell to Arms* (New York: Scribner, 1957), 185.

4. William Peterman and Philip Nyden, "Creating Stable Racially and Ethnically Diverse Communities in the United States: A Model for the Future," *Social Policy & Administration* 35/1 (March 2001): 34.

5. Chicago had 808,558 foreign-born residents. New York was the only other city in the country with more immigrants. U.S. Census, 1920.

6. John R. Commons, *Races and Immigrants in America* (New York: Macmillan, 1920), 165.

7. "Fresh-Air Pavilion True 'Melting Pot,'" *CDN*, July 15, 1919, 12.

8. James R. Barrett, "Unity and Fragmentation: Class, Race, and Ethnicity on Chicago's South Side, 1900–1922," *Journal of Social History* 18/1 (Autumn 1984): 43.

9. *NIC*, 13.

10. Mike Royko, *Boss: Richard J. Daley of Chicago* (New York: Plume, 1971), 31–32. Daley never discussed his role, if any, in what transpired in July 1919. Royko wrote: "The question has been raised by newspapers from time to time: Was young Daley a participant in the violence? Blacks passing through his neighborhood were beaten within screaming distance of his home. Daley has never answered, or even acknowledged, the question. The 1919 riot itself is something he has never talked about. But if he wasn't part of it, if he sat out his neighborhood's bloody battle, it is certain that some of his friends participated, because Daley belonged to a close-knit neighborhood club known as the Hamburg Social and Athletic Club." Daley became president of the Hamburg Club in 1924, 36–38.

11. "Crime Wave in Chicago," *NYT*, April 20, 1919, 17.

12. "1,500 'Blind Pigs' Here, 'Drys' Charge," *CDN*, July 17, 1919, 3.

13. Carl Sandburg, *Chicago Poems* (New York: Henry Holt, 1916), 4.

14. *NIC*, 79–80.

15. William Julius Wilson, *The Declining Significance of Race: Blacks and Changing American Institutions* (Chicago: University of Chicago, 1978), 72, Table 4.

16. Francis Taylor Long, "The Negroes of Clarke County, Georgia, During the Great War," *Bulletin of the University of Georgia* 19/8 (September 1919): 44–45.

17. Cary D. Wintz, ed., *African American Political Thought, 1890–1930, Washington, Du Bois, Garvey and Randolph* (Armonk, N.Y.: M. E. Sharpe, 1996), 61.

18. Thomas Jackson Woofter, *The Basis of Racial Adjustment* (New York: Ginn and Company, 1925), 44.

19. According to the 1920 Census, from 1910 to 1920, black populations in other northern cities also saw tremendous increases, including New York (66.3 percent), Cleveland (307.8 percent), and Detroit (611.3 percent). S. J. Holmes, "Will the Negro Survive in the North?" *Scientific Monthly* 27/6 (December 1928): 557–61.

20. Paul Street, "The Logic and Limits of 'Plant Loyalty': Black Workers, White Labor, and Corporate Racial Paternalism in Chicago's Stock Yards, 1916–1940," *Journal of Social History* 29/3 (Spring 1996): 660.

21. Howard R. Gold and Byron K. Armstrong, *A Preliminary Study of Inter-Racial Conditions in Chicago* (New York: Home Missions Council, 1920), 6.

22. Marvin Lazeron, "If All the World Were Chicago: American Education in the Twentieth Century," *History of Education Quarterly* 24/2 (Summer 1984): 165.

23. *CT*, March 15, 1917, quoted in Allan H. Spear, *Black Chicago: The Making of a Negro Ghetto, 1890–1920* (Chicago: University of Chicago Press, 1967), 140.

24. Lawrence Hogan, *A Black National News Service: The Associated Negro Press and Claude Barnett, 1919–1945* (Rutherford, N.J.: Fairleigh Dickinson University Press, 1984), 22.

25. *NIC*, 2.

26. Ibid., 98.

27. Hogan, *Black National News Service*, 23.

28. M. A. Majors, "The Devils Footprints," *Broad Ax*, May 31, 1919, 8.

29. Black relations with unions were not always contentious. In some industries in the South, blacks joined unions and even set up their own, despite Jim Crow restrictions. Black workers, from longshoremen in Savannah to miners in Tuscaloosa to tobacco workers in Winston-Salem, worked in concert with white unions to press management. U.S. Conciliation Service, Dispute Case Files, BWGM, Reel 1, 231–301.

30. *Report of Proceedings of the Thirty-ninth Annual Convention of The American Federation of Labor, held at Atlantic City, N.J., June 9 to 23, 1919* (Washington, D.C.: Law Reporter Printing Company, 1919), 221.

31. Mark Karson and Ronald Rodash, "The AFL and the Negro Worker, 1894–1949," in *The Negro and the American Labor Movement*, ed. Julius Jacobson (Garden City, N.Y.: Anchor Books, 1968), 159.

32. Wilson did not reply. Woodrow Wilson Papers, Series 2, Reel 1, 109566–109567.

33. William M. Tuttle Jr., *Race Riot: Chicago in the Red Summer of 1919* (New York: Macmillan, 1972), 136.

34. See August Meier and Elliott Rudwick, "Attitudes of Negro Leaders Toward the American Labor Movement from the Civil War to World War I," in *The Negro and the American Labor Movement*, chap. 1.

35. Tuttle, *Race Riot*, 143.

36. James R. Barrett, "Unity and Fragmentation: Class, Race, and Ethnicity on Chicago's South Side, 1900–1922," *Journal of Social History* 18/1 (Autumn 1984): 48. Economics professor John R. Commons summarized race and labor tensions in the North: "The Negro or immigrant strike breaker is befriended by the employer, but hated by the employee." John R. Commons, *Races and Immigrants in America* (New York: Macmillan, 1920), 114.

37. Arbitration hearings, Judge Samuel Altschuler presiding, U.S. Court of Appeals Courtroom, Chicago, June 20, 1919. BWGM, Reel 1, 773, 778.

38. Ibid., BWGM, Reel 1, 845–55.

39. Ibid., BWGM, Reel 1, 983–84.

40. See University of Chicago Library website, http://ecuip.lib.uchicago.edu/diglib/social/chi1919/aline/a3/a3focus.bmp.gif.

41. "Chicago Faces Fire Peril as Engineers Quit," *NYTrib*, July 20, 1919, 8.

42. Tuttle, *Race Riot*, 141.

43. "Race Riots in Chicago; Score of People Injured," *Hartford Courant,* July 28, 1919, 1.

44. *Chicago Tribune, Chicago Post,* June 23, 1919, NAACP-2, WTP.

45. The 1920 Census found 92,501 blacks in the Black Belt, up from 34,335 in 1910. See William Tuttle, "Contested Neighborhoods and Racial Violence: Prelude to the Chicago Riot of 1919," *JNH* 55/4 (October 1970): 270; Robert C. Weaver, *The Negro Ghetto* (New York: Harcourt, Brace, 1948), 274.

46. Tuttle, "Contested Neighborhoods and Racial Violence," 271.

47. Graham, *The Soul of John Brown,* 236.

48. William Howland Kenney, *Chicago Jazz: A Cultural History, 1904–1930* (New York: Oxford University Press, 1993), 10–11, 15.

49. Tuttle, "Contested Neighborhoods and Racial Violence," 266–88, 271–72.

50. Peter M. Hoffman, comp., *The Race Riots: Biennial* [Cook County Coroner's] *Report, 1918–1919* (Chicago: n.p., n.d.), 22–23.

51. "Reducing Friction," *CD*, May 3, 1919, 20.

52. "Race Segregation Ordinance Invalid," *Harvard Law Review* 31 (January 1918): 476.

53. Tuttle, "Contested Neighborhoods and Racial Violence," 276.

54. *Buchanan v. Warley* allowed an adjustment in the "free alienator" doctrine of common law so that courts could enforce restrictive covenants. The court allowed such private agreements until 1948. Clement Vose, *Caucasians Only: The Supreme Court, the NAACP, and the Restrictive Covenant Cases* (Los Angeles: University of California Press, 1959), 4–5. Such covenants developed as a popular substitute for outright segregation; however, they were not widely used in Chicago until the mid-1920s. Tuttle, "Contested Neighborhoods and Racial Violence," 277.

55. Tuttle, *Race Riot,* 179. These attacks in a northern metropolis came more than four decades before Birmingham, Alabama, would earn the moniker "Bombingham" for similar attacks.

56. Tuttle, "Contested Neighborhoods and Racial Violence," 267.

57. Tuttle, *Race Riot,* 172, 174. The handbill for the meeting White attended stated the group's goal was to "PREVENT INCURSION BY UNDESIRABLES." See Tuttle, "Contested Neighborhoods and Racial Violence," 281.

58. "Realty Feud Seen in Bombings of Negroes," *CDN*, July 16, 1919, 6. Duke and other prominent blacks organized the Anti-Vilification Society that summer to combat what they said was the unfair portrayal of black men as criminals. Carl Sandburg, *The Chicago Race Riots: July 1919* (1919; repr., New York: Harcourt, Brace & World, 1969), 6.

59. James T. Farrell, *Studs Lonigan, a Trilogy* (New York: Vanguard Press, 1935), 149. See Daniel Shiffman, "Ethnic Competitors in Studs Lonigan," *MELUS* 24/3 (Autumn 1999): 69.

60. Though blacks could vote in Chicago, they were still restricted from running for citywide office. "We admit frankly that if political equality had meant the election of Negro mayors, judges, and a majority of Negroes in the city council the whites would not have tolerated it," wrote *Chicago Tribune* editors in the summer of 1919. "We do not believe that the whites of Chicago would be any different from the whites of the South in this respect." "White and Black in Chicago," *CT*, August 3, 1919, F6.

61. Edward R. Kantowicz, *Polish-American Politics in Chicago, 1888–1940* (Chicago: University of Chicago Press, 1975), chap. 12, "Bill the Boisterous."

62. Herbert J. Seligmann, *The Negro Faces America* (New York: Harper & Brothers, 1920), 176.

63. In the 1920s Mayor Thompson became an ally of Al Capone.

64. Kenney, *Chicago Jazz,* 29.

65. Ibid., 28–29.

66. Tuttle interview with Chester Wilkins, WTP.

67. "'Stink' Bomb Cause Riotous Fight in Loop," *CT*, April 1, 1919, 2.

68. Walter White, "Chicago and Its Eight Reasons," *C*, October 1919, 295.

69. John M. Allswang, "The Chicago Negro Voter and the Democratic Consensus: A Case Study, 1918–1936," *Journal of the Illinois State Historical Society (1908–1984)* 60/2 (Summer 1967), WTP.

70. *The 45th Annual Report of the Citizens' Association of Chicago*, October 30, 1919, WTP.

71. Victor F. Lawson, editor of the *Chicago Daily News*, described Thompson in March 1919 as "a good advertiser, but of bad wares." Tuttle, *Race Riot*, 192.

72. "What Kind of a Man Is Lowden of Illinois?" *Leslie's Illustrated Weekly*, November 15, 1919, 759.

73. Chester Wilkins interview, WTP.

74. "Ragan's [sic] Colts Start Riot," *CD*, June 28, 1919, 1; *Chicago Herald Examiner*, June 23, 1919, NAACP-2, WTP.

75. Tuttle, *Race Riot*, 239.

76. Display advertisement, *CD*, July 5, 1919, 9.

77. Editorial note, *CD*, July 12, 1919, 20.

78. "The Race Problem in Chicago," letter to the editor, *CT*, July 7, 1919, 8.

79. The *Chicago Tribune* ran a similar series in May focusing on conditions in the Black Belt, May 4, 10, 11, and 16, 1919, WTP.

80. Sandburg, *Chicago Race Riots*, 6.

81. Sandburg's motives, though in the liberal progressive vein, were tainted by prejudice. He wrote to his father-in-law: "I have spent ten days in the Black Belt and am starting a series in the Chicago Daily News on why Abyssinians, Bushmen and Zulus are here." See C. K. Doreski, "From News to History: Robert Abbott and Carl Sandburg Read the 1919 Chicago Riot," *African American Review* 26/4 (Winter 1992): 647.

82. Penelope Niven, *Carl Sandburg: A Biography* (New York: Scribner, 1991), 342.

83. Sandburg, *Chicago Race Riots*, 6.

13. The Beach

1. The area today has been filled in as a waterfront park.

 2. William M. Tuttle Jr., *Race Riot: Chicago in the Red Summer of 1919* (New York: Macmillan, 1972), 6.

 3. Peter M. Hoffman, the Cook County coroner, ruled that Williams panicked and drowned from the rock throwing, but was not directly hit. Harris swore Williams was struck in the head. Either way, the rock throwing led to the drowning.

 4. "Report Two Killed, Fifty Hurt, in Race Riots," *CT*, July 28, 1919, 1.

 5. The Chicago Commission on Race Relations, *The Negro in Chicago: A Study of Race Relations and a Race Riot* (Chicago: University of Chicago Press, 1922), 596. A white man named George Stauber was reported beaten and cut. "Report Two Killed, Fifty Hurt, in Race Riots," *CT*, July 28, 1919, 1. Stauber was indicted on a manslaughter charge for throwing stones at Williams, but was acquitted on May 27, 1920. See Homicide in Chicago, 1870–1930, http://homicide.northwestern.edu/database/5420/?page= (accessed July 7, 2010).

 6. The white police officer had his badge taken after the incident, but after a hearing before the city's Civil Service Commission, it was restored (*NIC*, 5). Three other white officers who were at the beach with Callahan were also suspended. All were reinstated. Police Chief Garrity imposed the suspensions after black leaders brought him thirty pages of affidavits stating the officers refused to do their duty to arrest Stauber. Black leaders also submitted a petition demanding action. "Chief Suspends Four Police on Riot Charges," *CT*, September 4, 1919, 11.

 7. This account of the drowning is drawn from *NIC*, 4; Peter M. Hoffman, comp., *The

Race Riots: Biennial [Cook County Coroner's] *Report, 1918–1919* (Chicago: n.p., n.d.); news accounts and transcripts made by Professor William Tuttle of his interview, June 26, 1969, with John Turner Harris, WTP. Tuttle's interview with Harris formed the basis of Tuttle's account of Eugene Williams's drowning at the opening of *Race Riot: Chicago in the Red Summer of 1919.* On August 2, the *Chicago Defender* reported, with appropriate irony, that black lifeguards at the 26th Street beach saved three white boys whose raft drifted out into the lake. "Life Guards Save Boys from Watery Grave," *CD,* August 2, 1919, 14.

8. Frontispiece, *NIC.*
9. "Race Riots in Chicago; Score of People Injured," *Hartford Courant,* July 27, 1919, 1.
10. James T. Farrell, *Studs Lonigan Trilogy* (New York: Vanguard Press, 1935), 73–74.
11. "And Now It Is Chicago!" *New York Evening Mail,* July 28, 1919, editorial page.
12. *CT,* July 28, 1919. See Encyclopedia of Chicago, http://www.encyclopedia.chicago history.org/pages/3879.html (accessed July 15, 2009).
13. "Mayor Home in Happy Mood," *CDN,* July 28, 1919, 1; "Mayor Back from Ranges," *CDJ,* July 28, 1919, 1.
14. "300 Armed Negroes Gather; New Rioting Starts; Militia Next," *CDN,* July 28, 1919, 1.
15. Story in July 28, 1919, *Herald-Examiner,* quoted in *NIC,* 29.
16. "Mass Police in Race Riot," *CDJ,* July 28, 1919, 1.
17. "300 Armed Negroes Gather; New Rioting Starts; Militia Next," *CDN,* July 28, 1919, 1.
18. "Mass Police in Race Riot," *CDJ,* July 28, 1919, 1.
19. "3 Negro Policemen on Trial," *CDJ,* July 28, 1919, 1.
20. "300 Armed Negroes Gather; New Rioting Starts; Militia Next," *CDN,* July 28, 1919, 1.
21. "Chicago Police Kill Negroes, Fleet Speeding to San Diego," *San Francisco Chronicle,* July 29, 1919, 1.
22. Ibid.
23. "Street Battles at Night," *NYT,* July 29, 1919, 1.
24. *NIC,* 659–60.
25. Peter M. Hoffman, comp., *The Race Riots: Biennial Report, 1918–1919* (Chicago: n.p., n.d.), 40. The coroner found Metz led the crowd in assaulting the black men. Metz and another Jewish man were the first to be buried; Jewish religion requires corpses to be interred quickly. However, police did not allow black families to get their dead for days. Police said they feared black funeral parties would be attacked as they made their way through white areas to suburban cemeteries. "Father of Five and Boy, Riot Victims, Buried," *CT,* August 1, 1919, 2.
26. Hoffman, *The Race Riots: Biennial Report, 1918–1919,* 24–25.
27. Ibid., 28.
28. Police arrested Scott for murder but prosecutors later dropped the charges. The Cook County coroner's jury report ruled that Scott's arrest "was a travesty of justice and fair play." *NIC,* app.
29. "Street Battles at Night," *NYT,* July 29, 1919, 1.
30. *NIC,* 658, 663–64.
31. Hoffman, *The Race Riots: Biennial Report, 1918–1919,* 49–50.
32. *NIC,* 31–32, 661.
33. Hoffman, *The Race Riots: Biennial Report, 1918–1919,* 41.
34. From the annual report of the Provident Hospital Board of Trustees, quoted in Joanne Grant, ed., *Black Protest: History, Documents and Analyses, 1619 to the Present* (Greenwich, Conn.: Fawcett Publications, 1968), 190–91.
35. Dempsey J. Travis, *An Autobiography of Black Chicago* (Chicago: Urban Research Press, 1981), 25–26.
36. Roi Ottley, *The Lonely Warrior: The Life and Times of Robert S. Abbott* (Chicago: Henry Regnery Company, 1955), 179–82.

37. Alden Bland, *Behold a Cry* (New York: Scribner, 1947), 79.

38. Hoffman, *The Race Riots: Biennial Report, 1918–1919*, 20.

39. Tuttle, *Race Riot*, 44.

40. "Take Oaths Over Bodies," *CDJ*, July 30, 1919, 1.

41. Penelope Niven, *Carl Sandburg: A Biography* (New York: Scribner, 1991), 342.

42. Tuttle, *Race Riot*, 44. The strike lasted four days. "Bar Negroes From Stock Yards Work," *BG*, August 3, 1919, 10.

43. "Labor Conditions Depressed Corn," *AC*, July 30, 1919, 14.

44. "Traffic in Bad Mixup," *CDN*, July 29, 1919, 1.

45. *NIC*, 37.

46. Ibid., 666.

47. "Mobs in Loop Attack Negroes; Two Killed," *CDN*, July 29, 1919, 5.

48. "Troops Called Out in Chicago," *CSM*, July 31, 1919, 1.

49. *NIC*, 665.

50. Ibid., 659.

51. Ibid., 664–65.

52. "These Negro Policemen Appeal for Law and Order," *CT*, July 29, 1919, 3.

53. Ottley, *The Lonely Warrior*, 183; "Negro Business Men Act to Curtail Lawlessness," *CT*, July 30, 1919, 2.

54. Ottley, *The Lonely Warrior*, 184.

55. "Situation Well in Hand, Says Lowden," *CDN*, July 29, 1919, 1.

56. Ottley, *The Lonely Warrior*, 48–49.

57. "Storm Mayor With Demand for Troops to Quell Race Riots," *CDN*, July 30, 1919, 1.

58. "Situation Well in Hand, Says Lowden," *CDN*, July 29, 1919, 1.

59. *NIC*, 659.

60. "Chicago by SWING," *Variety*, August 6, 1919, 16.

61. "Citizen Soldiers Wanted for Police Duty," *CDN*, July 29, 1919, 1.

62. "6 Playgrounds Closed by Riot," *CDJ*, July 29, 1919, 3.

63. "150 Negro Prisoners at County Jail Riot; Machine Gun Put In," *CDN*, July 28, 1919, 1; "100 Colored Men Break from Pen and Riot in Jail," *CT*, July 30, 1919, 3.

64. Hoffman, *The Race Riots: Biennial Report, 1918–1919*, 42–43.

65. *NIC*, 667.

66. "Governor to Probe Riot Trouble," *Savannah Tribune*, August 9, 1919, 1.

67. "Help Two Booms Along; Efforts in Congress in Behalf of Both Harding and Lowden," *NYT*, July 27, 1919, 12.

68. Walter Lippmann was unimpressed with Lowden, describing him as "alien to the world of ideas," adding "his oratory is full of stock prejudice and canned platitude." Walter Lippmann, *Early Writings* (New York: Liveright, 1970), 178.

69. Diary of Florence Lowden, wife of Frank Lowden, entry of July 30, 1919, WTP. Given to Tuttle by Lowden's daughter, Mrs. C. Phillip Miller.

70. William T. Hutchinson, *Lowden of Illinois: Nation and Countryside*, vol. 2 (Chicago: University of Chicago Press, 1957), 399–400.

71. "150 Negro Prisoners at County Jail Riot; Machine Gun Put In," *CDN*, July 29, 1919, 1.

72. "Lowden of Illinois; Blacksmith's Son, a School Teacher at 15, Takes Field for Presidential Nomination," *NYT*, July 20, 1919, 35; "Order in Chicago," *NYT*, July 31, 1919, 8; Allen D. Grimshaw, ed., *Racial Violence in the United States* (Chicago: Aldine, 1969), 88.

73. Thompson fired Garrity in the fall of 1920. "Chicago Mayor Ousts Police Chief," *NYT*, November 11, 1920, 7.

74. *NIC*, 35; Allen Grimshaw, "Actions of Police and the Military in American Race Riots," *Phylon* 24/3 (1963): 280.

75. "New State Law Weapon to Curb Racial Clashes," *CT*, July 30, 1919, 3.

76. "Late Riot Bulletins," *CDJ*, July 30, 1919, 1.

77. "Race Riots Continue Despite Troops," *NYTrib*, August 1, 1919, 8.

78. "Governor to Probe Riot Trouble," *Savannah Tribune*, August 9, 1919, 1.

79. Walter F. White, "I Investigate Lynchings," *American Mercury*, January 1929, http://nationalhumanitiescenter.org/pds/maai3/segregation/text2/investigatelynchings.pdf (accessed December 10, 2009).

80. Hoffman, *The Race Riots: Biennial Report, 1918–1919*, 31–32; *NIC*, 662.

81. "Negroes Call on Mayor, Lowden, to Stop Riots," *CT*, July 31, 1919, 3.

82. "Late Riot Bulletins," *CDJ*, July 30, 1919, 1.

83. "Police Aid Starving Negroes," *CDN*, July 30, 1919, 1.

84. Tuttle, *Race Riot*, 54.

85. "Mayor Refuses Assent to Martial Law Demand," *CDJ*, July 30, 1919, 1.

86. "Soldiers Rescue Negroes in Clash with Chicago Mob," *NYT*, August 1, 1919, 1.

87. "Troops Act; Halt Rioting," *CT*, July 31, 1919, 1.

88. Notes: Field Orders No. 1, issued July 30, 1919, 10:30 p.m., WTP.

89. "Street Battles at Night," *NYT*, July 29, 1919, 1.

90. *NIC*, 41.

91. Ibid.

92. Ibid., 42.

93. Ibid., 41.

94. Ibid., 42.

95. "Riots Quiet in Face of Bayonets," *Aberdeen Daily American*, August 1, 1919, 1.

96. Notes: Minutes of the Meeting at the City Club of Chicago, February 25, 1920, WTP.

97. Sterling Morton, "The Illinois Reserve Militia During World War I and After" (unpublished manuscript, December 4, 1959), 9–11, WTP.

98. *NIC*, 42.

99. "Troops Quell Race Rioting," *Baltimore American*, August 1, 1919, 1; *NIC*, 7.

100. Henry A. Bellows, *A Treatise on Riot Duty for the National Guard* (Washington: Government Printing Office, 1920), 110.

101. Ibid., 128.

102. Hoffman, *The Race Riots: Biennial Report, 1918–1919*, 42–43; *NIC*, 667.

103. "Soldiers Rescue Negroes in Clash with Chicago Mob," *NYT*, August 1, 1919, 1.

104. Tuttle, *Race Riot*, 60.

105. Notes from NARA Military Intelligence, Record Group 60, Box 7 (Glasser File); Van Buren to Military Intelligence, July 29–July 30, 1919, WTP.

106. BWGM, Reel 21, Record Group 165, 463.

107. "Wilson May Appeal to Stop Race Riots," *CDN*, July 30, 1919, 1.

108. "St. Louis Fears Trouble," *LAT*, July 29, 1919, 3; "Omaha Fears Riots; Bars Film," *CDJ*, July 30, 1919; *CDJ*, August 1, 1919; *New York World*, July 31, 1919, NAACP-2, WTP.

109. Ottley, *The Lonely Warrior*, 191–93.

110. "Reaping the Whirlwind," *CD*, August 2, 1919, 16.

111. "Chicago Quiet; 35 Dead, 1,500 Hurt in Riots," *NYTrib*, August 2, 1919, 5.

112. "Patrol Burned Homes to Foil New Terrorism," *CT*, August 3, 1919, 1.

113. The next week, a soldier bayoneted and killed a white man who refused to move when ordered. The killing was ruled justified. *NIC*, 663.

114. Fifteen of the black people killed were born in the South; four were from the North, and four were from the British Commonwealth. Six of the whites killed were born in the United States and nine were foreign-born. Hoffman, *The Race Riots: Biennial Report, 1918–1919*, 16.

115. *NIC*, 1.

116. "List of Injured," *CD*, August 2, 1919, 1, 2.

117. "Police Bravery in Riots Wins Public Praise," *CT*, August 1, 1919, 2.
118. "Chicago Race Riot Bill Over $500,000," *New York Amsterdam News*, December 27, 1922, 1.
119. "Chicago Quiet; 35 Dead, 1,500 Hurt in Riots," *NYTrib*, August 2, 1919, 5.
120. "Troops Bring Bayonets, Peace, Grins and Handshakes to Riot Zone," *CT*, August 1, 1919, 3.
121. "Chicago by SWING," *Variety*, August 6, 1919, 16.
122. Herbert J. Seligmann, *The Negro Faces America* (New York: Harper & Brothers, 1920), 3.
123. "Devil Runs Riots, Says Dr. Boynton," *Broad Ax*, August 8, 1919, 5.
124. "Stop Exploiting of Negro Votes, Pulpits Demand," *CT*, August 4, 1919, 2.

14. Like a Great Volcano
1. "Liberty," Graggs to Grimké, July 22, 1919, AGHU. Historian John Hope Franklin later declared the casualty list for the riot "gave the appearance of the results of a miniature war." Terry Ann Knopf, *Rumors, Race and Riots* (New Brunswick, N.J.: Transaction Publishers, 2006), 34.
2. "The Racial Ruction," *Leslie's Illustrated Weekly*, August 16, 1919, 248.
3. Letter from League to Kelly Miller, vice chair, August 5, 1919, Emory University Archives and Rare Book Library, Kelly Miller Collection #1050, Box 6, Folder 2.
4. The Sixth Annual Conference of the American Society for Colonizing the Free People of Color of the United States," *North American Review*, vol. 18, n.s., vol. 9 (January 1824), 61.
5. W. S. Scarborough, "Race Riots and Their Remedy," *Independent*, August 16, 1919, 223.
6. "James Johnson Predicts Additional Race Riots," *Savannah Tribune*, August 7, 1919, 5.
7. "Report on the committee of the state of the country, for the Grand United Order of Odd Fellows of America, Lodge No. 18," *Atlanta Independent*, August 16, 1919, 4.
8. Minutes of meeting of Board of Directors, September 8, 1919, NAACPM, Part 1, Reel 1; Francis Grimké, "The Race Problem," AGHU.
9. Letter to James Weldon Johnson, July 29, 1919, in Guy J. Forgue, ed., *Letters of H. L. Mencken; Selected and Annotated* (Boston: Northeastern University Press, 1981), 151.
10. Letter to Ernest Boyd, August 9, 1919, ibid., 152.
11. Du Bois to Rev. John Joseph Glennon, August 9, 1919, and clipping from *St. Louis Argus*, "Catholic Priest Speaks Bitterly Against Negroes," August 1, 1919, NAACP Anti-Segregation Files, Reel 1, 466–67.
12. NAACP board meeting minutes, August 26, 1919.
13. "Negro Boasts of Riots; In Jail, Then Lynched," *CT*, August 6, 1919, 1.
14. "Negro Is Lynched in Wilcox County," August 14, 1919, publication unknown, enclosed in letter from Dorsey to Wilcox County sheriff, August 20, 1919, Governor's Subject Files, 1917–1921, Record Group 001-01-005, Georgia Archives.
15. "Negro's Charred Body Found in the Ashes of Church Building," *Eastman Times-Journal*, August 28, 1919, 1; Laurens County to Dorsey, August 29, 1919, and Laurens County sheriff to Dorsey, September 18, 1919, Governor's Subject Files, 1917–1921.
16. "Cadwell Negro Shot and Burned in Church," *AC*, August 29, 1919, 5.
17. "Georgia Mob Shoots Colored Leader Down in the Edifice," *NYT*, August 29, 1919, 3.
18. "Cadwell Blames Moonshine," *Eastman Times-Journal*, September 4, 1919, 1. Four white men were arrested and charged in the lynching. Cooper's widow testified and identified the men as part of the mob that took her husband away. The men were all acquitted. See "Four Acquitted Lynching Charge in Eastman Trial," *AC*, October 19, 1919, 16.

19. "Tried to Shoot a Soldier," *Cleveland Gazette*, August 8, 1919, 2.
20. "Thousands on Strike Because of Negroes," *AC*, August 9, 1919, 18.
21. Foster went on to head the Communist Party USA for years and run for president on its ticket.
22. William Z. Foster, *Problems of Solidarity* ([?]: Trade Union Educational League, 1926), http://www.marxists.org/archive/foster/1926/strikestrategy/ch02.htm (accessed August 10, 2009). See also Neil Betten and Raymond A. Mohl, "The Evolution of Racism in an Industrial City, 1906–1940: A Case Study of Gary, Indiana," *JNH* 59/1 (January 1974): 51–64. The packers were not in the good graces of the federal government at the time. Due to high prices for meat across the country, A. Mitchell Palmer threatened to file an antitrust case against them for price gouging.
23. "Race Riots Continue Despite Troops" *NYTrib*, August 1, 1919, 8.
24. Advertisement: "The Riot Is Over/ Everybody Is Doing Business," *Chicago Whip*, August 14, 1919.
25. Walter White, "Chicago and Its Eight Reasons," *C*, October 1919, 293.
26. "50 Graft and Riot Suspects Taken in Raids," *CT*, August 24, 1919, 1.
27. White, "Chicago and Its Eight Reasons," 293.
28. A coalition of 48 Chicago civic groups asked Lowden to create a committee. "Race Riots in Chicago," *Outlook*, August 13, 1919, 567.
29. The report was not completed until 1922, and its suggestions, for the most part, were not implemented.
30. "Commission Will Study Race Riots," *CSM*, August 21, 1919, 4.
31. "Troopers Restore Order in Chicago," *NYT*, August 2, 1919, 10.
32. "A Dangerous Experiment," *Chicago Whip*, August 9, 1919, 16. Ida Wells-Barnett opposed the commission, and later complained, "Many recommendations were made, but few, if any, have been carried out. Chicago has thus been left with a heritage of race prejudice which seems to increase rather than decrease." Alfreda M. Duster, ed., *Crusade for Justice: The Autobiography of Ida B. Wells* (Chicago: University of Chicago Press, 1991), 408.
33. William R. Thompson, "Anatomically the Same," *CT*, August 14, 1919, 8.
34. William M. Tuttle Jr., "Contested Neighborhoods and Racial Violence: Prelude to the Chicago Riot of 1919," *JNH* 55/4 (October 1970): 285–86.
35. George Harrison, *Chicago Race Riots* (Chicago: Great Western Publishing Company, 1919), 20.
36. "The National Race Crisis," *CDN*, July 30, 1919, 8.
37. "Rioting Is Battle of Hoodlums, Not the Races," *Chicago American*, August 1, 1919.
38. "The Grim Implacability of Fate," *Broad Ax*, August 9, 1919, 8.
39. David John Olson, "Racial Violence and City Politics: The Political Response to Civil Disorders in Three American Cities" (PhD diss., University of Wisconsin, 1971), 60.
40. Paula J. Giddings, *Ida: A Sword Among Lions* (New York: Amistad, 2008), 603.
41. White, "Chicago and Its Eight Reasons," 293–97.
42. Ibid., 293.
43. Carl Sandburg, *The Chicago Race Riots, July 1919* (1920; repr., New York: Harcourt, Brace & World, 1969), iii. Introduction by Walter Lippmann.
44. "Anniversary of Slaves to America," *C*, August 1919, 42.
45. "The Country Aflame," *Savannah Tribune*, August 2, 1919, 4.
46. "Racial Tension and Race Riots," *Outlook*, August 6, 1919, 534.
47. "President Wilson's Reply," *Southern Workman* 48/11 (November 1919): 590–91; Arthur S. Link et al., eds., *The Papers of Woodrow Wilson*, vols. 53, 60, 61, 62 (Princeton, N.J.: Princeton University Press, 1986), 292.
48. Link et al., eds., *The Papers of Woodrow Wilson*, vol. 62, 292. James Edward McCulloch and Edwin Courtland Dinwiddle to Wilson, August 14, 1919; Manuscript, Archives

and Rare Book Library, Emory University, Kelly Miller Collection, MSS 1050, Box 6, Item 9; Woodrow Wilson to J. E. McCulloch, August 4, 1919. Congress representatives did attend the governors' conference and issued a plan that called on each governor to establish a standing committee of whites and blacks to monitor relations in their state. They also called on the president to set up a federal committee. The president and the governors ignored the proposals. "The Race Problem," *Outlook*, September 10, 1919, 44.

49. William Howard Taft, "Taft Says Sympathetic Aid to Negro Will Halt Rioting," *WP*, August 4, 1919, 1.

50. Frank H. Giddings, "The Black Man's Rights," *Independent*, August 2, 1919, 153.

51. "What the South Has to Say About Northern Race Conflicts," *Chicago Whip*, August 23, 1919, 4.

52. Hannibal Duncan, "The Changing Race Relationship in the Border and Northern States" (PhD diss., University of Pennsylvania, 1922), 69.

53. "To Colored Labor Seeking Homes," *Broad Ax*, August 16, 1919, 8.

54. "Tennessee's Appeal to Negroes in Vain," *New York Call*, August 1, 1919.

55. Hugh E. Macbeth to Du Bois, August 6, 1919, DP, Reel 7. Similar ideas were floated to Du Bois during the Red Summer. On June 26, 1919, a retired captain in the U.S. Army Corps of Engineers who had commanded black troops suggested that a black colony be established in the Baja California section of Mexico, where blacks could take up fishing. "Circumstances compel this move as an experiment to see just what the American Negro can do," the captain wrote. Du Bois's response, if any, is unknown. DP, Reel 8, 640.

56. Theodore Kornweibel Jr. *"Seeing Red": Federal Campaigns against Black Militancy, 1919–1925* (Bloomington: Indiana University Press, 1998), 85.

57. "Reds Accused of Stirring Up Negro Rioters," *NYTrib*, July 29, 1919, 6.

58. "U.S. Seeks Hand of Bolsheviki in Race Riots," *CT*, August 3, 1919, 3.

59. Minutes of the Chicago Race Commission, December 4, 1919, Julius Rosenwald Papers, Box 6, Folder 4–5, Special Collections Research Center, University of Chicago Library.

60. Memorandum to the director of Military Intelligence, August 15, 1919, in William Cohen, "Riots, Racism, and Hysteria: The Response of Federal Investigative Officials to the Race Riots of 1919," *Massachusetts Review* 13/3 (Summer 1972): 387–88.

61. "Charges I.W.W. Incites Negroes," *NYTrib*, August 4, 1919, 7.

62. "By the Way," *Wall Street Journal*, August 2, 1919, 1.

63. "Propaganda Among Negroes," *New York Evening Sun*, July 28, 1919, editorial page.

64. One Hundred and Forty-Fourth Session, 1921, 18/50—Part 2. Revolutionary Radicalism. Report of the Joint Legislative Committee Investigating Activities, Filed April 24, 1920, in the Senate of the State of New York. Part I, *Revolutionary and Subversive Movements Abroad and at Home*, vol. 2 (Albany, N.Y.: J. B. Lyon, 1920), 1493–95. Document dated June 21, 1919.

65. Stephen Graham, *The Soul of John Brown* (New York: Macmillan, 1920), 109.

66. Frederick Blossom, "Justice for the Negro, How He Can Get It," in *One Big Union Monthly*, ed. George Knoles, vol. 1 (1919; repr., New York: Greenwood, 1968), 30.

67. *The Ohio Socialist*, September 10, 1919, from Marxists.org, http://www.marxists.org/history/usa/eam/cpa/cpa-clpfounders.html (accessed July 12, 2010).

68. Report from federal agent James O. Peyronnin, Marxist history website, http://www.marxisthistory.org/subject/usa/eam/cpa-cpa19delegates.html (accessed July 17, 2010).

69. Claude McKay to Marcus Garvey, December 17, 1919, Hubert Harrison Papers, Columbia University Rare Book and Manuscript Library, Box 2, Folder 66.

15. Austin

1. Cleveland Allen to Shillady, July 27, 1919, DP, Reel 8, 415.
2. "Liberty," Graggs to Grimké, July 22, 1919, AGHU.
3. "Palmer Told Negro Press Is Anti-American," *NYTrib*, August 26, 1919, 16; "Race Rioting Blamed on Negro Demagogues and I.W.W. 'Reds,' By Byrnes in a House Address," *WP*, August 26, 1919, 2; *Congressional Record*, 66th Cong. list, vol. 58, part 4, 4302.
4. David Robertson, *Sly and Able: A Political Biography of James F. Byrnes* (New York: W. W. Norton, 1994), 29.
5. Blacks did not forget Byrnes's segregationist stand. His nomination to the U.S. Supreme Court in the 1940s sparked complaints from black groups and newspapers. Byrnes went on to hold numerous key posts in the federal government during World War Two and beyond. Later he returned to South Carolina to become governor and lead that state's fight against desegregation.
6. "Plot to Stir Race Antagonism in U.S. Charged to Soviets," *NYTrib*, August 27 1919, 3.
7. W. E. B. Du Bois, "Byrnes," *C*, October 1919, 284.
8. DP, Reel 7, 751–52.
9. Ibid., 1020.
10. Mary White Ovington, "Is Mob Violence the Texas Solution of the Race Problem?" *Independent*, September 6, 1919, 320.
11. Steven Reich, "Soldiers of Democracy: Black Texans and the Fight for Citizenship, 1917–1921," *Journal of American History* 82/4 (March 1996): 1498–1500.
12. U.S. Railroad Administration, BWGM, Reel 6, 677.
13. Lewis L. Gould, *Progressives and Prohibitionists: Texas Democrats in the Wilson Era* (Austin: University of Texas Press, 1979), 253.
14. Mark Robert Schneider, *"We Return Fighting": The Civil Rights Movement in the Jazz Age* (Boston: Northeastern University Press, 2002), 30–31.
15. Mary White Ovington, *The Walls Came Tumbling Down* (New York: Arno, 1969), 173.
16. Shillady came directly from Chicago, where he met with the two black targets of the white riot in Longview.
17. "Shillady's Story of Assault," *AC*, August 23, 1919, 7.
18. Ovington, "Is Mob Violence the Texas Solution of the Race Problem?," 320.
19. "Negro Advocate Beaten by Texans," *AC*, August 23, 1919, 1, 7.
20. James Weldon Johnson, *Along This Way* (New York: Penguin, 2008 [reprint of 1933 edition]), 343.
21. "Shillady Got Deserts, Says Texas Governor," *AC*, August 24, 1919, 3.
22. NAACP, "Mass Meeting on Mob Violence," signed by Ovington, AGHU.
23. Shillady to Archibald Grimké, August 29, 1919, AGHU.
24. "Hiss Mayor's Name at Town Meeting," *NYT*, March 13, 1915, 9.
25. Shillady to Grimké, August 29, 1919.
26. "The Passing of Uncle Tom," *Chicago Whip*, August 2, 1919, editorial page.
27. Lillian Wald to Wilson, August 23 1919, in Arthur S. Link et al., ed., *The Papers of Woodrow Wilson*, vols. 53, 60, 61, 62 (Princeton, N.J.: Princeton University Press, 1986), 527.
28. Wilson to Joseph Patrick Tumulty, August 28, 1919, in ibid., 536.
29. House Committee on the Judiciary, *Part I—Segregation; Part II, Anti-Lynching. Hearings before the Committee on the Judiciary,* 66th Cong., 2nd sess., January 15 and January 29, 1920, 59.
30. NAACP board meeting notes, August 26, 1919; "Appeal to Wilson for Lynching Probe," *AC*, August 30, 1919, 15; "Asks Congressional Probe," *WP*, August 28, 1919, 1; Mark Robert Schneider, *"We Return Fighting,"* 32.

31. NAACP board minutes, August 26, 1919.
32. "What the South Thinks of Northern Race Riots," in *The Black Worker From 1900–1919*, vol. 5, Philip Foner and Ronald L. Lewis, eds., (Philadelphia: Temple University Press, 1980), 357; "What the South Has to Say About Northern Race Conflicts," *Chicago Whip*, August 23, 1919, 4.
33. "Government of the Negro," repr. in *The Crusader, September 1918–August 1919*, vol. 1 (New York: Garland, 1987), 402.
34. Percy L. Jones to Du Bois, August 6, 1919, DP, Reel 7, 1007.
35. Robert A. Hill, ed. *The Marcus Garvey and Universal Negro Improvement Association Papers, 27 August 1919–31 August 1920* (Berkeley: University of California Press, 1983), 2:502.
36. Cary D. Wintz, *African American Political Thought, 1890–1930: Washington, Du Bois, Garvey and Randolph* (Armonk, N.Y.: M. E. Sharpe, 1996), 194.
37. Ibid.
38. Du Bois to James Burghardt, August 27, 1919, in Hill, *Marcus Garvey*, 3.

16. Knoxville

1. Matthew Lakin, "'A Dark Night': The Knoxville Riot of 1919," *Journal of East Tennessee History* 72 (2000): 2.
2. Knoxville's population was 36,340 in 1910. By the 1920 census, it reached 77, 818 people, an increase of 114 percent. During the same time, the city's black population rose from 7,638 to 11,302, an increase of only 48 percent. So though the number of black people in Knoxville increased, the percentage of blacks in the city's overall population decreased, from 22.5 to 14.5 percent.
3. James Agee, *A Death in the Family* (New York: Vintage, 1998), 199–200.
4. Lakin, "A Dark Night," 3.
5. Advertisement, *KJT*, August 31, 1919, 12-B.
6. Stephen Graham, *The Soul of John Brown* (New York: Macmillan, 1920), 99.
7. The letter stated Governor Roberts was an organizing member, but Roberts publicly denounced the group and said his name was falsely added. "The South and Demobilization," *C*, April 1919, 290–291.
8. Lakin, "A Dark Night," 6.
9. Fountain City was later incorporated into Knoxville.
10. NAACPAL, Reel 2, 136.
11. "Gallows Needed to Stop Murder, Says Governor," *AC*, January 23, 1919, 1.
12. "Gov. Roberts Reviews Troops," *KJT*, August 30, 1919, 7.
13. Most news and historical accounts, as well as some court records, list the cousin's name as Smyth, but others list the name as Smith. "Bloody Race Riot Rages at Knoxville," *AC*, August 31, 1919, 1.
14. *Mays v. State, Southwestern Reporter* 238, April 19–May 10, 1922 (St. Paul, Minn.: West Publishing, 1922), 1097–104.
15. Ibid., 1101.
16. "Bloody Race Riot Rages at Knoxville," *AC*, August 31, 1919, 1.
17. *Southwestern Reporter*, 1101.
18. Lakin, "A Dark Night," 6.
19. Ibid., 7.
20. "Killed in Effort to Escape Negro," *KJT*, August 31, 1919, 2.
21. *Southwestern Reporter*, 1098.
22. "Crowd Partly Wrecks Jail," *KS*, September 1, 1919.
23. Ibid.
24. "Rioters Overrun Knoxville When Foiled in Lynching Attempt," *LAT*, August 31, 1919.

25. "Crowd Partly Wrecks Jail."
26. "12 Prisoners Are Liberated at Jail," *KJT*, September 1, 1919, 1, 2.
27. Lakin, "A Dark Night," 15.
28. William J. Bacon, *History of the Fifty-Fifth Field Artillery Brigade* (Memphis: William J. Bacon, 1920), 215.
29. "Crowd Partly Wrecks Jail."
30. Lakin, "A Dark Night," 17.
31. "Martial Law Stops Knoxville Bloodshed," *AC*, September 1, 1919, 1.
32. "Recent Race Riots," *NYTrib*, September 1, 1919, 1.
33. "Firearms in Stores Taken," *KS*, September 1, 1919.
34. "Bloody Race Riot Rages at Knoxville," *AC*, August 31, 1919, 1.
35. Henry A. Bellows, *A Treatise on Riot Duty for the National Guard* (Washington, D.C.: Government Printing Office, 1920), 126–27.
36. "Quiet Restored at Knoxville," *AC*, September 2, 1919, 5.
37. "Machine Guns in Main Battle of Riot," *Journal and Tribune*, September 1, 1919, 2.
38. Lakin, "A Dark Night," 21.
39. "Bloody Race Riot Rages at Knoxville," *AC*, August 31, 1919, 1.
40. "Martial Law Stops Knoxville Bloodshed."
41. Lakin, "A Dark Night," 22.
42. "Firearms in Stores Taken."
43. "Tennessee Troops Fight Negroes in Race Riot; 2 Dead," *NYTrib*, September 1, 1919, 1.
44. "Quiet Restored at Knoxville."
45. "Halt Knoxville Riot," *WP*, September 1, 1919, 1.
46. "Situation Seems Under Control," *KJT*, September 1, 1919, 3.
47. "Pleas for Order Made in Pulpits," *KJT*, September 1, 1919, 3.
48. "Guards Stop Hearse to Search the Negro Driver for Firearms," *KJT*, September 1, 1919, 3.
49. Lakin, "A Dark Night," 24.
50. *The Crusader September 1919–August 1920*, vol. 2 (New York: Garland Publishing, 1987), 476.
51. "Anxious Crowds Take Papers From Carriers," *KJT*, September 1, 1919, 6.
52. "Halt Knoxville Riot."
53. Troops returned to Knoxville two months later. Governor Roberts sent two militia battalions in late October to keep order during a bitter transit strike that took place at the same time 14 white men charged in the destruction of the jail were acquitted. "Knoxville Normal; Troops Withdrawn," *AC*, September 3, 1919, 3; "Knoxville Rioting Draws Troops," *AC*, October 27, 1919, 1.
54. McMillan left politics and went into business, with little success. In 1926, he committed suicide.
55. "Chattanooga Warned Ready for Attack," *San Francisco Chronicle*, August 31, 1919, 1; "Rioters Overrun Knoxville When Foiled in Lynching Attempt," *LAT*, August 31, 1919, 11.
56. Graham, *The Soul of John Brown*, 114.
57. "The Knoxville Mob—A Summing Up," *KJT*, September 1, 1919, 6.
58. *Minutes of Interracial Conference Including Committee on After War Program & Representatives of State YMCA Committees*, September 17, 1919, Atlanta University Center, Robert W. Woodruff Library, Commission on Interracial Cooperation Papers, 1919–1944, Series 2, Folder 1, Reel 20, 39–44.
59. "Teaching Negroes 'A Lesson,'" September 13, 1919, in *The Selected Writings of James Weldon Johnson*, vol. 1, The New York Age *Editorials (1914–1923)*, ed. Sondra Kathryn Wilson (New York: Oxford University Press, 1995), 70.

17. A New Negro

1. "Sailors and Sailors Menace Barbary Coast Negroes," *San Francisco Chronicle*, September 8, 1919, 1. Many of California's white politicians were obsessed with race at the time, but their fears were directed at Asians. They passed legislation barring Japanese immigrants from owning property, and debated how best to stop "the Japanese evil" of migration. James D. Phelan, "The Japanese Evil in California," *North American Review* (September 1919): 323. Phelan was a Democratic U.S. senator from California.
2. "One Man Slain in Clash with New York Police," *CT*, September 16, 1919, 1.
3. "Rescue Negro, White from Lynching," *LAT*, September 9, 1919, 12.
4. NAACP board minutes, September 8, 1919, 3; "Lynching Aftermath Expected in Pueblo," *LAT*, September 15, 1919, I2.
5. "Riot Guns Received by Savannah Police," *AC*, October 3, 1919, 3.
6. "Negroes Demand Race Amendment," *AC*, August 29, 1919, 11.
7. W. W. Kerr to Wilson, September 17, 1919, BWGM, Reel 22, Record Group 83, Bureau of Agricultural Economics, 395–98.
8. "Lack of Reason for Antagonism," *CSM*, September 4, 1919, 6; "Racial Bitterness Lamented by Moton," *AC*, September 4, 1919, 6.
9. W. S. Scarborough, "Race Riots and Their Remedy," *Independent*, August 16, 1919, 223.
10. His actions made him a national hero among law-and-order conservatives. He would be elected vice president in 1920.
11. William Z. Foster, *Misleaders of Labor* (Trade Union Educational League, 1927), 59; Edward P. Johanningsmeier, *Forging American Communism: The Life of William Z. Foster* (Princeton, N.J.: Princeton University Press, 1994), 112.
12. "First Stage of Dual Offensive Without Result," *Charlotte Observer*, September 30, 1919, 1.
13. "5 Strikers Killed; 15 Others Injured by Police," *AC*, September 10, 1919, 5.
14. Carl Ackerman, "Important Information to Be Given Committee Probing Steel Strike," *AC*, September 11, 1919, 11.
15. "Eugene Debs Sees Gravest Dangers in Steel Strike," *AC*, September 24, 1919, 1, 3.
16. "Riot Insurance Rates Trebled," *NYT*, September 23, 1919, 3.
17. The NAACP had been worried about this division between black workers and white union workers for years, and dedicated the September issue of *The Crisis* to labor. In one of the essays, George Haynes, director of Negro Economics for the United States Department of Labor, argued that black workers were a great source of unskilled labor, which was crucial to the American economy as it faced what he called "the greatest agricultural, industrial and commercial expansion in her history" following the war. Haynes, "The Opportunity of Negro Labor," *C*, September 1919, 236. Other essays urged blacks to join unions.
18. Neil Betten and Raymond Mohl, "The Evolution of Racism in an Industrial City, 1906–1940: A Case Study of Gary, Indiana," *JNH* 59/1 (January 1974): 52.
19. "Racial Conflict and Split Labor Markets: The AFL Campaign to Organize Steel Workers, 1918–1919," *Social Science History* 22/3 (Autumn 1998): 335.
20. Knoles, George, ed. *One Big Union, 1919*, ser. 1, vol. 1 (New York: Greenwood, 1968), 23. "The Awakening of the Negro."
21. DP, Reel 7, 629.
22. Newell Dwight Hillis, "What Is the Matter with the United States?" *McClure's Magazine*, September 1919, 13.
23. Black groups were not happy with the treaty. In August, William Monroe Trotter and others testified before the Senate Foreign Relations Committee, urging an amendment to the treaty that would guarantee equal rights for citizens of every nation. Others wanted the United States to take over the former German colony of Kamerun

(modern Cameroon) and make it a haven for African Americans. The proposals from black speakers went nowhere. Only five of the committee's 17 members showed up to hear them. "Negroes Demand Race Amendment," *AC*, August 29, 1919, 11.

24. "World Looks to America to Settle World Affairs, Says President Wilson," *AC*, September 14, 1919, 1.
25. Hearings on the Metropolitan Police in the District of Columbia, Committee on the District of Columbia, U.S. Senate, 66th Congress, 34.
26. John Milton Cooper Jr., *Woodrow Wilson: A Biography* (New York: Knopf, 2009), 530–31.
27. Arthur I. Waskow, *From Race Riot to Sit-In, 1919 and the 1960s* (Garden City, N.Y.: Doubleday & Company, 1966), 33.
28. *Cleveland Gazette* editors wrote on October 18, 1919, "It requires no stretch of imagination to remind the 12,000,000 Colored people of these United States that race prejudice has obtained to a far greater degree under the present national Democratic administration than at any time since the close of the War of the Rebellion."
29. The September *Crisis* was called the Labor Issue. The cover drawing showed silhouettes of haggard people trudging north, with the caption *Exodus*.
30. W. E. B. Du Bois, "Let Us Reason Together," *C*, September 1919, 231.
31. Johnson to Curtis, September 3, 1919, NAACPAL, Reel 2, 413–14.
32. The arguments outlined in Johnson's brief predicted some of the psychological arguments made against racial violence outlined in Gunnar Myrdal's 1944 report, *An American Dilemma: The Negro Problem and Modern Democracy*.
33. NAACPAL, Reel 2, 466–76.
34. NAACPAL, Reel 2, 449. On October 2, 1919, Representative Dyer of Missouri submitted a similar resolution to the House Judiciary Committee calling for hearings. Compared to Curtis, Dyer had much less political influence. NAACPAL, Reel 2, 449; NAACPAL, Reel 2, 448.
35. James Weldon Johnson telegram, September 30, 1919, NAACPAL, Reel 2, 434.
36. William Unrau, *Mixed-Bloods and Tribal Dissolution: Charles Curtis and the Quest for Indian Identity* (Lawrence: University of Kansas Press, 1989), 171.
37. See http://www.senate.gov/artandhistory/history/common/generic/VP_Charles_Curtis .htm (accessed May 13, 2009).
38. It would continue to grow in the 1920s. In 1928, he was elected vice president of the United States on the Republican ticket with Herbert Hoover.
39. Johnson report, September 25, 1919, NAACPAL, Reel 2, 422.
40. Trotter's National Equal Rights League held a two-day conference in Washington titled "To Make America Safe for Americans" to assert black citizens' rights guaranteed in constitutional amendments. The League planned simultaneous rallies in other cities. "An 'America Safe' Sunday," *Broad Ax*, September 13, 1919, 2. Black communities raised money for campaigns for better schools and legal defense funds for individuals accused of participating in the violence. Across the country, men and women were defended in court thanks to small donations made by family members, friends, and others in the black community.
41. Petition from Archibald Blackshear, September 6, 1919, notarized in Richmond County. SvR.
42. A. B. Lovett, Motion for Change of Venue, issued from Sylvania order, September 26, 1919. SvR.

18. Omaha

1. In subsequent years, the percentage of blacks rose slightly. In 2008, census estimates put the state's black population at 4.5 percent.
2. BWGM, Reel 20, Record Group 60, 353.

3. Michael Lawson, "Omaha, A City in Ferment: Summer of 1919," *Nebraska History* 58 (Autumn 1977): 405.

4. U.S. Census, 1920; War Department General Staff, BWGM, Reel 21, Record Group 165, 353.

5. Carl Ackerman, "National Crisis Is Not One of Industry, But of Human Life and Domestic Happiness," *AC*, August 28, 1919, 8.

6. Lawson, "Omaha," 395–97.

7. See http://www.omahahistory.org/Education_Mayors_Smith.htm (accessed July 7, 2010).

8. Orville Menard, "Tom Dennison, the *Omaha Bee*, and the 1919 Omaha Race Riot," *Nebraska History* 68/4 (Winter 1987): 152–53.

9. Lawson, "Omaha," 410–12.

10. Lee E. Williams II, *Post-War Riots in America, 1919 and 1946* (Lewiston, N.Y.: Edwin Mellen Press, 1991), 65.

11. Lawson, "Omaha," 412.

12. Benjamin Griffith Brawley, *A Social History of the American Negro* (New York: Macmillan, 1921), 301; Williams, *Post-War Riots in America*, 63.

13. After 1919, Parker aligned with Marcus Garvey. Views similar to Parker's were later espoused by another black man born in Omaha in 1925, Malcolm Little, who would take the name Malcolm X.

14. Mark Robert Schneider, *"We Return Fighting": The Civil Rights Movement in the Jazz Age* (Boston: Northeastern University Press, 2002), 33.

15. Herbert J. Seligmann, *The Negro Faces America* (New York: Harper & Brothers, 1920), 156.

16. Some accounts report Hoffman's name as Milton.

17. "Wave of Lawlessness Has Spread to Omaha," *The Monitor*, October 2, 1919, 1–2; Report from Omaha to U.S. Army Intelligence Department, Chicago, October 27, 1919, BWGM, Reel 20 (Glasser File), 534.

18. Menard, "Tom Dennison," 158.

19. Lawson, "Omaha," 415; Colonel Dade Report, October 15, 1919, BWGM, Reel 20, Record Group 60 (Glasser File), 527.

20. "Omaha's Riot in Story and Picture," NYPL Digital Gallery, http://digitalgallery.nypl .org/nypldigital/.

21. A military intelligence report later determined that the identification was not positive, BWGM, Reel 20, Record Group 60 (Glasser File), 534.

22. Menard, "Tom Dennison," 158.

23. BWGM, Reel 20, Record Group 60 (Glasser File), 527, 534.

24. See http://www.nebraskahistory.org/histpres/nebraska/douglas.htm (accessed August 10, 2009).

25. Menard, "Tom Dennison," 158.

26. Anonymous, *Omaha's Riot in Story and Picture—1919* (Omaha: Educational Publishing Company, 1919 or 1920), http://www.historicomaha.com/riot.htm (accessed August 10, 2009).

27. "Wave of Lawlessness Has Spread to Omaha," *The Monitor*, October 2, 1919, 1.

28. Clayton D. Laurie, "The U.S. Army and the Omaha Race Riot of 1919," *Nebraska History* 72/3 (Autumn 1991): 137.

29. Williams, *Post-War Riots in America*, 70–71.

30. "Wave of Lawlessness Has Spread to Omaha," *The Monitor*, October 2, 1919, 1.

31. American Legion, Omaha Post no. 1 official history, http://www.amlegomahapost1 .org/content.php?id=2 (accessed August 15, 2009).

32. Laurie, "The U.S. Army," 136, 138.

33. Ibid., 138.

34. Lt. Col. Jacob W. S. Wuest, Army Balloon School, Fort Omaha, to Co. D. Def. Chandler, October 28, 1919, Record Group 18, National Archives and Records Administration, Central Plains Divison.

35. Commanding Officer, Fort Omaha, to Commanding General, Central Department, October 2, 1919, BWGM, 524.

36. "Omaha City of Terror," *Nebraska State Journal*, September 30, 1919, 2.

37. Anonymous, *Omaha's Riot*.

38. Ibid.

39. "$1,000,000 Damage to Court House and Contents Result of Mob's Destructive Orgy," *The Monitor*, October 2, 1919, 2.

40. "Omaha Quiet after Riot," *Nebraska State Journal*, September 30, 1919, 1–2.

41. Ibid.

42. Laurie, "The U.S. Army," 136.

43. Telegram from Barrows to Baker, BWGM, Reel 20, Record Group 60 (Glasser File), 538.

44. Williams, *Post-War Riots in America*, 71.

45. Anonymous, *Omaha's Riot*.

46. "Rope About Neck, Mayor of Omaha Escapes the Mob," *AC*, September 30, 1919, 3.

47. Two months later, Smith made Norgaard a police chauffeur for his actions in saving Smith. Menard, "Tom Dennison," 159–60.

48. Williams, *Post-War Riots in America*, 82, 86.

49. "Omaha's Riot in Story and Picture," NYPL Digital Gallery.

50. Anonymous, *Omaha's Riot*.

51. "Troops Check Omaha Rioting," *BG*, September 30, 1919, 4.

52. Anonymous, *Omaha's Riot*.

53. "U.S. Troops Patrol Omaha," *San Francisco Chronicle*, September 30, 1919, 2.

54. Menard, "Tom Dennison," 160.

55. The prisoners included another black man, George Webb, who was charged with killing a white woman. "U.S. Troops Patrol Omaha," *San Francisco Chronicle*, September 30, 1919, 2.

56. Williams, *Post-War Riots in America*, 82.

57. Ibid., 84.

58. Menard, "Tom Dennison," 1.

59. Henry Fonda, as told to Howard Teichmann, *Fonda: My Life* (New York: New American Library, 1981), 23–25.

60. "Wave of Lawlessness Has Spread to Omaha," *The Monitor*, October 2, 1919, 1.

61. Du Bois was so shocked by the photograph that he purchased it to reprint in *The Crisis*. The *Chicago Tribune* photo editor who sold it called it "a splendid one." DP, Reel 8, 505.

62. Williams, *Post-War Riots in America*, 87.

63. Military intelligence report from H. T. Lewis, October 27, 1919, BWGM, Reel 20, Record Group 60 (Glasser File), 535.

64. "Lynching in Omaha," *NYT*, September 29, 1919, 1.

65. Laurie, "U.S. Army," 135.

66. Dade report to Commanding Central Department, October 15, 1919 BWGM, Reel 20, Record Group 60 (Glasser File), 529.

67. Ibid., 531.

68. O. W. Neidert, 1st Lieutenant, 64th Infantry, to Military Intelligence, October 16, 1919, BWGM, Military Intelligence, 533.

69. Federal military authorities took full credit for the restoration of order—and glossed over the hours of delay during which blacks were attacked and the courthouse pil-

Notes 313

laged. In subsequent reports, they laid blame for the riot on local police. Local business leaders, who opposed Smith and his administration, were quick to embrace this view. "There can be no question that the quick action on the part of the representatives of the War Department saved this city from a calamity that would have been many times more far-reaching than the disgraceful affair which took place," the Omaha Chamber of Commerce wrote to Wuest. Letter from the Omaha Chamber of Commerce to Wuest, October 11, 1919, Record Group 18, National Archives, Central Plains Division.

70. "Special Jury Will Sift Omaha Race Riot Evidence," NYTrib, October 1, 1919, 4.
71. "Monitor Editor Makes Statement," The Monitor, October 2, 1919, 1.
72. "The World-Pack," The Monitor, October 2, 1919, 4.
73. "Omaha Mob Rule Defended by Most of the Population," NYT, September 29, 1919, 1.
74. BWGM, Reel 20, Record Group 60 (Glasser File), 539.
75. John Holme, The Life of Leonard Wood (Garden City, N.Y.: Doubleday, Page & Company, 1920), 207.
76. Walter Lippmann, Early Writings (New York: Liveright, 1970), 169.
77. Jack Lane, Armed Progressive: General Leonard Wood (San Rafael, Calif.: Presidio Press, 1978), 232.
78. Holme, The Life of Leonard Wood, 210.
79. Lippmann, Early Writings, 167.
80. As Wood biographer Jack C. Lane wrote, "More than any other leading candidate for the Republican nomination, he played on the public's fear and intensified the hysteria by blaming radical activists for every American problem from race riots to labor strikes." Lane, Armed Progressive, 234.
81. Williams, Post-War Riots in America, 85–86.
82. "Leonard Wood in Omaha," Brooklyn Daily Eagle, October 1, 1919, editorial page.
83. Williams, Post-War Riots in America, 89–90. An investigation by military intelligence determined "it is not thought they were active in the beginning of the trouble" but afterward they tried to distribute some pamphlets. BWGM, Reel 20, Record Group 60 (Glasser File), 536.
84. George Knoles, ed., One Big Union, 1919, vol. 1 (New York: Greenwood Reprint Corp., 1968), 10.
85. New York Legislative Documents, One Hundred and Forty-Fourth Session, 1921, Vol. XVIII-No. 50—Part 2, Revolutionary Radicalism: Its History, Purpose and Tactics. Report of the Joint Legislative Committee Investigating Activities, filed April 24, 1920, in the Senate of the State of New York (Albany, N.Y.: J. B. Lyon Company, 1920), 1483.
86. "An American Worthy of His Splendid Citizenship," New York Evening Mail, September 29, 1919, editorial page.
87. Annual business meetings and correspondence, NAACPM, Part 1, Reel 13. 142–44; Ovington to Smith, December 11, 1919; Smith to Ovington, December 12, 1919.
88. Seligmann, The Negro Faces America, 167.
89. Menard, "Tom Dennison," 164.
90. Commissioner Ringer ran for mayor as the progressive candidate, and was roundly defeated by Dahlman, the Dennison associate Smith beat in 1918. Smith died in 1930. See http://www.omahahistory.org/Education_Mayors_Smith.htm.
91. Seligmann, The Negro Faces America, 44.
92. After numerous appeals, the newspaper paid a small fine. The Northwestern Reporter, December 23, 1921–February 3, 1922, vol. 185 (St. Paul, Minn.: West Publishing, 1922), 341–42.
93. The Crusader, September 1919–August 1920, vol. 2 (New York: Garland Publishing, 1987), 14.

94. Harvey Newbranch, "Law and the Jungle," in *Pulitzer Prize Editorials: America's Best Writing, 1917–2003*, ed. William David Sloan and Laird B. Anderson (Hoboken, N.J.: Wiley-Blackwell, 2003), 16–20.

95. "Contempt for Law," *The Youth's Companion*, October 23, 1919, 598.

96. NAACPAL, Reel 2, 436.

97. Sondra Kathryn Wilson, ed., *The Selected Writings of James Weldon Johnson: The New York Age Editorials (1914–1923)*, vol. 1 (New York: Oxford University Press, 1995), 71.

98. See Horace Green, ed., *American Problems: A Selection of Speeches and Prophecies by William E. Borah* (New York: Duffield & Company), 1924.

99. "Omaha Lynching in Senate Debate—John Sharp Williams Condones Action of Mob and Draws Sharp Reply From Senator Borah," *AC*, September 30, 1919, 1; "Williams Rips Senator Borah," *Charlotte Observer*, September 30, 1919, 1.

100. See Donald Wilhelm, "If He Were President: William E. Borah," *Independent*, October 4, 1919, 14.

101. LeRoy Ashby, *The Spearless Leader: Senator Borah and the Progressive Movement in the 1920s* (Chicago: University of Illinois Press, 1972), 251.

102. C. B. Wilmer, "Casting Out Demons Through Beelzebub," *AC*, October 1, 1919, 12.

103. "Three Negroes Dead, Two Sought by Mobs," *LAT*, October 1, 1919, 14; "Court to Order Inquiry into Alabama Lynchings," *NYTrib*, October 1, 1919, 4.

19. Phillips County

1. Francis to Wheeler, September 18, 1919, DP, Reel 7, 854. Seligmann also did not like the headline. See National Association for the Advancement of Colored People, *Tenth Annual Report for the Year 1919* (New York: NAACP, 1920), 26.

2. Wheeler to Francis, September 22, 1919, DP, Reel 7, 855.

3. M. Langley Biegert, "Legacy of Resistance: Uncovering the History of Collective Action by Black Agricultural Workers in Central East Arkansas from the 1860s to the 1930s," *Journal of Social History* 32/1 (Autumn 1998): 76.

4. The area produced several Confederate generals, including Patrick Cleburne, whose career suffered when he suggested slaves could earn their freedom if they fought for the Confederacy.

5. Fon Louise Gordon, *Caste & Class: The Black Experience in Arkansas, 1880–1920* (Athens: University of Georgia Press, 1995), 2–3.

6. "Swarming to Arkansas; Negro Laborers From Other States Welcomed by the Planters," *NYT*, January 20, 1890, 1.

7. Grif Stockley, *Blood in Their Eyes: The Elaine Race Massacres of 1919* (Fayetteville: University of Arkansas Press, 2001), 21.

8. Gordon, *Caste & Class*, 26–27.

9. Robert Whitaker, *On the Laps of Gods: The Red Summer of 1919 and the Struggle for Justice That Remade a Nation* (New York: Crown, 2008), 7–8.

10. Bratton to Sen. Charles Curtis, November 4, 1919, 3, WTP (Elaine file).

11. "30 Years of Lynching, 1889–1918," NAACPAL, Reel 1, 1092–209.

12. See http://www.encyclopediaofarkansas.net/encyclopedia/entry-detail.aspx?entryID=346 (accessed September 14, 2009).

13. Gordon, *Caste & Class*, 129.

14. Ibid.

15. Kieran Taylor, "'We Have Just Begun': Black Organizing and White Response in the Arkansas Delta, 1919," *Arkansas Historical Quarterly* 58/3 (Autumn 1999): 269.

16. Ibid., 280.

17. Ibid., 282.

18. U.S. Census, 1920.

19. Frank Lincoln Mather, *Who's Who of the Colored Race, 1915*, vol. 1 (Chicago: Frank Lincoln Mather, 1915), 199.

20. Richard Wright, *Black Boy* (New York: HarperPerennial, 1991), 57.

21. Ibid., 59.

22. Ibid., 65, 68.

23. Ibid., 58.

24. "Safer in the Trenches Than in the South," *Cleveland Gazette*, February 8, 1919, editorial page.

25. *The Crusader, September 1919–August 1920*, vol. 2 (New York: Garland Publishing, 1987), 505.

26. This includes the population of West Helena, an adjacent town incorporated in 1917; http://www.encyclopediaofarkansas.net/encyclopedia/entry-detail.aspx?entryID= 950 (accessed January 10, 2010).

27. Stockley, *Blood in Their Eyes*, 2.

28. Ida B. Wells-Barnett, *The Arkansas Race Riot* (Chicago: Ida B. Wells-Barnett, 1920), 49, http://lincoln.lib.niu.edu/cgi-bin/philologic/navigate.pl?lincoln.5069 (accessed July 8, 2010).

29. Ibid., 49.

30. Richard C. Cortner, *A Mob Intent on Death: The NAACP and the Arkansas Riot Cases* (Middletown, Conn.: Wesleyan University Press, 1988), 55.

31. Whitaker, *On the Laps of the Gods*, 11.

32. O. A. Rogers Jr., "The Elaine Race Riots of 1919," *Arkansas Historical Quarterly* 19/2 (Summer 1960): 144.

33. Wells-Barnett, *The Arkansas Race Riot*, 8.

34. *Ed Ware et al. v. State of Arkansas*, Supreme Court of Arkansas, 75, 108, WD.

35. Ibid., 74.

36. Ibid., 109.

37. Whitaker, *On the Laps of the Gods*, 16.

38. Wells-Barnett, *The Arkansas Race Riot*, 14.

39. Jeannie Whayne, "Low Villians and Wickedness in High Places: Race and Class in the Elaine Riots," *Arkansas Historical Quarterly* 58/3 (Autumn 1999): 306–7.

40. Rogers, "The Elaine Race Riots of 1919," 144.

41. Wells-Barnett, *The Arkansas Race Riot*, 13.

42. Taylor, "'We have just begun,'" 281.

43. Cortner, *A Mob Intent on Death*, 7.

44. Joey McCarty, "The Red Scare in Arkansas: A Southern State and National Hysteria," *Arkansas Historical Quarterly* 37/3 (Autumn 1978): 269.

45. See McCarty, "'The Red Scare in Arkansas,'" 264–77.

46. *Ed Ware et al. v. State of Arkansas*, 110.

47. Ibid., 74.

48. Ibid., 72.

49. Rogers, "The Elaine Race Riots of 1919," 147.

50. *Ed Ware et al. v. State of Arkansas*, 34.

51. *Arkansas Gazette*, October 1, 1919, WD.

52. *Ed Ware et al. v. State of Arkansas*, 15.

53. Ibid., 22.

54. Ibid., 31–32.

55. Ibid., 29.

56. Ibid., 19.

57. Ibid., 29.

58. "Alleged Plot Discovered," *Arkansas Gazette*, October 1, 1919, WD.

59. "10 Dead, Dozen Hurt, Race War at Elaine, Ark.," *Arkansas Gazette*, WD.

60. Rogers, "The Elaine Race Riots of 1919," 148.
61. Whayne, "Low Villains and Wickedness in High Places," 292.
62. Wells-Barnett, *The Arkansas Race Riot*, 18.
63. *Ed Ware et al. v. State of Arkansas*, 110.
64. "Bootleggers Ambush 3 Peace Officers," *Helena World*, October 1, 1919, WD.
65. Ibid.
66. Stockley, *Blood in Their Eyes*, 46.
67. Ibid., 203.
68. Ibid., 1.
69. Du Bois to *New York World*, November 20, 1919, DP, Reel 7, 1165.
70. Biegert, "Legacy of Resistance," 87.
71. Stockley, *Blood in Their Eyes*, xxiii.
72. Telegram sent October 1, 1919, BWGM, Reel 20, 375 (Glasser file). In 1921, then-governor Thomas McRae requested Camp Pike troops in anticipation of trouble when a black man in Little Rock was charged with rape. His request was denied. Ibid., 376–78.
73. "500 Camp Pike Soldiers Sent to Quell Riot," *Arkansas Gazette*, October 2, 1919; Ralph Desmairais, "Military Intelligence Reports on Arkansas Riots: 1919–1920," *Arkansas Historical Society* 33/2 (Summer 1974): 180–82.
74. Foy Lisenby, *Charles Hillman Brough: A Biography* (Fayetteville: University of Arkansas Press, 1996), 27.
75. Ibid., 14.
76. Charles Hillman Brough, "Work of the Commission of Southern Universities on the Race Question," *Annals of the American Academy of Political and Social Sciences* 49 (September 1913): 54–55.
77. His reelection in 1918 came with the support of white leaders of Elaine.
78. Lisenby, *Charles Hillman Brough*, 41, 45.
79. Ibid., 47.
80. Desmairais, "Military Intelligence Reports," 182. Report, Captain Edward P. Passailaigue, Third Ammunition Train, Headquarters, Camp Pike, October 7, 1919.
81. Desmairais, "Military Intelligence Reports," 182.
82. Grif Stockley and Jeannie Whayne, "Federal Troops and the Elaine Massacres: A Colloquy," *Arkansas Historical Quarterly* 61/3 (Autumn 2002): 276–77.
83. Desmairais, "Military Intelligence Reports," 184.
84. "Agitation Blamed for Negro Revolts," *Arkansas Gazette*, October 6, 1919, WD.
85. "Negroes Fire Upon Arkansas Governor," *CSM*, October 3, 1919, 9; "Federal Troops Check Race Riots," *BG*, October 3, 1919, 7.
86. Desmairais, "Military Intelligence Reports," 184.
87. "Agitation Blamed for Negro Revolts," *Arkansas Gazette*, October 6, 1919, WD.
88. Desmairais, "Military Intelligence Reports," 184.
89. Cortner, *A Mob Intent on Death*, 41–42; Butler Wilson to Archibald Grimké, November 15, 1919, AGHU.
90. *Moore v. Dempsey*, 261 U.S. 86 (1923). Argued January 9, 1923, decided February 19, 1923.
91. "Agitators Blamed for Negro Revolts," *Arkansas Gazette*, October 6, 1919, WD.
92. "Calm Prevails in Zone of Rioting," *Arkansas Gazette*, October 4, 1919, WD.
93. "No Lynching in Phillips County," *Arkansas Gazette*, October 4, 1919, WD.
94. Stockley, *Blood in Their Eyes*, 80.
95. "Called Out Negroes," *WP*, October 6, 1919, 1.
96. "Negro Leader Preys on Their Ignorance," *LAT*, October 7, 1919, I7.
97. "Negro Revolt Plan to Extort Money," *BG*, October 7, 1919, 1.
98. "Calm Prevails in Zone of Rioting," *Arkansas Gazette*, October 4, 1919, WD.

99. Bessie Ferguson, "The Elaine Race Riot" (History thesis, Hendrix College, Conway, Arkansas, August 1927, 71), WD.

100. "Negroes Plot White Massacre," *LAT*, October 6, 1919, 11.

101. Major Robert O. Poach to M.I.D. Washington, October 14, 1919, BWGM, Reel 20 (Glasser File), 429.

102. Ferguson, "The Elaine Race Riot," 83, 84.

103. James Weldon Johnson, *Black Manhattan* (New York: Knopf, 1930), 342.

104. L. S. Dunaway, *What the Preacher Saw Through a Key-Hole in Arkansas* (Little Rock, Ark.: Parke-Harper Publishing, 1925), 102, WTP.

105. Mark Robert Schneider, *"We Return Fighting": The Civil Rights Movement in the Jazz Age* (Boston: Northeastern University Press, 2002), 69.

106. "Trace Plot to Stir Negroes to Rise," *NYT*, October 4, 1919, 7.

107. "Confidence Everywhere Restored," *Helena World,* October 5, 1919, WD.

108. Whitaker, *On the Laps of the Gods*, 160.

109. Wells-Barnett, *The Arkansas Race Riot*, 17–18.

110. Whitaker, *On the Laps of the Gods*, 161.

111. Stockley, *Blood in Their Eyes*, 107–9.

112. Miller later won a special election to fill a U.S. Senate seat from 1931 to 1937. Before his term was up, President Franklin Roosevelt appointed him as a federal district judge in 1941. He retired in 1967 and died in 1981. In the 1950s, several of Miller's rulings from the federal bench supported the segregationist cause, leading up to the raucous desegregation of the Little Rock public schools in late 1957 (Cortner, *A Mob Intent on Death*, 198). See Congressional biography, http://bioguide.congress.gov/scripts/biodisplay.pl?index=M000738 (accessed July 7, 2009).

113. Whitaker, *On the Laps of the Gods*, 166.

114. Stockley, *Blood in Their Eyes*, 108.

115. Gordon, *Caste & Class*, 137.

116. Within weeks, Ware was caught in New Orleans and brought back to stand trial. Hill was found in Kansas, but the Kansas governor refused to allow Hill's extradition. An interstate legal battle ensued in 1920, but in the end Kansas did not hand over Hill to Arkansas. See Cortner, *A Mob Intent on Death*, chap. 4, "The Hill Extradition Fight."

117. Wells-Barnett, *The Arkansas Riot*, 55.

118. Cortner, *A Mob Intent on Death*, 16–17.

119. "Six to Death Chair in Race Riot Trial," *LAT*, November 4, 1919, 14.

120. Lisenby, *Charles Hillman Brough*, 47.

121. "Death Given Negro for Knoxville Riot," *AC*, October 5, 1919, A6. "I did not commit the crime," Mays declared at trial. "It is simply a case of prejudice." Also in October, 22 white men were tried for various crimes in the riot that destroyed the Knoxville jail. The all-white jury acquitted 14, deadlocked on 5 defendants, and dismissed 3 cases. Prosecutor Rufus Mynatt remarked, "There was never a more guilty set of men turned loose." Mays had that verdict thrown out, but he was reconvicted and executed in 1922. Matthew Lakin, "'A Dark Night': The Knoxville Riot of 1919," *Journal of East Tennessee History* 72 (2000): 28.

122. Curtis to Johnson, October 13, 1919, NAACPAL, Reel 2, 454.

123. Board meeting minutes, October 13, 1919; NAACP field secretary report, October 8, 1919, NAACP.

124. Schneider, *"We Return Fighting,"* 72.

125. Rep. Thaddeus Caraway, *Congressional Record* 58 (November 19, 1919): 8818–21.

126. Walter White, "I Investigate Lynchings," in *Anthology of American Negro Literature*, ed. V. F. Calverton (New York: Modern Library, 1929), 403.

127. Stockley, *Blood in Their Eyes*, 99.

128. Walter White, "'Massacring Whites' in Arkansas," *The Nation* 109 (December 6, 1919): 715.
129. White, "I Investigate Lynchings," 404.
130. White to Grimké, October 17, 1919, AGHU.
131. Grimké to Baker, October 27, 1919; Baker to Grimké, October 31, 1919, AGHU.
132. Paula J. Giddings, *Ida: A Sword Among Lions: Ida B. Wells and the Campaign Against Lynching* (New York: Amistad, 2008), 606–7.
133. Kerlin, *The Voice of the Negro, 1919*, 161.
134. Du Bois to *New York World*, November 20, 1919, DP, Reel 7, 1165.
135. Herbert Aptheker, ed., *Writings in Periodicals Edited by W. E. B. Du Bois, Selections from* The Crisis *1911–1925*, vol. 1 (Millwood, N.Y.: Kraus-Thomson Organization, 1983), 105.
136. Kerlin, *The Voice of the Negro, 1919*, 63.
137. Ibid., 69.
138. "Negroes Send Appeal to President Wilson for Doomed Negroes," *AC*, November 28, 1919, 3.
139. Robert Hill, ed., *The Marcus Garvey and Universal Negro Improvement Association Papers* (Berkeley: University of California Press, 1983), 47.
140. Some reports indicated that Garvey may have owed Tyler money. Tyler committed suicide in jail the next day.
141. Colin Grant, *Negro with a Hat: The Rise and Fall of Marcus Garvey* (New York: Oxford University Press, 2008), 212, 214–15.
142. "For Action on Race Riot Peril," *NYT*, October 5, 1919, 112.
143. "Camp Meade Men Attack Baltimore Negro Section," *WP*, October 3, 1919, 1.
144. "Negro Shoots Union Picket, Three Held," *BG*, October 4, 1919, 8; "Strikers Riot; Picket Is Shot," *LAT*, October 4, 1919, I3.
145. "Six Whites Shot by Enraged Negro; One Man Is Dead," *AC*, October 12, 1919, 9; "Negro Shoots Up a Bar; 1 White Dead, 5 Injured," *CT*, October 12, 1919, 1.
146. "Negroes Burned by Monster Mob at Lincolnton," *AC*, October 7, 1919, 13; "Two Negroes Are Lynched," *LAT*, October 7, 1919, I7; "Prepare a Lynching Orgy," *LAT*, October 6, 1919, I1. News accounts differ as to the second victim's name.
147. "Georgia Mob Slays Negro," *NYT*, October 29, 1919, 5.
148. Lynching of Eugene Hamilton, Governor's Subject Files, 1917–1921, Record Group 001-01-005, Georgia Archives.
149. Kristy Owens Griggs, "The Removal of Blacks from Corbin in 1919: Memory, Perspective, and the Legacy of Racism," *Register of the Kentucky Historical Society* 100/3 (Summer 2002): 293, 296.
150. "All Negroes Driven From Kentucky Town," *AC*, November 1, 1919, 15; Samantha Swindler, "The Thing That Happened in 1919 That No One Wants to Talk About," *Times-Tribune*, March 17, 2009, http://thetimestribune.com/editorials/x1065232998/The-thing-that-happened-in-1919-that-no-one-wants-to-talk-about/print (accessed July 7, 2010).
151. Griggs, "The Removal of Blacks from Corbin in 1919," 293.
152. "Our Own Race War," *North American Review* 210/767 (October 1919): 436–37.

20. Let the Nation See Itself

1. Herbert Seligmann, the NAACP's publicity director, offered the straightforward solution for large cities facing riots: "Call out five or six thousand militia, place them on street corners, put bullets in the magazines and bayonets on their guns and they will do much to prevent trouble." "'Rotten Politics' Caused Race Riots, Investigator Says," *NYTrib*, August 6, 1919, 6.

2. "Justice for Negro in America Urged," *BG*, November 10, 1919, 4.

3. Charles Spencer Smith, "The First Race Riot in Recorded History," speech delivered at the Bethel African Methodist Episcopal Church, Detroit, Sunday, November 30, 1919 (Commission on After-War Problems of the AME Church, January 1920), 10–11.

4. Stephen Graham, *The Soul of John Brown* (New York: Macmillan, 1920), 170. Graham visited Jenkins County, Georgia, site of the Carswell Grove killings, but made no mention of the trouble.

5. In January, the magazine's circulation fell to 77,000 due to production problems and irregular mail delivery. Board minutes, February 9, 1920, NAACP.

6. Pell to Shillady, November 6, 1919, NAACPAL, Reel 2, 478. Pell lost a reelection in 1920 in a Republican sweep. However, he continued to play a major role in Democratic politics, especially when fellow New York Democrat Franklin Roosevelt took the White House.

7. Anti-Lynching Committee meeting minutes, November 14, 1919, NAACPAL, Reel 2, 482–86.

8. James Lewis to NAACP, November 21, 1919, NAACPAL, Reel 2, 498.

9. "Try 6 Negroes; Death Verdict in 8 Minutes," *CT*, November 4, 1919, 7.

10. "Death for Rioters," *CD*, August 9, 1919, 1.

11. "Give to the Anti-Lynching Fund: Men on Trial in Chicago," *NAACP Branch Bulletin*, November 1919, 102, 104, WTP.

12. "Ruffin Will Hang in Chatham Jail Early Next Year," *AC*, November 21, 1919, 14.

13. In late December 1919, 249 radicals sailed on the United States Transport *Buford*, nicknamed the Soviet Ark, bound for Finland and the Soviet Union.

14. Stanley Coben, *A. Mitchell Palmer: Politician* (New York: Columbia University Press, 1963), 211, 219.

15. U.S. Department of Justice, *Report Submitted to Congress by Attorney General A. Mitchell Palmer, November 15, 1919. A Report on the Activities of the Bureau of Investigation of the Department of Justice Against Persons Advising Anarchy, Sedition, and the Forcible Overthrow of the Government* (Washington, D.C.: Government Printing Office, 1919), 101.

16. Ibid., 101–2.

17. Ibid., 102.

18. Ibid., 187.

19. "Radicalism and Sedition Among the Negroes, as Reflected in Their Publications," *NYT*, November 23, 1919.

20. Sondra Kathryn Wilson, ed., *The Selected Writings of James Weldon Johnson*, The New York Age *Editorials* (1914–1923), vol. 1 (New York: Oxford University Press, 1995), 221–22. "Report of the Justice Department on Sedition among Negroes," December 20, 1919.

21. Herbert J. Seligmann, *The Negro Faces America* (New York: Harper & Brothers, 1920), 144.

22. Coben, *A. Mitchell Palmer*, 248. "The Fighting Quaker" lost his bid to Governor James Cox of Ohio, who in turn lost the general election to Republican Warren Harding, also of Ohio. Palmer died in 1936.

23. Walter Lippmann, *Early Writings* (New York: Liveright, 1970), 281. "Unrest" was published November 12, 1919.

24. "Will Investigate Georgia Lynchings," *WP*, November 4, 1919, 8.

25. "Burns Negro in Public Square," *WP*, November 12, 1919, 1.

26. "Negroes Shoot 2 Police; Race Riot in Delaware City," *CT*, November 14, 1919, 1; "Negroes Are Barred from Wilmington Streets," *AC*, November 15, 1919, 19. Other news in November overshadowed racial violence. On November 11, a battle between

American Legionnaires and I.W.W. members on Armistice Day in Centralia, Washington, left six dead. On November 15, Attorney General A. Mitchell Palmer ordered the first of many raids against radical groups across the country. And on November 19, the Republican-dominated Senate rejected the Treaty of Versailles, the document upon which President Wilson had staked his legacy. Elsewhere in the world, "red" and "white" armies continued to battle for control of Russia; mobs attacked Jews in Austria; and strikes crippled nations across Europe.

27. *The Inauguration of J. Stanley Durkee, President of Howard University, November 12, 1919, and the Readjustment and Reconstruction Congress, November 13, 1919* (Washington, D.C.: Howard University, 1919), 40.

28. "Guards Patrol Bogalusa," *NYT*, November 24, 1919, 17.

29. Billy Wyche, "Paternalism, Patriotism, and Protest in 'The Already Best City in the Land': Bogalusa, Louisiana, 1906–1919," *Louisiana History* 40/1 (Winter 1999): 65–66, 78.

30. James Fickle, "Management Looks at the 'Labor Problem': The Southern Pine Industry During World War I and the Postwar Era," *Journal of Southern History* 40/1 (February 1974): 65.

31. Stephen H. Norwood, "Bogalusa Burning: The War Against Biracial Unionism in the Deep South, 1919," *Journal of Southern History* 63/3 (August 1997): 606.

32. Ibid., 613.

33. Ibid., 593.

34. Ibid., 613–14.

35. Ibid., 617.

36. *Williams v. Southern Lumber Co.*, 277 U.S. 19 (1928), decided April 16, 1928.

37. "Loyalty Leaguers Kill 3 Union Men," *NYT*, November 23, 1919, 1.

38. *Williams v. Southern Lumber Co.*

39. U.S. War Department, Annual Report, 1920, 71.

40. "Arrest Labor Riot Police," *NYT*, December 8, 1919, 16.

41. Norwood, "Bogalusa Burning," 620. A white union man also arrested was not indicted.

42. "Loyalty Leaguers Kill 3 Union Men," *NYT*, November 23, 1919, 1.

43. Norwood, "Bogalusa Burning," 592.

44. Issued November 5, 1919. John T. Woolley and Gerhard Peters, *The American Presidency Project*, University of California at Santa Barbara website, http://www.presidency.ucsb.edu/ws/?pid=72445 (accessed November 15, 2009).

45. Francis Grimké, "The Race Problem, as it respects the colored people and the Christian Church, in the light of the developments of the last year," sermon delivered at the Fifteenth Street Presbyterian Church, Washington, D.C., November 27, 1919, 5, AGHU.

46. "Lynched by Florida Mob," *WP*, November 30, 1919, 3.

21. Capitol Hill

1. Volstead became a strong supporter of Dyer's proposal in later years.

2. Moores's bill was similar to Dallinger's, but also allowed for anyone arrested and in fear of being lynched to ask for transfer of their case to a federal court. House Committee on the Judiciary, *Part 1, Segregation*, and *Part 2, Anti-Lynching*, 66th Cong., 2nd sess., January 15 and 29, 1920, 22–23.

3. Taft's legal gravitas was unquestioned at the time and Harding appointed him chief justice of the Supreme Court the next year. These bills were by no means the most severe offered during the 66th Congress. Representative Clarence MacGregor, a Republican from upstate New York, offered a bill that punished rioters with up to

twenty years in prison and a $10,000 fine. The bill did not pass. House Committee on the Judiciary, *Sedition, Syndicalism, Sabotage, and Anarchy*, 66th Cong., 2nd Sess., December 10 and December 16, 1919, 56–57.

4. House Committee on the Judiciary, *Part 1, Segregation, Part 2, Anti-Lynching*, 23.

5. Ibid., 34.

6. Ibid., 51.

7. Ibid., 50.

8. Ibid., 62–64.

9. Ibid., 74–75.

10. Before January 29, congressional committees had discussed the riots only a few times. At a September hearing about pay raises for District of Columbia police officers, the riot was discussed briefly, even though the hearing was called in response to the department's poor handling of the riot. In December, the House Judiciary Committee had held two hearings on "Sedition, Syndicalism, Sabotage, and Anarchy." The race riots were mentioned a couple of times.

11. Herbert J. Seligmann, *The Negro Faces America* (New York: Harper & Brothers, 1920), 298.

12. Ibid.

13. Ibid., 299.

14. Ibid., 4.

15. *NIC*, xxiv.

16. He also blasted the NAACP for its legal defense of black sharecroppers and attacked the Kansas governor who refused to extradite Robert Hill, the leader in the sharecroppers' union. The Kansas governor said the black man would not get a fair trial. U.S. House of Representatives, 66th Cong., 2nd Sess., Anti-Lynching Bill, Report No. 1027 (Washington, D.C.: Government Printing Office, 1920), 1. Submitted May 29, 1920. See minority report submitted by Caraway.

17. See Robert L. Zangrando, *The NAACP Crusade Against Lynching, 1909–1950* (Philadelphia: Temple University Press, 1980).

18. The NAACP sent a young lawyer, Thurgood Marshall, whose father had been chased in the Washington riot of 1919, to investigate the Detroit trouble.

19. Lowell Harrison and James Klotter, *A New History of Kentucky* (Lexington: University Press of Kentucky, 1997), 351,

20. "Success Certain for Reunion Fund," *AC*, August 9, 1919, 1.

21. Dr. Fuller to Du Bois, October 21, 1919; Du Bois to Mabel Ury, September 12, 1919, DP, Reel 7, 867.

22. James Weldon Johnson, *Black Manhattan* (New York: Knopf, 1930), 156.

23. "Strikes Proposed to Combat Lynchings," *CSM*, December 2, 1919, 4.

24. W. E. B. Du Bois, "As the Crow Flies," *New Amsterdam News*, October 21, 1939, 1.

25. W. E. B. Du Bois, *Darkwater: Voices from Within the Veil* (New York: Harcourt, Brace, 1920), 230.

26. NAACP, Tenth Annual Report, 11.

27. Ibid., 7.

28. Ibid., 61.

29. Ibid., 89.

30. Board minutes, February 9, 1920, NAACP.

31. JWJY.

32. In 1943, after the Detroit race riot, a committee of the American Civil Liberties Union headed by writer Pearl S. Buck distributed a pamphlet, *How to Prevent a Race Riot in Your Hometown*. It echoed many of the ideas outlined in the 1922 Chicago report.

33. "Harding Says Negro Must Have Equality in Political Life," *NYT*, October 27, 1921, 1; "Harding Supports New Policy in South," *NYT*, October 27, 1921, 11; "Praise and Assail Harding Negro Talk," *NYT*, October 28, 1921, 4.
34. Hugh M. Dorsey, "A Statement from Governor Hugh M. Dorsey as to the Negro in Georgia," Atlanta, 1921, 2. This is a pamphlet published by Dorsey.
35. BWGM, Reel 20 (Glasser File), 383, 384, 386.
36. Sidney Frissell, "Meeting the Negro Problem," *NYT*, December 14, 1919.
37. "Free 4 Negroes in Race Trials; Two Are Fined $1," *CT*, November 16, 1919, 1.
38. Ida B. Wells-Barnett, *The Arkansas Race Riot* (Chicago: Ida B. Wells-Barnett, 1920), 5.
39. "Charge Arkansas Supreme Court Railroaded Negro Peons to Death Sentences After Riots," *New York Amsterdam News*, January 17, 1923, 7.
40. *Moore v. Dempsey*, 261 U.S. 86 (1923). Argued January 9, 1923, decided February 19, 1923. Two justices, James McReynolds and George Sutherland, dissented.
41. Alfreda M. Duster, ed., *Crusade for Justice: The Autobiography of Ida B. Wells* (Chicago: University of Chicago Press, 1970), 404.
42. "Ruffin Does Not Pay Death Penalty," *AC*, January 10, 1919, 10.
43. Ibid.
44. SvR.
45. SvR.
46. SvR.
47. "Joe Ruffin Is Freed," *AC*, May 31, 1923, 2.
48. SvR.
49. "Joe Ruffin Is Freed."
50. "Joe Ruffin," *Savannah Tribune*, November 20, 1920, 4.
51. V. F. Calverton, ed., *Anthology of American Negro Literature* (New York: The Modern Library, 1929), opening page.
52. Langston Hughes notebook, 1919, JWJY, Box 511, Folder 12685.
53. Bogalusa, where white union men had fought and died to aid black union men in 1919, later became a major center of Klan activity.
54. Minutes of the Chicago Race Commission, University of Chicago Library, Special Collections Research Center, Papers of Julius Rosenwald, Box 6, Folder 4.
55. Scholars have speculated that the two men were lovers.
56. Claude McKay, *A Long Way from Home* (1937; repr., New York: Harcourt, Brace, 1970), 54–55.
57. He later returned. He died in Chicago in 1948.
58. *Defender* editorial of July 9, 1921, quoted in C. K. Doreski, "From News to History: Robert Abbott and Carl Sandburg Read the 1919 Chicago Riot," *African American Review* 26/4 (Winter 1992): 642.

Coda. Carswell Grove

1. King was a 1948 graduate of Morehouse.
2. Census records for Joe Ruffin could not be found after 1920. A death certificate also could not be found.
3. Jenkins County is one of the few counties in Georgia that lost population in recent decades. Today its population numbers about 8,000, roughly half what it was in 1920. In economic decline since the 1930s, it lost the greatest percentage of jobs of any county in Georgia during the recession of 2008–2009. Paul Donsky, "Georgia's Jenkins County Among Nation's Hardest-Hit by Recession," *Atlanta Journal-Constitution*, December 22, 2009, http://www.ajc.com/business/georgias-jenkins-county-among-252611.html (accessed July 8, 2010).
4. Ralph Ellison, *Shadow and Act* (New York: Vintage, 1972), 201.

5. Herbert J. Seligmann, *The Negro Faces America* (New York: Harper & Brothers, 1920), 36.
6. R. R. Wright Jr., editor of *The Christian Recorder* in Philadelphia, (undated) from 1919 warning to blacks, in Robert T. Kerlin, *The Voice of the Negro, 1919* (New York: E. P. Dutton, 1920), 22.

Bibliography

Selected Archives and Libraries
Arkansas Supreme Court Clerk
Atlanta University Center, Robert W. Woodruff Library, Archives and Special Collections
Atlanta-Fulton County Public Library, Auburn Avenue Research Library
Bulloch County (Ga.) Library
Chicago Historical Society Research Center
Chicago Public Library, Harold Washington Library
Chicago Public Library, Woodson Regional, Vivian G. Harsh Collection of Afro-American History and Literature
Columbia University, Butler Rare Book and Manuscript Library
Effingham County (Ga.) Court Clerk
Emory University, Manuscripts, Archives, and Rare Book Library
Emory University, Woodruff Library
Georgia Archives
Harvard University, Houghton Library
Harvard University, Widener Library
Historical Society of Washington, D.C., Kiplinger Research Library
Howard University, Moorland-Springarn Research Library
Jenkins County (Ga.) Court Clerk
Laurens County (Ga.) Historical Society
Library of Congress, Rare Book & Special Collections Reading Room
Library of Congress, Manuscripts Division
Mississippi Department of Archives and History
National Archives and Records Administration, College Park, Md.
National Archives and Records Administration, Southeast Region
National Archives and Records Administration, Central Plains Region
Nebraska Historical Society Archives
New York Public Library, Main Branch
New York Public Library, Schomburg Center for Research in Black Culture
New York University Library Archives
William Tuttle, personal archives
Supreme Court of Georgia, Clerk's Office
Tennessee State Library and Archives
University of Chicago, Joseph Regenstein Library, Special Collections Research Center

University of Georgia, Hargett Library, University Archives and Georgia Newspaper Project
Yale University, Beinecke Rare Book and Manuscript Library

Selected Books, Lectures, Speeches, and Pamphlets

Abu-Lughod, Janet L. *Race, Space, and Riots in Chicago, New York, and Los Angeles.* New York: Oxford University Press, 2007.

Aptheker, Herbert, ed. *The Correspondence of W. E. B. Du Bois, Selections, 1877–1934.* Vol. 1. Amherst: University of Massachusetts Press, 1973.

———. *Writings in Periodicals Edited by W. E. B. Du Bois: Selections from* The Crisis, *1911–1925.* Vol. 1. Millwood, N.Y.: Kraus-Thomson Organization, 1983.

Ashby, LeRoy. *The Spearless Leader: Senator Borah and the Progressive Movement in the 1920s.* Chicago: University of Illinois Press, 1972.

Bailey, Thomas Pearce. *Race Orthodoxy in the South and Other Aspects of the Negro Question.* New York: Neale Publishing, 1914.

Baldwin, Davarian L. *Chicago's New Negroes: Modernity, the Great Migration, and Black Urban Life.* Chapel Hill: University of North Carolina Press, 2007.

Barnes, Harper. *Never Been a Time: The 1917 Race Riot That Sparked the Civil Rights Movement.* New York: Walker & Company, 2008.

Bartlett, Bruce. *Wrong on Race: The Democratic Party's Buried Past.* New York: Palgrave Macmillan, 2008.

Bassiouni, M. Cherif, ed. *The Law of Dissent and Riots.* Springfield, Ill.: Thomas, 1971.

Bauerlein, Mark. *Negrophobia: A Race Riot in Atlanta, 1906.* San Francisco: Encounter Books, 2001.

Bay, Mia. *The White Image in the Black Mind: African-American Ideas About White People, 1830–1925.* New York: Oxford University Press, 2000.

Bellows, Henry A. *A Treatise on Riot Duty for the National Guard.* Washington, D.C.: Government Printing Office, 1920.

Bernstein, Iver. *The New York City Draft Riots: Their Significance for American Society and Politics in the Age of the Civil War.* New York: Oxford University Press, 1990.

Bilbo, Theodore G. *Take Your Choice: Separation or Mongrelization.* Poplarville, Miss.: Dream House Publishing, 1947.

Bird, Stewart, Dan Georgakas, and Deborah Shaffer. *Solidarity Forever, an Oral History of the IWW.* Chicago: Lake View Press, 1985.

Blackmon, Douglas A. *Slavery by Another Name: The Re-Enslavement of Black Americans from the Civil War to World War II.* New York: Doubleday, 2008.

Boesel, David, and Peter H. Rossi, eds. *Cities Under Siege: An Anatomy of the Ghetto Riots, 1964–1968.* New York: Basic Books, 1971.

Boyd, Herb, ed. *The Harlem Reader.* New York: Three Rivers Press, 2003.

Boyle, Kevin. *Arc of Justice: A Saga of Race, Civil Rights, and Murder in the Jazz Age.* New York: Henry Holt, 2004.

Boyle, Sheila Tully, and Andrew Bunie. *Paul Robeson: The Years of Promise and Achievement.* Amherst: University of Massachusetts Press, 2001.

Brawley, Benjamin. *A Social History of the American Negro.* New York: Macmillan, 1921.

———. *Doctor Dillard of the Jeanes Fund.* New York: Fleming H. Revell Co., 1930.

———. *Your Negro Neighbor.* New York: Macmillan, 1918.

Brissenden, Paul Frederick. *The I.W.W.: A Study of American Syndicalism.* New York: Columbia University Press, 1920.

Bruce Jr., Dickson D. *Archibald Grimké: Portrait of a Black Independent.* Baton Rouge: Louisiana State University Press, 1993.

Button, James W. *Black Violence: Political Impact of the 1960s Riots.* Princeton, N.J.: Princeton University Press, 1978.

Byrd, Rudolph P., ed. *The Essential Writings of James Weldon Johnson*. New York: Random House, 2008.

Calverton, V. F., ed. *Anthology of American Negro Literature*. New York: Modern Library, 1929.

Capeci Jr., Dominic J., and Martha Wilkerson. *Layered Violence: The Detroit Rioters of 1943*. Jackson: University of Mississippi, 1991.

Chikota, Richard A., and Michael C. Moran, eds. *Riot in the Cities: An Analytical Symposium on the Causes and Effects*. Rutherford, N.J.: Fairleigh Dickinson University Press, 1970.

Clarke, John Henrik, ed., with assistance of Amy Jacques Garvey. *Marcus Garvey and the Vision of Africa*. New York: Vintage Books, 1974.

Coben, Stanley. *A. Mitchell Palmer: Politician*. New York: Columbia University Press, 1963.

Collins, Winfield H. *The Truth About Lynching and the Negro in the South*. New York: Neale Publishing, 1918.

Commons, John R. *Races and Immigrants in America*. New York: Macmillan, 1920.

Cooper, Wayne F. *Claude McKay, Rebel Sojourner in the Harlem Renaissance*. Baton Rouge: Louisiana State University Press, 1987.

Cortner, Richard C. *A Mob Intent on Death: The NAACP and the Arkansas Riot Cases*. Middletown, Conn.: Wesleyan University Press, 1988.

Cronon, Edmund David. *Black Moses: The Story of Marcus Garvey and the Universal Negro Improvement Association*. Madison: University of Wisconsin Press, 1968.

Davis, Kenneth S. *FDR: The Beckoning of Destiny, 1882–1928*. New York: G. P. Putnam's Sons, 1972.

Deane-Drummond, Anthony. *Riot Control*. New York: Crane, Russak & Company, 1975.

Detweiler, Frederick G. *The Negro Press in the United States*. Chicago: University of Chicago Press, 1922.

Dickson, Harris. *An Old-Fashioned Senator: A Story-Biography of John Sharp Williams*. New York: Frederick A. Stokes, 1925.

Dillard, James Hardy. *Selected Writings of James Hardy Dillard*, Occasional Papers, no. 27. Washington, D.C.: John F. Slater Fund, 1932.

Dixon, Thomas. *The Fall of a Nation: A Sequel to the Birth of a Nation*. Chicago: M. A. Donohue, 1916.

Dorsey, Hugh. *A Statement from Governor Hugh M. Dorsey as to the Negro in Georgia*. Atlanta: n.p., 1921[?].

Douglas, Ann. *Terrible Honesty: Mongrel Manhattan in the 1920s*. New York: Noonday, 1995.

Drake, St. Clair, and Horace R. Cayton. *Black Metropolis: A Study of Negro Life in a Northern City*. New York: Harcourt, Brace, 1945.

Drimmer, Melvin, ed. *Black History, A Reappraisal*. Garden City, N.Y.: Anchor Books, 1969.

Drucker, A. P., Sophia Boaz, A. L. Harris, and Miriam Schaffner. *The Colored People of Chicago: An Investigation Made for the Juvenile Protective Association*. JPA, 1913.

Du Bois, W. E. B. *Darkwater: Voices From Within the Veil*. New York: Harcourt, Brace, 1920.

Duster, Alfreda M., ed. *Crusade for Justice: The Autobiography of Ida B. Wells*. Chicago: University of Chicago Press, 1991.

Duvall, C. H. *The Building of a Race*. Boston: Everett Print, 1919.

Elias, Sarah Davis. *Recalling Longview: An Account of the Longview, Texas Riot, July 11, 1919*. Baltimore: C. H. Fairfax, 2004.

Ellison, Ralph. *Shadow and Act*. New York: Vintage, 1972.

Embree, Edwin R. *Brown America: The Story of a New Race.* New York: Viking, 1931.

Eppse, Merl R. *The Negro, Too, in American History.* Chicago: National Educational Publishing, 1938.

Farrell, James T. *Studs Lonigan, a Trilogy.* New York: Vanguard Press, 1935.

Federal Writers' Project. *Washington: City and Capital.* Washington, D.C.: Workers' Progress Administration, 1937.

Feldman, Glenn. *Politics, Society, and the Klan in Alabama, 1915–1949.* Tuscaloosa: University of Alabama Press, 1999.

Flicker, Barbara, ed. *The Community and Racial Crises,* 2nd ed. New York: Practicing Law Institute, 1969.

Foley, Barbara. *Spectres of 1919: Class and Nation in the Making of the New Negro.* Chicago: University of Illinois Press, 2003.

Foner, Philip, ed. *W. E. B. Du Bois Speaks: Speeches and Addresses, 1890–1919.* New York: Pathfinder, 1970.

Forgue, Guy J., ed. *Letters of H. L. Mencken.* Boston: Northeastern University Press, 1981.

Fox, Stephen R. *The Guardian of Boston: William Monroe Trotter.* New York: Atheneum, 1970.

Franklin, John Hope, and Isidore Starr, eds. *The Negro in Twentieth Century America: A Reader on the Struggle for Civil Rights.* New York: Vintage, 1967.

Franklin, John Hope, and Alfred A. Moss Jr. *From Slavery to Freedom: A History of African Americans,* 8th ed. New York: Knopf, 2000.

Garvey, Amy Jacques, ed. *Philosophy and Opinions of Marcus Garvey or Africa for the Africans.* London: Frank Cass, 1967.

Giddings, Paula J. *Ida: A Sword Among Lions: Ida B. Wells and the Campaign Against Lynching.* New York: Amistad, 2008.

Giffin, William W. *African Americans and the Color Line in Ohio, 1915–1930.* Columbus: Ohio State University Press, 2005.

Gilje, Paul A. *The Road to Mobocracy: Popular Disorder in New York City, 1763–1834.* Chapel Hill: University of North Carolina Press, 1987.

———. *Rioting in America.* Bloomington: Indiana University Press, 1999.

Giles, James R. *Claude McKay.* Boston: Twayne Publishers, 1976.

Gilmore, Glenda Elizabeth. *Defying Dixie: The Radical Roots of Civil Rights, 1919–1950.* New York: W. W. Norton, 2008.

Ginzberg, Eli, and Alfred S. Eichner. *The Troublesome Presence: American Democracy and the Negro.* London: Collier-Macmillan, 1964.

Goggin, Jacqueline. *Carter G. Woodson: A Life in Black History.* Baton Rouge: Louisiana State University Press, 1993.

Gold, Howard R., and Byron K. Armstrong. *A Preliminary Study of Inter-Racial Conditions in Chicago.* New York: Home Missions Council, 1920.

Gompers, Samuel. *American Labor and the War.* New York: George H. Doran Co., 1919.

Graham, Stephen. *The Soul of John Brown.* New York: Macmillan, 1920.

Grant, Colin. *Negro With a Hat: The Rise and Fall of Marcus Garvey.* New York: Oxford University Press, 2008.

Grant, Joanne, ed. *Black Protest: History, Documents, and Analyses, 1619 to the Present.* Greenwich, Conn.: Fawcett, 1968.

Grant, Madison. *The Passing of the Great Race, or the Racial Basis of European History.* New York: Scribner, 1916.

Green, Constance McLaughlin. *The Secret City: A History of Race Relations in the Nation's Capital.* Princeton, N.J.: Princeton University Press, 1967.

———. *Washington: Village and Capital, 1800–1878.* Princeton, N.J.: Princeton University Press, 1962.

Green, Horace, ed. *American Problems: A Selection of Speeches and Prophecies by William E. Borah*. New York: Duffield, 1924.

Grimshaw, Allen D., ed. *Racial Violence in the United States*. Chicago: Aldine Publishing, 1969.

Gross, Ariela. *What Blood Won't Tell: A History of Race on Trial in America*. Cambridge, Mass.: Harvard University Press, 2008.

Hagedorn, Hermann. *Leonard Wood: A Biography*. Vols. 1 and 2. New York: Harper & Brothers, 1931.

Hahn, Steven. *A Nation Under Our Feet: Black Political Struggles in the Rural South from Slavery to the Great Migration*. Cambridge, Mass.: Harvard University Press, 2003.

Hale, Grace Elizabeth. *Making Whiteness: The Culture of Segregation in the South, 1890–1940*. New York: Vintage, 1998.

Hammond, L. H. *In the Vanguard of a Race*. New York: Council of Women for Home Missions and Missionary Education Movement of the United States and Canada, 1922.

Hapgood, Norman, ed. *Professional Patriots: An Exposure of the Personalities, Methods and Objectives Involved in the Organized Effort to Exploit Patriotic Impulses in These United States During and After the Late War*. New York: Albert & Charles Boni, 1927.

Haynes, George Edmund. *The Trend of the Races*. New York: Council of Women for Home Missions and Missionary Education Movement of the United States and Canada, 1922.

Headley, J. T. *The Great Riots of New York, 1712–1873*. New York: E. B. Treat, 1873.

Heaps, William A. *Riots, U.S.A., 1765–1965*. New York: Seabury Press, 1966.

Hendrick, George, and Willene Hendrick, eds. *Carl Sandburg: Poems for the People*. Chicago: Ivan R. Dee, 1999.

Hirsch, James S. *Riot and Remembrance: America's Worst Race Riot and Its Legacy*. Boston: Houghton Mifflin, 2002.

Hobbs, William Herbert. *Leonard Wood: Administrator, Soldier, and Citizen*. New York: Putnam, 1920.

Holme, John G. *The Life of Leonard Wood*. Garden City, N.Y.: Doubleday, Page, 1920.

Hoover, J. Edgar. *J. Edgar Hoover on Communism*. New York: Random House, 1969.

Horowitz, Donald L. *The Deadly Ethnic Riot*. Berkeley: University of California Press, 2001.

Hosher, John. *God in a Rolls-Royce: The Rise of Father Divine, Madman, Menace, or Messiah*. New York: Hillman-Curl, 1936.

Hutchinson, William T. *Lowden of Illinois*. Vol. 2. Chicago: University of Chicago Press, 1957.

Jacobson, Julius, ed. *The Negro and the American Labor Movement*. Garden City, N.Y.: Anchor Books, 1968.

Jacobson, Matthew Frye. *Whiteness of a Different Color: European Immigrants and the Alchemy of Race*. Cambridge, Mass.: Harvard University Press, 1998.

James, Winston. *Holding Aloft the Banner of Ethiopia: Caribbean Radicalism in Early Twentieth-Century America*. New York: Verso, 1998.

Janken, Kenneth Robert. *White: The Biography of Walter White, Mr. NAACP*. New York: New Press, 2003.

Johanningsmeier, Edward P. *Forging American Communism: The Life of William Z. Foster*. Princeton, N.J.: Princeton University Press, 1994.

Johnson, Charles S. *The Economic Status of Negroes*. Nashville: Fisk University Press, 1933.

Johnson, Claudius O. *Borah of Idaho*. New York: Longmans, Green, 1936.

Johnson, James Weldon. *Along This Way*. New York: Penguin, 2008. First published 1933.

———. *Black Manhattan*. New York: Knopf, 1930.

——. *Negro Americans, What Now?* New York: Viking, 1938.

——, ed. *The Book of American Negro Poetry.* New York: Harcourt, Brace, 1922.

Johnson, Julia E. *Selected Articles on the Negro Problem.* New York: H. W. Wilson, 1921.

Jordan, Winthrop D. *White Over Black: American Attitudes Toward the Negro, 1550–1812.* Baltimore: Penguin, 1968.

Kantowicz, Edward R. *Polish-American Politics in Chicago, 1888–1940.* Chicago: University of Chicago Press, 1975.

Katz, Michael B., and Thomas J. Sugrue, eds. *W. E. B. Du Bois, Race, and the City.* Philadelphia: University of Pennsylvania Press, 1998.

Keith, Michael. *Race, Riots and Policing: Lore and Disorder in a Multi-Racist Society.* London: University College London, 1993.

Kellogg, Charles Flint. *NAACP: A History of the National Association for the Advancement of Colored People: 1909–1920.* Vol. 1. Baltimore: Johns Hopkins University Press, 1967.

Kerlin, Robert T. *The Voice of the Negro, 1919.* New York: E. P. Dutton, 1920.

Kenney, William Howland. *Chicago Jazz: A Cultural History, 1904–1930.* New York: Oxford University Press, 1993.

Knight, Lucian Lamar. *A Standard History of Georgia and Georgians.* Vol. 6. Chicago: Lewis Publishing Company, 1917.

Knopf, Terry Ann. *Rumors, Race and Riots.* New Brunswick, N.J.: Transaction Publishers, 2006.

Kornweibel Jr., Theodore. *"Seeing Red": Federal Campaigns Against Black Militancy, 1919–1925.* Bloomington: Indiana University Press, 1998.

Kovel, Joel. *White Racism, a Psychohistory.* New York: Pantheon, 1970.

Lane, Jack C. *Armed Progressive: General Leonard Wood.* San Rafael, Calif.: Presidio Press, 1978.

Lane, Roger, and John J. Turner Jr., eds. *Riot, Rout, and Tumult: Readings in American Social and Political Violence.* Westport, Conn.: Greenwood, 1978.

Lemann, Nicholas. *The Promised Land: The Great Black Migration and How It Changed America.* New York: Vintage, 1992.

Lester, J. C., and D. L. Wilson. *Ku Klux Klan, Its Origin, Growth, and Disbandment.* New York: Neale Publishing, 1905.

Lewis, David Levering. *W. E. B. Du Bois: Biography of a Race, 1868–1919.* New York: Henry Holt, 1993.

——. *W. E. B. Du Bois: The Fight for Equality and the American Century, 1919–1963.* New York: Henry Holt, 2000.

Lewis, Rupert, and Maureen Warner-Lewis, eds. *Garvey: Africa, Europe, the Americas.* Kingston, Jamaica: Institute of Social and Economic Research, University of the West Indies, 1986.

Link, Arthur S., et al., eds. *The Papers of Woodrow Wilson.* Vols. 53, 60, 61, 62. Princeton, N.J.: Princeton University Press, 1986.

Lippmann, Walter. *Early Writings.* New York: Liveright, 1970.

Lipsky, Michael, and David J. Olson. *Commission Politics: The Processing of Racial Crisis in America.* New Brunswick, N.J.: Transaction Books, 1977.

Livesay, Harold C. *Samuel Gompers and Organized Labor in America.* Boston: Little, Brown, 1978.

Logan, Rayford W. *The Betrayal of the Negro, from Rutherford B. Hayes to Woodrow Wilson.* New York: Collier, 1954.

Logue, Cal M., and Howard Dorgan, eds. *The Oratory of Southern Demagogues.* Baton Rouge: Louisiana State University Press, 1981.

MacMillan, Margaret. *Paris 1919: Six Months That Changed the World.* New York: Random House, 2001.

McCallum, Jack. *Leonard Wood: Rough Rider, Surgeon, Architect of American Imperialism.* New York: New York University Press, 2006.

McCulloch, James E., ed. *Battling for Social Betterment.* Nashville: Southern Sociological Congress, 1914.

———, ed. *The Call of the New South: Addresses Delivered at the Southern Sociological Congress, Nashville, Tennessee, May 7 to 10, 1912.* Nashville: Southern Sociological Congress, 1912.

———, ed. *"Distinguished Service" Citizenship.* Washington, D.C.: Southern Sociological Congress, 1919.

McGill, Ralph. *The South and the Southerner.* Boston: Little, Brown, 1963.

McKay, Claude. *Home to Harlem.* Boston: Northeastern University Press, 1987.

McKoy, Sheila Smith. *When Whites Riot: Writing Race and Violence in American and South African Cultures.* Madison: University of Wisconsin Press, 2001.

Martin, Everett Dean. *The Mob Mind vs. Civil Liberty.* New York: American Civil Liberties Union, 1920.

Masotti, Louis H., and Don R. Bowen, eds. *Riots and Rebellion: Civil Violence in the Urban Community.* Beverly Hills, Calif.: Sage, 1968.

Maxwell, William J., ed. *Complete Poems: Claude McKay.* Chicago: University of Illinois Press, 2004.

Meacham, Jon, ed. *Voices in Our Blood: America's Best on the Civil Rights Movement.* New York: Random House, 2001.

Means, Philip Ainsworth. *Racial Factors in Democracy.* Boston: Marshall Jones Co., 1919.

Mecklin, John Moffatt. *The Ku Klux Klan: A Study of the American Mind.* New York: Russell and Russell, 1924.

Mencken, H. L. *Prejudices, First Series.* New York: Knopf, 1919.

Miller, Kelly. *An Appeal to Conscience: America's Code of Caste, A Disgrace to Democracy.* New York: Macmillan, 1918.

———. *Kelly Miller's History of the World War for Human Rights.* Washington, D.C.: Austin Jenkins, 1919.

———. *Race Adjustment, Essays on the Negro in America.* New York: Neale Publishing Co., 1909.

Miller, Kelly, and Joseph R. Gay. *Progress and Achievements of the Colored People.* Washington, D.C.: Austin Jenkins Co., 1917.

Mitchell, David. *1919: Red Mirage.* New York: Macmillan, 1970.

Mitchell, J. Paul, ed. *Race Riots in Black and White.* Englewood Cliffs, N.J.: Prentice-Hall, 1970.

Moton, Robert Russa. *Finding a Way Out: An Autobiography.* Garden City, N.Y.: Doubleday, Page, 1922.

Nichols, J. L., and William H. Crogman. *Progress of a Race, or the Remarkable Advancement of the American Negro.* Naperville, Ill.: J. L. Nichols & Company, 1929.

Niven, Penelope. *Carl Sandburg: A Biography.* New York: Scribner, 1991.

Northrup, Herbert R. *Organized Labor and the Negro.* New York: Harper & Brothers, 1944.

Oney, Steve. *And the Dead Shall Rise: The Murder of Mary Phagan and the Lynching of Leo Frank.* New York: Pantheon, 2003.

Osborn, George Coleman. *John Sharp Williams, Planter-Statesman of the Deep South.* Baton Rouge: Louisiana State University Press, 1943.

Ottley, Roi. *The Lonely Warrior: The Life and Times of Robert S. Abbott.* Chicago: Henry Regnery, 1955.

———. *New World A-Coming: Inside Black America.* Cleveland: World Publishing, 1943.

Ovington, Mary White. *The Walls Came Tumbling Down.* New York: Arno Press, 1969.

Painter, Nell Irvin. *Standing at Armageddon: The United States, 1877–1919.* New York: W. W. Norton, 1987.

Patler, Nicholas. *Jim Crow and the Wilson Administration: Protesting Federal Segregation in the Early Twentieth Century.* Boulder: University Press of Colorado, 2004.

Price, John Ambrose. *The Negro: Past, Present, and Future.* New York: Neale Publishing Co., 1907.

Powell, Lyman P. *The Social Unrest: Capital, Labor, and the Public in Turmoil.* New York: Review of Reviews Company, 1919.

Raushenbush, Winifred. *How to Prevent a Race Riot in Your Home Town.* New York: Committee on Race Discrimination of the American Civil Liberties Union, 1943.

Reuter, Edward Byron. *The Mulatto in the United States, Including a Study of the Role of Mixed-Blood Races Throughout the World.* Boston: Gorham Press, 1918.

Robertson, David. *Sly and Able: A Political Biography of James F. Byrnes.* New York: W. W. Norton, 1994.

Roediger, David R. *Colored White: Transcending the Racial Past.* Berkeley: University of California Press, 2002.

———. *Working Toward Whiteness: How America's Immigrants Became White, the Strange Journey from Ellis Island to the Suburbs.* New York: Basic Books, 2005.

Roman, C. V. *American Civilization and the Negro: The Afro-American in Relation to National Progress.* Philadelphia: F. A. Davis, 1916.

Ross, B. Joyce. *J. E. Spingarn and the Rise of the NAACP, 1911–1939.* New York: Atheneum, 1972.

Rudwick, Elliott. *Race Riot at East St. Louis, July 2, 1917.* Urbana: University of Illinois Press, 1982.

Russell, Charles Edward. *Bolshevism and the United States.* Indianapolis: Bobbs-Merrill, 1919.

Sandburg, Carl. *The Chicago Race Riots, July 1919.* New York: Harcourt, Brace & World, 1969.

Schechter, William. *The History of Negro Humor in America.* New York: Fleet Press, 1970.

Schneider, Mark Robert. *"We Return Fighting": The Civil Rights Movement in the Jazz Age.* Boston: Northeastern University Press, 2002.

Schuyler, George S. *Black No More.* New York: Random House/Modern Library, 1999.

Scott, Emmett J. *Negro Migration During the War.* New York: Oxford University Press, 1920.

Sears, Joseph Hamblen. *The Career of Leonard Wood.* New York: D. Appleton, 1919.

Seligmann, Herbert J. *The Negro Faces America.* New York: Harper & Brothers, 1920.

Senechal de la Roche, Roberta. *In Lincoln's Shadow: The 1908 Race Riot in Springfield, Illinois.* Carbondale: Southern Illinois University Press, 1990.

Shay, Frank. *Judge Lynch, His First Hundred Years.* New York: Ives Washburn, 1938.

Shapiro, Herbert. *White Violence and Black Response, from Reconstruction to Montgomery.* Amherst: University of Massachusetts Press, 1988.

Shufeldt, R. W. *The Negro: A Menace to American Civilization.* Boston: Gorham Press, 1907.

Simmons, William Joseph. *America's Menace or the Enemy Within.* Atlanta: Bureau of Patriotic Books, 1926.

Slotkin, Richard. *Lost Battalions: The Great War and the Crisis of American Nationality.* New York: Henry Holt, 2005.

Sochen, June. *The Unbridgeable Gap: Blacks and Their Quest for the American Dream, 1900–1930.* Chicago: Rand McNally, 1972.

Spargo, John. *Bolshevism, the Enemy of Political and Industrial Democracy.* New York: Harper & Brothers, 1919.

Spear, Allan H. *Black Chicago: The Making of a Negro Ghetto, 1890–1920.* Chicago: University of Chicago Press, 1967.

Spengler, Oswald. *Spengler Letters, 1913–1936*. London: George Allen & Unwin Ltd., 1966.

Steel, Ronald. *Walter Lippmann and the American Century*. Boston: Little, Brown, 1980.

Stockley, Grif. *Blood in Their Eyes: The Elaine Race Massacres of 1919*. Fayetteville: University of Arkansas Press, 2001.

Stoddard, Lothrop. *The Rising Tide of Color Against White World-Supremacy*. New York: Scribner, 1920.

Storey, Moorfield. *Obedience to the Law, An Address at the Opening of Petigru College, Columbia, S.C., June 9, 1919*. Boston: Geo. H. Ellis Co., 1919.

Stowell, Jay S. *J. W. Thinks Black*. New York: Methodist Book Concern, 1922.

Sweeney, William Allison. *History of the American Negro in the Great World War*. Chicago: G. G. Sapp, 1919.

Theoharis, Athan G., and John Stuart Cox. *The Boss: J. Edgar Hoover and the Great American Inquisition*. Philadelphia: Temple University Press, 1988.

Thompson, Fred, and Patrick Murfin. *The I.W.W.: Its First Seventy Years, 1905–1976*. Chicago: Industrial Workers of the World, 1976.

Thompson, Holland. *The New South, a Chronicle of Social and Industrial Evolution*. New Haven, Conn.: Yale University Press, 1921.

Travis, Dempsey J. *An Autobiography of Black Chicago*. Chicago: Urban Research Press, 1981.

Tuttle Jr., William M. *Race Riot: Chicago in the Red Summer of 1919*. New York: Atheneum, 1970.

Twombly, Robert C. *Blacks in White America Since 1865*. New York: David McKay, 1971.

Vivian, James F., ed. *William Howard Taft: Collected Editorials, 1917–1921*. New York: Praeger, 1990.

Vogel, Richard. *Reading the Riot Act: The Magistracy, the Police, and the Army in Civil Disorder*. Philadelphia: Open University Press, 1991.

Vought, Hans P. *The Bully Pulpit and the Melting Pot: American Presidents and the Immigrant, 1897–1933*. Macon, Ga.: Mercer University Press, 2004.

Wade, Wyn Craig. *The Fiery Cross: The Ku Klux Klan in America*. New York: Simon and Schuster, 1987.

Waskow, Arthur I. *From Race Riot to Sit-In, 1919 and the 1960s*. Garden City, N.Y.: Doubleday, 1966.

Weatherford, W. D. *Present Forces in Negro Progress*. New York: Association Press, 1912.

Wedin, Carolyn. *Inheritors of the Spirit: Mary White Ovington and the Founding of the NAACP*. New York: John Wiley & Sons, 1998.

Weiss, Nancy J. *The National Urban League, 1910–1940*. New York: Oxford University Press, 1974.

Wendt, Lloyd, and Herman Kogan. *Big Bill of Chicago*. Evanston, Ill.: Northwestern University Press, 2005.

Werner, John M. *Reaping the Bloody Harvest: Race Riots in the United States During the Age of Jackson, 1824–1849*. New York: Garland, 1986.

Whitaker, Robert. *On the Laps of the Gods*. New York: Crown, 2008.

Williams, Juan. *Thurgood Marshall: American Revolutionary*. New York: Times Books, 1998.

Williams II, Lee E. *Post-War Riots in America, 1919 and 1946*. Lewiston, N.Y.: Edwin Mellen Press, 1991.

Wilson, Sondra Kathryn, ed. *In Search of Democracy: The NAACP Writings of James Weldon Johnson, Walter White, and Roy Wilkins (1920–1977)*. New York: Oxford University Press, 1999.

———, ed. *The Selected Writings of James Weldon Johnson, The New York Age Editorials (1914–1923)*. Vol. 1. New York: Oxford University Press, 1995.

Wilson, William Julius. *The Declining Significance of Race: Blacks and Changing American Institutions.* Chicago: University of Chicago Press, 1978.

Wintz, Cary D., ed. *African American Political Thought, 1890–1930; Washington, Du Bois, Garvey and Randolph.* Armonk, N.Y.: M. E. Sharpe, 1996.

Wolters, Raymond. *Du Bois and His Rivals.* Columbia: University of Missouri Press, 2002.

Woodson, Carter G. *A Century of Negro Migration.* Washington, D.C.: Association for the Study of Negro Life and History, 1918.

———. *The Negro in Our History.* Washington, D.C.: Associated Publishers, 1922.

Woofter, Thomas Jackson. *The Basis of Racial Adjustment.* New York: Ginn and Company, 1925.

———. *Negro Problems in Cities.* New York: Doubleday, Doran, 1928.

Work, Monroe N., ed. *The Negro Year Book, 1921–1922.* Tuskegee Institute, Ala.: Negro Year Book Publishing, 1922.

Yafa, Stephen. *Big Cotton: How a Humble Fiber Created Fortunes, Wrecked Civilizations, and Put America on the Map.* New York: Viking, 2005.

Zangrando, Robert L. *The NAACP Crusade Against Lynching, 1909–1950.* Philadelphia: Temple University Press, 1980.

Selected Journal Articles and Theses

Alexander, Charles C. "Kleagles and Cash: The Ku Klux Klan as a Business Organization, 1915–1930." *Business History Review* (Autumn 1965): 39, 348–67.

Anonymous. "Riot Control and the Fourth Amendment." *Harvard Law Review* 81/3 (January 1968): 625–37.

Anonymous. "Riot Control and the Use of Federal Troops." *Harvard Law Review* 81/3 (January 1968): 638–52.

Arensen, Eric. " 'Like Banquo's Ghost, It Will Not Down': The Race Question and the American Railroad Brotherhoods, 1880–1920." *American Historical Review* 99/5 (December 1994): 1601–33.

Barrett, James R. "Unity and Fragmentation: Class, Race, and Ethnicity on Chicago's South Side, 1900–1922." *Journal of Social History* 18/1 (Autumn 1984): 37–55.

Beck, E. M., and Stewart E. Tolnay. "The Killing Fields of the Deep South: The Market for Cotton and the Lynching of Blacks, 1882–1930." *American Sociological Review* 55/4 (August 1990): 526–39.

Berthoff, Rowland T. "Southern Attitudes Toward Immigration, 1865–1914." *Journal of Southern History* 17/3 (August 1951): 328–60.

Betten, Neil, and Raymond A. Mohl. "The Evolution of Racism in an Industrial City, 1906–1940: A Case Study of Gary, Indiana." *Journal of Negro History* 59/1 (January 1974): 51–64.

Blumenthal, Henry. "Woodrow Wilson and the Race Question." *Journal of Negro History* 48/1 (January 1963): 1–21.

Brown, Cliff. "Racial Conflict and Split Labor Markets: The AFL Campaign to Organize Steel Workers, 1918–1919." *Social Science History* 22/3 (Autumn 1998): 319–47.

Brown, Sterling A. "The American Race Problem as Reflected in American Literature." *Journal of Negro Education* 8/3 (July 1939): 275–90.

Byrd, Rudolph P. "Jean Toomer and the Afro-American Literary Tradition." *Callaloo*, no. 24 (Spring–Summer 1985): 310–19.

Capozzola, Christopher. "The Only Badge Needed Is Your Patriotic Fervor: Vigilance, Coercion, and the Law in World War I America." *Journal of American History* 88/4 (March 2002): 1354–82.

Clarke, John Henrik. "Marcus Garvey: The Harlem Years." *Transition*, no. 46 (1974): 14–15 and 17–19.

Coben, Stanley. "A Study in Nativism: The American Red Scare of 1919–20." *Political Science Quarterly* 79/1 (March 1964): 52–75.

Cooper, Wayne. "Claude McKay and the New Negro of the 1920's." *Phylon* 25/3 (1964): 297–306.

Crouthamel, James L. "The Springfield Race Riot of 1908." *Journal of Negro History* 45/3 (July 1960): 164–81.

Cryer, Daniel Walter. "Mary White Ovington and the Rise of the NAACP." (PhD diss., University of Minnesota, June 1977).

Cuban, Larry. "A Strategy for Racial Peace: Negro Leadership in Cleveland, 1900–1919." *Phylon* 28/3 (1967): 299–311.

Doreski, C. K. "From News to History: Robert Abbott and Carl Sandburg Read the 1919 Chicago Riot." *African American Review* 26/4 (Winter 1992): 637–50.

Duncan, Hannibal. "The Changing Race Relationship in the Border and Northern States." (PhD diss., University of Pennsylvania, Philadelphia, 1922).

Durham Jr., Kenneth R. "The Longview Race Riot of 1919." *East Texas Historical Journal* 18/2 (1980).

Ellis, Mark. "'Closing Ranks' and 'Seeking Honors': W. E. B. Du Bois in World War I." *Journal of American History* 79/1 (June 1992): 96–124.

Ellison, Ralph. "No Apologies." *Harper's Magazine*, July 1967, 4–20.

Farber, Naomi. "Charles S. Johnson's The Negro in Chicago." *American Sociologist* (Autumn 1995): 78–88.

Farley, Reynolds. "The Urbanization of Negroes in the United States." *Journal of Social History* 1/3 (Spring 1968): 241–58.

Fickle, James E. "Management Looks at the 'Labor Problem': The Southern Pine Industry During World War I and the Postwar Era." *Journal of Southern History* 40/1 (February 1974): 61–76.

Frazier, E. Franklin. "The Status of the Negro in the American Social Order." *Journal of Negro Education* 4/3 (July 1935): 293–307.

Gilbert, Ben W. "Toward a Color-Blind Newspaper, Race Relations and the Washington Post." *Washington History* 5/2 (Fall/Winter 1993–1994): 4–27.

Glazier, Kenneth M. "W. E. B. Du Bois's Impressions of Woodrow Wilson." *Journal of Negro History* 58/4 (October 1973): 452–53.

Grimshaw, Allen D. "Actions of Police and the Military in American Race Riots." *Phylon* 24/3 (1963): 271–89.

———. "Police Agencies and the Prevention of Racial Violence." *Journal of Criminal Law, Criminology, and Police Science* 54/1 (March 1963): 110–13.

Harrold Jr., Stanley C. "The Pearl Affair: The Washington Riot of 1848." *Records of the Columbia Historical Society* (1980): 140–60.

Hellwig, David J. "Black Leaders and United States Immigration Policy, 1917–1929." *Journal of Negro History* 66/2 (Summer 1981): 110–27.

Hirsch, Arnold R. "Massive Resistance in the Urban North: Trumbull Park, Chicago, 1953–1966." *Journal of American History* 82/2 (September 1955): 522–50.

Hixson Jr., William B. "Moorfield Storey and the Defense of the Dyer Anti-Lynching Bill." *New England Quarterly* 42/1 (March 1969): 65–81.

Holmes, S. J. "Will the Negro Survive in the North?" *Scientific Monthly* 27/6 (December 1928): 557–61.

Hopkins, George W. "From Naval Pauper to Naval Power: The Development of Charleston's Metropolitan-Military Complex." In *The Martial Metropolis: U.S. Cities in War and Peace*. Edited by Roger W. Lotchin. New York: Praeger, 1989.

Hutchinson, Edward P. "Immigration Policy Since World War I." *Annals of the American Academy of Political and Social Science* 262 (March 1949): 15–21.

Johnson, Charles S. "The Rise of the Negro Magazine." *Journal of Negro History* 13/1 (January 1928): 7–21.

Knopf, Terry Ann. "Race, Riots, and Reporting." *Journal of Black Studies* 4/3 (March 1974): 303–27.

Korstad, Robert, and Nelson Lichtenstein. "Opportunities Found and Lost: Labor, Radicals, and the Early Civil Rights Movement." *Journal of American History* 75/3 (December 1988): 786–811.

Laurie, Clayton D. "The U.S. Army and the Omaha Race Riot of 1919." *Nebraska History* 72/3 (Autumn 1991): 135–43.

Lawson, Michael L. "Omaha, a City in Ferment: Summer of 1919." *Nebraska History* 58/3 (Autumn 1977): 395–416.

Lighter, Jonathan. "The Slang of the American Expeditionary Forces in Europe, 1917–1919: An Historical Glossary." *American Speech* 47/1–2 (Spring–Summer 1972): 5–142.

Lyons, Richard L. "The Boston Police Strike of 1919." *New England Quarterly* 20/2 (June 1947): 147–68.

Meier, August. "The Racial and Educational Philosophy of Kelly Miller, 1895–1915." *Journal of Negro Education* 29/2 (Spring 1960): 121–27.

Meier, August, and John H. Bracey Jr. "The NAACP as a Reform Movement, 1909–1965: 'To Reach the Conscience of America.'" *Journal of Southern History* 59/1 (February 1993): 3–30.

Meier, August, and Elliott Rudwick. "The Rise of Segregation in the Federal Bureaucracy, 1900–1930." *Phylon* 28/2 (1967): 178–84.

Menard, Orville D. "Tom Dennison, the *Omaha Bee,* and the 1919 Omaha Race Riot." *Nebraska History* 68/4 (Winter 1987): 152–65.

Mennell, James. "African-Americans and the Selective Service Act of 1917." *Journal of Negro History* 84/3 (Summer 1999): 275–87.

Merritt, Russell. "Dixon, Griffith, and the Southern Legend." *Cinema Journal* 12/1 (Autumn 1972): 26–45.

Miller, Robert Moats. "The Protestant Churches and Lynching, 1919–1939." *Journal of Negro History* 42/2 (April 1957): 118–31.

Murray, Robert K. "Communism and the Great Steel Strike of 1919." *Mississippi Valley Historical Review* 38/3 (December 1951): 445–66.

Noon, Mark. "'It Ain't Your Color, It's Your Scabbing': Literary Depictions of African American Strikebreakers." *African American Review* 38/3 (Autumn 2004): 429–39.

Norwood, Stephen H. "Bogalusa Burning: The War Against Biracial Unionism in the Deep South, 1919." *Journal of Southern History* 63/3 (August 1997): 591–628.

Norvell, Stanley B., and William M. Tuttle Jr. "Views of a Negro During 'The Red Summer' of 1919." *Journal of Negro History* 51/3 (July 1966): 209–18.

Olzak, Susan. "Labor Unrest, Immigration, and Ethnic Conflict in Urban America, 1880–1914." *American Journal of Sociology* 94/6 (May 1989): 1303–33.

Olzak, Susan, and Suzanne Shanahan. "Racial Policy and Racial Conflict in the Urban United States, 1869–1924." *Social Forces* 82/2 (December 2003): 481–517.

O'Reilly, Kenneth. "The Jim Crow Policies of Woodrow Wilson." *Journal of Blacks in Higher Education,* no. 17 (Autumn 1997): 117–19.

———. "The Roosevelt Administration and Black America: Federal Surveillance Policy and Civil Rights During the New Deal and World War II Years." *Phylon* 48/1 (1987): 12–25.

Palmer, Dewey H. "Moving North: Migration of Negroes During World War I." *Phylon* 28/1 (1967): 52–62.

Perloff, Richard M. "The Press and Lynchings of African Americans." *Journal of Black Studies* 30/3 (January 2000): 315–30.

Puttkammer, Charles, and Ruth Worthy. "William Monroe Trotter, 1872–1934." *Journal of Negro History* 43/4 (October 1958): 298–316.

Reich, Steven. "Soldiers of Democracy: Black Texans and the Fight for Citizenship, 1917–1921." *Journal of American History* 82/4 (March 1996): 1478–1504.

Reid, Ira De A. "A Critical Summary: The Negro on the Home Front in World Wars I and II." *Journal of Negro Education* 12/3 (Summer 1943): 511–20.

Robinson, Bernard F. "The Sociology of Race Riots." *Phylon* 2/2 (1941): 162–71.

———. "War and Race Conflicts in the United States." *Phylon* 4/4 (1943): 311–27.

Rogers Jr., O. A. "The Elaine Race Riots of 1919." *Arkansas Historical Quarterly* 19/2 (Summer 1960): 142–50.

Rudwick, Elliott M. "East St. Louis and the 'Colonization Conspiracy' of 1916." *Journal of Negro Education* 3/1 (Winter 1964): 35–42.

Schaich, Warren. "A Relationship Between Collective Racial Violence and War." *Journal of Black Studies* 5/4 (June 1975): 374–94.

Schuler, Edgar A. "The Houston Race Riot, 1917." *Journal of Negro History* 29/3 (July 1944): 300–38.

Senechal de la Roche, Roberta. "Collective Violence as Social Control." *Sociological Forum* 11/1 (March 1996): 97–128.

Shiffman, Daniel. "Ethnic Competitors in Studs Lonigan." *MELUS* 24/3 (Autumn 1999): 67–79.

Street, Paul. "The Logic and Limits of 'Plant Loyalty': Black Workers, White Labor, and Corporate Racial Paternalism in Chicago's Stock Yards, 1916–1940." *Journal of Social History* 29/3 (Spring 1996): 659–81.

Strickland, Arvarh E. "The Strange Affair of the Boll Weevil: The Pest as Liberator." *Agricultural History* 68/2 (Spring 1994): 157–68.

Sutton, William A. "Personal Liberty Across Wide Horizons: Sandburg and the Negro." *Negro American Literature Forum* 2/2 (Summer 1968): 19–21.

Taylor, Kieran. "'We have just begun': Black Organizing and White Response in the Arkansas Delta, 1919." *Arkansas Historical Quarterly* 58/3 (Autumn 1999): 265–84.

Taylor, Nikki. "Reconsidering the 'Forced' Exodus of 1829: Free Black Emigration from Cincinnati, Ohio, to Wilberforce, Canada." *Journal of African American History* 87 (Summer 2002): 283–302.

Tolnay, Stewart E., Glenn Deane, and E. M. Beck. "Vicarious Violence: Spatial Effects on Southern Lynchings, 1890–1919." *American Journal of Sociology* 102/3 (November 1996): 788–815.

Tuttle, Jr., William M. "Contested Neighborhoods and Racial Violence: Prelude to the Chicago Riot of 1919." *Journal of Negro History* 55/4 (October 1970): 266–88.

———. "Violence in a 'Heathen' Land: The Longview Race Riot of 1919." *Phylon* 33/4 (1972): 324–33.

Whayne, Jeannie M. "Low Villains and Wickedness in High Places: Race and Class in the Elaine Riots." *Arkansas Historical Quarterly* 58/3 (Autumn 1999): 285–313.

Willborn, Steven. "The Omaha Riot of 1919." *The Nebraska Lawyer*, December 1999/January 2000, 56–60.

Williams II, Lee E. "The Charleston, South Carolina, Riot of 1919." In *Southern Miscellany: Essays in History in Honor of Glover Moore.* Edited by Frank Allen Dennis. Jackson: University of Mississippi Press, 1981.

Wolgemuth, Kathleen L. "Woodrow Wilson and Federal Segregation." *Journal of Negro History* 44/2 (April 1959): 158–73.

Woodson, Carter G. "The Beginnings of the Miscegenation of the Whites and Blacks." *Journal of Negro History* 3/4 (October 1918): 335–53.

Wright, W. D. "The Thought and Leadership of Kelly Miller." *Phylon* 39/2 (1978): 180–92.

Index

Abbott, Robert S., 90, 118, 122, 137–38, 147, 154, 264
ABC of the Invisible Empire (KKK pamphlet), 64–65
Aberdeen Daily American, 144
abolitionists, 25, 96–97
Ackerman, Carl William, 66, 193
Adkins, Will, 216–17, 222
Adler, Herman M., 141
African Blood Brotherhood, 168, 186
Afro-American, 109
Agee, James, 171
Alabama, 65, 73, 95, 207, 266
Alexander, Burris, 12, 14
Allen, E. M. "Mort," 215, 223
American Colonization Society, 150
American Federation of Labor (AFL), 119, 153, 185, 186, 243, 244
American Legion, 50, 196, 200, 202, 217, 219
American Negro as a Dependent, Defective and Delinquent, The (McCord), 60
American Protective League, 57
Amritsar, India, massacre, 24
anarchism, 39, 55–56, 58, 159, 186, 239–40, 263. *See also* radicalism
Annapolis, Maryland, race riot, 73
Anniston, Alabama, 95
Anthology of American Negro Literature (Calverton), 261
anti-lynching laws, 35, 38–39, 89, 151, 166, 172, 206, 235–36, 238–39, 246–51, 256, 259
"Appeal to Conscience, An" (Miller), 96

Arkansas, 13, 52, 73, 209–32, 239–41, 256, 258–59
    desegregation and, 251
    state legislature, 209
Arkansas Gazette, 217, 222
Ashley, Bob, 94–95
Atlanta, 64
    race riot (1906), 4, 28, 53–54
Atlanta Constitution, 9, 36, 42, 52, 54, 112
Atlanta Independent, 9, 106
Atlanta NAACP, 28, 40
Augusta Chronicle, 8
Austin attack on Shillady, 164–69, 190, 263
Austin NAACP, 89
Autobiography of an Ex-Colored Man, The (Johnson), 37

Baker, Newton, 12, 47, 100, 102, 108–10, 140, 196–97, 200, 202, 219–20, 230
Baltimore Daily Herald, 72
Baltimore race riot, 233
Barbare, John, 207
Barchton, Robert, 131
Barnes, Robert, 50
Barnett, F. L., 142
Barrows, Pelham, 197
Bass, Samuel, 137
Beatty, Frank Edmund, 43–46, 49
Bedford, Robert, 120
Behavior of Crowds, The (Martin), 72
Behold a Cry (Bland), 135
Bellows, Henry A., 41, 47, 145, 177–78
Belzoni, Mississippi, 29–30

Berkman, Alexander, 239
Bickett, Thomas Walter, 72
Biga, Frank, 136
Bilbo, Theodore, 29–30, 69, 71–72
Binga, Jesse, 143
biracial committees, 23
Birth of a Nation (film), 60–61, 64, 146
Bisbee, Arizona, race riot, 90–92
Black, Joseph A., 45
"Black Belt" (Sandburg), 126, 156
Black Boy (Wright), 212
Black Dispatch, 231
black education, 22, 27, 35, 38, 39, 43, 117,
    157, 171, 185, 190, 220, 254, 256
black farmers, 2–3, 117, 184, 210–11, 215.
    See also sharecroppers
black leadership, 142–43, 166–67, 184–85,
    210–11, 236–37, 240
Black No More (Schuyler), 26
black political awakening, 14–16, 22–23,
    57–58, 67, 76–77, 81, 95, 108, 184–85,
    209–10, 252–53, 255, 261–63
black resistance (self-defense), 22, 53, 58, 79,
    84–87, 94, 101, 103, 105, 112–13, 135,
    141–43, 148, 150–52, 168–69, 176–79,
    182, 186, 188–91, 188, 199–200, 208–9,
    212–13, 236–38, 240, 244–45
black rights, 31, 36, 39, 172, 206, 210, 213,
    245, 256, 257–61. *See also* civil rights
    movement; equality; legal rights;
    voting rights
Blackshear, Archibald, 75, 191, 260
black soldiers, 12–15, 23, 30–34, 49–50,
    56–57, 74–76, 78, 88, 91–92, 112–13,
    52, 94, 97, 105, 111, 120, 210–12, 251.
    See also veterans
Black Star Line, 67, 169, 186, 232
Blanco, Jose, 142
Bland, Alden, 135
Bloomington, Illinois, 146
Blossom, Frederick, 161
Bodenheim, G. A. "Bodie," 84, 87–89
Bogalusa, Louisiana, 152, 242–44
Bolshevik Revolution, 16, 221.
    See also radicalism
Bonaparte, Augustus, 42
Booker, Paul, 241
Borah, William, 205–6
Boston Guardian, 25
Boston police strike, 185
Bouchillon, J. P., 244
Boughton, Rev. Len G., 180

"Bound for the Promised Land" (poem),
    118
Boynton, Rev. M. P., 148
Brainerd, Chauncey, 100, 111
Bramlette, Erskine H., 83, 87–89
Bratton, Ocier, 222
Bratton, Ulysses A., 210, 222–24, 258
Briggs, Cyril, 58, 168, 180, 204
Brignadello, Harold, 137
Broad Ax, 85, 147, 155
Brooklyn Daily Eagle, 100, 111
Brough, Charles Hillman, 219–23, 226–27,
    229–31, 256
Brown, W. Clifford, 4–8, 11
Brown, William (Charleston), 45
Brown, Willie (Omaha), 194–200, 204–5
Brownlow, Louis "Brownie," 100–103, 106,
    109–11
Brown v. Board of Education, 266
Bruce, Roscoe Conkling, 97–98
Buchanan v. Warley, 34, 122
Bullard, Eugene, 50
Bundy, Leo, 20–21
Burke County, Georgia, 10, 267
Burton, Cyril, 42, 49
Bush, Marion, 88, 89
Butler, Hilton, 70–71
Butler, Sol, 92
Byrd, Thomas, 131
Byrnes, James Francis, 163–64, 241

Cadwell, Georgia, 152, 263
California, 73, 159, 183, 253
Call, 112
Callahan, Daniel, 129, 147
Calverton, V. F., 261–62
Campbell, James, 212
Cane (Toomer), 261
Cansler, Charles Warner, 171, 180
Capone, Al, 116
Caraway, Thaddeus, 247, 250
Carswell, Porter W., 4
Carswell Grove Baptist Church, 1–11, 13,
    22, 24–25, 75, 191, 239, 257, 259–61,
    263, 265–70
Carter, Frank, 98, 111
Catts, Sidney Johnston, 29
Challenge, 106
Charleston NAACP, 43, 48, 79
Charleston News and Courier, 43, 48, 49
Charleston race riot (1822), 42

Charleston race riot (1919), 41–50, 79, 99, 220, 232
  background of, 42–44
  events of, 41–42, 44–48
  legal aftermath of, 48–51, 257
Chattanooga, Tennessee, 181
Chester, Pennsylvania, 233
Chesterton, Cecil, 60
Chicago American, 115, 155
"Chicago and Its Eight Reasons" (White), 156–57
Chicago Commission on Race Relations, 154, 250, 255
Chicago Daily News, 126, 146, 155, 156, 229
Chicago Defender, 9, 15, 18, 21, 26, 50, 58, 82–84, 87, 90, 118, 122, 125, 137–38, 147, 154, 159, 264
Chicago Herald-Examiner, 131
Chicago Law and Order League, 116
Chicago race riot, 13, 114–48, 167, 202, 208, 220, 224, 240
  background of, 15, 19, 114–26
  deaths and injuries in, 147
  events of, 127–48, 264
  film on, 262
  joint emergency committee and, 155–56
  legal aftermath of, 190, 239, 257
  political blocs and, 120, 123–25, 255
  responses to, 149–50, 153–61, 168
  state militia and, 139–46
  street gangs and, 19, 116, 121, 125, 127–28, 130–36, 144–45
  transit strike and, 136, 141
Chicago Tribune, 57, 118, 125, 130, 148, 155
Chicago Tribune, 111–12
Chicago Whip, 154, 167
Cicero, Illinois, race riot, 251
Civil Rights Act (1965), 253
civil rights movement, 25–26, 251, 254–55, 266–70
civil service, segregation of, 107
Civil War, 3, 12, 34, 42–43, 69, 111, 170, 209, 237, 252
Clansman, The (Dixon), 60, 63
Clark, Frank, 110
Clark, Michael, 196, 198
Clarksdale, Mississippi, 68, 159
Clay, Lloyd, 51–52, 257
Cleveland, 74, 117, 152. *See also* NAACP National Convention of 1919

Cleveland Gazette, 24, 31, 39, 153, 212
Clinton, Mississippi, race riot (1875), 220
Coatesville, Pennsylvania, 92–93
Cochran, Georgia, 152
Cohen, Jacob, 45, 48
Coleman, Ed, 218
Coleman, Roscoe, 45, 48
Collins, "Kidd," 216, 217
Colored Knights of Pythias, 94, 151, 211
Columbia State, 49
Commission of Southern Universities on the Race Question, 220
Commission on Interracial Cooperation, 22–23, 110, 181, 256
Committee of Seven, 223–26, 259
communism, 56, 58, 65–66, 159–61, 262–63. *See also* radicalism
Communist Labor Party, 16, 59, 149, 161, 186
Communist Party of America, 16, 58, 59, 161, 185, 186
Confederacy, 3, 69, 163, 209, 252
Congressional Record, 163
Cook, George William, 248, 249
Coolidge, Calvin, 185
Cooper, Eli, 152, 263
Cooper, John, 233–34
Corbin, Kentucky, 234
Cornhuskers (Sandburg), 126
Cotton Futures Act (1919), 2
cotton, 2, 117, 209–11, 214–15, 224
Crall, Kenneth, 105
Crawford, James, 129
Crawford, Joe, 134
crime, 156, 172, 194, 204, 205
Crisis, 14, 15, 31–32, 38, 50, 57–59, 65, 77–78, 81, 90, 96, 156, 157, 163–64, 183, 188, 219, 229, 231, 238, 255
  launched, 27–28
Crosky, Robert, 207
Crusader, 58, 168, 204, 213
Current Opinion, 208
Curtis, Charles, 111, 182, 188–90, 228, 232, 250

Dacus, Sol, 242–44
Dahlman, "Cowboy" Jim, 193
Daley, Richard J., 116
Dallas, 164
Dallas Dispatch, 162
Dallinger, Frederick W., 35, 39–40, 167, 247

Daniels, Josephus, 48, 99–101
Darkwater (Du Bois), 61, 107, 231, 246, 254
Daughters of the Confederacy, 61
Davis, Dr. Calvin P., 83–88, 90
Davis, Charles, 137
Davis, C. L., 264
Davis, Jefferson, 252
Davis, Jim, 8
Death in the Family, A (Agee), 171
Debs, Eugene, 59, 185
Decline of the West, The (Spengler),
    62, 66
Democratic Party, 34, 57, 108, 110, 123–24,
    138, 140, 154, 163, 172, 205, 209–10,
    238, 240–41
Demper, Mose, 53
Denmark, South Carolina, race riot, 105
Dennison, Tom, 193, 204
De Priest, Oscar, 124, 131–32, 230
Detroit, 117
    race riot (1943), 251
    race riot (1967), 253
Dillard, James Hardy, 22–23, 181
"Divine, Father" (George Baker), 77
Dixon, Thomas, Jr., 60, 63
Doctor, Isaac, 41, 45, 48
"Dominant White, The" (McKay), 21–22
Domingo, W. A., 203
Dorsey, Hugh, 10–11, 36, 52, 71–73, 94–95,
    220, 234, 256
Douglass, Frederick, 29
Doyle, Thomas C., 138
Dozier, William H., 145
Dublin, Georgia, 52–53, 79, 94–95
Du Bois, W. E. B., 14–15, 25, 40, 53, 59, 61,
    77–78, 81, 90, 106–7, 110–11, 159,
    163–64, 255, 183, 194, 219, 231, 246,
    253–54, 262
    background of, 26–29, 37
    on black soldiers, 30–32, 50, 163, 241
    board and, 95, 238
    personality of, 36, 63, 101
    separatism and, 38, 168–69, 186
    on slavery, 157
    on "veil" between races, 263
due process, 72, 257, 259
Duke, Charles S., 123
Dumas, Arkansas, 256
Dunaway, L. Sharpe, 225
Durkee, J. Stanley, 242
Duvall, D. H., 77
Dyer, Leonidas, 34, 40, 247, 250

Eastman, Max, 86
East St. Louis, Illinois, race riot (1917),
    20–21, 26, 34, 66, 96, 108, 112, 125,
    141, 247
Eatonton, Georgia, 53
Eberstein, Marshal, 195–96
Effingham County, Georgia, 260
Eighteenth Amendment, 4, 16
Elaine, Arkansas, massacre, 13, 211–13,
    217–19, 221–26, 229, 231, 256–57
El Dorado, Arkansas, 52
elections
    1912, 107
    1915, 124
    1916, 37
    1918, 193
    1919, 124, 140, 172, 180–81
    1920, 34, 139–40, 187, 201, 206, 240–41,
    255
Ellison, John Gordon, 9
Ellison, Ralph, 269–70
Ellisville, Mississippi, 68–71, 252
Emancipation Proclamation, 209
Emancipator, 203
Emerson, Henry Ivory, 35
Emerson, Ralph Waldo, 34
equality, 23, 34, 61, 71, 74–75, 105, 111,
    150–51, 156–57, 168, 189, 206, 243,
    248, 250–56, 268
Equal Rights League, 112
espionage law, 163
Etter, Joe, 176–77, 179
eugenics movement, 62

Fall of a Nation, The (Dixon), 63
Farewell to Arms, A (Hemingway), 115
Farrell, James T., 123, 130
Federal Bureau of Investigation (FBI), 263
federal troops, 47, 49, 71, 140, 146, 196–97,
    200, 202–3, 219–22, 224–25, 230, 251,
    256. *See also* specific riots and units
Ferguson, Bessie, 225
15th Infantry Regiment, 73
Fifteenth Amendment, 60
First Amendment, 147
Fisher, B. Harrison, 76, 80
Fitzgerald, Georgia, 18
Flanagan, Tom, 84–85, 87
Florida, 19, 29, 68, 183, 245, 251
Foch, Ferdinand, 123
Fonda, Henry, 192, 198–99

Foster, William Z., 153, 185
Fourteenth Amendment, 122, 246, 258
Fourth of July, 90–92, 125
France, 30–31, 50, 71, 92
Francis, William (Omaha), 195
Francis, William T. (St. Paul), 208–9
Frank, Leo, 10, 64
Franklin, Chester A., 112
Franklin, John Hope, 13
Freedmen's Bureau, 237
Fridie, W. G., 45, 46

Gaddy, Monroe, 137
Gaines, Thomas, 244
Garrity, James T., 131–32, 141
Garvey, Marcus, 25–26, 66–67, 149, 161,
    168, 186, 213, 231–32, 250, 255
Gary, Elbert, 153
Gary, Indiana, 117, 153, 185
Georgia, 18, 65, 79, 184, 191, 236–38,
    259–61, 265–70
  anti-lynching bills and, 10–11, 52,
    72–73, 94, 234, 256
  lynchings, 35, 51–53, 94–95, 152, 183,
    233, 241, 262
  race riots, 1–11, 13, 22, 24–25, 75, 191,
    212, 239, 263
  school desegregation, 267
Georgia Court of Appeals, 233, 260, 265–67
Giddings, Frank H., 158
Gish, Lillian, 60
Gladden, Moses, 49
Goldman, Emma, 239
Gompers, Samuel, 119
Goodman, Henry, 133
Gordon, Jack, 233
Grace, John P., 44, 49
Graggs, Charles R., 149
Graham, Stephen, 121, 161, 171, 181, 238
Grant, Jim, 152
Grant, Madison, 62–63
Great Britain, 16, 24, 73–74
  race riots, 73–76
Great Migration, 9–10, 17, 19, 93, 116–23,
    126, 159, 171, 181, 192, 211, 264–65
Great Southern Lumber Company,
    242–44
Green, Clyde, 94
Green, Eugene, 29–30
Green, George, 94
Gregg, G. A., 80

Gregg County, Texas, 82–90
Gregory, Thomas W., 57
Griffith, David Wark, 60–61
Grimké, Archibald H., 31, 72, 97, 101, 103,
    112, 166, 230, 248–49
Grimké, Rev. Francis J., 31, 72, 97, 244–45,
    248

Haan, Gen. William G., 109–10
habeas corpus, 258
Halbfinger, Isaac, 110
Hamby, Charles, 164–65
Hamilton, Eugene, 233
Hamitic League of the World, 194
Harcourt, Brace and Co., 28, 126
Harding, Warren, 255–56
Harlem, 73, 183
  Renaissance, 15, 112
Harleston, Edwin A., 43, 48, 79
Harris, John Turner, 128–29
Harrison, Hubert, 58, 66
Harrison, Pat, 110
Hartfield, John, 68–71, 252, 257, 263
Hawkins, W. E., 112
Hawkinsville, Georgia, 52
Haynes, Edward M., 174
Haynes, George Edmund, 13, 63, 85
Helena, Arkansas, 209, 211–13, 215, 217,
    219, 221–22, 226, 229
Helena Business Men's League, 215, 223
Helena Negro Business League, 211
Helena World, 211, 215, 218, 223
Henson, Jim, 177
Hill, Robert, 214, 226
Hillis, Newell Dwight, 65–66, 186–87
*History of the American Negro in the Great
    World War* (Sweeney), 15
History of the American People (Wilson), 61
History of the United States, A
    (Chesterton), 60
Hobby, William P., 35, 88–89, 166
Hobson City, Alabama, 95
Hoffman, Millard, 194–95
Hoffman, Peter, 136
Holden, George, 18
Holliday, Frank, 45, 48
Holmes, Oliver Wendell, 259
Hoop Spur, Arkansas, 213–14, 216–19,
    222, 224–26
Hoover, J. Edgar, 56, 159, 188, 209, 240,
    262–63

housing restrictions, 121–23, 126, 152, 156–57, 159, 210, 262
Houston Chronicle, 158–59
Houston Informer, 208, 231
Houston mutiny (1917), 50
Houston NAACP, 164–65
Howard University, 26, 96, 99, 102–4, 242, 249, 267
Hoyne, Maclay, 124, 154, 257
Hughes, Charles Evans, 33–34, 37
Hughes, Langston, 121, 262
Humphrey, John Walter, 134
Hurst, John, 78
Hyde, Tristram T., 43–44, 46, 48–49
Hyde Park-Kenwood Association, 122–23, 262
Hykell, James, 197

"If We Must Die" (McKay), 22, 85–86, 263
"I Have a Dream" (King), 252–53
"I Investigate Lynchings" (White), 261
Illinois, 13, 15, 19–21, 29, 34, 66, 96, 108, 112, 114–48, 153–55, 167–68, 185, 202, 208, 220, 224, 232, 240, 247, 251, 257, 262, 264
    state militia, 132, 140–49
immigrants and ethnic whites, 65, 92, 115–17, 120–25, 131, 141, 144–45, 153, 155, 161, 186, 192, 239.
    See also specific nationalities
Indiana, 117, 153, 185, 233
Indiana Harbor, Indiana, 233
Industrial Savings Bank, 96
inflation, 120, 172, 185, 193
integration, 66, 253
intelligence agencies, 149, 159–60
Inter-Allied games (France), 92
International Workers of the World (I.W.W., "Wobblies"), 39, 56, 59, 79, 91, 159–61, 163, 186, 202–3, 215, 228, 231
interracial marriage, 97, 108
Invisible Man (Ellison), 269
Irish immigrants, 115–16, 120, 123–25, 127, 131, 141
Italian immigrants, 120, 123, 131, 138

Jackson, Robert R., 151
Jackson Daily News, 17, 30, 68, 70, 74
Jacksonville, Florida, 19, 68, 183

Jameson, Jordan, 241
Jasper County, Georgia, 233
Jeffries, James, 97
Jenkins County, Georgia, race riot, 1–11, 75, 212–13
    aftermath of, 265–66
    background of, 2–4
    events of, 4–11, 13, 25
    legacy of, 265–70
    legal aftermath of, 11, 191, 239, 257, 259–61
Jenkins County Superior Court, 191
Jenks, Isaac, 220–22
Jernagin, Rev. William H., 97
Jim Crow, 3, 9, 16–17, 34, 67, 79, 94, 97, 117, 151, 163, 210–11, 252, 262, 268
jobs, 93–94, 116–18, 120, 193. *See also* labor
Johnson, Carrie Minor, 104, 257
Johnson, Charles S., 154, 250
Johnson, Henry, 183
Johnson, Jack, 97
Johnson, James Weldon, 13, 20–21, 23, 33, 36–38, 108, 110–11, 149, 151, 162, 166, 182, 188–89, 205, 225, 228, 232, 236–37, 238, 248–49, 253–54
    background of, 27–28, 37
    board and, 30, 238
    leadership of, 166–67, 253–54
    Palmer report and, 240–41
    Red Summer named by, 13, 269
    writing and speaking by, 37, 74–75, 77–78, 95, 237, 261
Johnson, M. G., 7
Johnson, Sol C., 157
Johnson County, Georgia, 52–53
Johnston brothers, 219
Jones, Horace, 40
Jones, Howard, 40
Jones, Percy L., 168
Jones, Samuel L., 82–90, 95, 264
Jones, Scipio A., 210, 229, 258–59
Jones, Thomas Jesse, 110
Jones County, Mississippi, 69
Jungle, The (Sinclair), 115
Justice Department, 58, 108, 159, 163–64, 188, 232, 239, 241, 262–63
"Justice for the Negro" (I.W.W. pamphlet), 161

Keese, T. W., 226
Kendrick, S. M., 112

Kentucky, 122, 159, 234, 251
   anti-lynching bills, 239
   state militia, 251
Kenwood Improvement Association, 123
Kerr, W. W., 184
Kilgore, Texas, 82–83, 89
"Kind of Democracy the Negro Expects,
   The" (Pickens), 67
King, Rev. Martin Luther, Jr., 237, 252–53,
   266
Kirksey, J. D., 95
Kitchens, Fred, 217–18, 223
Kleinmark, Nicholas, 133
Knight, J. C., 217, 223
Knoxville Journal and Tribune, 168, 174,
   181
Knoxville NAACP, 167, 171
Knoxville race riot, 13, 170–82, 220, 227,
   240
   aftermath of, 179–82
   background of, 170–73
   events of, 173–79
   legal aftermath of, 257
   response to, 181–82, 188–89
   state militia and, 177–79
Knoxville Sentinel, 174
Ku Klux Klan, 28, 52–54, 60–61, 64–65,
   72, 80, 95, 149, 168, 171–72, 186, 203,
   250, 262, 266

labor
   cheap, 19, 93–94, 116–17, 209, 211, 262
   unrest, 16, 39, 47, 65, 202, 215
Labor Department, 13, 93, 211
labor unions
   black, 186, 242–43
   white, black relations with, 24, 58–59,
      93, 116–17, 119–20, 126, 136, 146, 153,
      155, 172–73, 180, 185–86, 242–43
Lake City, Florida, 245
Lamar, Missouri, 39
Laney, William, 105
Laurens County, Georgia, 94
Lazzeroni, Casmere, 133
League of Nations, 34, 106, 146, 187–88,
   205–6
Lee, Clinton, 219
Lee, Edward, 134
Leech, Harper, 162
left, 58–59, 163–64, 185, 186, 234.
   See also radicalism; *and specific groups*

legal rights, 38–39, 72, 163, 204, 210, 212,
   226–27, 229–30, 255–61, 265–68
Leggett, Texas, 164
Leslie's Illustrated Weekly, 150
Lexington, Kentucky, 251
Liberator, 21, 86
Liberty League, 58
"Lift Every Voice and Sing" (Johnson and
   Johnson), 37
Lilly, O. R., 219
Lincoln League of America, 25
Lincoln Memorial Association, 35
Lincolnton, Georgia, 233
Lindsay, Vachel, 63
Lindsey, Bertie, 173–74
Lippmann, Walter, 156, 202, 241
Livingston, Frank, 52
Lockett, Will, 251
Loebeck, Agnes, 194–95
Lokal Anzeiger (German newspaper), 107
Longview, Texas, race riot, 82–90, 220
   aftermath of, 90–91, 95, 125, 126, 164, 264
   background of, 83–84
   black resistance and, 85–86
   events of, 82–84, 86–88
   legal aftermath and, 257
   state militia and, 88–90
Longview Chamber of Commerce, 83
Longview Negro Business League, 83, 87
Los Angeles race riot (1992), 253
Los Angeles Times, 90, 224
Louisiana, 18, 152, 183, 210, 242–44,
   252–55
Louisville, Kentucky, 122, 159
Lovecraft, H. P., 63
Lovett, Archibald B., 191
Lovings, Joseph, 138
Lowden, Frank, 21, 124–25, 139–45, 154,
   159, 202, 220, 231, 255
Loyalty League, 203
Lynch, Jay, 39
lynching. *See also* anti-lynching laws;
      National Association for the
      Advancement of Colored People;
      and specific locations
   AFL resolution vs., 119
   authority to stop, 47, 73
   black literature on, 261
   federal investigation of, 189
   goal of stopping, and NAACP, 255
   history and statistics on, 10, 13, 20–21,
      35–36, 90, 189

lynching (*cont'd*)
national conference on, 28, 33–40
post-1919, 251–53
White's investigations of, 28
Woodrow Wilson and, 108, 158

Macon, Georgia, 241
Macon, Mississippi, 73
Macon Telegraph, 8
Magnolia, Arkansas, 241
Manchester Guardian (British newspaper), 73
Maninichi (Japanese newspaper), 106
March, Peyton, 100
March on Washington (1963), 252–53
Marcosson, Isaac Frederick, 24
Marcus, David, 134
Marshall, Thomas R., 71
Marshall, Thurgood, 104
Marshall, Willie, 104
Martin, Everett Dean, 72
Marton, J. A., 53
Marxists, 16, 186, 239
Maryland, 73, 97, 233
Massachusetts, 185
Matthews, Sam, 84
May Day labor riot, 39
Mays, Maurice, 173–76, 227, 257
McClure's Magazine, 187
McCord, Charles H., 60
McCullough, Will, 215–16
McKay, Claude, 21–22, 85–86, 161, 263–64
McKelvie, Samuel, 200
McMillan, John E., 172, 174–76, 180–81
meatpacking and stockyards, 115–20, 132–33, 136, 138, 141–42, 145–47, 153, 192–93, 224
Meeks, Ruth, 69, 70
Memphis, 54, 173, 183
Memphis Commercial Appeal, 54, 54
Mencken, H. L., 24, 37, 65, 149, 151
Messenger, 58, 85, 112, 163
Metcalfe, Mississippi, 18
Metz, Clarence, 133
Mexican immigrants, 142, 183–84, 251
Micheaux, Oscar, 262
Milan, Georgia, 52
military tribunals, 48, 50
Milledgeville, Georgia, 53
Millen, Georgia, 1, 8–9
Miller, Jim, 216

Miller, John E., 218, 222, 226–27
Miller, Kelly, 26, 96, 101, 262
Mims, Edwin, 170, 181
Mississippi, 18, 29–30, 51–53, 68–72–73, 152, 159, 210, 217, 220, 241, 249, 252, 257
Constitution of 1898, 108
Money, Mississippi, 252
Monitor, 199, 200
Monroe, Louisiana, 18, 183
Montgomery, Alabama, 207
bus boycott (1955), 266
Montgomery Advertiser, 94
Moore, H. D., 223
Moores, Merrill, 35, 247
Moore v. Dempsey, 259
Morris, Rev. Elias Camp, 211
Morton, Sterling, 144–45
Mosely, Sam, 245
Moses, Isaac, 45
Moton, Robert, 157, 184
Mulatto in the United States, The (Reuter), 62

Nation, 229
National Association for the Advancement of Colored People (NAACP), 9, 13–14. *See also* specific branches and individuals
anti-lynching campaign, 29–30, 38–40, 57, 93, 95, 157, 166, 206, 235, 238–39
Arkansas and, 210
Austin attack on, 162–69
Birth of a Nation and, 60
black leadership and, 26–29, 37, 78, 184–85
changing black attitudes and, 22–23
Chicago and, 142, 149, 151, 154, 156
Coatesville and, 93
congressional hearings and, 208, 232, 246–50
East St. Louis and, 20–21
Ellisville and, 68–69, 71–72
federal investigations of, 57–59, 160
founding of, 27–29, 34
Garvey vs., 66–67, 168–69
growth and finances of, 25–32, 38, 40, 77–78, 81, 149, 162, 166–67, 186, 190, 228, 238, 253–54
housing and, 122
Judge Ruffin and, 267
Knoxville and, 188–89

legacy of Red Summer and, 253–55
legal defenses by, 228–31, 239, 258–59
lobbying by, 187–88, 236–37
Mississippi and, 51–52
Omaha and, 200–201, 203–5
Phillips County and, 227–31, 258–59
radicalism and, 89
southern branches, 252–53
Washington riot and, 99, 101, 110–11,
    149, 151
Woodrow Wilson and, 108
NAACP Annual Meeting (New York,
    1920), 255
NAACP Annual National Convention
    (Cleveland, June, 1919), 38, 40, 76–81
NAACP board, 27–32, 35, 38, 78, 80–81,
    95, 101, 111, 126, 167, 190, 228, 238
NAACP Legal Defense and Educational
    Fund, 104, 190, 228, 247
NAACP National Conference on
    Lynching (May, 1919), 33–40, 57
NAACP state branches, 30, 189–90
NAACP Tenth Annual Report (1920), 254
National Baptist Convention, 211
National Brotherhood of Workers of
    America, 186
National Defense Council, 19
National Equal Rights League, 25, 184, 230
National Race Congress, 97, 231
National Security League, 160
Neale, Randall, 104
Neely, Charles, 233
Negro, A Menace to American Civilization,
    The (Shufeldt), 60
Negro Faces America, The (Seligmann),
    127, 148, 249–50
Negro Fellowship League, 230
Negro in Chicago, The (Chicago
    Commission report), 154
"Negro Problem," 23, 150, 184
Negro World, 26, 66
Newark race riot (1967), 253
Newbranch, Harvey, 204–5
New Brunswick, New Jersey, 73
New Hebron, Mississippi, 53
"New Idealism, The" (Robeson), 76–77
New London, Connecticut, 51
New Negro, 38, 101, 112, 248
Newport News, Virginia, 18
New Republic, 36, 156
"New South," 220
New York Age, 37, 182, 240

New York Call, 112, 160
New York City race riot (1900), 37
New York Evening Mail, 20, 130, 203
New York Evening Sun, 160
New York Times, 17, 22–23, 36, 91, 141,
    152, 200, 201, 225, 232, 240, 244
New York Tribune, 103, 163–64
New York World, 14, 111, 231
1919 (Dos Passos), 24
North. *See also* specific cities and states
    racism in, 118–19, 149, 238, 252
    race riots in, 35, 73, 93, 270
Norfolk, Virginia, 105
Norgaard, Russell, 198
North American Review, 235
Norvell, Stanley B., 15
Norwood, Stephen H., 244

O'Connor, Thomas, 138
Oglethorpe County, Georgia, 183
Omaha Bee, 193, 194, 204
Omaha Evening World Herald, 204–5
Omaha lynching (1891), 194
Omaha NAACP, 194, 200–201
Omaha race riot, 146, 192–207, 220, 240
    aftermath of, 200–201, 263
    background of, 192–94
    events of, 194–200
    federal troops and, 200
    Fonda on, 198–99
    legal aftermath of, 257
    responses to, 201–7
O'Neal, Newman, 95
One Big Union, 161, 203
organized crime, 116, 154
O'Rourke, Stanley, 244
Ottley, Roi, 135, 138
Outlook, 157
Ovington, Mary W., 28–29, 80, 165–66

Pace, Harry, 40
Palmer, A. Mitchell, 36, 55–57, 163, 188,
    231, 239–41, 248, 262–63
Pan-African Congress (1919), 30
Parents' League of Washington, 97, 100
Parker, George Wells, 194
Passing of the Great Race, The (Grant), 62
Payne, James W., 178
Pell, Herbert Claiborne, Jr., 238
Pennsylvania, 51, 92–93, 233

Perry, Oliver Hazard, 54
Perry County, Mississippi, 71
Pershing, John "Black Jack," 92, 202
Phagan, Mary, 10
Phifer, Miles, 207
Philadelphia Public Ledger, 66, 193
Philadelphia race riot, 51
Phillips County, Arkansas, race riot,
    209–32, 256
  background of, 209–16
  as "black revolt," 209, 223–24, 227–31
  deaths and injuries, 224–25
  events of, 216–22
  federal troops and, 212, 220–22, 224–25
  Garvey on, 231–32
  legal aftermath of, 222–31, 258–59
Pickens, Mississippi, 51
Pickens, William, 9–10, 67
Pickle, David, 162, 164–66
Pleasant, Ruffin, 244
Police, Harry, 41
Polish immigrants, 120, 124, 137, 147
Pope City, Georgia, 152
Port Arthur, Texas, 90
Pratt, Charles, 216–17
Price, John Ambrose, 60
Prince, Henry, 52
Progressive Farmers and Household Union
    of America, 213–15, 223, 226–27
Progressive Party, 107
progressives, 123–25, 154, 172, 193, 206–7,
    220–21
Prohibition (Volstead Act, 1919), 4, 16, 88,
    116, 220, 234
Protocols of the Elders of Zion, The
    (Ackerman), 66
Pueblo, Colorado, 183–84
Pullman, Raymond W., 100–101
Putnam County, Georgia, 53

race
  definitions of, 62, 142
  pseudoscientific theories of, 59–67,
    220–21
Race Business Men's Exposition (1919), 153
race relations
  arc of, and Ruffin family, 265–69
  need to explore history of, 270–71
  Red Summer and shift in, 14–16, 21–23,
    148, 150, 182, 184–85, 212–13, 237,
    249–50, 252–56, 263–64

race riots. *See also* lynching; *and specific*
    agencies; individuals; locations; and
    organizations
  authority and tactics to stop, 46–48, 73,
    145, 232–33
  black literature on, 261
  black press blamed for, 163–66
  equality as remedy for, 151
  exploitation of, 17
  moral framing of, 37–38
  number of, in 1919, 13, 90
  Palmer report on, 239–41
  post-1919, 104, 251–53
  trauma of, 263–64
racism, 50, 121–23, 151, 190, 194.
    See also race; segregation; *and specific*
    issues
  North vs. South and, 118–19
radicalism (Bolshevism; subversion),
    16–17, 39, 56–60, 65–67, 79, 89, 91,
    105, 110, 125, 146, 149, 159–61,
    163–64, 185–88, 202–3, 215, 218, 221,
    223–24, 227–28, 231, 234, 239–40,
    243, 250, 257, 262–63. *See also* left;
    and specific groups
Ragen's Colts, 116, 125, 143
Railroad Administration, 74, 165
Randall, William, 42
Randolph, A. Philip, 58
Rand School of Social Science, 160
Rankin, Bill, 265–66
rape accusations, 36, 51–52, 60, 69, 71–72,
    93, 98, 111, 172–75, 194, 206, 245, 267
recession of 1919, 120
Reconstruction, 59, 209, 220, 237
Red Scare, 17, 56, 160, 215
Reed, John, 59
Republican Party, 25, 34–35, 37–38, 94,
    106–7, 110–11, 114, 123–25, 139–40,
    154, 161, 187, 187–90, 193, 202,
    205–6, 209–10, 255
"Returning Soldiers" (Du Bois), 25, 31, 50,
    163
Reuter, Edward Byron, 62
Richards, Benny, 51
Ringer, John Dean, 193, 195, 204
Rising Tide of Color, The (Stoddard), 63, 256
Roberts, Albert, 73, 172–73
Robeson, Paul, 76–77
Robinson, Robert, 125
Roosevelt, Franklin D., 55, 96, 108–9, 251
Roosevelt, Theodore, 37, 61, 107, 140, 201

Rosenwald, Julius, 154
Rosewater, Edward, 193, 194
Rosewood, Florida, race riot (1923), 251
Ruffin, Henry (son of Joe), 2–3, 7–8, 257,
    263
Ruffin, Joe
    Carswell Grove lynching and, 1–11, 75
    flight from Georgia, 265–66
    legacy of, 261, 268–70
    legal battle of, 191, 239, 259–61
Ruffin, Joe Andrew (son of Joe), 2
Ruffin, Chief Judge John H. "Jack"
    (great-grandson of Joe), 265–69
Ruffin, John H., Sr. (grandson of Joe;
    father of Judge), 267–68
Ruffin, John Holiday (son of Joe;
    grandfather of Judge), 2, 5–8, 11, 257,
    263, 266
Ruffin, Louis (son of Joe), 2, 5–9, 75
Russian Revolution, 16, 221
Rutgers University, Robeson address,
    76–77

St. Louis, Missouri, 146, 152, 212.
    See also East St. Louis
Sandburg, Carl, 116, 126, 136, 156
Sanford, Joseph, 134
San Francisco race riots, 73, 183
Savannah, Georgia, 184, 239
Savannah Tribune, 10, 157, 261
Scarborough, William S., 151, 184–85
Schoff, Joseph, 142
school desegregation, 251, 267
Schuyler, George S., 26
Scott, Edmund, 4–7, 11, 260–61
Scott, Emmett J., 12–13, 19, 78–79
Scott, Joseph, 133
"Second Coming, The" (Yeats), 16
sedition laws, 57, 59, 185
segregation, 27, 30–31, 34, 43, 60, 89, 97,
    102, 107–8, 110–12, 121–23, 127–29,
    131, 152, 154–55, 163, 170–71,
    184–85, 210, 243, 250, 252, 255–57,
    262, 264
Self-Preservation and Loyalty League, 243
Seligmann, Herbert, 52, 77, 104, 127, 148,
    208, 249–50, 253, 270
separatism, 66–67, 168–69, 238, 255
"Shall the Mob Govern?" (Shillady), 205
sharecroppers, 2–4, 79–80, 83–84, 93–94,
    209–16, 218–19, 225–27, 229

Shillady, John R., 29–30, 39–40, 72, 77,
    79–81, 101, 205, 228, 236, 238
    Austin attack on, 162–69, 190, 263
Shufeldt, R. W., 60
Simmons, William Joseph, 53–54, 64–65
Simpson, John, 147
slavery, 42, 59, 60, 96, 150, 157, 209
Smiddy, H. F., 218, 219
Smith, Charles Spencer, 237–38
Smith, Edward Parsons, 193–98, 203–5,
    231, 263
Smith, Harry, 39
Smith, Jim, 173
Smyth, Ora, 173–74
Snyder, F. S., 91
socialism, 161–62, 168, 224
"Socialism Imperiled" (Rand School),
    160–61
Socialist Party, 28, 58–59, 160, 185, 186
Souls of Black Folk, The (Du Bois), 27, 29
South Carolina, 41–51, 79, 99, 105, 152,
    163, 220, 232, 257, 260
    state legislature, 35
Southern Race Congress, 39
Southern Sociological Congress, 38–39,
    71, 157–58, 220
Southern University Race Commission, 22
Spanish-American War, 201
Spengler, Oswald, 62, 66
Spingarn, Arthur, 29, 34, 247–48
Spingarn, Joel, 27–29, 110–11, 126, 247
Springfield, Illinois, race riot (1908), 29
Stars and Stripes, 50
state militias, 47, 49, 72, 132, 140–41, 184,
    220. See also specific locations
Stauber, George, 129, 147
steel industry, 92–93
steel strike, 153, 185–86, 233
steelworkers union, 153
Stephens, Thomas, 4–7, 11
Stewart, Jack, 183
Stoddard, Lothrop, 63, 256
Stonewall, Mississippi, 241
Storey, Moorfield, 22, 34–35, 39, 55, 59, 77,
    122, 167, 238, 258
Straton, John Roach, 111
Straub, Sebastian, 215, 218, 223, 226
strikebreakers, 117, 120, 122, 153, 185, 193,
    233
strikes, 16, 91, 108, 119–20, 131, 141, 153,
    185–86, 193, 215, 233
Studs Lonigan (Farrell), 123, 130

Sweeney, Edward Baxter, 176–77, 179–80
Sweeney, William Allison, 15
Sweitzer, Robert M., 124
Swing, Mayor A. H., 93

Taft, William Howard, 77, 158, 201, 247
Talbert, James, 48
Talented Tenth, 27
Tappan, John, 219
Taylor, Hymes, 134
Taylor, Julius F., 85
Temple, Eugene, 134
Temple, John, 207
Tennessee, 13, 54, 159, 170–83, 188–89, 217, 220, 227, 240, 257
    anti-lynching legislation, 73, 172
    National Guard, 172–73, 175–80
Tenth Cavalry Regiment ("Buffalo Soldiers"), 91–92
Texas, 60, 82–91, 95, 125–26, 164–69, 190, 220, 257, 263–64
    state legislature, 88–89
    state militia, 88–89
Texas NAACP, 35, 81, 164–69
Texas Rangers, 88, 89, 164–65
Thirty Years of Lynching in the United States, 1889–1918 (NAACP), 35–36, 189
Thomas, Francis, 103
Thomas, Moses, 131
Thomas, Neval Hollen, 101, 103–4, 248
Thompson, William H. "Big Bill," 19, 114, 123–25, 131, 139–41, 143, 153–54, 202, 255
369th Infantry Regiment (Harlem Hellfighters), 13–14, 31
Till, Emmett, 252
Tillman, Ben "Pitchfork," 163
Toomer, Jean, 15–16, 112, 261
Treatise on Riot Duty, A (Bellows), 41, 47
Trotsky, Leon, 66, 186–87
Trotter, William Monroe, 25, 107, 112–13, 184, 230
Tulsa race riot (1921), 251
Tuscaloosa News, 93
Tuskegee Institute, 12, 157, 184, 251
Tyler, George, 232

Union of Timber Workers, 243
United Brotherhood of Carpenters and Joiners, 243, 244

U.S. Army, 2, 16, 50, 78, 91–92, 125, 183, 201, 210–11, 220, 224, 244
    military intelligence, 146, 159–60, 239
    segregation of, 30–32, 252
    Work or Fight laws and, 117
U.S. Congress, 2, 4, 57, 34–38, 40, 73, 110–11, 157, 167, 187–90, 182, 208, 228, 231, 234–35, 238–39, 246–50
    black press and, 163–64
    lack of blacks in, 15, 108
    lynching supported in, 205–7
    Palmer report and, 239–41
    Washington, D.C., riot and, 110
U.S. Constitution, 12, 34, 47, 204, 206, 213, 247, 262
U.S. Court of Appeals, 119–20
U.S. House of Representatives, 108, 167
    anti-lynching hearings, 246–50
U.S. Marines, 45, 51
U.S. Navy, 43–44, 46, 48–49, 51, 99–101, 183
U.S. Senate, 106, 108, 187, 205–6, 228, 239
U.S. Supreme Court, 34, 122, 159, 258–59, 266
Universal Negro Improvement Association (UNIA), 25–26, 66–67, 149, 168–69, 186, 188, 213, 232, 255
Urban League, 25, 63, 142, 150, 156, 231

Valdinoci, Carlo, 55–56
Vardaman, James K., 107–8
Variety, 138–39, 148
Versailles Treaty (1919), 24, 30, 33–34, 206
Vesey, Denmark, 42
Veteran, 58
veterans, 17, 19, 31, 49–50, 123, 125, 133, 135, 152, 168, 177, 194, 202, 207, 212, 214, 219, 243. See also black soldiers
Vicksburg, Mississippi, 51–52, 249
Vicksburg Herald, 159
Villard, Oswald Garrison, 108
Voice, 58
Volstead, Andrew J., 234, 246–47, 247
voting rights, 2, 15, 23, 39, 60, 79, 107–8, 123–24, 156, 170, 181, 206, 209–10, 221, 231, 253–56

wages, 117, 120, 172
Wald, Lillian, 167

Walker, Madame C. J., 35
Walker, Zachariah, 92–93
Wall Street Journal, 93, 160
Walters, Lemuel, 82–83
"War After the War, The" (Marcosson), 24
Ward, Walter, 226
War Department, 78, 230
     General Order No. 147, 47, 50
Ware, Ed, 213–18, 226–27, 230, 258
Warrenton, Georgia, 51
Washington, Berry, 52
Washington, Booker T., 27, 37, 66, 107,
     117–18, 184, 220
Washington, D.C., NAACP, 97, 101, 112,
     248
Washington, D.C., race riot (1848), 96–97,
     187
Washington, D.C., race riot (1910), 97
Washington, D.C., race riot (1919), 13,
     98–113, 125, 126, 149, 167, 208, 220,
     240, 245
     background of, 35, 61, 96–98
     black crime and, 111–12
     black population and, 117
     black resistance and, 112–13
     deaths and injuries, 104, 110
     events of, 98–100, 103–6
     federal action delayed in, 100–103
     federal troops brought in, 109–10
     legal aftermath of, 257
     response to, 106–11, 149–51
     subversives and, 104–5, 110
     Wilson's inaction and, 106–8
Washington, Louis C., 133
Washington Bee, 9
Washington Evening Star, 98
Washington Herald, 98
Washington Post, 98, 102, 103, 224, 233
Washington Star, 106
Washington Times, 98
Waters, James, 52–53
Watts race riot (1964), 253
Wells-Barnett, Ida, 114, 125–27, 142, 156,
     159, 227, 230–31, 259
"What Is Behind the Negro Uprisings?"
     (Seligmann), 208
"What Is the Matter with the United
     States?" (Hillis), 187
Wheeler, Edward, 208–9
Wheeler, Harry, 91
White, Ernest, 87
White, George Henry, 108

White, Walter, 23, 30, 38, 40, 77, 78, 95,
     124, 142, 154, 156, 188–89, 228–30,
     238, 253–54, 261
     background of, 28
     leadership of, 166–67
white liberals, 20, 22–23, 38, 156–57,
     166–67, 209
white merchants and planters, 214–15,
     229
whites. *See also* immigrant and ethnic
     whites; race; race relations; racism;
     and specific individuals and locations
     black attitudes toward, 21–23
     equality resisted by, 74–75, 150
     impact of Red Summer on, 255–56
     lynching defended by, 36, 205–6
     lynching of, 35, 39
     race riots started by, 13–14, 208–9, 241
     Red Summer misremembered by, 250
white supremacists, 17
Williams, Austin "Heavy," 119
Williams, Charles, 127
Williams, Eugene, 127–29, 131
Williams, Rev. G. W., 79–80
Williams, Irvin, 270
Williams, Rev. John A., 200–201
Williams, John S., 205–7
Williams, Rev. Lacey Kirk, 142, 148
Williams, Lawrence, 127
Williams, L. E., 243, 244
Williams, Paul, 127
Williams, Robert, 136
Williams, Willie, 6, 8
Wilmer, C. B., 206
Wilmington, Delaware, 241–42
Wilmington Dispatch, 98, 111
Wilson, Harry, 104, 257
Wilson, J. C., 38
Wilson, T. Webber, 70
Wilson, William, 248
Wilson, Woodrow, 12, 20–21, 24, 34, 38,
     50, 61, 140, 146, 157–58, 167, 184, 196,
     208, 231, 234, 244, 249
     blacks and, 107–9
     election of, 37, 201–2
     illness of, 187–88, 221
     labor and, 119, 153, 185
     League of Nations and, 33–34, 106, 187,
     205
     race riot comment by, 187
     Red Scare and, 56–57
     Washington riot and, 100–102, 106–9

Wilson Efficiency Club, 119
Within Our Gates (film), 261–62
women's suffrage, 16, 28, 88, 220
Wood, Gen. Leonard, 140, 160, 201–4
Woodson, Carter Godwin, 99–100
Woofter, Thomas Jackson, 117
Wordlow, William, 225–26
Work or Fight laws, 117
World War One, 2, 12–17, 22–24, 30–32,
    36, 43, 61–62, 97, 109, 117, 120,
    123–24, 150, 156, 171, 173, 176,
    192, 201–2, 210–11, 220–21, 238,
    242–43
World War Two, 251
Wright, Richard (novelist), 211–12
Wright, Richard R. (minister), 265, 271
Wuest, Jacob, 196–97, 200

Yeats, William Butler, 16
Young, Louis, 196
Youth's Companion, 205

About the Author

CAMERON MCWHIRTER is a reporter for the *Wall Street Journal*. He previously worked for other news organizations, including the *Atlanta Journal-Constitution*, the *Detroit News*, and the *Chicago Tribune*. He has reported in cities across the United States, as well as the Horn of Africa, Bosnia, Iraq, and Central America. He graduated Phi Beta Kappa, summa cum laude with history honors from Hamilton College and earned a master's degree from Columbia University's Graduate School of Journalism. He was awarded a Thomas J. Watson Fellowship in the Sudan and Eritrea and a Nieman Fellowship at Harvard University. He lives in Decatur, Georgia, with his wife and two children.